Education, Migration and Development

Also Available from Bloomsbury

Education, Migration and Development

Critical Perspectives in a Moving World

Amy North and Elaine Chase

BLOOMSBURY ACADEMIC
LONDON • NEW YORK • OXFORD • NEW DELHI • SYDNEY

BLOOMSBURY ACADEMIC
Bloomsbury Publishing Plc
50 Bedford Square, London, WC1B 3DP, UK
1385 Broadway, New York, NY 10018, USA
29 Earlsfort Terrace, Dublin 2, Ireland

BLOOMSBURY, BLOOMSBURY ACADEMIC and the Diana logo are trademarks of
Bloomsbury Publishing Plc

First published in Great Britain 2023
This paperback edition published 2024

Cover design: Charlotte James
Cover image © Mohamed Keita www.mohamedkeita.it

A catalogue record for this book is available from the British Library.

A catalog record for this book is available from the Library of Congress.

ISBN: HB: 978-1-3502-5754-2
PB: 978-1-3502-5758-0
ePDF: 978-1-3502-5755-9
eBook: 978-1-3502-5756-6

Typeset by Deanta Global Publishing Services, Chennai, India

To find out more about our authors and books visit www.bloomsbury.com
and sign up for our newsletters.

Education, Migration and Development

Critical Perspectives in a Moving World

Amy North and Elaine Chase

BLOOMSBURY ACADEMIC
LONDON • NEW YORK • OXFORD • NEW DELHI • SYDNEY

BLOOMSBURY ACADEMIC
Bloomsbury Publishing Plc
50 Bedford Square, London, WC1B 3DP, UK
1385 Broadway, New York, NY 10018, USA
29 Earlsfort Terrace, Dublin 2, Ireland

BLOOMSBURY, BLOOMSBURY ACADEMIC and the Diana logo are trademarks of
Bloomsbury Publishing Plc

First published in Great Britain 2023
This paperback edition published 2024

Copyright © Amy North and Elaine Chase and contributors, 2023

Amy North and Elaine Chase and contributors have asserted their right under the
Copyright, Designs and Patents Act, 1988, to be identified as Author of this work.

For legal purposes the Acknowledgements on p. xiii constitute an extension of this
copyright page.

Cover design: Charlotte James
Cover image © Mohamed Keita www.mohamedkeita.it

Bloomsbury Publishing Plc does not have any control over, or responsibility for, any third-
party websites referred to or in this book. All internet addresses given in this book were
correct at the time of going to press. The author and publisher regret any inconvenience
caused if addresses have changed or sites have ceased to exist, but can accept no
responsibility for any such changes.

A catalogue record for this book is available from the British Library.

A catalog record for this book is available from the Library of Congress.

ISBN: HB: 978-1-3502-5754-2
PB: 978-1-3502-5758-0
ePDF: 978-1-3502-5755-9
eBook: 978-1-3502-5756-6

Typeset by Deanta Global Publishing Services, Chennai, India

To find out more about our authors and books visit www.bloomsbury.com
and sign up for our newsletters.

Contents

Illustrations

Figures

Tables

Contributors

Mai Abu Moghli is Lecturer in Education and International Development at the Institute of Education, University College London, UK, and Senior Researcher at the Centre for Lebanese Studies, Lebanese American University, Lebanon. Her research interests focus on decolonizing research and research ethics, education in emergencies and critical approaches to human rights education.

Jennifer Allsopp is Birmingham Fellow at the University of Birmingham, UK. Her research centres on how people move and mobilize to support what they perceive to be viable futures for themselves, their families and their societies in contexts of migration, and explores the relationship between immigration control, welfare and wellbeing, with a focus on gender, ageing and the politics of membership and belonging.

Veronica Cadavid-González is a Colombian lawyer and researcher at the University of Minnesota Law School Human Rights Center, United States. She previously held a position as a researcher for the Memorias Vivas (Living Memories) research group at the Museo de la Casa Memoria (Casa de la Memoria Museum) in Medellín, Colombia. Her research centres on human rights approaches to social justice, inequality and gender, and economic, social and cultural rights in rural communities.

Elaine Chase is Professor of Education, Wellbeing and International Development at the Institute of Education, University College London, UK. Her teaching, research and writing explore the sociological dimensions of health, wellbeing and rights of individuals and communities, particularly those most likely to experience marginalization and exclusion. A core focus of her work is the impact of immigration controls and displacement on the wellbeing of children, young people and families.

Sondra Cuban is Professor of Health & Community Studies at Western Washington University, United States. Her research interests focus on gender, care labour, migration and new technologies. Her books include *Deskilling Migrant Women in the Global Care Industry* (2013), *Transnational Family*

Communication: Immigrants & ICTs (2017) and *Mapping Southern Routes of Migrant Women: A Case Study of Chile* (forthcoming, 2022).

Kavita Datta is Professor of Development Geography and Director of the Centre for the Study of Migration at Queen Mary University of London, UK. Her interdisciplinary research spans migration studies and development and financial geography. Contributing to critical understandings of transnational migration, financialization and migrants' financial practices, her research has particularly focused on migrant labour, financial and food remittances, gender and intersectionality.

Rian de Villiers is Professor in the Department of Science, Mathematics and Technology Education, Faculty of Education, University of Pretoria, South Africa. His interdisciplinary research focus areas are inter- and intra-continental teacher migration studies and teacher training for life sciences education. In 2019 he received the international Science-Made-Sensible Award from Miami University, United States.

Caroline Dyer is Professor of Education and International Development at the University of Leeds, UK. Her research focuses on the intersections of education, livelihood-related mobility and social inclusion in countries across South and East Asia, and sub-Saharan Africa. She explores these themes in her 2014 monograph *Livelihoods and Learning: Education for All and the Marginalisation of Mobile Pastoralists* and 2021 paper (with Vijitha Rajan) in *Compare* 'Left Behind? Internally Migrating Children and the Ontological Crisis of Formal Education Systems in South Asia'.

Sowmya J. is a research associate with the Centre for Budget and Policy Studies, Bengaluru, India. She has a master's in economics from Bangalore University, India. Her research focuses on public finance and local governance.

Jyotsna Jha is Director of the Centre for Budget and Policy Studies (CBPS), Bengaluru, India. She has a PhD in economics from Jawaharlal Nehru University (JNU), India. Her research primarily focuses on education and gender. She has several publications in the form of book chapters, co-authored books and papers. Before her association with CBPS, she worked as an education advisor at the Commonwealth Secretariat, London, UK.

Priyadarshani Joshi is Senior Analyst with the Global Education Monitor (GEM) Report Team, UNESCO. Her research interests include the equity and other systemic consequences of private schooling growth and the role of education in the Sustainable Development Goals, especially to improve gender equality and urban inclusion.

Ziyuan Lu is a doctoral student at Renmin University of China, China, in the School of Agricultural Economics and Rural Development (SARD).

Faith Mkwananzi is Senior Researcher with the Centre of Development Support at the University of the Free State, South Africa. Her academic work has generally centred on higher education, migration, youth and development in sub-Saharan Africa. She is specifically interested in pursuing research which develops operationalizations of the capability approach and engages more creative participatory methodologies to bridge the gap between researchers and development practitioners and civil society at large.

Sugandha Nagpal is Assistant Professor of Sociology at the School of International Affairs at O.P. Jindal Global University, India. Her research interests focus on youth mobility, migration and gender.

Anneke Newman is a postdoctoral fellow in the Department of Anthropology (Laboratoire d'Anthropologie des Mondes Contemporains) at the Université Libre de Bruxelles, Belgium. She is interested in the intersections between epistemologies, identities, mobility and school preference; postcolonial critiques of education and development theory and practice; debates around 'indigenous' or endogenous knowledges in African contexts; and decolonial approaches to the study of Islamic education and Muslim societies.

Amy North is Associate Professor of Education and International Development at the Centre for Education and International Development (CEID) at the Institute of Education, University College London, UK. Her research, writing and teaching are concerned with understanding gendered and other inequalities in relation to education, particularly in low-income contexts. She has particular interests in literacy, women and girls' education, and migration, with a focus on the ways in which ideas, policies or practices move and are understood between different local, national and global settings.

Xiaopeng Pang is Professor at Renmin University of China, China, in the School of Agricultural Economics and Rural Development (SARD). Her research interests include development economics, anti-poverty and rural development, women in rural governance, gender inequality and economic growth, and public policy. Her articles are published in *The China Quarterly*, *Contemporary Economic Policy*, *Journal of Development Effectiveness*, *Asian Survey*, *China Economic Review*, *American Journal of Ophthalmology*, *Computers & Education* and so on.

Ishita Patil is a research associate at the National Institute of Advanced Studies, India. Her research interests include labour, migration and livelihood studies.

Archana Purohit is Senior Research Advisor at the Centre for Budget and Policy Studies, Bengaluru, India. She has a PhD in public policy from the Indian Institute of Management Bangalore, India. Her research focuses on poverty, inequality and inclusive growth.

Nitya Rao is Professor of Gender and Development, at the School of International Development, University of East Anglia, UK. She has worked extensively in the field of women's rights, employment and education for over three decades. Her research interests focus on exploring the gendered changes in land and agrarian relations, migration and livelihoods, especially in contexts of climatic variability and economic precarity, and literacy and creative communication. She has published extensively on these themes in international peer-reviewed journals and books.

Hiba Salem is a research associate at the Refugee Studies Centre, University of Oxford, UK. Her research focuses on education, well-being and inclusion in forced displacement. Her work seeks to bridge discussions between academia and policy, and she has published on learner experiences, voice and school structures in Jordan.

Zenzele Weda is a teacher at St Charles College, Pietermaritzburg, South Africa. He is affiliated as a researcher to the Department of Educational Foundations, College of Education, University of South Africa. His research niche is international teacher migration.

Acknowledgements

Many people have been involved in supporting the development of this book. In particular, we are grateful to colleagues and students at the UCL Centre for Education and International Development (CEID), who have provided invaluable encouragement and critical feedback throughout the process, and to Mark Richardson at Bloomsbury Publishing. Thanks also to Cyrine Saab, who provided careful proofreading and formatting of the manuscript with funding provided by the Department of Education, Practice and Society at UCL IoE. We would also like to extend our thanks to the anonymous peer reviewers who reviewed and provided extremely helpful comments on both the full manuscript and the proposal for the book. Finally, as a collaborative project, this book would not have been possible without the generous contributions of all its chapter authors. We look forward to future collaborations as we take forward the discussions and conversations initiated in this volume.

Introduction

Elaine Chase and Amy North

Despite a growing literature bridging the disciplines of education and international development on the one hand (e.g. McCowan and Unterhalter 2022; Harber 2014) and migration and development on the other (e.g. Bastia and Skeldon 2020; de Haas 2010; Raghuram 2009), and an emerging body of work attending to aspects of the relationship between migration and education (e.g. Culp and Zwarthoed 2020; Bartlett and Ghaffer-Kucher 2013), the migration, education and development nexus remains largely under-theorized, with research in these areas disjointed and siloed. Migration, mobility and, importantly, immobility have thus become the missing links in theory, policy and practice pertaining to the role of education in international development.

The Sustainable Development Goals (SDGs), adopted by all UN Member States in 2015, provide a broadly normative aspirational framework for global human development. However, although the SDG framework gives prominence to education as a key means to achieving sustainable development, there is only limited attention given to the role of migration in education and development processes and, where this does happen, it tends to be limited to concerns such as facilitating international student mobility through the provision of scholarships (Target 4.b). Moreover, related work in the field often fails to acknowledge the often rapidly shifting political, social and economic landscape within which the education, migration and development nexus operates. At the time of writing, for example, the Covid-19 pandemic raises important new challenges for education and development, and highlights the significance of migration and increased global connections as potential buffers to these impacts, which are in turn limited by additional restrictions on movement and mobility. As such, migrant communities are playing key roles in alleviating the impact of the pandemic (e.g. through sustaining resources for care and education and as skilled workers providing core services across the globe) while simultaneously being made particularly vulnerable as a result of a range of governance and public health policy responses which discriminate against and marginalize them.

The aim of this edited interdisciplinary volume is to bring together a selection
of original and critically engaged bodies of work which examine the education,
migration and development nexus from multiple perspectives and which, at the
same time, capture the complex and fluid dynamics which shape it. A number of
key questions underpin the contributions to the book:

- What new considerations for education and international development arise
  when we apply a migration lens?
- What sorts of theoretical frameworks and approaches are most useful
  in understanding the intersections between education, migration and
  development?
- What opportunities and challenges do migration and (im)mobility create for
  education in contexts of international development?
- What are the implications of migration processes for education policy and
  systems, curricula, pedagogy, training and learner experiences and well-
  being?
- What approaches to policy, practice and research are most likely to promote
  justice, equity and well-being in and through education in the context of
  migration?
- How do gendered and other inequalities intersect with the possibilities
  and constraints emerging from the education, migration and development
  nexus?

Throughout the volume we explore some of the different ways in which the
education, migration and development nexus is emerging in contemporary
global scholarship and practice. Migration and mobility are understood broadly
as processes of movement not just of people but also of resources, ideas, norms
and values. We suggest that, in order to understand such processes of movement,
it is important to steer away from the mobility bias (Schewel 2020) and also
explore the dynamics of non-movement or immobility, whether voluntary or
involuntary, (Carling 2002; Schewel 2020) as well as ideas about 'motility' – that
is, the potential or capability for spatial and/or social mobility, irrespective of
whether this takes place (see Chapter 7). Equally we give attention to processes
of movement and (im)mobility both within and across national borders;
movement within countries of the Global South as well as the less frequent,
though highly politicized and excessively monitored, movement of people from
countries in the Global South to the Global North. With respect to education,
the volume explores the diverse purposes of education and learning in different
contexts, the range of formal, non-formal and informal settings within which

education and learning takes place as well as how education both generates and responds to multiple flows of movement. Finally, we recognize the contested nature of ideas around development and the need to understand the historical and political dynamics which shape development processes. Through the diverse chapters of the volume, the aim is thus to engage more fully with the complex ways in which diverse forms of migration and (im)mobility can simultaneously be drivers of, obstacles to and mediators of both education and development in different settings.

In the following sections of this introduction we briefly outline some core theoretical, methodological, ethical and definitional debates and reflections of relevance to the volume, before mapping out the structure of the book and the different thematic contributions of its authors.

Understanding the Education, Migration and Development Nexus: Theoretical Perspectives and Approaches

The chapters in the book engage with a range of theoretical lenses and approaches for understanding the intersections between education, (im)mobility and development in multiple global contexts. Three main principles permeate the volume as a whole. The first is the emphasis on adopting postcolonial and decolonial lenses in migration, education and development scholarship. Such an approach builds on the work of postcolonial and decolonial scholars who, despite engaging with different geographies and timeframes (Bhambra 2014), are broadly concerned with the continuing legacy of colonialism in the Global South, including the role played by formal education systems and development actors in reproducing colonial hierarchies (e.g. Kapoor 2008; Tikly 2019; Del Monte and Posholi 2021), and the need to understand the historical and political dynamics that shape patterns of migration and mobility (Samaddar 2020). Such a stance is underpinned by a number of important core principles, including a commitment to diversifying the accounts and insights of different actors within the education, migration and development nexus; giving attention to the historical, social, political and economic factors that have shaped dynamics of migration and mobility and peoples' uneven opportunities in and through education; and recognizing the plurality of learning spaces, knowledges and processes of knowledge production and their contextualized value. In particular, chapters by Abu Moghli, Newman and Rao and Patil provide some important illustrations of the importance of applying such lenses to thinking about what education means in contexts of displacement, migration, mobility and immobility, and attending to the historical and political situatedness of the interactions between migration, education and development.

The second overarching principle is that of interdisciplinarity, and the volume brings together scholarship from across the fields of education, sociology, anthropology, geography, development studies, economics and the arts to illustrate the potential for dialogue across disciplinary perspectives, each offering different ways of understanding the education, migration and development nexus. Taking an interdisciplinary approach helps make sense of the multifaceted nature of the relationship between migration, education and development. For example, some people may move as skilled workers to share knowledge and ideas and boost economies elsewhere in the world, while sending home resources to support education or economic development in their communities of origin; while others may go in search of new employment opportunities, learning ideas, skills or expertise. Some people are forced to move across borders and continents as a result of conflict, persecution, extreme poverty, climate change or the impacts of globalization and 'development', while for others mobility is intrinsic to their lives and livelihoods (as in the case of nomadic communities). All require forms of education and learning which can sustain their lives while at the same time offering opportunities in a changing world. As various chapters suggest, the impact of such movement and forms of (im)mobility, and the ways in which they intersect with education, may have economic, social, emotional, cultural and political dimensions. Such complexity is best understood through diverse disciplinary lenses and employing different methodologies.

A third cross-cutting principle is a concern with understanding intersectionality in relation to experiences of, and responses to, migration and education. The term 'intersectionality', first used by Kimberlie Crenshaw (1989) to describe the way in which African American women in the United States experienced subordination on the basis of their sex, their race and their class, is used to refer to the ways in which multiple forms of inequality and discrimination may intersect, generating overlapping systems of disadvantage. This has implications for thinking about both migration and education. Intersecting forms of discrimination, disadvantage or inequality can combine in complex ways to shape educational opportunities, trajectories and outcomes in contexts of migration and (im)mobility and may be transformed, reproduced or exacerbated by institutional structures and processes, such as those associated with schools, immigration systems or labour markets. Several chapters in the book, for example, illustrate how women's experiences of migration, mobility and immobility, as well as their engagement with education, are affected by gendered norms and expectations, as well as by hierarchies and inequalities linked to race, class and, in some cases, caste. Despite this, as Cuban notes in her chapter, much policy analysis remains gender blind and fails to fully engage with the specific needs of female and male learners across the life course or to consider the impact of intersecting inequalities on their experiences of, or as a result of, education in contexts of migration and (im)mobility.

Researching the Education, Migration and Development Nexus: Methodological and Ethical Considerations

Reflecting their different disciplinary leanings, the studies presented in the volume draw on diverse methodological approaches enabling explorations of the education, migration and development nexus from a range of different perspectives. Each approach raises distinct ethical, epistemological and ontological dilemmas and considerations. While ethical approval was secured for all the studies, individual chapters go further to highlight the significance of positionality, power, voice and agency; the relationship between research, policy and practice; and the ethics of research in relation to 'marginalized communities' in often complex contexts.

Contributors to the volume share a commitment to research that seeks to unsettle dominant norms, ideas and values which perpetuate inequalities. For example, Abu Moghli in her chapter and related work (Abdelnour and Abu Moghli 2021) explores how, in relation to displacement, there is a tendency to normalize violent contexts of, say, conflict, natural disasters or revolutions. Rather than accepting such adversity as normal, it is argued, researchers have a moral and a political duty to be reflexive and engage ethically with the contexts, people, societies and topics which form the foci of their work.

One particular intention of the book is to unsettle normative ideas that tend to underpin 'modern' education and what it is and should be for in contexts of migration and mobility. Dyer's work, for example, speaks to the sedentary norm in education which means that educational policies frame pastoralism as a problem that needs to be fixed rather than thinking about how education might function within a nomadic pastoralist society. Meanwhile, in her chapter, Newman argues that while 'eduscape' offers a useful concept for understanding the effects of globalization on educational phenomena, its typical application in related literature reflects Eurocentric biases, focusing on Western schooling to the neglect of non-Western or indigenous knowledges and education systems. Thus, she used exploratory ethnography as a deliberate methodological strategy to move past these biases and consider how what is uncovered on the ground defines the direction of the research, which can then in turn recentre the knowledges, epistemologies and forms of education most valuable to communities participating in the research. This provides an example of how ethnographic methods combined with an open-ended research design can provide the tools for scholars to '"re-narrativise" (Hall 1996) the globalisation story in a way that places historically marginalised parts of the world at the centre, rather than at the periphery of the education and globalisation debate' (Tikly 2001: 151). Other chapters in the book similarly seek to centre the experiences and perspectives of research participants from communities whose voices are often excluded or marginalized in policy and academic debates by drawing on ethnographic (Nagpal) and narrative methods (Cuban, Salem, De Villiers and Weda, Mkwananzi), participatory and peer-led research approaches (Allsopp and Chase), and the use of the arts and participatory dialogue (Cadavid-González and Allsopp).

Such methodological reflections raise questions of positionality and power within research on migration and education particularly in contexts of inequality and disadvantage. While efforts to hear from the perspectives of pastoralists, refugee communities or other marginalized groups about what is important to them in terms of education are laudable, other dilemmas emerge about the value and ethics of such research in contexts where it is unlikely to shape or inform changes to notoriously slow policy machineries. This is a particular challenge in the often highly charged political space associated with education and migration research, which is riddled with normative discourses surrounding who should move and who should stay, and where educational policies are often politics-driven rather than evidence-based. In this context, at the very least, researchers need to understand the contexts in which they are working and acknowledge their positionality in terms of their backgrounds, privilege, connection to funding and governments, and in relation to knowledge production dynamics including their historical dimensions. In preparing this manuscript, we encouraged authors to reflect on these questions of positionality. Nagpal, for example, in her work with young Dalit women in India, reflected on the significance of her status as a woman of Indian origin from an upper-caste identity, highly educated and living in Canada, while Jha and colleagues spoke about the dilemmas of when and how best to interview migrant workers whose work and living conditions are so closely controlled by their employers and their precarity exacerbated by the impact of the Covid-19 pandemic.

The chapters in the book also highlight other methodological challenges and evidence gaps. For example, across the field there appears to be a lack of relevant statistical and other data which speaks directly to the scale of the issues being observed in the education, migration and development nexus. This is compounded by the fact that people on the move, particularly nomadic and pastoralist communities and those who migrate internally or who do not have regularized immigration status, are often excluded from household surveys and other official censuses (Carr-Hill 2013). The chapter by Pang and Lu, which brings together diverse studies on the education and well-being trajectories of children whose parents have migrated from rural to urban areas in China, highlights the value of systematically reviewing the available statistical data in order to give as complete a picture as possible and begin to make sense of conflicting findings from research, but also notes the limitations of only working with existing quantitative evidence. It thus points to the importance of bringing together both qualitative and quantitative data and approaches in education, migration and development research.

Definitions, Classification and Nomenclature

The process of researching and writing about the education, migration and development nexus raises a number of challenges in relation to terminology. As noted earlier, for example, the term 'education' may have multiple meanings; while it is often used to refer to different levels of formal education (from early years through to university), it also encompasses non-formal education and informal learning spaces and processes. The concept of 'development', meanwhile, is highly contested. McCowan and Unterhalter (2022, 5) note that although the term is often associated with 'the process of change of the less wealthy and often newly independent countries of Africa, Asia and Latin America, in conjunction with an increasingly elaborate architecture of development agencies' in the period following the Second World War, this dominant view of development has been challenged from multiple perspectives. Post-development scholars, for example, have problematized 'development' as a 'eurocentric and hierarchic construct defining non-Western, non-modern,

non-industrialised ways of life as inferior and in need of "development"'
(Ziai 2017: 2547) and linked it to the maintenance of colonial hierarchies
and relationships (McCowan and Unterhalter 2022). In official development
discourse and global development frameworks (such as the Millennium
Development Goals (MDGs) and the SDGs), meanwhile, normative ideas
about rights, freedoms and capabilities often sit uneasily alongside economistic
perspectives linked to economic growth and increased GDP. In this context,
terms such as 'developing countries', 'the Global South' or 'low and middle-
income', used to describe those countries considered to be the intended
beneficiaries of development interventions, are often highly value-laden or
viewed as problematic in terms of their geographical or historical accuracy
(ibid., p. 6).

Defining the parameters of who is being referred to in migration research
is also notoriously challenging and highly politicized (Zetter 2007). The terms
'migrant', 'immigrant', 'expatriate', 'asylum-seeker' and 'refugee' reflect wider
social cleavages of class and status (Long 2014). Within migration governance
and policy speak, people are frequently assigned reductionist acronyms such
as 'IDP' (internally displaced person), 'UASC' (unaccompanied asylum-seeking
child) or LBC (left-behind children) or are invisibilized in research and policy.
As a result, any volume on migration, education and development is bound to
run into a number of definitional challenges, particularly when we are interested
in the educational and developmental impacts for those who move as well as
those who remain immobile.

Such challenges are explored explicitly in a number of the book's chapters.
Jyotsna Jha, Archana Purohit and Sowmya J. in their chapter, for example,
speak about the diversity of internal migrants in India and the lack of
consensus in defining who a migrant is. The census of India, for example,
considers a migrant as someone who is enumerated at a place different from
his/her place of birth, while the National Sample Survey defines a migrant
as someone who is being enumerated at a place different from his/her usual
place of residence (UPR). Women who move to live with their husbands
after marriage (a traditional cultural practice in India) constitute the largest
number of migrants as per official data on migration within India. Hence, in
their study, decisions were made to purposively sample migrants from the
most marginalized or vulnerable backgrounds, to take into account whether
their movement was inter-state or intra-state, and to draw some distinctions
between the lengths of time spent in the place of destination. Similarly,
Sondra Cuban speaks about the mobility of women in the Latin American

and Caribbean (LAC) region, in the context of the region's particular developmental trajectory, and the lack of relevant policy frameworks which engage with their educational experiences, raising questions of interregional migration and its growing relevance in some contexts over international migration.

We attempt to circumnavigate some of these definitional dilemmas by focusing on the processes of education, migration and development and all their protagonists rather than solely on those who migrate. This requires attending to the relational aspects of migration and (im)mobility (White 2016; Villalon 2021), including consideration of the historical, political and economic relationships between contexts (including those that people migrate to and from), and the nature of social relationships between people (including those who migrate and those who remain immobile). This, while fundamentally important in migration scholarship, is an area that has received relatively limited attention. Pang and Lu's chapter on the educational trajectories of the children of migrants who move to urban centres for work, for example, highlights important political, social and economic insights on the dynamics of internal migration in China and the educational implications. Dyer and other contributors highlight the hybrid nature of family formations and mobility, with some family members staying while others leave and family formations being constantly reconfigured in response to shifting social, economic and educational demands. The varied intergenerational dynamics are equally important. While migration is normatively associated with the search for a 'better life', for many it actually entails much sacrifice and reverse social mobility (such as when highly skilled women end up in low-skilled work) so that future generations might benefit through increased educational and other opportunities. In some cases, it is the younger generation who migrate to improve the lives of those left behind, sometimes, as is the case for some young people in the chapter by Allsopp and Chase, resulting in them becoming conflicted in whether to opt for educational or work trajectories.

The chapters within the volume thus invite reflection on the complex and multidirectional nature of the relationships between processes associated with education, migration and development. They encourage readers to think in mobile and dynamic ways as we engage with a world which itself is in a constant state of change and flux, where people are connected at an unprecedented scale through national, transnational and global networks and in which, as noted earlier, immobility can be as crucial to the education, migration and development nexus as mobility itself.

Structure of the Book

The chapters that follow this introduction explore diverse aspects of the education, migration and development nexus through three sections.

In the first section, Chapters 1–5 consider key and emerging themes and trends in relation to internal and international migration and mobility, and their implications for education and development processes. In Chapter 1, Kavita Datta examines debates around skilled migration, looking at the movement of both skilled workers and international students. Drawing on multidisciplinary scholarship, the chapter engages critically with the dominant 'brain drain/ gain/circulation' analytical lens often used to understand the skilled migration, education and development nexus, and considers the need to problematize the framing of 'skills', noting that these are socially and politically constructed. The chapter highlights the value of taking an intersectional approach to understanding experiences of skilled migration, focusing in particular upon gender, race and class. Amy North and Priyadarshani Joshi also consider issues of intersectionality in Chapter 2, in their discussion of the 'feminization' of migration. Focusing on the experiences of women who migrate (whether internally or internationally) as domestic workers, they discuss existing literature and empirical research with migrant domestic workers in London to consider the role that formal and non-formal education may play in influencing how women experience, and are able to make decisions about, migration and domestic work.

In Chapter 3, Caroline Dyer turns to consider internal forms of migration, with a focus on mobile pastoralist communities who herd livestock in the highly variable conditions of the global drylands. The chapter provides comparative perspectives on how education policies in Mongolia, Ethiopia and India approach or ignore education inclusion for mobile pastoralists and reflects on the implications of these cases for the provision of education and equitable and sustainable development, which, informed by pastoralist values, is conducive to the environmental stewardship essential for a sustainable future.

Chapters 4 and 5 are concerned with aspects of the relationship between education and forced displacement. In Chapter 4, Mai Abu Moghli examines refugee education in Lebanon and Jordan, highlighting the failure to fulfil the right to education and critically examining the nature of donor investments, which, she argues, have led to the commodification of refugee education, turning refugeehood into a profitable label. The chapter examines possibilities of moving beyond reactionary humanitarian response(s) and considers alternative possibilities for funding and education programming. Chapter 5, by Verónica Cadavid-González and Jennifer Allsopp, considers the significance of museums as educational spaces in contexts of displacement. Drawing on a case of the Memory Museum in Medellín, Colombia, the chapter argues that museums have an important role in creating critical spaces to assess the topic of migration and displacement.

In the second section (Chapters 6–10), the focus shifts to a concern with understanding how the education, migration and development nexus plays out in particular national and local settings. Chapters in this section engage critically with and unsettle commonly held assumptions about the relationship between education and development in contexts of migration and (im)mobility. They raise questions about the meaning and purpose of education in such settings, and highlight the complex social, cultural and economic impacts of migration and the implications of this for educational systems, aspirations, outcomes and experiences. In Chapter 6, Anneke Newman draws on a critical, postcolonial engagement with the concept of 'eduscape' to explore ethnographic data on youth's educational trajectories in Senegal. Focusing on a commune in the Senegal River valley basin, which has experienced high levels of male outward migration, her analysis reveals how young people's aspirations and educational engagements are shaped by the availability of Islamic schooling, aspirations to migrate overseas and intersecting identities of gender and position in the local caste-like hierarchy.

Chapters 7 and 8 consider the significance of migration and outward mobility on communities and views of education in communities in two different states in India. In both chapters, ideas about immobility, as well as mobility, take on particular salience. In Chapter 7, Nitya Rao and Ishita Patil present an in-depth study of a large fishing village in the western Indian state of Maharashtra. In the context of rapid transformations, including climate change and environmental degradation, the development of industrial estates and infrastructure projects, and the decline of the local fishing industry, they consider the case of the state-run local 'fishing school', exploring how perceptions towards schooling and skills training have changed in the fishing community and how these are shaped by gender and class. In Chapter 8, Sugandha Nagpal focuses on young Dalit women from upwardly mobile families residing in Chaheru, a predominantly Dalit village in the Doaba region of Punjab with a strong culture of migration. Drawing on ethnographic data to probe the importance of education in a context where migration is seen as the main pathway to mobility, it considers how, in the absence of opportunities for mobility, young women use college education to construct middle-class identities while remaining in the village.

Chapters 9 and 10 look specifically at issues of internal migration associated with people moving from rural to urban locations in search of employment. In Chapter 9, Jyotsna Jha, Archana Purohit and Sowmya J. report on findings from a household survey in Bangalore, one of the fast-growing cities of Southern India. In the context of the Covid-19 pandemic, the chapter explores the impact of migration on the educational outcomes of the children of migrant parents. The chapter demonstrates the extremely precarious existence of many migrants but suggests that despite this, life in the city is seen as preferable to their circumstances 'back home', and, in some cases, is associated with a desire for upward mobility and increased educational aspirations for their children. In Chapter 10, Xiaopeng Pang and Ziyuan Lu systematically review studies which used rigorous multi-regression methods to examine the impact of internal migration in China on the education, nutrition and health of children who remain behind in their communities of origin when one or both of their parents migrate to find work in urban centres. Their analysis highlights some of the challenges faced by the children of migrants, who are often prevented from accompanying their parents and attending school in the city as a result of the *hukou* registration system.

The final section (Chapters 11–15) is concerned with understanding lived experiences of migration. Chapters in the section explore the migration journeys of both learners and teachers. They consider the place of education in relation to their wider aspirations, identities and well-being, and social relationships with others. Chapters 11 and 12 both focus on the narratives and educational engagements of migrant women, highlighting the intersecting forms of disadvantage that contribute to shaping their experiences. In Chapter 11, Sondra Cuban explores the issues faced by women in the Latin American and Caribbean region, focusing specifically on the experiences of intraregional migrant women in Chile. Drawing on a mobilities framework for examining educational progress in migrant women's lives, the chapter highlights not only the centrality of education and sought-after opportunities in the women's narratives and experiences but also the challenges and discrimination they face. In doing so, she makes the case for a transnational feminist perspective in migration and education research. In Chapter 12, Faith Mkwananzi discusses data from a qualitative study in Johannesburg, South Africa, on refugees and asylum-seeking young women's aspirations for post-secondary education and their perceptions of whether and how education might contribute to their desired futures. Drawing on the capability approach and the concept of possible selves, the chapter highlights the value that the women in the study placed on vocational education, which they saw as creating opportunities for increased levels of independence and well-being.

Chapter 13, by Jennifer Allsopp and Elaine Chase, draws on data from a three-year study exploring the well-being outcomes of unaccompanied asylum-seeking and migrant young people as they become adult in England and Italy. It considers how young men's decisions to pursue educational progress or alternative work-based trajectories were significantly influenced by a range of structural and institutional opportunities and constraints as well as their broader identities as migrant young people intimately tied to others through their transnational obligations and commitments for collective better futures. In Chapter 14, Hiba Salem explores the experiences of Syrian refugee students in Jordan's double-shift school system. Her data and analysis shed light on how well-being, aspirations and perceptions of self are influenced by the educational spaces that refugee young people navigate and highlight the need for education policies and structures for refugee young people which, rather than being exclusionary, seek to promote positive interactions with their non-refugee peers and wider communities.

Finally, in Chapter 15, Rian de Villiers and Zenzele Weda remind us that it is not only learners but also educators who move. Their chapter focuses on the experiences of Zimbabwean teachers in South Africa. Drawing on interview data, their chapter points to multiple factors that impede the reconstruction of migrant teachers' personal and professional identities, and, in a context of increasing xenophobia, emphasizes the importance of supporting migrant teachers to integrate into host country communities.

Conclusion

The chapters in this book illustrate some of the multiple ways in which the relationship between education, migration and development plays out in relation to particular communities and geographical settings, and the lives and experiences both of those who move and those who stay behind. However, despite the range of contexts and topics covered, we are fully aware that in many respects we are scratching the surface of a complex and under-researched and underdeveloped field. For example, although chapters by Newman, Rao and Patil, Dyer, and Allsopp and Cadavid-González all highlight the significance of environmental change for livelihoods and related engagements with education and processes of migration, the complex interconnections between climate change, migration and education remain underexplored. Similarly, as Jha, Purohit and Sowmya J., and Datta's chapters indicate, the Covid-19 pandemic highlights the need for greater attention to the interactions between the education, migration and development nexus and health and well-being, including the impacts of pandemics and other health crises. Furthermore, in the current volume we have not had scope to begin to explore the burgeoning field of digital learning and literacy and its relevance to migratory contexts, particularly in relation to forms of transnational connections and shifting family dynamics. We pick up some of these themes in the volume's conclusions as we consider future directions for a developing research agenda. Meanwhile, although the volume brings together scholars working in diverse geographical and linguistic contexts, we recognize the English-centric nature of this work as a limitation and how it falls short of our decolonial intentions.

Nonetheless, in bringing together a diverse and global group of scholars, and a rich body of empirical and theoretical work, we hope we have gone some way towards opening up this emerging field of enquiry and laying the basis for new collaborations and networks of global scholars who share this interest. We are excited at the prospect of the volume providing a springboard for ongoing dialogue and debate about the role and function of education in a rapidly changing world in which migration and (im)mobility are increasingly core features of our existence.

References

Abdelnour, S., & Abu Moghli, M. (2021). 'Researching Violent Contexts: A Call for Political Reflexivity', *Organization*, 13505084211030646.

Bartlett, L., & Ghaffar-Kucher, A. (Eds). (2013). *Refugees, Immigrants, and Education in the Global South: Lives in Motion*. Abingdon: Routledge.

Bastia, T., & Skeldon, R. (Eds). (2020). *The Routledge Handbook of Migration and Development*. Abingdon: Routledge.

Bhambra, G. K. (2014). 'Postcolonial and Decolonial Dialogues', *Postcolonial Studies*, 17(2), 115–21.

Carling, J. (2002). 'Migration in the Age of Involuntary Immobility: Theoretical Reflections and Cape Verdean Experience', *Journal of Ethnic and Migration Studies*, 28(1), 5–42.

Carr-Hill, R. (2013). 'Missing Millions and Measuring Development Progress', *World Development*, 46, 30–44.

Crenshaw, K. (1989). 'Demarginalizing the Intersection of Race and Sex: A Black Feminist Critique of Antidiscrimination Doctrine, Feminist Theory and Antiracist Politics', *University of Chicago Legal Forum*, 1(8), 139–167

Culp, J., & Zwarthoed, D. (Eds). (2020). *Education and Migration*. Abingdon: Routledge.

de Haas, H. (2010). 'Migration and Development: A Theoretical Perspective', *International Migration Review*, 44(1), 227–64.

Del Monte, P., & Posholi, L. (2021). 'Decolonial Perspectives on Education and International Development', in T. McCowan & E. Unterhalter (Eds), *Education and International Development: An Introduction*, second edition. London: Bloomsbury, 79–92.

Long, K. (2014). *Huddled Masses: Immigration and Inequality*. London: Thistle Publishing.

Hall, S. (1996). '"When Was the Post-colonial"? Thinking at the Limit', in I. Chamber & L. Curtis (Eds), *The Post-colonial Question: Common Skies, Divided Horizons*. London: Routledge, 65–77.

Harber, C. (2014). *Education and International Development: Theory, Practice and Issues*. Oxford: Symposium Books Ltd.

Kapoor, I. (2008). *The Postcolonial Politics of Development*. London: Routledge.

McCowan, T., & Unterhalter, E. (Eds). (2022). *Education and International Development: An Introduction*, second edition. London: Bloomsbury Publishing.

Raghuram, P. (2009). 'Which Migration, What Development? Unsettling the Edifice of Migration and Development', *Population, Space and Place*, 15, 103–17.

Samaddar, R. (2020). *The Postcolonial Age of Migration*. India: Routledge.

Schewel, K. (2020). 'Understanding Immobility: Moving beyond the Mobility Bias in Migration Studies', *The International Migration Review*, 54(2), 328–55.

Tikly, L. (2001). 'Globalization and Education in the Postcolonial World: Towards a Conceptual Framework', *Comparative Education*, 37(2), 151–71. https://doi.org/10.1080/03050060124481.

Tikly, L. (2019). *Education for Sustainable Development in the Postcolonial World: Towards a Transformative Agenda for Africa*. Abingdon: Routledge.

Villalon, R. (2021). *Migration, Health and Inequalities: Critical Activist Research across Ecuadorean Borders*. Bristol: Bristol University Press.

White, S. (2016). *Cultures of Wellbeing: Method, Place, Policy*. Basingstoke: Palgrave Macmillan.

Zetter, R. (2007). 'More Labels, Fewer Refugees: Remaking the Refugee Label in an Era of Globalization', *Journal of Refugee Studies*, 20(2), 172–92.

Ziai, A. (2017). 'Post-development 25 Years after the Development Dictionary', *Third World Quarterly*, 38(12), 2547–58. https://doi.org/10.1080/01436597.2017.1383853.

Skilled Migration, Education and International Development

Kavita Datta

Introduction

Skilled or knowledge migration goes against the trend of a *hostile* age of migration (Raghuram 2021). Labelled as 'expatriates', 'human capital', 'knowledge workers', 'transnational elites' and a 'creative class',[1] skilled migrants are a much sought-after resource globally (Cranston 2017; Friesen and Collins 2017; Liu-Farrer et al. 2020). 'Talented' labour is credited for securing competitive advantage at the firm level while also revitalizing transnational cities. Indeed, cities emerge as critical nodes in skilled mobilities with most migrants moving from, to and between large cities with intercity mobility underpinning career development (Skeldon 2020). Skilled migrants are accepted as less threatening and more easily integrated in comparison to their 'unskilled' counterparts, those who are forced to migrate or those who move to join families (Boucher 2020; also, Liu-Farrer et al. 2020; Yeoh and Lam 2016). Importantly, mobility is integral to delimiting the skilled transnational worker who 'is by definition (and in fact *produced* by being) internationally mobile' (Yeoh and Lam 2016: 638).

Comprising two main 'types' of migrants – skilled workers and international students – the significance of skilled migration is evidenced by a 200 per cent global growth in tertiary educated migrants in the period 2000–17 (UNESCO 2019). Its relative importance is illustrated by a 130 per cent increase in skilled migration to OECD countries between 1990 and 2010 as compared to the far more modest 40 per cent growth in less-skilled migration (Skeldon 2020). A diversity of migration pathways and destinations is increasingly apparent. While the dominant trajectory of movement, and scholarly interrogation, is from the Global South to the Global North, and specifically the United States, Canada and the United Kingdom as primary destinations alongside Singapore and Dubai, the geographies of skilled migration are now recognized as being more diverse, including the Gulf States, Malaysia, Taiwan, South Africa and the East African region (Izaguirre and Walsham 2021). Cross-border south-to-south intraregional mobility of university students, professionals and scholars is also on the rise in Latin America and Asia, attributed in the latter case to increased intraregional investment, expansion of the middle classes, improving education levels and reduced restrictions on travel (Lee and Piper 2003).

Drawing upon multidisciplinary scholarship,[2] this chapter explores the nexus of skilled migration, education and international development, moving between and across the sites of home nations, host countries and migrants. It begins by unpacking the intersections between migration, education and development, highlighting the extent to which scholarship has been dominated by the 'brain drain/gain/circulation' framework. It assesses recent policy interventions such as the Global Skills Partnerships which have purportedly been designed to benefit home and host countries, and migrants, alike. The chapter then moves on to explore how skills are defined, drawing attention to social and political constructions which are temporally and spatially varied. The third and final section is dedicated to international student migration specifically, exploring intersectional gendered, racialized and class-based embodied experiences of migration particularly amplified during the Covid-19 pandemic, as well as wider structural and institutional dynamics shaping these mobilities.

Unpacking the Intersections of Skilled Migration, Education and Development

The importance of education for development has long been recognized with investments in primary, secondary and tertiary education a priority in many postcolonial states. Notwithstanding a nomenclature shift from education to 'human capital' and 'knowledge economies', key global organizations such as the World Bank (2007: xiii) continue to stress the need to 'put [knowledge] to work to accelerate and deepen the development process', particularly in relation to enhancing economic growth and competitiveness (see also Robertson 2008). In turn, migration scholars note the propensity for educated men and women to migrate. A UNESCO (2018) study reports that in comparison to those with no education who are least likely to migrate, primary school leavers are two times, secondary school educated three times and tertiary qualified four times more likely to migrate. Furthermore, skilled migrants are prone to migrate permanently to maximize incomes, highlighting the extent to which mobility might be beneficial at individual levels (Friesen and Collins 2017). Although emerging research has begun to explore Global South-to-South migrations, skilled migration, as noted earlier, is predominantly investigated in relation to Global South-to-North mobilities and identified as being driven by the labour market demands, demographic transitions and selective immigration policies instigated by advanced economies (Chikanda and Crush 2014; Skeldon 2009; Skeldon 2020).

'Brain drain, gain, waste, abuse, return and circulation' reflect the trajectory of skilled migration and development scholarship (Dodson 2021). The term 'brain drain' was first coined to capture the migration of skilled British workers moving to the United States in the 1950s and 1960s (Adams 1968). Since then, it has been predominantly deployed to understand emigration from the Global South to North, with the attrition of 'medical brains' – or health workers – a particular focus of attention (Friesen and Collins 2017). This said, and particularly salient in this context, is the loss of teachers through both North-to-South but also South-to-South migration with implications for the delivery of education (Weda and De Villiers 2021). Given this context, skilled migration has been widely perceived as being against the national interest of home countries due to knock-on economic and financial effects such as the depletion of the local knowledge and science base, erosion of tax revenues and adverse impacts on public institutions and service delivery (Liu-Farrer, Yeoh and Baas 2020). Cumulatively, the brain drain is blamed for entrenching global patterns of inequality (see also Crush and Hughes 2009).

Meanwhile, from the host country and migrant perspective, researchers have tracked the potentially deleterious outcomes of skilled migration on migrant men and women through the lens of 'brain waste' or 'abuse' with experiences of deskilling and de-professionalization widely noted (Wills et al. 2010). This is explained in relation to an oversupply of skilled labour, the fact that skills do not retain their value over space and obstacles to accreditation. Oftentimes, a lack of time, money or desire among migrants results in failure to obtain prerequisite credentials in host countries (Skeldon 2020). Importantly, deskilling is also the result of intersecting racist, nationalist and gender hierarchies which manifest in the particular (de)valuing of skills held by women and racialized minorities. Liu-Farrer, Yeoh and Baas (2020) argue that while migrants from the Global South are assumed to be 'unskilled', being white and/or having European citizenship translates into economic and social privilege. More broadly, the competition to capture the 'best talent' is increasingly evident in immigration policies which pay limited attention to the subsequent potentially deleterious impacts on countries of origin and/or the social and emotional costs of downward socio-economic mobility on migrants themselves (Datta et al. 2007). Exploring lived experiences of deskilling, Buckley, McPhee and Rogaly (2017) identify waiting as an active strategy adopted by migrant workers in low-paid sectors whereby deskilling is temporarily accepted as a short-term tactic on the premise that there will be opportunities to upskill or reskill while also building social networks to facilitate socio-economic mobility. This ambition is not necessarily realized.

More recent research has sought to illustrate the developmental gains generated by skilled migrations. There are various dimensions to the 'brain circulation' thesis which rests upon the movement of skills and/or skilled migrants. For a start, research highlights the beneficial educational impacts resulting from both financial and social remittances (defined as the circulation of ideas, skills and technologies) sent by workers to their families and countries of origin (see Levitt 1998). The expenditure of migrant remittances on children's education is commonplace across the globe while the anticipation of future emigration might stimulate skill development among aspiring migrants (Crush and Hughes 2009). In turn, transnational networks facilitate socio-economic, political, cultural and knowledge exchange while the return migration of knowledge workers with enriched entrepreneurial, financial and social capital is actively promoted by home governments through dual nationality initiatives as well as tax and other financial incentives (Crush and Hughes 2009; Weda and De Villiers 2021). This said, again, the acquisition of skills might not necessarily translate into economic or welfare increases while also distorting national education priorities. As an example, Dodson (2021) reports on the disruption of gendered patterns of nursing education in India and the Philippines attributable to the increased enrolment of men in this hitherto feminized sector. Furthermore, pressures on migrants to remit might hinder their own economic and social mobility.

Amidst perceptions that host countries benefit disproportionately from skilled migration, policy initiatives such as Global Skills Partnerships have sought to ameliorate the tension between home and host country interests by purportedly seeking to create a 'triple win' situation (Yeates and Pillinger 2018). Backed by international organizations such as the World Bank, International Labour Organization, International Organization for Migration, International Trade Union Confederation and OECD, Global Skills Partnerships are aligned to the Global Compact for Safe, Orderly and Regular Migration ambition to 'invest in skills development and facilitating mutual recognition of skills, qualifications and competence', with pilot initiatives in the health, and specifically nursing, sector (Van de Pas and Hinlopen 2018). Distinct from previous publicly funded bilateral agreements, these initiatives seek to mobilize private capital to invest in human capital in return for a (promise of a) solid return. The 'wins' for home countries include enhanced training capacities, while host countries benefit from filling skilled labour vacancies with well-educated relatively cheap workers and migrants given access to decent jobs and income security. However, despite these ambitions, concerns around sustainability, guarantees of decent work and labour rights associated with Global Skills Partnerships are prevalent (Yeates and Pillinger 2018; Van de Pas and Hinlopen 2018).

Critiquing the 'brain drain/gain/circulation' triad for being narrowly focused on outcomes and patterns, and suggestive of a particular directionality and temporality promoting a binary analysis of 'source-destination', 'permanent-temporary' and 'cost-benefit' analysis, Friesen and Collins (2017) propose the concept of 'brain chains'. The authors argue that this concept 'draws attention to the constitutive features of knowledge migration, the policies, processes and institutions that facilitate the development and movement of skilled workers and the knowledge they embody . . . as well as the intermediary actors and networks involved in generating and channelling flows, from families and communities to profit seeking agents' (Friesen and Collins 2017: 324). Encapsulating research which illustrates the chain migrations that are set in motion due to the emigration of knowledge workers, 'brain chains' are more attentive to complex multidirectional and multidimensional processes, and bring different stakeholders – home and host states, migrant intermediaries, migrants, their families and communities – into purview.

(Re/de) Valuing Skills: Social and Political Constructions

The definition of what constitutes as skills is largely unproblematized in migration, education and development scholarship. Yet, skills, critical scholars agree, are not objectively determined but rather socially and politically constructed (Boucher 2021). Indeed, as Boucher (2021: 190) argues, 'the process of defining skills is in itself an integral step in exercising power'. Defined by international organizations and national governments in different ways, the simplistic equation of (some level of) tertiary education with skills has given way to more expansive interpretations. As such, skills are identified in relation to human capital which encompasses education, occupation and linguistic skills;

by wage levels; by occupational skills benchmarked against the International Standard of Occupation;[3] as defined by employers and as 'extraordinary' talent associated with sportspeople, scientists, investors and artistic performers (Boucher 2021; Liu-Farrer et al. 2020; Skeldon 2020). While new distinctions such as 'extraordinary', 'highly' and 'super' skilled seek to differentiate among skilled populations, Skeldon (2020) maintains that the basic correlation between tertiary education, professional occupation and levels of income holds across many different contexts in relation to defining skills and shaping immigration approaches (Boucher 2020).

Despite these technical definitions, the ability to utilize skills is fundamentally shaped by social and political negotiation (Liu-Farrer et al. 2020). Gracia Liu-Farrer and her colleagues (2020: 3) cogently argue that the distinctions between high-, low- and mid-skilled labour are the outcome of 'economic demand and political calculation'. Skills, they point out, are not an intrinsic quality that individuals possess but are acquired, quantified and credentialed. Given that this sorting is generally done nationally, migrants who cross borders face particularly complex negotiations in the de/re/valuing of their skills in both spatially and temporally contingent ways. In turn, 'a constellation of actors' (Liu-Farrer et al. 2020: 4) comprising home and host states, employers and migrant intermediaries play a significant role in manipulating the conceptualization and categorization of skills to align with political and economic priorities.

Migration policies are key in reinforcing a hierarchical categorization of migrants' skill levels. Reflecting a shift in emphasis from occupational classification to more employer-targeted approaches, a UN survey conducted in 2013 found that two-thirds of its 172 member states were interested in developing skilled migration policies. This is particularly evident in managed migration approaches that seek to maximize the impact of knowledge migration by (i) attracting and managing skilled migration; (ii) facilitating international student migration as knowledge generators and (iii) tapping the knowledge flows of diasporic migrant communities (Friesen and Collins 2017). Ensuing 'points-based' immigration systems, such as the UK's Post Brexit 'New Plan for Immigration', aim to sort migrants into skilled, semi-skilled and unskilled categories, and to enhance the economic advantage of host countries by attracting the skilled and 'super skilled' (Boucher 2021; Liu-Farrer et al. 2020). As such, Buckley et al. (2017) argue the state plays a significant role in both producing *and* intensifying 'unfreedoms' and precarity in migrant labour markets, particularly evidenced in relation to low-paid work, the tying of migrants to employers and debt-financed migrations. More broadly, the authors argue that non-citizenship shapes the time-geographies of migrant work and employment. Importantly, and reflecting the extent to which definitions of skills are politically constructed, the trajectory from 'unskilled' to 'skilled' is not linear or unidirectional such that 'lesser' skilled work – for example carers – might be re-categorized as skilled in response to labour market vacancies (Boucher 2021).

Feminist scholarship illustrates that gender, race and nationality crucially shape understandings of skills, determining the exclusion of certain types of skills while overestimating skill levels associated with other professions (see earlier; also, Boucher 2021; Dodson 2021; Raghuram and Kofman 2004). While gender-disaggregated data are scarce, Lim (2019) details that two-thirds of the UK's Tier 1 visa holders (identified as businesspeople, investors and those with 'exceptional talent') are men, while 78 per cent of Tier 2 highly skilled workers are also male. Gender and racial discrimination are endemic in labour markets across the world as evidenced by wage gaps. Particularly evident in highly skilled work, and in sectors such as health and education where female workers predominate, women migrants are disadvantaged due to intersecting gender, racial and migrant divisions of labour (see Wills et al. 2010; also, Boucher 2020). Furthermore, a shift in occupational lists – which are determined by labour market vacancies – has the potential to shape the gender composition of skilled immigration admissions (see previous discussion). Boucher (2021) reports on horizontal segregation in Australian and Canadian occupational classifications whereby women are more likely to enter via the health and academic routes and men predominate in the IT sector. Equally problematic is that skill-based immigration policies can implicitly endorse race and gender biases despite purported commitments to equality (Boucher 2020). For example, employer-sponsored models whereby employers and/or their agents petition governments for visas for prospective employees are underpinned by 'soft skills' such as appearance, accent and demeanour which implicitly favour men and/or particular racialized women in relation to specific occupations. Women often fare far worse than men when it comes to leadership positions (ibid.).

As such, it is clear that the lived experiences of skilled migration are not frictionless illustrating that socio-economic privilege does not necessarily travel well particularly for skilled women (Raghuram and Kofman 2004). A range of studies illustrate the 're-domestication' of highly educated migrant women who may not be primary visa applicants and enter host countries as dependent spouses. Research undertaken in Malaysia and Qatar, for example, reflects that immigration rules delineate migrant women's status as mothers, wives and workers, and how intersections of gender and 'foreignness' produce disadvantage and control, resulting in the subordination, marginalization and exclusion of skilled migrant women in work and social spaces (Lee and Piper 2003; Rodriguez and Scurry 2019). A fruitful area for further enquiry, as identified by Izaguirre and Walsham (2021), is to explore, from a gendered and intersectional perspective, how skilled migration experiences differ for highly skilled individuals heading to Northern and Southern destinations.

International Student Migrations and Education

International students comprise a significant cohort of skilled migration who are either already skilled at the time of departure as they migrate to acquire further qualifications or who represent the 'future skilled' by virtue of studying abroad (Pitkänen and Takala 2012). Sidhu and her colleagues (2021) point to the particular significance of Anglophone destinations which are valued by international students for enabling the acquisition of critical social and cultural capital partly through the experience of living and studying in different linguistic and cultural contexts. As such, dominant Global South–North geographies are reproduced in international student migration flows, with China[4] and India standing out as source countries, and the United States, Australia, the United Kingdom, Canada and New Zealand emerging as significant destinations (Madge et al. 2015; Sondhi 2019). Singapore is increasingly noteworthy among the latter as it seeks to position itself as a 'global knowledge hub' with implications for intra-regional student mobilities (see later; also, Sidhu et al. 2021). Notwithstanding this focus on 'source' and 'destination' countries, it is important to remember that in the context of the internationalization of higher education, some countries fulfil both roles. For example, China ranks third, behind the United States and the United Kingdom, as a destination for international students, while Chinese international students are themselves very significant (Brooks and Waters 2021). International student migration has become a highly intermediated field brokered by education representatives, employment agencies, visa and immigration authorities and travel agents (Raghuram and Sondhi 2022).

Positioned at the juncture of education and migration, theorizations of international student migrations have entailed advances in both education and pedagogy, and mobilities and migration scholarship (Madge et al. 2015; Paul and Yeoh 2020; Raghuram 2021). Madge et al. (2015: 685) argue that the conceptual frame of 'international study' as opposed to 'international students' better 'locate[s] . . . life stories of mobility in the context of academic cultures and the demands of knowledge production, reproduction and circulation'. In reasoning that international students play an active role in knowledge production and circulation as opposed to being passive consumers, they argue for a two-way dialectic which recognizes the circulation of both bodies and knowledge. As such, greater appreciation is needed of the mutually constitutive nature of student mobility, education and pedagogy. In turn, there is increased consensus that student mobility should be situated within a broader trajectory of mobile careers and lives, and cognizant of diverse yet interrelated corporeal, knowledge and finance mobilities (Hari, Nardon and Zhang 2021; Madge et al. 2015; Raghuram and Sondhi 2022). Seeking to capture the lifetimes of these mobilities, Paul and Yeoh (2020: 4) propose that 'multinational migrations' capture the 'complex, dynamic and open-ended multinational trajectories that are contingent on shifting and uneven capitals, structured by fluid multinational migratory infrastructures and shaped by migrants evolving geographical imaginaries, aspirations and sense of themselves'.

In recognition of the potential benefits that international students stand to make to labour markets and economies, host countries often seek to capitalize on student mobility by linking it to skilled migration policies (Kim and Sondhi 2015). For example, Hari and her colleagues point to several Canadian immigration policy initiatives to retain students once they complete their education through schemes such as the Express Entry system whereby international students acquire additional points if they have Canadian qualifications. Yet despite the assumption that students who have these credentials will face fewer barriers to accessing and integrating into local labour markets, this is not necessarily the case (Kim and Sondhi 2015). Indeed, even while international student mobilities entail movement between visa categories, there is relatively limited work which examines the transitionary stages between being students and becoming workers which are highly contingent upon local political, economic and legal contexts (Hari, Nardon and Zhang 2021). The benefits to host countries and economies are restricted not only to students who remain but also with regard to those who return where they continue to exert 'soft power' on their behest (ibid.).

Meanwhile the position of home countries in relation to international students and potential aggravation of 'brain drain' is perhaps less well explored (although see Gribble 2008; Brooks and Waters 2021). In part this is attributable to a failure to apprehend international student migration as part of 'knowledge diasporas' and a tendency to view their mobilities as temporary (Brooks and Waters 2021). Yet, this said, home countries do/can operationalize strategies to 'retain, return and engage' with international students via initiatives such as bond arrangements whereby students on state sponsorships are required to return to work for a prerequisite number of years, encouraging students to enrol on shorter sandwich courses as well as motivating repatriation through economic and social incentives (Gribble 2008; Brooks and Waters 2021). While national identity is operationalized, for example, by the Singapore state to 'name and shame' scholars who fail to return home, other strategies deployed to engage students include professional-based networks (Brooks and Waters 2021).

Research demonstrates the wider structural and systemic dimensions of international student migrations, with particular foci on urban development, demographic compositions and retail environments. Perhaps unsurprisingly, large cities feature significantly as destinations for international student migration, which is particularly evident in the United States, Australia, New Zealand and Canada but less so in the United Kingdom where the international student population is more dispersed with only 15 per cent of international students studying and living in London (Collins 2010). The interplay between student migration and urban form has largely been interrogated in relation to domestic mobility, and then through the lens of 'studentification' or the social, cultural, economic and physical impact of seasonal student in-migrations on towns and cities. In extending this work to explore international student migrations, Collins (2010) calls for a broader approach that is cognizant of migratory regimes, the negotiation of different cultures, linguistic barriers and so on. He argues that international students are important urban agents, who symbolically and materially impact upon urban form and morphology. Various examples demonstrate this. Global rankings such as 'best student cities' are critically shaped by international students. Housing infrastructures – such as student accommodation – make a significant imprint on urban morphology while also playing a vital role in rental economies. Sidhu et al.'s (2021) report on rising vacancies and falling rents in a number of New Zealand and Australian cities in response to Covid-19-related travel restrictions is illustrative of the importance of international students for urban rental markets. International student migrations can also result in shifts in ethnic economies of food, service, retail and entertainment (Madge et al. 2015; Sidhu et al. 2021). Furthermore, they potentially reshape demographic profiles of minoritized communities as students are generally younger and more educated in comparison to settled diasporic populations as illustrated in Sondhi's (2019) examination of Indian students in Canada.

The experience of being an international student has received much attention. Scholars point to diverse socio-economic and political agential capacity, partly attributed to complex simultaneously occupied subjectivities as migrants, students, workers, refugees, sons, daughters and parents which interplay with gender, race and class regimes (Madge et al. 2015). In their rather sombre assessment, Kim and Sondhi (2015) argue that there is a real disconnect between imagined and real experiences. Thus, while for some international mobility can reproduce class privilege and help cement cosmopolitan identities, for others the experience is considerably less positive (Madge et al. 2015; Raghuram and Sondhi 2022). International student experiences are explored in relation to academic outcomes, social dimensions and psychosocial well-being and adaptation, and regarding encounters with local populations, other international students and co-ethnic diasporic populations (Sondhi 2019). There is significant evidence that international students struggle to extend their friendship groups to include local students, partly due to linguistic and cultural differences, while also encountering significant racism. In her exploration of the relationship between old settled and new student Indian communities, Sondhi (2019) draws attention to the gendered and sexual negotiations that women and gay students undertake to either make themselves intelligible or remain unintelligible in the context of a more conservative heteronormative diasporic milieu. In an interesting twist, while the assumption is that student migrants move from traditional to progressive societies, this may not be their lived experience.

The Covid-19 pandemic has been instructive in both revealing and intensifying experiences of deprivation, marginalization and exclusion among international students. An early casualty of the travel restrictions instituted in response to the pandemic, student mobilities began to decline as far back as February 2020 (Sidhu et al. 2021). The irony that the 'costs' of this decline were largely considered in terms of implications for the higher education sector is not lost on scholars who have long noted that the operational budgets of Northern universities are underpinned by the inflated fees paid by international students (Hari, Nardon and Zhang 2021; Raghuram and Sondhi 2022). In the UK alone, the loss in real and potential revenue was estimated at £790 million in 2019–20 and £6.9 billion in 2020–1 (ibid.). In thinking through the implications of the pandemic on UK-based international students, Raghuram and Sondhi (2022) reflect that they fell into one of three categories. The first comprised students who chose to remain in the UK largely due to fears that a potentially protracted period away might have deleterious implications on post-study visas which require a minimum period of residence. The second category included those who left – identified by some as being 'healthy and wealthy' enough to do so – but have then faced difficulties re-entering (see also Sidhu et al. 2021). This is attributable to volatile travel bans and 'red lists' that were subject to frequent and unanticipated changes as the pandemic has itself peaked and subsided in different parts of the globe; prohibitive airfares which have accompanied enforced immobility; mandatory isolation periods and third-country clearance policies. The third, and final group, is made up of students who have delayed their plans to move to study with some uncertainty of their future plans (see later).

The restrictions put in place to contain the coronavirus disrupted 'taken-for-granted mobility' and sociality across two or more nations that underpin transnationalism (Hari, Nardon and Zhang 2021). In their research on the impact of the Covid-19 pandemic on international students in Canada, Hari and her colleagues (2021) examine students' transnational sensemaking, transnational families and transnational futures. Clearly evidenced in their broader research are significant experiences of deprivation across a range of Northern contexts as stories of hunger, isolation and abandonment have surfaced (Datta et al. 2021). These illustrate the heterogeneity of 'international students', who are not uniformly privileged and among whom a significant proportion rely upon part-time work to make ends meet while they study. As these opportunities to work failed to materialize or disappeared during the pandemic, so dependence on food banks, diasporic communities and reverse remittances from parents has become evident (ibid.). Pandemic-related experiences of racism, particularly directed at East Asian students, have also been noted, while universities have been criticized for failing to adjust their education, housing and visa structures to respond to student deprivation (Hari, Nardon and Zhang 2021; Raghuram and Sondhi 2022).

The pandemic raises specific educational and pedagogical challenges with three potential scenarios put forward by Sidhu et al. (2021). The first is the entrenchment of hybrid learning whereby physical presence and virtual presence are facilitated and enable both short- and long-term mobilities. It is clear that the pandemic necessitated broader structural changes in the provision of education with a shift towards digital and online teaching. While the pros and cons of online teaching are extensively discussed elsewhere, in relation to international students, the following points are worth noting. For those in favour, digital infrastructures potentially broaden social and geographical access, allow students to actively choose immobility over mobility in educational settings and enable significant reductions in the carbon footprint associated with international student migrations (Sidhu et al. 2021). However, critics counter-argue that while 'low-level' educational activities might be deliverable online, higher-quality, enquiry-led educational activities require face-to-face encounters. As such, effective and quality learning is associated with embodied learning that is situated and place-reliant and underpinned by, and building upon, social capital (ibid.). Digital poverty remains a significant challenge, as does teaching across different time zones. Identifying the very real threat of the 'surveilled, datafied classroom' as digital technologies are used to monitor student engagement and educational and pedagogic content and practice, Sidhu et al. (2021: 317) warn against the threats posed by rapid digitalization, the (further) privatization and commercialization of universities as digital infrastructures and services are outsourced and the emergence of what they term as the 'platform university'.

A redrawing of international student migrations away from traditional Anglophone destinations to more intraregional mobilities is a second alternative future. This can be partly attributed to ongoing pandemic travel restrictions but also due to xenophobic racist attacks and health concerns prompting movement to destinations closer to home. Here the evidence is varied. While Sidhu and her colleagues (2021) point to the pivoting of Chinese student migration to destinations in East Asia, others predict a 'return to normal' partly engineered by the global industry which underpins student mobility as well as the entrenched valuing of Anglophone knowledges and social capital. The third set of arguments relates to the forging of a responsibility and ethics of care *for* international student migrants who were abandoned during the pandemic, with home and host states, and universities stepping up to this responsibility (Sidhu et al. 2021).

Conclusion

This chapter has explored the linkages between skilled migration, education and development, highlighting the extent to which these are co-constituted. The key lines of enquiry include a critical assessment of the dominant frames deployed to interrogate this nexus: the definition, and social and political construction, of skills and the specific dynamics of international student mobilities which comprise a significant part of skilled migration. In so doing the chapter has sought to elaborate on the interplay between structural and systemic processes and agential capacities, as well as the extent to which experiences of skilled migration are far from frictionless and heavily intermediated by gender, race and nationality.

Notes

1 There are important distinctions between these terms, although they are often used interchangeably with 'skilled migrant' (see Cranston 2017).
2 Skilled migration has been studied from a diverse range of disciplinary perspectives, including geography, sociology, politics, anthropology, economics, philosophy, migration studies and human resource management (Raghuram 2021).
3 The top three categories – namely managers, social officials and legislators; professionals and technicians and associated professionals - are identified as skilled occupations (Boucher 2021).
4 Almost 43 per cent of international students coming to New Zealand originate from China alone, while Chinese international students are estimated to have generated AU\$1.1 billion for the eight research intensive universities in Australia (Go8) (Sidhu et al. 2021).

References

Adams, W. (1968). *The Brain Drain*. New York: Macmillan.
Boucher, A. (2020). 'How "Skill" Definition Affects the Diversity of Skilled Immigration Policies', *Journal of Ethnic and Migration Studies*, 46(12), 2533–50.
Boucher, A. (2021). 'Gender Bias in Skills Definition, Labour Market Dynamics and Skills Recognition', in C. Mores & N. Piper (Eds), *Palgrave Handbook of Gender and Migration*. Switzerland: Palgrave Macmillan, 187–202.
Brooks, R., & Waters, J. (2021). 'International Students and Alternative Visions of Diaspora', *British Journal of Educational Studies*. https://doi.org/10.1080/00071005.2021.1948501.
Buckley, M., McPhee, S., & Rogaly, B. (2017). 'Labour Geographies on the Move: Migration, Migrant Status and Work in the 21st Century', *Geoforum*, 78, 153–8.
Chikanda, A., & Crush, J. (2014). 'Diasporas of the South', in R. Anich, J. Crush, S. Melde, & J.O. Oucho (Eds), *A New Perspective on Human Mobility in the South*. New York: Springer, 65–88.
Collins, F. L. (2010). 'International Students as Urban Agents: International Education and Urban Transformation in Auckland, New Zealand', *Geoforum*, 41(6), 940–50.
Cranston, S. (2017). 'Expatriate as a "Good" Migrant: Thinking through Skilled International Migrant Categories', *Population, Space and Place*, 23(6). https://doi.org/10.1002/psp.2058.
Crush, J., & Hughes, C. (2009). 'Return Migration', in R. Kitchen & L. Lees (Eds), *International Encyclopaedia of Human Geography*. Elsevier, 342–7.
Datta, K., McIlwaine, C., Wills, J., Evans, Y., Herbert, J., & May, J. (2007). 'The New Development Finance or Exploiting Migrant Labour? Remittance Sending among

Low-Paid Migrant Workers in London', *International Development Planning Review*, 29(1), 43–67.

Datta, K., Hammond, L., & Majeed-Hajaj, S. (2021). 'Shifting Contours of Care: How UK Indian Diasporas Give and Receive Care in the Time of COVID-19, World Bank People Move Blog Series'. https://blogs.worldbank.org/peoplemove/shifting-contours -care-how-uk-indian-diasporas-give-and-receive-care-time-covid-19 (accessed 12 October 2021).

Dodson, B. (2021). 'Gender and Gender Relations in Skilled Migration: More Than a Matter of Brains', in C. Mores and N. Piper (Eds). *Palgrave Handbook of Gender and Migration*. Switzerland: Palgrave Macmillan, 203–20.

Friesen, W., & Collins, F. L. (2017). 'Brain Chains: Managing and Mediating Knowledge Migration', *Migration and Development*, 6(3), 323–42.

Gribble, C. (2008). 'Policy Options for Managing International Student Migration: The Sending Country Perspective', *Journal of Higher Education Policy and Management*, 30(1), 25–39.

Hari, A., Nardon, L., & Zhang, H. (2021). 'A Transnational Lens into International Student Experiences of the COVID-19 Pandemic', *Global Networks*. https://doi.org /10.1111/glob.12332.

Izaguirre, L., & Walsham, M. (2021). 'South to South Migration from a Gender and Intersectional Perspective: An Overview', Working Paper, MIDEQ. https:// www.mideq.org/en/resources-index-page/south-south-migration-gender-and -intersectional-perspective/ (accessed 20 August 2021).

Kim, A. H., & Sondhi, G. (2015). 'Bridging the Literature on Education Migration', *Population Change and Lifecourse Strategic Knowledge Cluster*, Discussion Paper Series/Un Réseau stratégique de connaissances Changements de population et parcours de vie Document de travail, 3(1), Article 7. https://ir.lib.uwo.ca/pclc/vol3/ iss1/7 (accessed 20 August 2021).

Lee, M., & Piper, N. (2003). 'Reflections on Transnational Life-course and Migratory Patterns of Middle-class Women: Preliminary Observations From Malaysia', in N. Piper & M. Roces (Eds), *Wife or Worker? Asian Women and Migration*. Lanham, MD: Rowman and Littlefield, 121–36.

Levitt, P. (1998). 'Social Remittances: Migration Driven Local-level Forms of Social Diffusion', *The International Migration Review*, 32(4), 926–48.

Lim, D. (2019). 'The Indirect Gender Discrimination of Skill – Selective Immigration Policies', *Critical Review of International Social and Political Philosophy*, 22(7), 906–28.

Liu-Farrer, G. Yeoh, B. S., & Baas, M. (2020). 'Social Construction of Skill: An Analytical Approach toward the Question of Skill in Cross-border Labour Mobilities', *Journal of Ethnic and Migration Studies*. https://doi.org/10.1080 /1369183X.2020.1731983.

Madge, C., Raghuram, P., & Noxolo, P. (2015). 'Conceptualizing International Education: From International Student to International Study', *Progress in Human Geography*, 39(6), 681–701.

Paul, A. M., & Yeoh, B. S. A. (2020). 'Studying Multinational Migrations, Speaking Back to Migration Theory', *Global Networks*. https://doi.org/10.1111/glob.12282.

Pitkänen, P., & Takala, T. (2012). 'Using Transnational Lenses to Analyse Interconnections between Migration, Education and Development', *Migration and Development*, 1(2), 229–43.

Raghuram, P. (2021). 'Injecting the *Geographies of Skills* into International Skilled Migration Research', *Population, Space and Place*. https://doi.org/10.1002/psp.2463.

Raghuram, P., & Kofman, E. (2004). 'Out of Asia: Skilling, Re-skilling and Deskilling of Female Migrants', *Women's Studies International Forum*, 27, 95–100.

Raghuram, P., & Sondhi, G. (2022). 'The Entangled Infrastructures of International Student Migration: Lessons from Covid-19', in A. Triandafyllidou (Ed), *Migration Pandemics: Spaces of Solidarity and Spaces of Exception*. Springer International Publishing. https://doi.org/10.1007/978-3-030-81210-2.

Robertson, S. L (2008). 'Producing' Knowledge Economies: The World Bank, the KAM, Education and Development', in M. Simons, M. Olssen & M. Peters (Eds), *Re-reading Education Policies: Studying the Policy Agenda of the 21st Century*. Netherlands: Sense Publishers, 235–56.

Rodriguez, J. K., & Scurry, T. (2019). 'Female and Foreign: An Intersectional Exploration of the Experiences of Skilled Migrant Women in Qatar', *Gender, Work and Organization*, 26(4), 480–500.

Sidhu, R., Cheng, Y., Collins, F., Ho, K. C., & Yeoh, B. (2021). 'International Student Mobilities in a Contagion: (Im)mobilising Higher Education?', *Geographical Research*, 59(3), 313–23.

Skeldon, R. (2009). 'Of Skilled Migration, Brain Drains and Policy Responses', *International Migration*, 47(4), 3–29.

Skeldon, R. (2020). 'Skilled Migration', in T. Bastia and R. Skeldon (Eds), *Routledge Handbook of Migration and Development*. London and New York: Routledge, 136–45.

Sondhi, Gunjhan. (2019). '"Settlers" Meeting the "Settled": International Students Encountering South Asian "Diasporas" in Ontario, Canada', in OUM Book', in M.-J. Kwak & A.H. Kim (Eds), *Outward and Upward Mobilities: International Students in Canada, Their Families, and Structuring Institutions*. Toronto: University of Toronto Press, 159–76.

UNESCO (United Nations Educational, Scientific and Cultural Organisation) (2018). *Migration, Displacement and Education: Building Bridges Not Walls*. Global Education Monitoring Report. Paris: UNESCO.

UNESCO (2019). *Defending the 'Right to the City': How Cities Include Migrants and Refugees in and Through Education*. Paris: UNESCO.

UN (2013). *International Migration Policies: Government Views and Priorities*. Economic and Social Affairs. New York: UN.

Van de Pas, R., & Mans, L. (2018). *Global Skills Partnerships and Health Workforce Mobility: Pursuing a Race to the Bottom?* Public Services International. http://world

-psi.org/sites/default//files/attachment/news/web_2018_mig_report_marrakesh.pdf (accessed 19 October 2021).

Weda, Z., & de Villiers, R. (2021). 'Partial and Virtual Return: The Willingness of Migrant Zimbabwean Teachers in South Africa to Participate in Skills Transfer', *International Migration & Integration*, 22, 849–64. https://doi.org/10.1007/s12134 -020-00778.

Wills, J., Datta, K., Evans, Y., Herbert, J., May, J., & McIlwaine, C. (2010). *Global Cities at Work: New Migrant Divisions of Labour*. London: Pluto Press.

World Bank (2007). *Building Knowledge Economies: Advanced Strategies for Development, World Bank Institute Development Series*. Washington, DC: World Bank.

Yeates, N., & Pillenger, J. (2018). 'International Healthcare Worker Migration in Asia Pacific: International Policy Responses', *Asia Pacific Viewpoint*, 59(1), 92–106.

Yeoh, B. S. A., & Lam, T. (2016). 'Immigration and Its (Dis)Contents: The Challenges of Highly Skilled Migration in Globalising Singapore', *American Behavioral Scientist*, 60(5–6), 637–58.

2

Education, Domestic Work and the 'Feminization of Migration'

Amy North and Priyadarshani Joshi[1]

Introduction

Processes and experiences of internal and international migration are fundamentally shaped by gendered norms, relations and inequalities in both countries and communities of origin and countries and communities of settlement, and by the gendered nature of global and local labour markets. These, in turn, both affect and are affected by education in often complex ways: access to and engagement with education is in itself a highly gendered process, which may facilitate – or hinder – migration and be enabled or limited by it, while gendered opportunities for and engagements with education may have a significant influence on how processes of migration and settlement are experienced.

The gendered dynamics of the migration–education relationship affect both women and girls, and men and boys in different ways (North 2019). This chapter is concerned with the experiences of migrant women in particular, in the context of what has been termed the 'feminization of migration' (Castles and Miller 1993), and focuses on the experiences of women who migrate as domestic workers. In the sections that follow, we consider the wider literature that has explored the experiences of migrant domestic workers and then look at issues relating to aspects of their engagement with education more specifically. Through the discussion we examine some of the tensions between the ways in which the experiences of migrant women have been understood in terms of vulnerability on the one hand and agency on the other, and how ideas about education play out within this.

The 'Feminization of Migration'

Since the 1990s, a growing body of literature has been concerned with the relationship between gender and migration. While women are estimated to make up just under 50 per cent of migrants globally (ILO 2015), there is significant regional variation, with women comprising up to 70–80 per cent of migrants in some countries (Fleury 2016). Much of the recent growth in female migration has been within the Global South, with increased numbers of women migrating from South and Southeast Asia to West Asian countries in the Gulf and more affluent East and North Asian countries (Tittensor and Mansouri 2017). Moreover, although the overall proportion of women among international migrants globally has increased only slightly since the 1960s,[2] the past three decades have witnessed significant shifts in the type and nature of this migration. In particular, in contrast to traditional 'male breadwinner' models of migration, which assumed that women largely migrate to join male family members as dependents, research has pointed to the increased numbers of women migrating independently for work (Gutierrez-Rodriges 2010; Hondagneu-Sotelo 2017).

A significant proportion of women migrating internationally work in a relatively small number of highly gendered sectors of employment, in which conditions are often extremely precarious and the work demanding and low-paid. These include domestic work, the care economy more broadly – which includes childcare, healthcare, care for the elderly, and cleaning in private households and institutional settings – as well as in manufacturing and the garment industry (Kofman and Raghuram 2015; Gonçalves and Schluter 2020). Similar patterns of factory labour, domestic work and care are highly prevalent among rural to urban internal migrants in African, Asian and Latin American countries (ILO 2013; Alaluusua 2017; Mitra and Damle 2019). In China, for example, the *dagongmei* (female migrant workers) often symbolize the feminized workforce that supported China's tremendous industrialization and economic progress through a gendered division of labour (Ngai 1999; Fan 2003). However, ethnographic research has shown that young women are often encouraged to marry migrant men before returning to their households of origin to perform domestic labour, with factory work portrayed as risky and not feminine (Chuang 2015), and analysis finds that married migrant women have worse working conditions, pay and benefits than single women (An, Broadbent and Yuan 2018).

Domestic Labour and 'Global Care Chains'

Migrant domestic work is particularly gendered: according to the International Labour Organization (ILO), of the estimated sixty-seven million domestic workers globally, approximately 80 per cent are women (ILO 2017). While male domestic workers tend to take on the relatively prestigious roles of butlers, valets or gardeners (Cox 2006), migrant women tend to carry out the reproductive work associated with caring for children, as well as general housekeeper tasks. This reproductive labour is generally considered to be low-status 'women's work' and, as such, often not viewed as 'real work' (Hondagneu-Sotelo 2007; Lutz and Palenga-Möllenbeck 2011) or stigmatized as 'dirty work' (Anderson 2000; Zarembka 2002).

The role played by migrant women, who are often mothers themselves, in carrying out reproductive work for other families has resulted in what Parreñas, drawing on Glenn's (1992) formulation of the 'racial division of international labour', has described as the 'international division of reproductive labour' (Parreñas 2001; 2012) and what Hochschild (2000) has referred to through the term 'global care chains'. Both conceptualizations draw attention not only to the role that global inequalities and processes of uneven development play in shaping both demand and supply for migrant domestic work but also to the way in which migrant domestic work itself may serve to reinforce such inequalities. Thus, the concept of the 'international division of reproductive labour' is a way of 'accounting for the costs of migrant reproductive labour to families and communities in countries of origin and juxta-positioning such costs against the gains made by the households of employers in the host countries' (Parreñas 2012: 271). Meanwhile, Hochschild associates 'care chains' – which describe how a migrant domestic worker caring for someone else's children in the Global North may use her wages to pay for someone else to care for her own children in her country of origin, who may, in turn, pay another woman from a rural community to look after her children – with the extraction of care labour as 'emotional surplus value' from the Global South and the provision of 'surplus love' to children in the Global North (Hochschild 2000; King-Dejardin 2019).

Such discussions highlight the significance of the relationships between migrant domestic workers and their communities of origin and the impact that migrant domestic work has not only for migrant women themselves but also for those they leave behind. The nature of this relationship is complex and has emotional and social, as well as economic dimensions. The economic role that the migrant domestic workers play in sending remittances back to their home countries is well documented (see Abrantes 2012; Deshingkar et al. 2014). For Sassen (2002), this is associated with the emergence of 'survival circuits' and the 'feminization of survival', as, in the context of high levels of global inequality, exacerbated by the structural adjustment programmes of the 1980s and 1990s, the increasingly significant role played by migrant women in providing financial support to their communities of origin has meant that 'not only are households, indeed whole communities, increasingly dependent on women for their survival but so too are governments' (265).

Taking on the role of economic provider in this way has the potential to enhance migrant women's economic and social status and standing in their communities of origin (Batnitzky et al. 2012). However, it also binds women into networks of obligation, which may limit their ability to leave abusive employers or make the decision to return home (Lai 2011). Meanwhile, the emotional challenges associated with trying to maintain close family relationships from a distance are often considerable. Research into the experiences of migrant domestic workers and their families suggests that, for women who are mothers, the relationships sustained with families back home can be particularly intense, as they attempt to navigate 'transnational motherhood' (Hondagneu-Sotelo and Avila 1997) and play an active role in bringing up their children from a distance (Parreñas 2005; Madianou and Miller 2011). And, although remittances may enable the children of migrant mothers to access educational opportunities which otherwise might not have been available to them, the social and emotional costs of separation for children who stay behind are often significant (Lam and Yeoh 2019).

Exploitation, Agency and/in Constraint

Research that has engaged with the experiences of migrant women reveals how these are shaped by their marginal positioning within structures of power and inequalities, which are mediated by gender, class, race, ethnicity and immigration status (Crenshaw 1991; Brah and Phoenix 2004). Intersecting forms of disadvantage and inequality mean that migrant women are often vulnerable to sexual and racial abuse, harassment and discrimination, as well as to exploitation and abuse in the workplace, and, for migrant domestic workers, this vulnerability is exacerbated by the hidden nature of domestic work within private households, which are often exempt from normal processes of labour regulation (Ehrenreich and Hochschild 2002; Mactaggart and Lawrence 2011).

Moreover, the contradictions between the home as both an intimate private space and a workplace mean that the relationship between domestic workers and their employers, and the power dynamics that are entailed, may be particularly complex (Lan 2002; Hondagneu-Sotelo 2007).

Numerous studies have revealed the exploitation and abuse often experienced by migrant domestic workers (e.g. Cox 2006; Wadhawan 2013; Näre 2014). Research with female domestic workers who travel from Nepal to the Gulf and other countries, for example, demonstrates how they experience multiple layers of exploitation, often facilitated by labour brokerage networks, which are inadequately controlled by government enforcement. Migrant domestic workers are often misinformed about their working conditions and incur major debt at high credit rates, which traps them into continuing in domestic work, even when faced with abuse, harassment and other abhorrent working conditions (Amnesty International 2017). Bridget Anderson's research among domestic workers in London similarly documents multiple instances of physical and sexual abuse in the workplace, as well as imprisonment, being 'sold' to other employers, and having food and wages withheld. This has led her to compare migrant domestic work to slavery and argue that 'the commonly accepted transition from traditional to modern, from un-free labour to free labour is incomplete' (Anderson 2000: 4). However, researchers have also cautioned against simply characterizing migrant domestic workers as 'victims', emphasizing their agency in resisting exploitative working conditions and pointing to the potential for migration to represent a process of liberation from restrictive family control or gender norms (e.g. Barber 2000; Williams 2010).

Studies with migrant domestic workers that have engaged explicitly with understanding agency in their lives suggest that the relationship between liberation and agency, on the one hand, and slavery and exploitation, on the other, is complex (see Parreñas 2001; Briones 2009). Rhacel Salazar Parreñas's (2001) seminal study of the experiences of Filipina domestic workers in Rome and Los Angeles, for example, suggests that domestic workers' 'marginal location in multiple discursive spaces of race, gender, nation and class' leaves them 'decentred' and 'fragmented' subjects (32). However, her research also reveals how, despite this, migrant domestic workers can and do take action to attempt to ease and resist the dislocations they experience and counteract their marginal status and quasi-citizenship in their places of work. This includes, for example, turning to 'the construction of the Philippines as "home" so as to envision a place of rightful membership in the global labor market' or building relationships of solidarity with other migrant domestic workers (252). Importantly, though, these actions do not necessarily result in 'concrete benefits in their lives' (254) and, indeed, may contribute to the maintenance of wider inequalities. Parreñas thus argues that while migrant domestic workers do have agency, that agency is not only highly constrained but may in fact be binding rather than liberating.

Such research points to a need to better understand how, and under what circumstances, migrant women may exercise forms of agency 'in constraint' (McNay 2000) as they attempt to navigate the tensions and dislocations generated by migration and domestic work, combined with the wider inequalities that may limit the impact of such agency on their working conditions, material circumstances or ability to pursue alternative forms of employment and livelihood. Several factors have been identified as potentially significant here, including connections to social networks, as well as, importantly, immigration status and the nature of the immigration and employment regimes in the host country. In the following sections, we turn our attention to considering the role of education in influencing women's agency and experiences in relation to migrant domestic work.

The Significance of Education

Education can play multiple roles in gendered decision-making and experiences with regard to migration and migrant domestic work. At the individual level, opportunities – or a lack of opportunities – to engage in schooling, themselves shaped by gendered norms and socio-economic conditions in countries and communities of origin, may influence the ability of women and girls to make decisions regarding their migratory trajectories, and affect their ability to deal with informational and other challenges during migration. However, there may also be important, and gendered, intergenerational and intrafamily dynamics affecting decision-making regarding both migration and education. The need to provide economically for family members, or to support the education of the younger generation, for example, can be major motivators for entering and continuing in migrant domestic work (North 2013).

Although educated women may have more employability options, and therefore be less likely to have to enter vulnerable employment such as domestic work, a number of studies have underlined the fact that many women who migrate for domestic work are highly educated (Parreñas 2001; Lutz 2011; Abrantes 2012). This means that in undertaking domestic work, they may experience processes of downward mobility, as their educational experiences and qualifications are not recognized in the countries and households in which they find work. Such studies, alongside research with migrant women working in the care sector more broadly (Cuban 2008), suggest that having higher levels of education does not automatically translate into better working conditions or career opportunities, and that this is a result of the way in which the qualifications and skills of migrant women lose value when they leave their countries or communities and professions of origin (see also Datta, Chapter 1). However, it is also clear that there is considerable diversity with regard to the educational backgrounds of migrant domestic workers. Anderson (2009), for example, when discussing migrant domestic workers in London, notes the contrast between well-educated Filipino migrants 'with a specific migratory project' coming to London with employment agencies via the Middle East, and Indian migrant domestic workers who had come to the UK with wealthy Indian employers and who 'themselves were rural to urban migrants, often with little English or education' (ibid.: 68). The educational backgrounds of domestic workers may also vary depending on the location and type (internal or international) of migration. Despite this, relatively few studies include specific consideration of the experiences of migrant domestic workers with little formal education or examine how migrant domestic workers' engagement with learning (prior to or following migration) may interact with their experiences of domestic labour.

Research with women who have migrated internally as domestic workers suggests that the relationship between education and experiences of domestic work is a complex one. Rao's (2011) study of the experiences of adolescent girls from a rural village in Jharkhand state who migrate to work in private households in urban Delhi, for example, considers how the girls' ability to exercise agency in dealing 'with the contradictions they face between earning incomes, acquiring markers of status and gaining respect across the urban and rural worlds they straddle' (ibid.: 758) is affected by previous engagement with formal schooling. It shows how for domestic workers formal education does not provide many of the skills and attributes that are valued by employers, but that nonetheless schooling does contribute to improving their ability to engage in workplace negotiation and enhance their terms of employment. Research by Chatterjee and Schulter (2020) considers the informal tutoring in English provided by female employers to the daughters of the domestic workers they employ in Kolkata. Their study points to the aspirational value that learning English holds for the domestic workers 'as a vehicle through which they can imagine a higher status' for their daughters, if not for themselves, but also highlights the tensions apparent in the ways in which the tutoring process plays out within the asymmetrical, and interdependent, relationship between domestic workers and their employers.

Such complexity is also reflected in the findings of studies concerned with the learning experiences of internationally mobile migrant domestic workers. Sondra Cuban's research, for example, with domestic workers in New York and the Bay Area (Cuban 2007), points to the challenges to learning that arise from their employment as domestic workers, but also shows how, despite these difficulties, 'women participate and persist in community-based literacy and ESOL programmes as part of a self-determination strategy to cope with the strains and stresses of low paying demanding work in the service sector' (ibid.: 4). This echoes Rockhill's earlier research with Latina domestic workers in Los Angeles, which highlighted the symbolic value placed on literacy learning as representing the possibility of escape from domestic labour, but also pointed to the way in which domestic workers' engagement with such learning may be constrained by the nature of their work in the private sphere, which both isolates them and renders invisible the literacy practices they engage in (Rockhill 1993).

Research with migrant women more widely points to the value of non-formal education programmes which both recognize the constraints of migrant women's lives and build on their 'funds of knowledge' (the existing skills and experience that they bring with them into the classroom space), and highlights the importance of ensuring that learning opportunities support migrant women to develop skills which are relevant to their lives and aspirations (e.g. Choi and Najar 2017; Klenk 2017). For migrant domestic workers, educational interventions that are attentive to the financial pressures they experience, linked to responsibilities for supporting families at home, debt accrued during migration and vulnerability to exploitation by financial intermediaries, may be particularly important. However, although financial education programmes for migrant women have been valuable in informing them how to access and use financial services and improve their savings, there is often less focus on the more challenging protective and preventive aspects, such as providing information and mechanisms to help them tackle problematic credit rates and exploitation by moneylenders; tackling misinformation regarding working conditions and providing them with tools to protect themselves when they face mistreatment on the job. Research with migrant domestic workers in Hong Kong and Italy suggests that education programmes that link financial literacy with wider issues affecting the well-being of migrant domestic workers, such as employment rights or the challenges of managing family expectations, can play an important role not only in building financial skills but also in increasing confidence and self-esteem (Zhou et al. 2020; Prandini and Baconguis 2021).

The extant literature thus points to some of the tensions and contradictions apparent in the relationship between education, learning and the ways in which women experience migration and domestic work. While having some formal education may contribute to increased power of negotiation within the workplace, it is clear that increased education does not automatically translate into better working conditions or alternative career options outside domestic work. Despite this, the value that many migrant domestic workers place on learning – whether formal or non-formal – is significant. This is explored further in the following case study, which is based on empirical research conducted by North with migrant domestic workers in London.[3]

Case Study: Learning, Literacy and Transnational Connection

> Maybe if we had a good education, we could find a nice job but we don't, we didn't get an education, we can't read and write, all we can be is domestic workers.

The aforementioned quote is from Nhanu,[4] one of a group of ten migrant domestic workers from Nepal and India, who, between 2008 and 2013, attended an informal literacy support group at the Migrant Resource Centre in London. This case study draws on interviews and observations conducted with the group by North over this period. It considers three key ways in which the women in the group spoke about education in relation to their lives and experiences.

An Education Lost

> My parents didn't force me to go to school. . . . When I was 11, I went to make carpets. . . . Then I went to India when I was 15, working as a domestic worker. I was still a child then, I hadn't even got my period, but I was working.

In contrast to the highly educated women who are often the focus of studies of migrant domestic work, all the women in the group described limited opportunities to engage in formal education: one had completed primary school, three had attended school for a short time, while the others had never enrolled at all. In describing their first experiences of migration, the women emphasized their sadness at the loss of opportunities for schooling, as well as the loss of childhood entailed by the responsibility of providing for family at a very young age. None of them saw migrant domestic work as something they entered into by choice. Rather, they linked having to migrate and become domestic workers to their lack of education, as well as to high levels of poverty and poor economic opportunities in their rural communities. Meanwhile, migration clearly curtailed their opportunities to complete school or gain qualifications that might have opened up different options. This was a source of regret: in sessions they often compared themselves to friends who had been able get 'office jobs', commenting that 'life would have been easier' if they had learned to read and write.

The women's negative view of domestic work was shaped by their own experiences of often severe exploitation and abuse. These included physical abuse, being held captive in employers' houses (in one case for a whole year), being 'lent out' to other families, having passports confiscated and salaries unpaid. Meanwhile, being required to work excessively long hours and on days-off were common and ongoing experiences across the group. However, group members also spoke with enormous pride of their achievements as migrant women, who, despite their lack of formal schooling, had crossed the world, travelling from rural communities in Nepal and India to London, often via countries in the Middle East, and provided significant support to families and communities at home.

Learning in London

> Now if someone asks me my surname at least I know how to spell it, if they ask my house number or road, I can write it. . . . Now it is much easier to know how to go places. . . . Before I had to get a taxi if I got lost and would be charged so much because I couldn't read the places, the street names to find my way.

For all the women in the group coming to London not only brought new literacy and language demands but also opened up new opportunities to learn. As well as the informal literacy support sessions, they all also attended other English or ESOL and citizenship classes. However, despite having good spoken English, they described the challenges of language classes which assumed prior experience of formal education, explaining how they struggled to copy things from the board or fill out grammar worksheets. Nevertheless, they were determined to make the most of opportunities to improve their literacy and language skills. This was, in part, linked to their perceived importance for securing 'indefinite leave to remain' in the UK and to enable them to apply for visas for family members, but it was also linked to their wider aspirations and hope that education might help them realize their dreams of finding jobs outside of domestic work. However, although several of the women were successful in regularizing their immigration status and changing employers during the period of the research, none were able to move out of domestic work altogether.

Nonetheless, although the new skills they developed did not result in the transformation of their working conditions, they were considered important as they moved beyond the workplace. This was in part due to the increased confidence they gave them as they navigated life in London, reducing their reliance on – and vulnerability to exploitation by – others as they travelled around the city or negotiated financial transactions. Being able to draw on their developing language and literacy skills as they managed their transnational relationships and connected with family and friends at home and across the globe was also important. Here, being able to assume a literate identity as they filled in the documentation associated with travel between the UK and Nepal, or read and responded to SMS messages, was particularly valued.

Supporting Others

> If [my nephews and nieces] can read and write they will find a nice job in a hotel or in an office, they won't have to be housekeepers.

When the women in the group discussed their own learning, they often spoke about how proud family members at home were that they had learned to read and write in English. One described how her own learning success had enabled her to persuade her husband to learn to read and write in India. Another, Sudha, talked often about her son, a teenager, who, at the beginning of the research, attended a private school in India, paid for by her wages. She explained that the thought that her son was proud of her was one of the reasons she was so happy to have learnt to read and write in English.

In Sudha's case, her aspirations for her son's education entailed supporting him to come to London for college (something that she had achieved by the end of the research period). More often, group members spoke about the support they provided to the schooling and university education of family members back home, describing the achievements of not just their own children but also nieces, nephews and extended family members. However, continuing to provide this support came at a cost. All the women spoke of their longing to one day be able to leave domestic work and return home to their villages but said that this would not be easy as the role they played in sending home remittances was essential, not just for their families' immediate material well-being but also to enable the next generation to receive the education and opportunities that they had missed out on, and to ensure that they wouldn't have to become domestic workers like they had.

Conclusion

Despite growing academic attention to the experiences of migrant domestic workers since the 1990s, the position of education in women's migratory journeys and the role it may play in influencing experiences of migrant domestic work, and supporting women's agency and ability to overcome discrimination and exploitation, remain underexplored. The experiences of the women discussed in the case study earlier, like those in the wider literature, suggest that the position of education in migrant domestic workers lives may be complex and often contradictory. In the narratives of the women discussed earlier, education takes on multiple meanings. It is talked about in in terms of loss, and in terms of opportunity, and is bound up in wider aspirations for – and sense of obligation to – family at home. It is seen as important and may enhance agency in often quite subtle ways but, on its own, is not transformative; it does not necessarily enable migrant women to overcome the constraints and the wider structural inequalities that led to them having to migrate in the first place and which affect their gendered positioning vis-à-vis the global labour market and tie them into low-status work in the domestic sphere. Despite this, it is highly valued, not only for its practical significance in enabling women to negotiate new literacy demands and manage transnational communication with family and friends, but also for its symbolic promise linked to hopes for a different future not just for the women themselves but also for the future generation.

Migrant women, including those employed as domestic workers, play a significant role in supporting education and development in their communities of origin through the provision of remittances, and, in the context of the feminization of migration, and the continued demand for migrant women's labour in domestic work and other sectors of the care economy, this is likely to continue. However, this contribution comes at a cost. The research literature shows that women who migrate, whether internally or internationally, experience intersecting forms of inequality and discrimination linked to their sex, class, ethnicity and (im)migration status, and that migrant domestic workers are especially vulnerable to exploitation and abuse, particularly in contexts where local labour laws provide little or no protection. There is therefore a need for continuing research in order to better understand the needs of migrant domestic workers and the factors that influence their experiences of domestic work, as well as those that might enable them to resist exploitation and support them to pursue aspirations and opportunities beyond the domestic space. This must include paying closer attention to education and to understanding the role that formal and non-formal educational opportunities – both prior to and following migration – may play in shaping the way in which women experience, and are able to make decisions about, migration and domestic work.

Notes

1 The designations employed and the presentation of material throughout this chapter do not imply the expression of any opinion whatsoever on the part of UNESCO concerning the legal status of any country, territory, city or area, or its authorities or concerning the delimitation of its frontiers or boundaries. The author is responsible for the choice and the presentation of the facts contained in this chapter and for the opinions expressed therein, which are not necessarily those of UNESCO and do not commit the organization.
2 Rising from 46.6 per cent in 1960 to 48.8 per cent in 2006 (Marchetti 2018).
3 For more details, see North 2013, 2017, 2018.
4 All names are pseudonyms.

References

Abrantes, M. (2012). 'You're Not There to Make the World Any Cleaner', *European Societies*, 14(3), 320–37. https://doi.org/10.1080/14616696.2012.676661.

Alaluusua, S. (2017). 'Rural to Urban Migration and Young Female Domestic Workers in the 21st Century Lima, Peru', *Migrating Out of Poverty: From Evidence to Policy*, London, 28–29 March. http://www.migratingoutofpoverty.org/files/file.php?name=alaluusua-rural-to-urban-migration-and-young-female-domestic-workers-update.pdf&site=354.

Amnesty International (2017). 'Nepal: Turning People into Profits: Abusive Recruitment, Trafficking and Forced Labour of Nepali Migrant Workers'. https://www.amnesty.org/en/documents/asa31/6206/2017/en/ (accessed 15 October 2021).

An, F., Broadbent, K., & Yuan, F. (2018). 'Employment Inequality among Women Migrant Workers in China: Comparative Analysis from the 2014 Guangdong Migrant Workers Survey', *Asia Pacific Journal of Human Resources*, 56(4), 518–38. https://doi.org/10.1111/1744-7941.12180.

Anderson, B. (2000). *Doing the Dirty Work? The Global Politics of Domestic Labour*. London and New York: Zed Books.

Anderson, B. (2009). 'Mobilizing Migrants, Making Citizens: Migrant Domestic Workers as Political Agents', *Ethnic and Racial Studies*, 33(1), 60–74. https://doi.org /10.1080/01419870903023660.

Barber, P. (2000). 'Agency in Philippine Women's Labour Migration and Provisional Diaspora', *Women's Studies International Forum*, 23(4), 399–411. http://dx.doi.org/10 .1016/S0277-5395(00)00104-7.

Batnitzky, A., McDowell, L., & Dyer, S. (2012). 'Remittances and the Maintenance of Dual Social Worlds: The Transnational Working Lives of Migrants in Greater London', *International Migration*, 50(4), 140–56. https://doi.org/10.1080 /01419870903023660.

Brah, A., & Phoenix, A. (2004). 'Ain't I a Woman? Revisiting Intersectionality', *Journal of International Women's Studies*, 5(3), 75–86. https://vc.bridgew.edu/jiws/vol5/iss3/8.

Briones, L. (2009). *Empowering Migrant Women: Why Agency and Rights Are Not Enough*. Farnham: Ashgate.

Castles, S., & Miller, M. (1993). *The Age of Migration: International Population Movements in the Modern World*. Basingstoke: Palgrave Macmillan.

Chatterjee, A., & Schluter, A. (2020). '"Maid to Maiden": The False Promise of English for the Daughters of Domestic Workers in Post-colonial Kolkata', *International Journal of the Sociology of Language*, 2020(262), 67–95. https://doi.org/10.1515/ijsl -2019-2070.

Choi, J., & Najar, U. (2017). 'Immigrant and Refugee Women's Resourcefulness in English Language Classrooms: Emerging Possibilities through Plurilingualism', *Literacy and Numeracy Studies*, 25(1), 20–37. http://dx.doi.org/10.5130/lns.v25i1 .5789.

Chuang J. (2015). 'Factory Girls After the Factory: Female Return Migrations in Rural China', *Gender & Society*, 30(3), 467–89. https://doi.org/10.1177/0891243215621718.

Cox, R. (2006). *The Servant Problem: Domestic Employment in a Global Economy*. London and New York: I.B. Tauris.

Crenshaw, K. (1991). 'Mapping the Margins: Intersectionality, Identity Politics, and Violence against Women of Color', *Stanford Law Review*, 43(6), 1241–99. https://doi .org/10.2307/1229039.

Cuban, S. (2007). 'For Some Reason, I'm Just Tired': Women Domestic Workers Persisting in Community-Based Programmes', *Journal of Adult and Continuing Education*, 13(1), 3–18. https://doi.org/10.7227/JACE.13.1.2.

Cuban, S. (2008). 'Home/Work: The Roles of Education, Literacy, and Learning in the Networks and Mobility of Professional Women Migrant Carers in Cumbria', *Ethnography and Education*, 3(1), 81–96. https://doi.org/10.7227/JACE.13.1.2.

Deshingkar, P., Zeitlyn, B. & Holtom, B. (2014). 'Does Migration for Domestic Work Reduce Poverty? A Review of the Literature and an Agenda for Research', *Migrating*

Out of Poverty Research Programme Consortium, Working Paper 15. Brighton: University of Sussex.

Ehrenreich, B., & Hochschild, A. (2002). 'Introduction', in B. Ehrenreich & A. Hochschild (Eds), *Global Women: Nannies, Maids and Sex Workers in the New Economy*. London: Granta Books, 193–7.

Fan, C. (2003). 'Rural-Urban Migration and Gender Division of Labor in Transitional China', *International Journal of Urban and Regional Research*, 27(1), 24–47. https://doi.org/10.1111/1468-2427.00429.

Fleury, A. (2016). 'Understanding Women and Migration: A Literature Review', *Knomad*, Working Paper 8. Washington, DC: Knomad. http://www.atina.org.rs/sites/default/files/KNOMAD%20Understaning%20Women%20and%20Migration.pdf (accessed 15 October 2021).

Glenn, E. (1992). 'From Servitude to Service Work: Historical Continuities in the Racial Division of Paid Reproductive Labor', *Signs: Journal of Women in Culture and Society*, 18(1), 1–43. https://doi.org/10.1086/494777.

Gonçalves, K., & Schluter, A. (2020). 'Introduction: Language, Inequality and Global Care Work', *International Journal of the Sociology of Language*, 2020(262), 1–15. https://doi.org/10.1515/ijsl-2019-2067.

Gutierrez-Rodriges, E. (2010). *Migration, Domestic Work and Affect: A Decolonial Approach on Value and the Feminization of Labor*. New York: Routledge.

Hochschild, A. (2000). 'Global Care Chains and Emotional Surplus Value', in W. Hutton & A. Giddens (Eds), *On the Edge: Living with Global Capitalism*. London: Jonathan Cape, 130–46.

Hondagneu-Sotelo, P. (2007). *Domestica: Immigrant Workers Cleaning and Caring in the Shadows of Affluence*. Berkeley, LA: University of California Press.

Hondagneu-Sotelo, P. (2017). 'Gender and Migration Scholarship: An Overview from a 21st Century Perspective', *Migraciones Internacionales*, 6(20), 219–34. https://doi.org/10.17428/rmi.v6i20.1066.

Hondagneu-Sotelo, P., & Avila, E. (1997). '"I'm Here, But I'm There": The Meanings of Latina Transnational Motherhood', *Gender & Society*, 11(5), 548–71. https://doi.org/10.1177/089124397011005003.

ILO (2013). 'Rural-Urban Migrants Employed in Domestic Work: Issues and Challenges'. https://in.one.un.org/wp-content/uploads/2016/09/wcms_214732.pdf (accessed 15 October 2021).

ILO (2015). *Labour Migration Highlights No. 3: Migrant Domestic Workers*. Geneva: ILO (International Labour Office). https://www.ilo.org/wcmsp5/groups/public/---ed_protect/---protrav/---migrant/documents/publication/wcms_384860.pdf (accessed 15 October 2021).

ILO (2017). 'Implementation of International Labour Standards for Domestic Workers'. https://www.ilo.org/global/research/publications/what-works/WCMS_572156/lang--en/index.htm (accessed 15 October 2021).

King-Dejardin, A. (2019). *The Social Construction of Migrant Care Work: At the Intersection of Care, Migration and Gender.* Geneva: International Labour Office. https://www.ilo.org/wcmsp5/groups/public/---ed_protect/---protrav/---migrant/documents/publication/wcms_674622.pdf (accessed 15 October 2021).

Klenk, H. (2017). 'An Alternative Understanding of Education and Empowerment: Local-Level Perspectives of Refugee Social Integration in the United Kingdom', *European Education*, 49(2–3), 166–83. https://doi.org/10.1080/10564934.2017.1341290.

Kofman, E., & Raghuram, P. (2015). *Gendered Migrations and Global Social Reproduction.* Basingstoke: Palgrave Macmillan.

Lai, M.-y. (2011). 'The Present of Forgetting: Diasporic Identity and Migrant Domestic Workers in Hong Kong', *Social Identities*, 17(4), 565–85. https://doi.org/10.1080/13504630.2011.587309.

Lam, T., & Yeoh, B. (2019). 'Parental Migration and Disruptions in Everyday Life: Reactions of Left-behind Children in Southeast Asia', *Journal of Ethnic and Migration Studies*, 45(16), 3085–104. https://doi.org/10.1080/1369183X.2018.1547022.

Lan, P.-C. (2002). 'Among Women: Migrant Women and Their Taiwanese Employers across Generations', in B. Ehrenreich & A. Hochschild (Eds), *Global Women: Nannies, Maids and Sex Workers in the New Economy.* London: Granta Books, 169–89.

Lutz, H. (2011). *The New Maids: Transnational Women and the Care Economy.* London and New York: Zed Books.

Lutz, H., & Palenga-Möllenbeck, E. (2011). 'Care, Gender and Migration: Towards a Theory of Transnational Domestic Work Migration in Europe', *Journal of Contemporary European Studies*, 19(3), 349–64. https://doi.org/10.1080/14782804.2011.610605.

Mactaggart, F., & Lawrence, M. (2011). *Service Not Servitude: Protecting the Rights of Domestic Workers.* London: IPPR.

Madianou, M., & Miller, D. (2011). 'Mobile Phone Parenting: Reconfiguring Relationships between Filipina Migrant Mothers and Their Left-behind Children', *New Media & Society*, 13(3), 457–70. https://doi.org/10.1177/1461444810393903.

Marchetti, S. (2018). 'Gender, Migration and Globalisation: An Overview of the Debates', in A. Triandafylidou (Ed.), *Handbook of Migration and Globalisation.* Cheltenham: Edward Elgar Publishing, 443–57.

McNay, L. (2000). *Gender and Agency: Reconfiguring the Subject in Feminist and Social Theory.* Cambridge: Polity Press.

Mitra, R., & Damle, A. (2019). 'Female Migrant Workers and Domestic Employees Need a Security Net', *The Wire*, 11 November. https://thewire.in/labour/women-labour-domestic-work (accessed 15 October 2021).

Näre, L. (2014). 'Moral Encounters: Drawing Boundaries of Class, Sexuality and Migrancy in Paid Domestic Work', *Ethnic and Racial Studies*, 37(2), 363–80. https://doi.org/10.1080/01419870.2012.729669.

Ngai, P. (1999). 'Becoming Dagongmei (Working Girls): The Politics of Identity and Difference in Reform China', *The China Journal*, 42, 1–18. https://doi.org/10.2307/2667638.

North, A. (2013). 'Reading and Writing between Different Worlds: Learning, Literacy and Power in the Lives of Two Migrant Domestic Workers', *International Journal of Educational Development*, 33(6), 595–603. https://doi.org/10.1016/j.ijedudev.2012.12.001.

North, A. (2017). 'What Kind of Literacy? Reflections on the Experiences of Migrant Domestic Workers Negotiating Learning in London', *European Education*, 49(2–3), 184–200. https://doi.org/10.1016/j.ijedudev.2012.12.001

North, A. (2018). 'Domestic Work, Learning and Literacy Practices across Transnational Space', *International Studies in Sociology of Education*, 27(2–3), 217–38. https://doi.org/10.1080/09620214.2018.1425101.

North, A. (2019). 'Gender, Migration and Non-formal Learning for Women and Adolescent Girls', *2019 Global Education Monitoring Report Gender Report*. Paris: UNESCO. https://gem-report-2019.unesco.org/background-papers/ (accessed 15 October 2021).

Parreñas, R. (2001). *Servants of Globalization: Women, Migration and Domestic Work*. Stanford, CA: Stanford University Press.

Parreñas, R. (2005). 'Long Distance Intimacy: Class, Gender and Intergenerational Relations between Mothers and Children in Filipino Transnational Families', *Global Networks*, 5(4), 317–36. https://doi.org/10.1111/j.1471-0374.2005.00122.x.

Parreñas, R. (2012). 'The Reproductive Labour of Migrant Workers', *Global Networks*, 12(2), 269–75. https://doi.org/10.1111/j.1471-0374.2012.00351.x.

Prandini, M., & Baconguis, R. (2021). 'Changing Lives: Transformative Learning and Financial Attitudes of Filipino Women Migrants in Italy', *Studies in the Education of Adults*, 53(1), 61–81. https://doi.org/10.1080/02660830.2020.1813956.

Rao, N. (2011). 'Respect, Status and Domestic Work: Female Migrants at Home and Work', *European Journal of Development Research*, 23(5), 758–73. https://doi.org/10.1057/ejdr.2011.41.

Rockhill, K. (1993). 'Gender, Language and the Politics of Literacy', in B. Street (Ed.), *Cross Cultural Approaches to Literacy*. Cambridge: Cambridge University Press, 156–75.

Sassen, S. (2002). 'Global Cities and Survival Circuits', in B. Ehrenreich & A. Hochschild (eds), *Global Women: Nannies, Maids and Sex Workers in the New Economy*. London: Granta Books, 254–74.

Tittensor, D., & Mansouri, F. (Eds). (2017). *The Politics of Women and Migration in the Global South*. London: Palgrave Macmillan.

Wadhawan, N. (2013). 'Living in Domesti-City: Women and Migration for Domestic Work from Jharkhand', *Economic & Political Weekly*, 48(43), 47–54. https://www.jstor.org/stable/23528839.

Williams, F. (2010). 'Migration and Care: Themes, Concepts and Challenges', *Social Policy and Society*, 9(3), 385–96. https://doi.org/10.1017/S1474746410000102.

Zarembka, J. (2002). 'America's Dirty Work: Migrant Maids and Modern-Day Slavery', in B. Ehrenreich & A. Hochschild (Eds), *Global Women: Nannies, Maids and Sex Workers in the New Economy*. London: Granta Books, 142–53.

Zhou, H., Dai, H., & Jung, N. (2020). 'Empowering Migrant Domestic Helpers through Financial Education', *International Journal of Social Welfare*, 29(2), 129–41. https://doi.org/10.1111/ijsw.12385.

3

Policies and Practices of Education Inclusion for Mobile Pastoralists

Caroline Dyer

Introduction: Mobile Pastoralists and Policy Discourses of Inclusion

The Education for All (EFA) movement recognized, and made a specific pledge to address, the widespread exclusion of mobile pastoralists from formal education provision (WDEFA 1990). Since that pledge was made, UN-led Global (Education) Monitoring Reports have repeatedly highlighted that migrating groups in general continue to be marginalized in education provision (e.g. GMR 2010; GEMR 2019) and that mobile pastoralists are among the globally most excluded (Dyer 2014).

'Migrants' might now be more firmly in the gaze of scholars and development actors, but this gaze has begun to see 'migrants' in ways that may perpetuate, rather than tackle, education inequalities. Migration studies persistently focus on international/cross-border migration, reflecting a politicization of migration that is linked to perceptions of security threats and what many in the Global North see as a 'refugee crisis', which prompts scholarly concern over multiple related injustices for international migrants. This concern, justifiable though it is, deflects attention from the numerically more significant scale of internal (within country) migration (Dyer 2014) and its implications for equitable education inclusion (Dyer and Rajan 2021). But even if this semantic elision is recognized, mobile pastoralists remain a 'migrating' population segment that lies outside the general, albeit lopsided, purview of migration studies altogether.

Mobile pastoralists are people who raise domestic livestock, using mobility as a strategy to access natural resources in the highly variable conditions that characterize global drylands (de Jode 2010). In pastoralist-dominated regions, rates of school enrolment, retention and progression lag behind – usually far behind – national averages (Ruto et al. 2009; GMR 2010; GEMR 2019). These statistical profiles reflect structural disadvantages of urban-centric development approaches that leave 'remote rural' areas with poor physical infrastructure, poor access to services and, often, weak governance (Onwu and Agu 2010; Davies et al. 2010). This has given rise to labels such as 'hard to reach' and, in the Sustainable Development Goal (SDG) framework, 'left behind', which imply that efforts should be intensified to reach and include pastoralists in existing, albeit more 'flexible', forms of provision. Policy approaches framed by this kind of discourse tend to assume mobility is *the* key barrier to be overcome and promote alternative delivery models to enable access and address 'terms of inclusion' (Dyer 2013) that obviously disadvantage migrating children, such as the requirement of being in the same place every day to attend school.

Access-focused strategies are important but do not address 'terms of inclusion' at the level of normative framings that formal education systems – through both their overt and their hidden curricula – reflect and reproduce (Dyer and Rajan 2021). These norms reflect the historical antecedents of modern education itself, as a means of developing citizens who embody the dominant values of sedentary modernity (e.g. residential fixity, being formally educated, being able to contribute to/compete in/benefit from a (globalized) market economy, being a consumer). Exclusion and marginality are situated in tensions between these kinds of norms, and the mobile, moral economies of pastoralist communities and their practices of situated, contextual learning: childhood is not sharply demarcated from adulthood in terms of labour contributions, so children have to attend to livelihood-related tasks at the times when schools run; mobility patterns counter sedentary norms around physical accessibility of fixed place provision and the curricular content of formal education does not provide knowledge or skills that support the pursuit of pastoralism and can be socially divisive (Scott-Villiers et al. 2015).

It is also important to recognize that mobile pastoralists are not a homogenous group. In contexts of often rapid change, some are 'stepping up' (intensifying pastoralism, with large animal holdings and significant wealth); others are 'staying in' (staying within pastoralism, but often diversifying to include other income-generating activities at household level) and others again are 'stepping out' (leaving pastoralism altogether) (Catley 2017). These categories are not fixed, but this broad typology points to the need for education provision to respond to the differences between, and within, them (Figures 3.1 and 3.2).

The term 'mobile' pastoralist, now widely used in scholarly literature, differentiates pastoralists who move from those who rear domesticated animals in a sedentary setting. Mobility is a deliberate livestock management strategy used in zones of high variability to ensure animals have continuous access to fodder and water resources. Mobile pastoralism is highly dependent on 'common property' (as well as private) resources.

Many mobile pastoralists have a 'home', in a particular location, and they migrate away from this home in an annual, seasonal cycle (this is called transhumance). 'Nomadic' pastoralist is another term in use, sometimes meaning the same as 'mobile' pastoralist but also meaning people who permanently move and do not have a 'home' location. Agro-pastoralists are people who farm and keep animals, migrating locally.

Migration can be *vertical*, between high summer / low winter pastures in mountainous regions; or *horizontal*, across the plains. Pastoralist mobility is carefully planned: the routes taken by particular groups are broadly similar each year but mobility *en route* is responsive to local conditions and movement may, accordingly, be very frequent (a stay of just a few days) or longer. Pre-planning helps to avoid clashes with other land users and competition for resources.

'Land grabbing' and development-induced displacement are everywhere undermining mobile pastoralism by constraining access to resources. In Sub-Saharan Africa, in areas where small arms circulate because of conflict, clashes have sometimes become very violent. Climate change, which makes rains more erratic, is also enforcing change to migration patterns in the constant search for resources. It can also mean that 'shocks' (events that have a significant negative welfare effect, such as drought or flood) are more frequent. They can increase vulnerability by leaving less time to re-stock before the next shock, which may lead to 'exiting' from pastoralism.

Figure 3.1 Mobile pastoralism: Definitions, migration and mobility. *Source*: Davies et al. (2010); Catley (2017); Dyer (2014).

The next section presents case studies of Mongolia, Ethiopia and India that illustrate how policy initiatives, through both their presence and absence, approach (or ignore) education inclusion for mobile pastoralists. The conclusion reflects on implications of these cases for education in equitable and sustainable development.

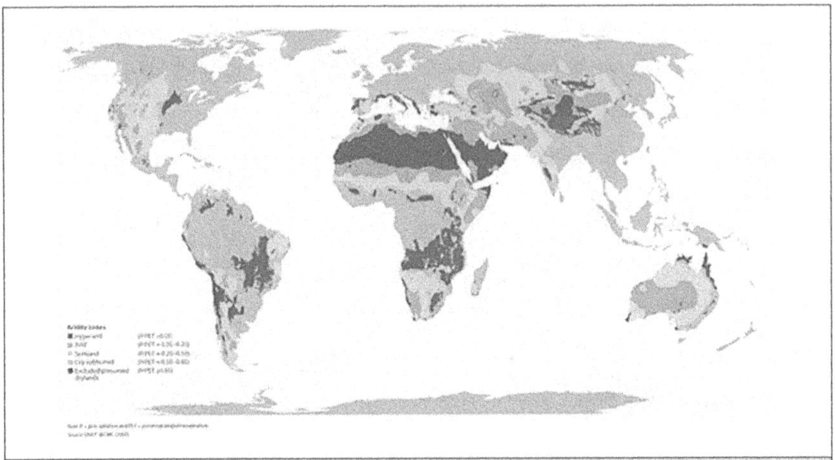

Drylands cover approximately 41% of the world's surface, are highly vulnerable to climate change and are commonly marginalised in national development plans. They typically show very low health and education indicators, and high poverty levels, and are prone to violent conflict, outmigration and youth unemployment. Policy engagement with drylands development has widely been misinformed by inaccurate science and/or inappropriate knowledge of natural resource-based livelihoods which are a major driver of dryland economies.

Figure 3.2 The global drylands. *Source*: de Jode (2010); Davies et al. (2010).

Policy and Practices of Educating Mobile Pastoralists: Cases of Mongolia, Ethiopia and India

Our first case is of Mongolia, which in 2018 embarked on a review of education sector policy to inform its planned 2020–30 Education Sector Master Plan. I worked there (as lead international consultant) with UNESCO representatives and national stakeholders on the Education Policy Review (EPR 2020). The review focused, at the government's request, on questions of quality, relevance, equity and inclusion, in response to national concerns that the sector, while meeting existing policy goals and numerical targets, was nevertheless 'in crisis' when it came to these issues. The next case is of Ethiopia, where the federal Ministry of Education had developed a Pastoralist Education Strategy in 2008 and sought, in 2016–17, to evaluate and update it within the scope of the externally supported Quality Education Sector Support Programme. I co-conducted an empirically based situation analysis covering four pastoralist regions in 2016 and then co-authored the 2017 Pastoralist Education Strategy. The third case of Western India draws on my work there for over twenty years as a 'pracademic' (researcher/teacher/learner) with pastoralists (Dyer 2014, 2019). In this context, in contrast with Mongolia and Ethiopia, strategic engagement by the state with the specificities of mobile pastoralists' educational needs or aspirations is notable by its complete absence.

The Rural Past, Present and Future in Mongolia

Mongolia is one of the world's most sparsely populated countries, with a dispersed population of 3.2 million people living across a vast territory. About three-quarters of national land area is pastureland, which supports immense herds of grazing livestock, and in rural areas the population density is just two persons per km² (MIER 2019). In stark contrast, the capital Ulaanbaatar – a magnet for rural–urban migration – is heavily overcrowded, with 311.3 persons per km² (MIER 2019). By 2017, just 32 per cent of the population was living in rural areas (MIER 2019). Mongolia's distinctive ancient culture of extensive herding is integral to national identity. The country's geographic location, extreme and highly seasonal climate, fragile ecosystems and dependence on extractive industries to power economic growth have combined to make Mongolia particularly vulnerable to climate change, with an increasing frequency of *dzud* (extremely harsh winters), and desertification.

Mongolia began the transition to a multiparty, democratic polity and market economy in 1990 after the collapse of the Soviet Union and its sphere of influence. Structural adjustment reforms privatized public assets and enterprises, introduced liberalized markets to drive economic growth and rolled back the state. Donor agencies became critical sources of funds, technical advice and 'policy borrowing' solutions (Steiner Khamsi 2006), against a backdrop of high political instability. The extensive, high-mobility pastoralism for which Mongolia is known, and which had been integrated into the command economy via collectives, was subjected to de-collectivization, marketization and land privatization. This rural re-structuring, and lifting of regulations that tightly controlled movement, ushered in a trend of migration to urban locations where markets, better job opportunities and higher education are available (Ahearn and Bumochir 2016; UNICEF 2017). Nevertheless, some 30–40 per cent of the population are herders (sources are inconsistent) and about quarter of the population own livestock (MIER 2019), although it is heavy industry that drives national economic growth. In Ulaanbaatar, where 47 per cent of the population now lives, public services are under severe pressure, air pollution is notorious and levels of human well-being are low for many (IoM 2018).

Like other formerly socialist states, Mongolia's education sector came close to collapse following the break-up of the Soviet Union. Soviet subsidies, which had supported free education for every child from primary school to tertiary education, suddenly ceased, and teachers left the profession. Mongolia saw the most rapid fall in school life expectancy among Central Asian transition economies. Families lacked incentives to invest in education, which, with the economy in collapse, was bringing reduced rates of returns, at least at secondary and tertiary levels. Two decades on, Mongolia had configured a new system in which, by 2015–16, the net primary enrolment rate was 96.3 per cent, and retention to grade 5 runs at 94 per cent (MIER 2019). The percentage of out-of-school children (OOSC) is higher in rural areas (1.4 per cent urban, 2.4 per cent rural). Boys comprise two-thirds of OOSC, and their dropout rate at secondary level is higher than girls', which is widely attributed to leaving school to work in pastoralism. The adult literacy rate, nevertheless, is claimed to be 98.5 per cent (MIER 2019). Tertiary provision has mushroomed, with high reliance on private sector investment: by 2018, 23 per cent of all women and 17 per cent of all men had a bachelor's or master's degree (IoM 2018). Beneath apparently healthy statistics, however, are major policy concerns over quality, notably highly didactic teaching at all levels, and relevance (EPR 2020).

In socialist times, in rural areas, children studied at the primary school in their *soum* (district), enrolled for lower secondary education in inter-*soum* secondary schools and went for upper secondary education to *aimag* (province) centres or secondary schools in large settlements. Boarding facilities were resource-intensive but well-funded and part of the rural social fabric. Children were required to complete eight years of schooling within a ten-year period, and the enrolment age was eight. But in 2005, the school entrance age was lowered from eight to seven; and just three years later, in 2008, it was lowered again, from seven to six. Structural reform aligned provision with the international norm of twelve years but had a catastrophic set of effects for pastoralists: it curtailed the period in which situated livelihood learning could take place; and it exposed children to dormitory environments at a younger age. Boys and girls in pastoralist communities comprised more than two-thirds of the 25,063 children using dormitories in 2016–17 (MIER 2019). Dormitory quality has deteriorated, due to insufficient budget and staffing constraints, to an extent that there are calls for a child protection system to address not only inadequate heating and water, sanitation and hygiene (WASH) facilities but also intimidation, group discrimination and corporal punishment (Save the Children Japan 2015).

Pastoralist families' coping strategies have various effects on schooling participation. Sometimes a child is simply sent later. Another common response is to split households during the winter months (Ahearn 2018; Batkhuyag and Dondogdulam 2018), which enables age-for-grade enrolment but avoids using dormitories. Children, usually with their mother, migrate to *soum* centres for school in the autumn, where they usually live with a family member. Men are left behind to tend animals and maintain the rural household. This response undermines rural schools, as enrolments decline (Batkhuyag and Dondogdulam 2018); and the social structure of pastoralist families is being changed. 'Winters without women' (Ahearn 2018) make divorce more common; and because women often cannot gain employment in urban settings, material poverty increases (IoM 2018) which puts pressure on the state to alleviate it.

The 2014–24 State Policy on Education requires that every child be enrolled in Early Childhood Education (ECE) provision, using different modalities of provision. Pastoralist children comprise a disproportionately low 11.5 per cent of the current total (EPR 2020), and the alternative programmes provided for them are 'not sufficient to close the school readiness gap' (Batkhuyag and Dondogdulam 2018). Almost 70 per cent of access to ECE for young pastoralist children is provided by mobile '*ger* kindergartens' which move from community to community during spring and summer. These typically offer just 21–62 days of instruction, about one-third of the learning opportunity of the 190 days offered in formal kindergartens (Batkhuyag and Dondogdulam 2018). Alternative ECE services were innovations intending to improve equity and parity of participation, but such provision relies on time-bound projects and programmes offered by development partners; and the sector itself has become fragmented in ways that undermine policy objectives of holistic, good quality ECE for all children.

Poor employability is a key focus of policy discourse around relevance. This prompted a 2019 reform of technical and vocational education that vigorously focuses on closing the gap between qualifications and employment within industries on which national development is seen to depend, such as mining and construction. Consideration of skills for those who wish to stay in mobile pastoralism is almost entirely excluded (EPR 2020). Although development partners have supported programmes aiming to blend farming and herding (Batkhuyag and Dondogdulam 2018), 'policy borrowing' is imposing norms of a sedentary ranching model rather than extensive high-mobility pastoralism.

Nor is there any relationship between mobile livestock herding and teaching programmes in the higher education sector, which is oriented towards formal professions, although the economy is not generating enough graduate level jobs (MIER 2019). Since almost all tertiary provision is in Ulaanbaatar (93 per cent of all students at this level), higher education is a significant driver of migration to the capital (IoM 2018).

Internal migration, with its dynamic effects on both rural and urban areas, is a core policy concern in Mongolia. It is driven by unequal economic and social development, and largely undertaken by movement of economically active, educated and young working-age individuals (IoM 2018), many from pastoralist backgrounds. There are high levels of participation in an education system that is, nevertheless, (re)creating forms of structural disadvantage and contributing to an ecologically and socially unsustainable development trajectory.

Alternative Basic Education in Ethiopia

Four-fifths of Ethiopia's population live in the temperate highland regions and just one-fifth in the arid lowlands. Those lowlands, however, cover 60 per cent of the country's land mass and are home to an estimated 12–15 million pastoralists (approximately 14 per cent of the population) (MoE 2015). The lowlands are optimistically now termed the 'emerging' regions but have a long history of socio-economic and political marginalization.

Under Emperor Haile Selassie (1930–74), education was used instrumentally to build national unity and identity, but since schools were concentrated in urban areas, pastoralist populations were not drawn in. The subsequent Derg regime also saw education as a means of inspiring patriotism and nationalism, and used schooling to disseminate its socialist philosophy, in the service of its project to unify the country by assimilation and homogenization (Desta 2017). Inclusion of pastoralists was limited to enrolling the children of chieftains in urban boarding schools, to prepare them to serve the regime (MoE 2008; Desta 2017). In 1991, the regime was overthrown. In 1994, the incoming government promulgated a national Education and Training Policy (ETP), which aimed to decentralize the system, included non-formal education and proposed a new curriculum that affirmed principles of equality, democracy and justice (MoE 2008). From 2005 onwards, educating pastoralists began to be mainstreamed, via Education Sector Development Plans (ESDP III onwards) which identified pastoralist education as a priority. In 2008, a specific Pastoral Areas Education Strategy (PEAS 2008), which primarily focused on access strategies and the need to institutionalize different delivery modalities, including Alternative Basic Education (ABE), noted the need to improve the quality and relevance of primary education to Ethiopia's pastoralists.

Successive ESDPs sustain the focus on pastoralists as among Ethiopia's 'hard-to-reach' children. ESDP IV's strategic approach for such learners (alongside supportive measures such as multi-grade classes, scholarships, school feeding and provision of special support) was to expand the number of primary schools to reduce home-school distance, and to provide more ABE centres, upgrade some of those already existing into regular schools but, in the longer term, to phase out ABE provision (MoE 2010). ESDP V (2015/16–2019/20) continues the specific focus on pastoralists, via its commitment to 'broadening access for out-of-school children, with a focus on adolescent girls, children from pastoralist communities and children in emergency contexts' (MoE 2015, 82). In a notable policy shift, however, ESDP V departs from its predecessor and firmly embeds ABE as an enduring feature of the education system that will enable objectives of improving retention rates and increasing transition to higher levels (Figure 3.3).

In 2016, investigation of PEAS 2008 implementation in four pastoralist regions revealed that despite the range of possible delivery modalities that had been suggested, 'of other strategies it seems there is nothing – just total reliance on ABE' (personal communication Afar Regional Education Bureau (REB) representative 2016) (Dyer 2018). There was no evidence of any distance provision or radio-based education, mobile schools or extra investment in residential schools or hostels, a handful of which were operating. The ABE centres we visited had recently received books, although sometimes they were in Amharic when people spoke other languages; some were in makeshift structures where 'students' aged from three to twenty-two were crammed into a small space; were usually staffed by facilitators with no teaching qualifications or prioritized functioning as feeding centres (Figure 3.4). Sporadic excellence, in the shape of a well-functioning ABE centre operating as a satellite for the formal school, just as the policy had envisioned, underlined how uneven and unequal provision was.

Discussions with staff of Regional Education Bureaus revealed known weaknesses of decentralized governance in pastoralist-dominated regions (Onwu and Agu 2010; Dyer 2018). Staff turnover was often high (spectacularly so in the Afar region, where a new bureau head had been appointed every year for the last twelve years), and some REB officials were unfamiliar with the standards/implementation manual that framed operationalization of the national ABE strategy. REBs' own institutional arrangements had not evolved to keep up with

1996: ActionAid Ethiopia develops ACCESS (Accessible, Cost-effective Centres of Education within the School System), a non-formal education programme intending to improve access to basic education (particularly of girls). Gains would be made sustainable by integrating ABE into the state education system, to achieve 'a single unitary education system that is flexible, responsive to local needs and that integrates best practice from NFE experiences' (Action Aid 2002).

2003: a national Conference on ABE provided a definition of ABE, reflected in ESDP III, as non-formal education that offers those 'unable to use the formal schooling system' the chance to 'benefit from alternative educational opportunities designed to meet their basic learning needs such as literacy, numeracy, oral expressions and problem-solving' (Redd Barna 2007: 20).

2004: USAID contracts PACT Ethiopia and its 27 Ethiopian partner NGOs to deliver the TEACH 1 (Transforming Education for Adults and Children in the Hinterlands) project. TEACH 1 rolled ABE out in eight regions, enrolling over 150,000 children from pastoralist and other groups not reached by formal schools' in 531 ABE Centres where primary (Cycle 1) equivalent education was offered. Plan Ethiopia and the Save the Children federation are active in mainstreaming ABE to enable access to basic education in 'cost-effective, flexible, easily reachable, and community-based basic education centers that are closely linked with, and that effectively serve as satellites or feeders to formal primary schools' (Bedanie et al. 2007). Key features that would enable ABE to respond to pastoralist livelihoods and mobility include learner-centred teaching; flexible timings; low cost construction; teaching in the local language; facilitator selected from local community; and a focus on under-served populations.

Thereafter: ABE provision became part of government strategy in major pastoral regions particularly Somali, Afar and also pastoral areas of Oromia (EU 2008). As a systemic innovation, ABE began as school equivalency programme for children aged 7-14. It offered a compressed curriculum, covering the equivalent of the first four primary grades in three years, as an opportunity to over-age learners who had missed out to catch up and then transition into the formal system. By 2017, ABE was a recognised 'mainstream' modality, offering levels that mirror those of the formal system (ABE levels 1-4 = Grades 1-4), with no emphasis on accelerated learning. But emergence of a flexible and equitable system has been compromised by 'uncontrolled expansion' of ABE centres with poor infrastructure, inadequate resources and learning facilities, since from early on, scaling up failed to ensure 'minimum criteria' in the ABE setup were met (SCD 2003: 60). This situation persists (C4ED 2017). Nevertheless, two more Grades are to be added to larger ABE centres, so they offer the full primary cycle, but otherwise learners are expected to transition to formal schools for higher levels – all as envisaged in ESDP V.

Figure 3.3 The emergence of ABE in Ethiopia.

policy change, so attention to ABE was ad hoc and based on extending already thin arrangements for formal schooling:

> There is just one officer for ABE, special needs and adult education in the region. ABE needs support and monitoring. The office is established for formal education, so you may get a bit, but mostly it's for formal education. (Afar REB officer 1, March 2016)

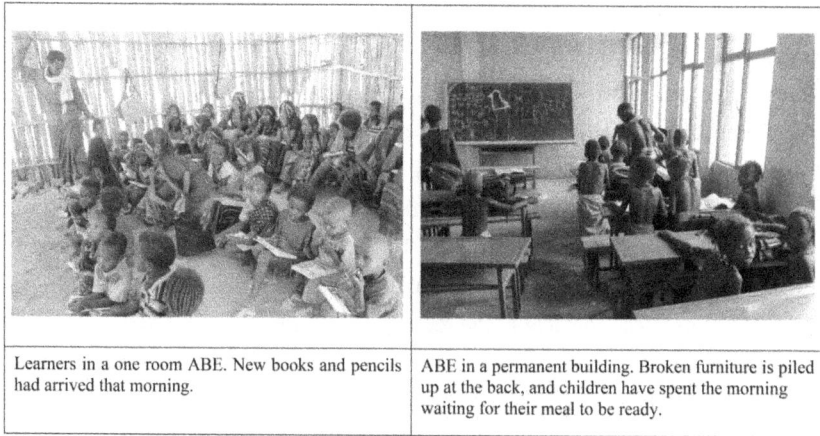

| Learners in a one room ABE. New books and pencils had arrived that morning. | ABE in a permanent building. Broken furniture is piled up at the back, and children have spent the morning waiting for their meal to be ready. |

Figure 3.4 Snapshots of ABE centres. Photo credit: Caroline Dyer.

Poor policy clarity meant that some responsible officials thought that ABE is 'a temporary intervention so no due attention is given'. Severe budgetary constraints and unrealistic recruitment norms for teachers were implicated in quality shortcomings that were widely noted, but officials' reluctance was also shaped by an understanding of context that centralized directives were not seen to recognize:

> ABE focuses on the pastoralist child but practically it doesn't work. It is not mobile, also it's based on the regular curriculum. It's a bit different from primary but the way we are acting is for primary schools. (Afar REB officer 2, March 2016)

However, an innovative programme of 'networked schooling' (Dyer and Echessa 2019) in the Somali region, introduced by Save the Children in 2013 and later scaled up by UNICEF, demonstrated different possibilities. The intervention hinges on an understanding of education as a resource that, just like water and fodder, needs to be continuously available and is made so by prediction and preparation, which is how pastoralists manage uncertainty. It adopts the three stages of a drought management cycle. During the 'normal' phase at home, a learner card is issued to a child enrolled in a school/ABEC and likely to migrate; community/officials map the planned migration route and available education provision. The 'alert' stage triggers migration: learners collect their card, and schools on the planned route are alerted. At the 'emergency' stage, learners migrate, presenting their card to each school on their route to enable schools cumulatively to sustain an individual's learning programme. If there is no school, the alert stage enables the local education office to re-deploy teachers from seasonally vacated provision and to pre-position blackboards, chalk and identify community resources to create learning spaces. The cycle completes and reverts to 'normal' when families return, and the home school/ABE centre re-enrols children and provides catch-up classes if needed.

This innovation is promising but highly resource-intensive for 'emerging' regions, where the infrastructure can still be too sparse to ensure continuity, and adding temporary learners puts further pressures on a fragile system. But perhaps the greatest obstacle is the federal government's insistence that mobile schools are a better solution, written into policy (in ESDP V). In this regard, Ethiopia has its own experience of failure, and international evidence shows that setting up, running and monitoring mobile schools for pastoralists are fraught with difficulties (see summaries in Krätli and Dyer 2009; Dyer 2014).

Despite proactive policy, Ethiopia's approach to pastoralists' education inclusion has often resulted in poor quality provision, and opportunities to transition to higher education levels are circumscribed by limited infrastructure, which is demotivating. From a policy perspective, ABE is promoted as a low-cost 'solution' to 'reach' where 'alternative' applies to vestiges of flexibility in timings and location but does not ensure adequate material conditions for contextualized learning or progression.

Aspirations and Realities of Schooling for Sedentarizing Pastoralists in Western India

There are an estimated thirty-five million pastoralists in India, and although mobile pastoralism is practised all over the country, it has been marginalized in policies for rural development. Kachchh, a district of Gujarat state in Western India, is a major pastoralist zone, located within in a semi-arid zone that stretches across the politically divided territories of India and Pakistan. Pastoralism in Kachchh has recently undergone rapid changes, linked specifically to an earthquake in 2001 and subsequent reconstruction, and generally, to the Gujarat's neoliberal political economy (Figure 3.5).

The Rabaris, on whom we focus here, are a major grouping of pastoralists in Kachcch. Not all Rabaris are now active in pastoralism; some are but migrate only very locally; some keep their animals permanently outside Gujarat but migrate back and forth for social events; and many practise transhumant pastoralism within Gujarat, migrating out of their home village once the rain-fed resources there are exhausted to other areas, until they return in the next monsoon.

While India's Prime Minister, and former Chief Minister of Gujarat, Narendra Modi, claims that Gujarat is a 'model' for India in terms of economic growth, Gujarat's growth is not translating into high human development. Rather, the 'co-operation between capitalists, politicians and bureaucrats at the expense of labour' which characterises Gujarat's political economy, means that inequalities are rising and disparities are widening. Gujarat spends less on the social sector than all other States in India, bar one (5.1 percent against the national average 5.8 percent). In the decade until 2013, Gujarat's average budget spend on education was 13.22 percent, compared with the national average of just over 15 percent.

Figure 3.5 The Gujarat model: Economic growth without human development? *Source*: Jaffrelot (2016).

Before the earthquake, 'extensive' pastoralism was a viable livelihood, although increasingly constrained by diminishing access to land and natural resources. As resource constraints squeezed, pastoralist parents recognized the instrumental importance of schooling as a means of diversifying out of pastoralism in the future and accessing employment. They saw being 'educated' as a marker of 'progress' that they wanted for their children and their community, and mobile pastoralism as a livelihood that only 'backward' and 'uneducated' people pursue; and they labelled themselves 'left behind' long before this term became part of the SDG 2030 Agenda lexicon. But mostly, the presumed advantages of schooling remained only idealistic, since for much of the year, schools are inaccessible to children who are actively engaged in mobile pastoralism, unless a child is left behind with relatives in the village or families split.

After the January 2001 earthquake, reconstruction cast in the 'Gujarat model' (Figure 3.5) transformed the region. Barren, but state-owned, land was transferred to private ownership, to be built over with factories or allocated for wind farms, which reduced the pastures available on the return to Kachchh. Rebuilt villages made new housing available; and the transforming economy generated new job opportunities. Some Rabari families adapted by settling in their home villages and reducing animal holdings or divesting altogether: an oft-cited motivation was that, as these changes would free children from responsibilities in pastoralism, they could access schooling and be able to compete for local jobs that had never before been available. This trend of settlement intensified with the passage of time, fuelled by shrinking pastures, a sense of deteriorating security and experience of organized animal theft. Some families carried on as before, migrating as a family; some split, leaving men migrating with reduced animal holdings and women and children living permanently in Kachchh; others sold off their animals and divested from mobile pastoralism altogether.

For newly settled adults with no qualifications or abilities to read and write, the experience of sedentarization has often been one of a material poverty that they had not known while they kept animals. In many of the villages where Rabaris live, the land is dry, labour work is hard to get, wages are low and daily living expenses are high. Industrial expansion created factory jobs, but amidst competition from migrant labour from outside the state, hoped-for opportunities do not always go to local people. For older Rabari women, work that requires them to relinquish the clothing that is integral to their social identity for a factory uniform is a condition too far, although they accept this for their daughters.

The experience of Rabari children, as first-generation learners, illustrates many challenges associated with education 'inclusion'. Although there is no disaggregated information about Rabaris specifically, there is often a vast gap between aspirations of schooling and actual outcomes. While school enrolment is high, children's (especially boys') attendance is reportedly erratic, and promotion without learning is common. The village schools that sedentarizing makes available reflect the national scenario of 'learning poverty' (Beteille et al. 2020) that Gujarat has failed to tackle (Table 3.1).

Rabaris' engagement with schooling often ends when they sit the external grade 8 board examination (end of upper primary), which many fail. Boys are under pressure around that time, as marriage begins to loom. Within Rabaris' relatively egalitarian, yet still patriarchal, society, a boy should provide for his (future) family, and it is unseemly to be less educated than his (future) wife. In sedentary contexts, youths are drawn into local cultures of consumption, which puts pressures on often slender family finances to afford public markers of affluence, particularly for boys, such as smartphones and motorbikes. Many swell the ranks of those locally known as the 'half-educated': uncompetitive in the formal job market, lacking the skills, confidence and capital to be self-employed, and unwilling to do manual work. Ironically, where schooling has failed to significantly improve prospects, mobile pastoralism is being re-evaluated as an occupation that, amidst economic uncertainty, provides boys with a steady income. Boys who have dropped out of school are being called back into pastoralism, to work with their fathers, or others. Ambivalent pragmatism may be the best way to describe this trend: it is a poor return on the investment made in schooling; and there are many reservations among both boys and girls about migrating, living in the 'jungle' and the hard work associated with pastoralism.

Table 3.1 Reading and Numeracy Levels in Kachchh and across Gujarat (Rural), from ASER 2019

	% Children (age 6–14) enrolled in private schools	% Children (age 6–14) not enrolled in school	Std. III to V: Learning levels		Std. VI to VIII: Learning levels	
			% Children who can read Std. II– level text	% Children who can do at least subtraction	% Children who can read Std. II– level text	% Children who can do division
Kachchh	15.4	4.9	40.1	29.8	65.6	35.2
Gujarat	12.4	1.8	45.5	39.4	68.8	32.7

Source: Annual Status of Education (ASER) 2019.

Intergenerational conflicts have become sharp, as values that were part of the social fabric of pastoralism are challenged by new exigencies of sedentary living and contested by youths exposed to the values that schooling espouses. Youths conduct themselves, and their social interactions in person or via WhatsApp, in ways that contravene older Rabaris' notions of propriety. Social distance and the *mariyada* (strict moral code) that guides interactions are being eroded by freer social intermingling, both between sexes and between different communities. Because Rabari women are seen to be custodians of the community's social norms, new freedoms that girls can enjoy are also sources of pressure sometimes so extreme that they have taken their own lives.

This focus on experience among newly settled pastoralist families highlights an often vast gap between the 'education' that is idealized as a pathway to livelihoods outside pastoralism and a respectable identity, and the realities of using state-managed schools, as first-generation learners, in rural settings. It is worth remembering, too, that although splitting is a common trend, children who still migrate with families are not at all in the policy gaze. The Right to Education Act of 2009 has tied its concept of 'quality' provision to an idea of the 'neighbourhood' school that reflects an unarticulated sedentary norm which, de facto, excludes mobile pastoralist learners (Dyer 2019).

Conclusion

Successful pastoral management in extensive livestock systems depends on mobility (de Jode 2010), although patterns of that mobility are changing as pastoralists adapt to pressures – notably constraints to resource access. Those pressures themselves are often reflections of state failure to invest in pastoralist systems (Davies et al. 2010), linked to ambivalence about the contemporary relevance of mobile pastoralism.

Underinvestment in education services in pastoralist areas, facets of which these case studies illustrate, is common around the world (GMR 2010; GEMR 2015, 2019), and widely deprives pastoralists of their rights not only to but also through and from education. Improving flows of funds and changing funding formulae that are out of step with rural realities (Ruto et al. 2009; EPR 2020) would undoubtedly help to address operational constraints that existing forms of provision experience, some of which these case studies illuminate (see also Dyer 2014 and 2018). Policy concerns tend to focus on this axis of 'quality', expecting that such investment will deliver improved rates of enrolment, retention and learning achievements.

Without denying the need for financial investment, the 2030 Agenda and its lens of 'sustainable development' requires a kind of investment that goes above and well beyond this. In pastoralist regions, formal education services are currently conceived and organized in ways that leave them very poorly able to respond to the contexts of high variability in which they are situated; and they envisage 'development' largely in terms of supporting an exit from pastoralism. The investment that the 2030 Agenda calls for, fundamentally, is in mobile pastoralism itself, and in the knowledge of people whose understanding of these uncertain and fragile environments, and how to manage them, is unparalleled. Once the myths and faulty science surrounding it are revealed as such (Krätli and Dyer 2009; Dyer 2014), mobile pastoralism is, as Davies et al. (2010) point out, 'conducive to environmental stewardship' (20). Yet pastoralist voices are rarely heard when it comes to articulating curricular content, training teachers or designing the school year, all of which are ways in which non-pastoralist values inform what is desirable. All too often, those values are not conducive to environmental stewardship. This call for an alternative conception of 'investment' may sound highly idealistic, but it is perhaps ultimately also highly pragmatic. A sustainable future for the global drylands matters not only to mobile pastoralists but also to our planet and, therefore, to us all.

References

Action Aid (2002). *Global Education Review, International Education Unit.* London: Action Aid.

Ahearn, A. (2018). 'Winters Without Women: Social Change, Split Households and Gendered Labour in Rural Mongolia', *Gender, Place & Culture*, 25(3), 399–415. https://doi.org/10.1080/0966369X.2018.1443910.

Ahearn, A., & Bumochir, D. (2016). 'Contradictions in Schooling Children among Mongolian Pastoralists', *Human Organization*, 75(1), 87–96. https://doi.org/10.17730/0018-7259-75.1.87.

ASER (2019). *Annual Status of Education Report (Rural).* New Delhi: ASER Centre. http://img.asercentre.org/docs/ASER%202018/Release%20Material/aserreport2018.pdf (accessed 15 October 2021).

Batkhuyag, B., & Dondogdulam, T. (2018). 'Mongolia Case Study: The Evolving Education Needs and Realities of Nomads and Pastoralists', 2019 Global Education Monitoring Report. https://unesdoc.unesco.org/ark:/48223/pf0000266056 (accessed 15 October 2021).

Bedanie, M., Baraki, Z., Hailemariam G., & Assefa, G. (2007). 'A Study on the Quality of Alternative Basic Education in Amhara Region', *Save the Children Denmark and Save the Children Norway.* https://norad.no/globalassets/import-2162015-80434-am/www .norad.no-ny/filarkiv/ngo-evaluations/docs-133283-v1-the_quality_of_alternative_ basic_education_in_amhara-ethiopia---final-report_.pdf (accessed 15 October 2021).

Beteille, T., Tognatta, N., Riboud, M., Nomura, S., & Ghorpade, Y. (2020). 'Ready to Learn: Before School', in *School, and Beyond School in South Asia, South Asia Development Forum, World Bank.* https://openknowledge.worldbank.org/handle /10986/33308 (accessed 15 October 2021).

Catley, A. (2017). 'Pathways to Resilience in Pastoralist Areas', *A Feinstein International Center Brief.* https://fic.tufts.edu/assets/FIC-Briefing-Q1_12.26.pdf. (accessed 15 October 2021).

C4ED (2017). 'Impact Evaluation of ABE in Ethiopia: The Case of the Regions Afar', *Oromia and Somali Final Evaluation Report.* The Center for Evaluation and Development (C4ED).

Davies, J., Niamir-Fuller, M., Kerven, C., & Bauer, K. (2010). 'Extensive Livestock Production in Transition: The Future of Sustainable Pastoralism'. https://www .researchgate.net/publication/285360020_Extensive_livestock_production_in _transition_the_future_of_sustainable_pastoralism (accessed 15 October 2021).

De Jode, H. (Ed.) (2010). *Modern and Mobile. The Future of Livestock Production in Africa's Drylands.* London: International Institute for Environment and Development (IIED).

Desta, A. (2017). 'Political Socialization in the Era of Globalization in Ethiopian Schools', *Institute of Development and Education for Africa.* http://www.africanidea .org/Political_socialization_Ethiopia.html (accessed 15 October 2021).

Dyer, C. (2013). 'Does Mobility Have to Mean Being Hard to Reach? Mobile Pastoralists and Education's "Terms of Inclusion"', *Compare: A Journal of Comparative and International Education,* 43(5), 601–21. https://doi.org/10.1080/03057925.2013.821322.

Dyer, C. (2014). *Livelihoods and Learning: Education for All and the Marginalisation of Mobile Pastoralists.* London: Routledge.

Dyer, C. (2018). 'Education Inclusion as a Border Regime: Implications for Mobile Pastoralists in Ethiopia's Afar Region', *International Studies in Sociology of Education,* 27(2–3), 145–65. https://doi.org/10.1080/09620214.2018.1426998.

Dyer, C. (2019). 'Rights, Entitlements and Education Inclusion for Mobile Pastoralist Children in India', in N. Varghese & M. Bandhopdyay (Ed.), *Education, Democracy and Development: Equity and Inclusion.* New Delhi: NIEPA, 275–88.

Dyer, C., & Echessa, E. (2019). 'Sustaining Learner Participation and Progression through Networked Schooling: A Systemic Approach for Mobile Out of School Children', *International Journal of Educational Development,* 64, 8–16. https://doi.org /10.1016/j.ijedudev.2018.11.002.

Dyer, C., & Rajan, V. (2021). 'Left Behind? Internally Migrating Children and the Ontological Crisis of Formal Education Systems in South Asia', *Compare: A Journal of Comparative and International Education*, 1–18. https://doi.org/10.1080/03057925 .2021.1907175.

EPR (2020). *Mongolia, Education Policy Review: Towards a Lifelong Learning System*. UNESCO. https://unesdoc.unesco.org/ark:/48223/pf0000373687 (accessed 15 October 2021).

European Union (2008). 'Updated Mapping Study of Non-State Actors in Ethiopia'. http://eeas.europa.eu/archives/delegations/ethiopia/documents/eu_ethiopia/ ressources/main_report_en.pdf. (accessed 15 October 2021).

GEMR (2015) 'Education for All 2000-2015: Achievements and Challenges'. Global Education Monitoring Report. Paris: UNESCO. https://en.unesco.org/gem-report /report/2015/education-all-2000-2015-achievements-and-challenges (accessed 06 April 2022)

GEMR (2019). 'Migration, Displacement and Education: Building Bridges, Not Walls', 2018–2019 Global Education Monitoring Report. Paris: UNESCO. https://unesdoc .unesco.org/ark:/48223/pf0000265866 (accessed 15 October 2021).

GMR (2010). 'Reaching the Marginalised', 2010 Global Monitoring Report. Paris: UNESCO. https://en.unesco.org/gem-report/report/2010/reaching-marginalized (accessed 15 October 2021).

IoM (2018). *Mongolia: Internal Migration Study*. Ulaanbaatar: International Organization for Migration. https://publications.iom.int/system/files/pdf/mongolia _internal_migration_study.pdf (accessed 15 October 2021).

Jaffrelot, C. (2016). 'What "Gujarat Model"?—Growth without Development—and with Socio-Political Polarisation', *Journal of South Asian Studies*, 39(4), 830–28. https://doi .org/10.1080/00856401.2015.1087456.

Krätli, S., & Dyer, C. (2009). 'Mobile Pastoralists and Education: Strategic Options', Education for Nomads Working Papers #1. London: IIED. https://www.researchgate .net/publication/295078437_Mobile_Pastoralists_and_Education_Strategic _Options. (accessed 15 October 2021).

MIER (2019). *Education in Mongolia. A Country Report*. Ulaanbaatar: Mongolian Institute of Education Research.

MoE (2008). *The Development of Education. National Report of the Federal Democratic Republic of Ethiopia*. Addis Ababa: Federal Ministry of Education.

MoE (2010). *Education Sector Development Program IV (ESDP IV) 2010/2011– 2014/2015 (2003 EC–2007 EC)*. Addis Ababa: Federal Ministry of Education. https://planipolis.iiep.unesco.org/sites/default/files/ressources/ethiopia_esdp_iv.pdf (accessed 15 October 2021).

MoE (2015). *Education Sector Development Programme (ESDP V) 2015–2020*. Addis Ababa: Federal Ministry of Education, Ethiopia.

Onwu, G., & Agu, A. (2010). 'Examining Some Aspects of Alternative Basic Education Programmes in Ethiopia', *Perspectives in Education*, 28(2), 75–85. https://journals.co .za/doi/10.10520/EJC87571.

PEAS (2008). *Pastoralist Area Education Strategy*. Addis Ababa: Federal Ministry of Education, Ethiopia.

Redd Barna (2007). 'A Study on the Quality of Alternative Basic Education in Amhara Region'. Save the Children–Norway. Oslo: Redd Barna. https://www.norad.no/en /toolspublications/publications/ngoevaluations/2009/a-study-on-the-quality-of -alternative-basic-education-in-amhara-region/

Ruto, S., Ongwenyi Z., & Mugo, J. (2009). 'Educational Marginalisation in Northern Kenya', 2010 EFA Global Monitoring Report. http://unesdoc.UNESCO.org/images /0018/001866/186617e.pdf (accessed 15 October 2021).

Save the Children Japan (2015). *Child Rights Situation Analysis in Mongolia*. Ulaanbaatar: Save the Children.

Scott-Villiers, P., Wilson, S., Kabala, N., Kullu, M., Ndung'u, D., & Scott-Villiers, A. (2015). 'A Study of Education and Resilience in Kenya's Arid and Semi-Arid Lands', *UNICEF Eastern and Southern Africa Regional Office*.

Steiner Khamsi, G. (2006). 'The Economics of Policy Borrowing and Lending: A Study of Late Adopters', *Oxford Review of Education*, 32(5), 665–78. https://doi.org/10.1080 /03054980600976353.

UNICEF (2017). 'Mining-related In-migration and the Impact on Children in Mongolia'. www.unicef.org/mongolia/reports/mining-related-migration-and-impact -children-mongolia (accessed 15 October 2021).

WDEFA (1990). 'World Declaration of Education for All: Meeting Basic Learning Needs', World Conference on Education for All. Jomtien: UNESCO. http://unesdoc .unesco.org/images/0012/001275/127583e.pdf (accessed 15 October 2021).

4

Education as an Emergency Response

Time for Radical Change

Mai Abu Moghli

Refugees are people fleeing conflict or persecution. They are protected under international law and must not be expelled or returned to situations where their life and freedom are at risk (UNGA 1951). In 2019, the number of refugees under the United Nations High Commissioner for Refugees' (UNHCR) mandate was 20.4 million. This number does not include the 5.6 million registered Palestinian refugees under the mandate of the United Nations Relief and Works Agency for Palestine Refugees in the Near East (UNRWA) (UNHCR 2021). Under Article 22 of the United Nations (UN) Refugee Convention of 1951, 'States shall accord to refugees the same treatment as is accorded to nationals with respect to elementary education.' The convention requires that states recognize foreign school certificates, diplomas and degrees, and allow for the remission of fees and charges and award scholarships to the refugee population (UNGA 1951). While these rights for refugees are enshrined in international law, some host countries such as Lebanon and Jordan are not signatories to the UN Refugee Convention of 1951, hence the law does not apply. However, these countries are signatories to other conventions and covenants that ensure the right to education to all children, regardless of their legal status, such as the UN Convention on the Rights of the Child of 1989 and the International Covenant on Economic, Social and Cultural Rights of 1966. Nonetheless, these legal obligations have not ensured the fulfilment of the right to education for refugee children and hundreds of thousands of learners remain out of school.

In Lebanon, organizations such as United Nations International Children's Emergency Fund (UNICEF) and UNHCR have raised hundreds of millions of dollars since 2011 to develop an education programme with the Lebanese government for Syrian children within the Lebanese public school system

(RACE[1] I and RACE II). Over US$300 million has been spent on this programme (Shuayb 2021). Yet, the challenges for Syrian refugee children accessing formal education are huge (Shuayb 2021). These include difficulties in finding a place in the public school second-shift system, discrimination practised against Syrian children by teachers and students, a reduced learning timetable and poor quality of teaching in second shifts, restrictions on using school space and amenities, the language used for instruction and exams,[2] and the confused policy regarding residencies and other legal documentation required for school enrolment (ibid.; Abu Moghli 2020). These challenges have left 40 per cent of school-age Syrian children out of education, with less than 4 per cent making it to the secondary stage and only 1 per cent enrolled in grade 9 (Shuayb 2020).

In Jordan, while the political and economic situation is considerably better than in Lebanon, Syrian refugee children also face various challenges to accessing education. By the end of 2017 over 131,000 refugee children aged 5–18 were in formal education, the majority in double-shift schools (Salem, Chapter 14), while some 40 per cent remained outside of formal schooling (Karasapan and Shah 2018). Obstacles to accessing education are most acute for children ages twelve and older and include poverty-driven child labour and child marriage, a lack of affordable school transportation, government policies that limit access to education and a lack of inclusive education that keeps children with disabilities out of school (HRW 2020).

The situation for Palestinian refugees is also dire, particularly in Lebanon, where for more than 70 years they have lived in overcrowded camps and been deprived of basic rights including fair access to public education and have been unable to afford the high tuition fees of private schools (Shuayb 2014), resulting in many dropping out of school (Shuayb 2014; Abu Moghli 2020). At the same time, only 61 per cent of Palestinian young people between the ages of sixteen and eighteen are enrolled in UNRWA schools (UNRWA 2017), in which the pass rate in the Brevet Official exams[3] was as low as 13.6 per cent in some schools. This educational haemorrhage among young Palestinians has been attributed to the deteriorating socio-economic conditions and a growing disillusionment with schooling as Palestinians suffer legal discrimination and social marginalization (Abu Moghli 2020).

In this chapter, I examine various aspects of refugee education programmes in both Lebanon and Jordan, where, despite substantial investments, the fulfilment of the right to education has not been achieved in relation to either access or quality. The chapter critically engages with these investments and how they have led to the commodification of refugee education, turning refugeehood into a profitable label. The chapter examines the possibilities of moving beyond short-term and reactionary humanitarian response(s) that produce and sustain two-tiered systems of education and considers alternative possibilities for educational funding and programming.

The Refugee Experience: Labelling, Commodification and Securitization

When engaging with Education in Emergencies (EiE), it is imperative to consider how the human experience of becoming a 'refugee', an experience of loss and dispossession, is completely different from how it is portrayed and capitalized on by governments and institutions; this difference is where refugeehood turns into a profitable label.

The migration policies of Syria's neighbouring states have dramatically changed post 2011 (Doraï 2018). Before 2011, Syrians had relative freedom of cross-border mobility towards Lebanon and Jordan and nearly 400,000 Syrians were working in Lebanon (Chalcraft 2009). However, in 2014, with the deteriorating economic and political situation in Syria, Syrians arriving in Lebanon were used as an excuse by the Lebanese government to suspend a bilateral agreement between Syria and Lebanon that facilitated movement across borders (ibid.). Since Lebanon is not a signatory to the Refugee Convention of 1951, there is no national asylum system, hence no protection or right to live and work for refugees in the country. It is the UNHCR that establishes asylum procedures in cooperation with the government. Lebanon has signed a Memorandum of Understanding (MOU) with the UNHCR that specifies the mandate of the international organization (Kagan 2011). In spite of this MOU, Syrian refugees remain vulnerable to arbitrary government procedures that might expose them to imprisonment and refoulement, in addition to discriminatory practices on all levels. Syrians in Lebanon are treated in the same way as any foreign national who needs a residency to live and work in the country. According to HRW[4] (2016), residency regulations adopted in January 2015 have resulted in most Syrians losing their legal status. Under these residency regulations, refugees applying to renew their residency permits are sorted into two categories: those registered with UNHCR, and those who are not and must find a Lebanese sponsor to remain in the country legally. Prohibitive paperwork requirements and fees,[5] combined with arbitrary application of the regulations, effectively bar Syrians in both categories from renewal. Additionally, Syrian refugees reported that the renewal process is itself abusive and arbitrary and that some government employees use the renewal process to interrogate them about security issues (ibid.).

In Jordan, the situation is not any better. Like Lebanon, Jordan is not a signatory to the 1951 convention and so there are no protection mechanisms for refugees. Since mid-2014, the vulnerability of Syrian refugees has deepened as Jordan has restricted refugee inflows, violated international non-refoulement laws and restricted services to Syrians already in the country (Francis 2015). The opening of the Zaatari refugee camp in July 2012 can be considered a first turning point to regulate entries of Syrian refugees (Doraï 2018). In early 2015, tens of thousands of refugees from Syria ended up stranded in the no-person's land known as the berm, between Jordan and Syria. An estimated 75 per cent of the berm's population have returned to Syria since mid-2015. Still, 10,000 people live in the deserted camp with no facilities, water or health services (Forestier 2020).

Palestinian refugees from Syria[6] are among the most vulnerable; they are stateless and have been denied rights granted to other refugees in Jordan and Lebanon. In January 2013, the Jordanian government announced a non-entry policy for Palestinian refugees from Syria. Since then, Palestinians who had been able to cross into Jordan (usually relying on forged documents or smugglers) have lived in fear of being arrested and deported back to Syria. Palestinians who fled to Jordan cannot legally live in refugee camps established for Syrians; at the same time they cannot legally work to earn money for rent. The one exception is Cyber City, which is more of a detention centre than a refugee camp to which Jordanian authorities have been transferring Palestinians who are in the country clandestinely since April 2012. Palestinians are confined to Cyber City unless they decide to return to Syria. In 2013 Lebanese authorities began requiring that Palestinians from Syria apply for a visa before entering the country and, as of May 2014, were allowing Syria-registered Palestinian refugees entry into the country only if they had the documents needed to travel to a third country, limiting their stay in Lebanon to a maximum of nine hours. Restrictions were placed on the ability of Palestinians from Syria to legally renew their residency papers. The majority of Palestinians from Syria who are currently in Lebanon live under the threat of arrest and deportation (Abu Moghli et al. 2015). Such discriminatory government policies exacerbate the hardships experienced by those who have lost their homes, livelihoods and possibly loved ones. These policies are designed to keep out those seeking safety or make life so unbearable in host countries to make them leave.

The label of 'refugee' permits the violation of basic rights such as freedom of movement, work, housing and education and negatively impacts people's socio-economic status and causes long-term stigmatization that is passed through generations. Some displaced communities have resisted this label; for example, 'a central element in the Palestinians' first struggle after exile was to reject the refugee designation and redefine themselves as Palestinians' (Sayigh 1988: 13). This rejection, however, does not sit well with the representation(s), language and agendas of donor agencies, international organizations and host governments. According to Malkki (1996: 378) the refugee is conceptualized as a 'universal humanitarian subject' – an apolitical and de-historicized figure, reduced to the role of aid beneficiary. To be categorized as a 'good refugee', worthy of aid, refugees are expected to behave in a certain way and 'to display characteristics that justify the provision of aid, [such as] poverty and passivity' (Szczepanik 2016: 30). Such objectification (Abdelnour and Abu Moghli 2021), that is, reducing someone to the status of an object, without appreciation for her agency or voice, or subsuming her within generalized categories and labels (such as refugees), fundamentally undermines her humanity (Nussbaum 1995; Papadaki 2010) and erases the diversity and significance of lived experiences (Abdelnour and Abu Moghli 2021). Objectification is a political act, especially when complicit in the generalized dehumanizing of entire categories of people (Said 1978). Though 'refugee' is a legal status, this labelling, categorization and erasure of human experiences allow for commodification. According to Tsourapas (2019), displaced populations are being commodified by host states who view them as a source of economic rent. Such commodification has been encouraged through diplomatic measures such as Europe's introduction of socio-economic and political aid to states of first asylum via migration and refugee deals (ibid.).

In 2016 the idea of refugee compacts was introduced. In line with the practice of objectification, Jordan and Lebanon agreed to these compacts (deals of financial and political rent) without considering the needs of the refugee populations or consulting with them (Barbelet et al. 2018). These compacts continue to shape the two countries' responses (Tsourapas 2019) negatively impacting the well-being of refugees and in many cases prioritizing the security agenda of governments who frame the plight of refugees as a crisis and a potential source of terrorism. For example, in the 2016 compact, the EU provided 1 million euros to the Lebanese security agencies; this is in addition to 1.2 million euros for projects on Countering Violent Extremism and promoting Social Cohesion (European Commission 2016). As for the UK, in 2015 the government created a five-year,

£1.5 billion Global Challenges Research Fund (GCRF) to procure research that will 'contribute to realizing the UK aid strategy'. The GCRF is itself aid funding, diverted from the UK DfID, and is legally required to support the government's aid agenda. This aid agenda was redefined in 2015 by the UK government so that all foreign aid must directly serve UK 'national security and foreign policy' interests, and controlling migration flows triggered by the Syrian conflict was explicitly highlighted as a priority concern for these interests (HM Treasury 2015, 3 cited in Sukarieh and Tannock 2019). Within this discourse, refugee communities have become bargaining chips between host and donor countries and their well-being features low in the list of priorities of governments and international agencies who implement donor-funded projects, including those within the education sector.

The humanitarian response to the refugee 'crisis' has been characterized as geopolitical, racist and xenophobic and exploited by many politicians in Lebanon for political and financial gains (Shuayb 2020). Within this context there are dire implications for education as one of the main sectors supported and funded under the above-mentioned compacts and operationalized via partnership deals. Shuayb (2020) pointed out how an EU official, during the peak of the refugee 'crisis' in 2015, reported that the EU was willing to cover the costs of the Syrian children's education programme in Lebanon at any cost as long as they stay there. As a result of this practice hundreds of thousands of Syrian learners remain out of school in both Lebanon and Jordan while others, such as Palestinians, Iraqis and Sudanese, alongside children of migrant workers, are not even considered in the equation.

Education

UNHCR (2019) claims that education provides stability and security for children when everything else in their lives seems to have fallen apart. For many refugee children, a classroom can be the first peaceful and reliable environment they encounter. Similarly, the Inter-Agency for Education in Emergencies (INEE) Minimum Standards Handbook (2010) states that EiE ensures dignity by offering safe spaces for learning and that quality education saves lives by providing physical protection from the dangers and exploitation of a crisis environment such as being sexually or economically exploited, forced or early marriage, recruitment into armed forces and armed groups or organized crime. Here I argue that such an approach to EiE is simplistic and dangerous. It assumes that education can be apolitical, provided to learners in a vacuum and homogenizes all refugees as one group with the same needs and aspirations. With the proliferation of the EiE industry, which is based on values of liberal humanitarianism, that is, 'a market-driven moral economy and a state-driven political morality within a humanitarian endeavour' (Reid-Henry 2014: 418), the assumption is that education is neutral, limited to schooling, and leads to a better future through expanding opportunities for employability. Within this narrative, the violent face of schooling particularly in 'crisis' contexts, where bullying, corporal punishment, discrimination and xenophobia (Shuayb 2014; 2020) are rampant, is overlooked for the sake of keeping agreements (compacts) in place and providing proof that they are leading to successful and effective educational programming.

In many cases, the needs of teachers, caregivers and learners are overshadowed by the demand for evidence of this success from governments, policymakers, international donors and aid agencies. This evidence is provided via funded EiE research where teachers, caregivers and learners are merely subjects and sources of data. Moreover, there is evidence that shows a picture contrary to what the EiE industry claims: in cases of complex and extreme hardship the demand for education falls. Through their independent research in Jordan during the Covid-19 pandemic, for example, Batshon and Shahzadeh (2020: 3) show that for the most marginalized 'Maslow comes before Bloom'. They found that 'at the time of crisis, access to education might be of least concern for refugees and other vulnerable communities [. . .] access to food, healthcare, and cash assistance are crucial in order for education interventions to be considered or adopted'. Similarly, Abu Moghli and Shuayb (2020) conducted research to assess the impact of the Covid-19 lockdown on access to and quality of education from the perspectives of teachers, learners and caregivers in Jordan, Lebanon and the Occupied West Bank and Gaza Strip. The results of the research showed that learners, particularly male learners, who dropped out of school during complex crises, including economic collapse, ongoing colonial occupation, political upheaval and a pandemic, did so to look for work and support their families. These findings contradict the narrative of the EiE industry that promotes schooling as a mechanism to save lives and calls for increased funding for EiE interventions during crisis. Such interventions can become smoke screens for institutional violations, structural discrimination and inequalities impacting the most marginalized (Love 2019). Additionally, interventions targeting refugee children, in effect, contribute to their further marginalization, enforcing the state of exception. This is done by the power of omission and the creation of parallel education systems.

There is ample literature documenting the emergence and proliferation of the EiE industry. The main milestones include the formation of INEE in 2000 in response to the Dakar Framework for Action on Education for all (EFA), the development of the INEE Minimum Standards in 2003 and the adoption of the Global Education Cluster in 2006 (Nicolai and Hine 2015). INEE is a source of knowledge production and documentation for researchers and practitioners. While having this entity is important, it is problematic that almost all written material, activities and initiatives included in the INEE timeline (INEE 2020) are linked to the establishment of UN agencies such as UNRWA in 1949 and UNHCR in 1950 (Kagawa 2005) or UN declarations and conventions such as the Universal Declaration of Human Rights in 1948 and the UN Convention on the Rights of the Child of 1989, constituting what Zembylas and Keet (2019) define as a declarationist approach. This approach leads to omitting theories, knowledges and community approaches that ensure the continuation of education in times of emergencies, including mass displacement (INEE 2002; Abu Moghli 2021). However, there is limited documentation of these efforts (Burde et al. 2017), which leads to a false perception that communities affected by crisis are waiting for well-intentioned aid workers and advocates to develop EiE programmes (Burde 2007) through emancipatory projects intended to liberate individuals from the causes of suffering and increase their capacity to determine their fates (Barnett 2011). This omission does not allow for displaced communities and their hosts, the majority of which are in the Global South struggling against similar conditions of discrimination and injustice, to share their experiences and knowledges. The increasingly institutionalized and standardized EiE efforts draw hard lines between the displaced and the host, hindering the identification of commonalities and sharing of experiences and knowledge, largely ignoring the aspirations of those most impacted and creating a sense of exception where the displaced populations are categorized as the incapable *Other*. This is typified by the financial support by Western governments for segregated shifts in public schools in Jordan and Lebanon and the non-formal education sector designed specifically for refugee children. In its 2016 compact, the EU pledged 16 million euros for non-formal education programmes in 2016–17 (European Commission 2016). While approved by the Lebanese government, these programmes are uncertified and do not guarantee that learners will be integrated into formal education. There are hardly any advocacy campaigns or pressure from donor governments or international institutions to change this situation, which leaves displaced learners in a state of prolonged exception and educational marginalization.

Debunking the Myths

In this section I encourage critical engagement with how EiE programming is framed, designed and implemented by donor governments, host governments and international organizations in relation to three commonly held myths: education as a humanitarian response; equitable partnerships for education and education for a better future. I am aware of my privileged positionality as an academic based in the UK, working on government-funded projects in Lebanon, Palestine and Jordan, and admit that I am part of the problem. Hence, this is an opportunity for me to reflect on the work I am engaged in and to continue my journey of auto-critique and unlearning.

Education as a Humanitarian Response

'Education needs to be woven into planning and funding for refugee emergencies, at national and international levels, and systematically included in national development and education sector planning and budgeting' (UNHCR 2017). This statement by UNHCR reflects the increasing push for the humanitarian-development nexus (Lie 2020) which refers to the 'the transition or overlap between the delivery of humanitarian assistance and the provision of long-term development assistance' (Strand 2020: 104). This nexus includes various contradictions particularly for EiE budgeting, planning and programming. When considering EiE in cases of mass displacement, the nexus is problematic as the efforts of 'long-term development' are diminished in order to maintain the temporary and exceptional status of refugees. EIE can also exacerbate the unwelcoming context of refugees' supposedly temporary presence. For example, by supporting second-shift schools and segregated non-formal education, EiE programming can fuel conditions of conflict by unevenly distributing access and quality across regions and social groups, reproducing existing socio-economic inequalities, repressing languages and cultures of the most marginalized (Bush and Saltarelli 2000) and, most importantly, excluding refugee populations from access to quality learning and disallowing them opportunities to forge social relationships with the wider community (Pherali and Abu Moghli 2019). These contradictions make the nexus a harmful oxymoron rather than a positive strategy.

The solution is not giving up on the idea of long-term development, as education is a long-term investment. Instead, the nexus needs to take into account the needs of the most affected communities, include advocacy efforts to end the state of exception of refugees and ensure that displaced populations are not commodified through financial and political agreements between governments that disregard the capabilities and voice of the displaced and their host communities. EiE efforts should respect the knowledges and experiences of individuals and communities who are most affected rather than enforce universalist solutions that may or may not work.

Equitable Partnerships for Education

'Partnership' is a buzzword in development and has become a mandatory component of fundable research or programme implementation in international development (Pherali and Abu Moghli 2019: 12). For example, the UK GCRF fund was created to procure research through forming 'high-quality', 'equitable' partnerships with academic staff in the Global South to create a 'global community of researchers', who together can tackle global development challenges (BEIS 2017, 3-6-7 cited in Sukarieh and Tannock 2019). Downes (2013: 2) claims that such partnerships emerged as 'a reaction against the "former" power asymmetry between the North and South'. The aim was to promote horizontal educational partnerships, which would produce higher impacts in education-development projects. Hence, humanitarian and development projects need to improve the involvement of affected communities as equal contributors (Pherali and Abu Moghli 2019). Despite such aspirations, these partnerships are not without caveats. According to Pherali and Abu Moghli (2019), educational partnerships in humanitarian and conflict-affected settings are often risky, sensitive and difficult to implement in terms of sustainability and accountability. Moreover, such partnerships often benefit already privileged elitist institutions in the Global South such as the American University of Beirut in Lebanon and the Queen Rania Foundation in Jordan, rather than more marginalized grass-roots organizations, thus exacerbating socio-economic inequalities. In terms of sustainability of funding, donor interests diminish as new humanitarian crises arise and draw away donor support from ongoing programming (ibid.). Additionally, changes in financial and political conditions in certain countries or globally, such as during the Covid-19 pandemic, make governments redirect their funds, possibly to their internal needs rather than abroad, as was the case with the 2021 cuts to UKRI's GCRF funds which negatively impacted multiple international partnerships established through this fund, with partners in the Global South being hardest hit. Finally, the claim to equality and end of power asymmetry through these partnerships is dubious. For example, Sukarieh and Tannock (2019) have demonstrated how young, educated and highly skilled researchers in countries in the Global South where these partnership projects are taking place can become an indigenous, proletarian overseas workforce, subcontracted to perform research that UK academics direct from afar, separated as they often are by a gulf of language, culture, geography and politics of research production in the twenty-first-century marketized university sector. This power asymmetry also impacts academics in the Global South who are in many cases not treated as equals but as convenient fixers, whose time and effort might not even be accounted for.

Sustainable and effective partnerships require appropriate coordination so that limited resources and capacities are utilized efficiently (Pherali and Abu Moghli 2019) and are contingent on engaging refugee and host communities not merely as potential beneficiaries, but also as key contributors in design, planning and implementation of education programmes. Moreover, aid and development workers as well as academics and researchers who are in positions of power need to be aware of their positionality in relation to the space and people they work with. Being sensitive to context, being aware of our limitations, the geopolitical dynamics and the colonial ties of the countries from which they work or obtain the funding and acknowledge the contribution of partners in countries and contexts we work in are vital in countering cycles of exploitation, objectification and commodification.

Education for a Better Future

Education is a long-term investment involving far more than the acquisition of skills for the job market. Education is vital for building and harnessing social and cultural capital. However, investing in education for a better future contradicts the majority of EiE models continuously growing in funds, size and reach. EiE programming focuses on primary education, while secondary and higher education in refugee contexts have been largely under-prioritized (Dryden-Peterson 2010; Pherali and Abu Moghli 2019). This is in spite of UNHCR's Education Strategy (2012–16) and their strategic directions for 2017–21 (UNHCR UK n.d.) which emphasize strengthening access to higher education for refugee young people. Lack of higher education opportunities prevents refugee learners from enrolling in secondary education (Abu Moghli 2020) alongside other legal, financial and security barriers which have resulted in less than 2 per cent of refugee learners being enrolled in grade 9 in Lebanon after almost a decade of education interventions. In Jordan, the numbers are similar (Shuayb and Brun 2020). Higher education has been almost totally neglected due to the economic justification that supported investment in primary education bears higher rates of returns (Psacharopoulos 1989; 1994; Psacharopoulos and Patrinos 2004) and the idea that it is a luxury rather than a part of the educational continuum (Pherali and Abu Moghli 2019). Such prioritization by the EiE sector reproduces inequalities, sustains the commodification of refugees and, at the same time, suggests that they are unworthy of investment.

Despite limited access for refugees to orthodox secondary and higher education through schools, universities or vocational centres, a number of online alternatives have emerged such as Massive Open Online Courses (MOOCS). While often presented as a panacea to issues of accessibility, high costs and legal barriers, these can gloss over structural issues of inequality and disregard learners' needs and aspirations. For example, many programmes are not available in Arabic (Pherali and Abu Moghli 2019), and hence are not tailored to the needs of students. Most are not certified or part of a university course, and it is difficult to distinguish short-term project-based experimentation in online education from carefully designed academic training programmes that enable refugees to support their personal and professional development or gain academic qualifications (ibid.). Online courses can also contribute to further marginalization of young refugees who consider physical spaces of higher education as an opportunity to integrate in the host community and exchange knowledge and culture (Abu Moghli 2020). Additionally, online courses create an illusion of access, deflecting the attention from the real issue of access, quality and equity in provision as well as the lack of resources that are needed to operate the education system. Limited monitoring and poor completion rates in online programmes can lead to educational failures which might be invisible in the immediate term (Wagner 2017; Pherali and Abu Moghli 2019).

The idea of future education is critical in contexts of mass displacement; however, there are a number of issues that need to be considered. In situations of upheaval and rapid change in socio-economic conditions, young people have the ability to find creative solutions and formulate new aspirations. Displacement unleashes new habitus for young refugees (Morrice 2013 cited in Pherali and Abu Moghli 2019) and provides new opportunities for equitable education programmes (Pherali and Abu Moghli 2019). This concept is useful in explaining the potential of education to provide learning opportunities which align with the aspirations of refugees and their circumstances, and what they see as possible to the logic of their surroundings (Dryden-Peterson and Giles 2010).

Consequently, the idea of future education needs to accommodate a range of possibilities and engage with a rich network of learners and educators from the refugees' own communities and beyond.

In any EiE programming, whether primary, secondary or tertiary, it is imperative to recognize that refugees are not a homogeneous group, and refugee-ness is not a brand or a category that people fit into. Consequently, any programme needs to consider their different needs and aspirations. Additionally, assumptions of imminent return should not be the basis of programme design and programmes should be designed to cater for the most vulnerable and not for the easiest groups to access. Issues of security, parenthood and disability should be integral to the design of any refugee education programmes.

Conclusion

UNHCR (2014) suggests that the average length of time that refugees spend in camps is seventeen years. While refugee populations in the Global North remain the exception, countries in the Global South, such as Jordan and Lebanon, host millions of refugees and require long-term solutions that fall within the realm of development rather than humanitarian responses. Sustainable financial and technical solutions, based on the vision and needs of the concerned populations, would improve the quality of education not only for refugee children but for everyone in these countries. By contrast, donors and aid agencies overwhelmingly consider education as part of their humanitarian response, particularly in contexts of mass displacement. For refugees, this exacerbates their state of exception and precarity and reinforces the false perception that displacement is temporary.

The intent here was not to dismiss education interventions in contexts of displacement as useless or harmful in their entirety. It was rather to highlight that as international interventions (humanitarian, development and whatever is in-between) become increasingly important with the rise in protracted displacement across the world, it is imperative to find better ways of conceptualizing, designing and implementing such programmes not only for effective programming but also for ethical and moral considerations. This involves re-examining ideas of universality, professionalization and standardization of EiE and allowing systems of education within host and refugee communities, with appropriate resources and support, to lead the way rather than remain recipients of pre-packaged 'one size fits all' solutions.

As researchers, humanitarian or development workers in the field of education, we need to acknowledge that this is a process that involves mistakes; a process where we need to learn from our failures as much as our successes. There is no solution to the difficult relationships that shape knowledge production and power dynamics; there is no single process that will resolve everything. However, from an ethical standpoint, we need to be honest about the mistakes we make; be aware of our positionality, power and privilege; and demand a fundamental rethinking and restructuring of the EiE industry, where powerful institutions, not the displaced communities and their hosts, bear the weight of any mistakes.

Notes

1 Reaching all Children with Education.
2 Language used is either French or English, particularly for science, technology, engineering, math (STEM) subjects.
3 The Lebanese national exams for grade 9.
4 Human Rights Watch.
5 $200 annual renewal fee for any Syrian aged fifteen or over.
6 For the purposes of this chapter, I will only discuss the situation of Palestinian refugees from Syria.

References

Abdelnour, S., & Abu Moghli, M. (2021). 'Researching Violent Contexts: A Call for Political Reflexivity', *Organization*, 1–24. https://doi.org/10.1177/13505084211030646

Abu Moghli, M. (2020). 'Situational Analysis to Inform Interventions to Increase Access to Higher Education for Refugees and Host Community Members in Lebanon', [Unpublished], American University of Beirut.

Abu Moghli, M. (2021). 'A Contested Terrain: Education in Emergencies Research', *World Humanities Report (WHR)*. https://www.arwhr.com/post/a-contested-terrain-education-in-emergencies-research (accessed 15 October 2021).

Abu Moghli, M., Gabiam, N., & Bitarie, N. (2015). 'Palestinian Refugees from Syria: Stranded on the Margins of Law', *Al-Shabaka: The Palestinian Policy Network*. https://al-shabaka.org/briefs/palestinian-refugees-from-syria-stranded-on-the-margins-of-law/#easy-footnote-bottom-6-4788.

Barbelet, V., Hagen-Zanker, J., & Mansour, D. (2018). *The Jordan Compact Lessons Learnt and Implications for Future Refugee Compacts*. ODI. https://odi.org/en

/publications/the-jordan-compact-lessons-learnt-and-implications-for-future
-refugee-compacts/ (accessed 15 October 2021).

Barnett, M. (2011). 'Humanitarianism as a Scholarly Vocation', *Humanitarianism in Question*, 235–63, Cornell University Press. https://doi.org/10.7591/9780801461538 -012.

Batshon, D., & Shahzadeh, Y. (2020). 'Education in the Time of COVID-19 in Jordan: A Roadmap for Short, Medium, and Long-Term Responses'. https://lebanesestudies .com/education-in-the-time-of-covid-19-in-jordan-aroadmap-for-short-medium -and-long-term-responses/ (accessed 15 October 2021).

BEIS – Department for Business, Energy and Industrial Strategy (2017). *UK Strategy for the Global Challenges Research Fund*. London: BEIS.

Burde, D. (2007). 'Empower or Control? Education in Emergencies and Global Governance', *Current Issues in Comparative Education*, 9(2), 55–64.

Burde, D., Kapit, A., Wahl, R., Guven, O., & Skarpeteig, M. (2017). 'Education in Emergencies: A Review of Theory and Research', *Review of Educational Research*, 87(3), 619–58. https://doi.org/10.3102/0034654316671594.

Bush, K., & Saltarelli, D. (2000). *Two Faces of Education in Ethnic Conflict: Towards a Peacebuilding Education for Children*. UNICEF. https://www.unicef-irc.org/ publications/pdf/insight4.pdf (accessed 15 October 2021).

Chalcraft, J. (2009). *The Invisible Cage Syrian Migrant Workers in Lebanon*. Stanford: Stanford University Press.

Doraï, K. (2018). 'Conflict and Migration in the Middle East: Syrian Refugees in Jordan and Lebanon', *E-International Relations*. https://www.e-ir.info/2018/09/04/ conflict-and-migration-in-the-middle-east-syrian-refugees-in-jordan-and-lebanon/ (accessed 15 October 2021).

Downes, G. (2013). 'A Critical Analysis of North-South Educational Partnerships in Development Context', *Policy & Practice – A Development Education Review*, 16, 1–12.

Dryden-Peterson, S. (2010). 'The Politics of Higher Education for Refugees in a Global Movement for Primary Education', *Refuge*, 27(2), 10–18. https://doi.org/10.25071 /1920-7336.34718.

Dryden-Peterson, S., & Giles, W. (2010). 'Introduction: Higher Education for Refugees', *Refuge*, 27(2), 3–10.

European Commission (2016). 'EU – Lebanon Partnership: The Compact'. https://www .ecbproject.org/help-library/eu-lebanon-partnership-the-compact (accessed 15 October 2021).

Forestier, M. (2020). *Jordan: Stop Forcible Transfer of Syrian Refugees to a No-Man's Land in the Desert*. Amnesty International, September 15. https://www.amnesty.org /en/latest/news/2020/09/jordan-stop-forcible-transfer-of-syrian-refugees-to-a-no -mans-land-in-the-desert/ (accessed 15 October 2021).

Francis, A. (2015). 'Jordan's Refugee Crisis', *The Carnegie Endowment for International Peace*. https://carnegieendowment.org/2015/09/21/jordan-s-refugee-crisis-pub -61338 (accessed 15 October 2021).

HRW (2016). "'I Just Wanted to be Treated Like a Person": How Lebanon's Residency Rules Facilitate Abuse of Syrian Refugees'. https://www.hrw.org/report/2016/01/12 /i-just-wanted-be-treated-person/how-lebanons-residency-rules-facilitate-abuse (accessed 15 October 2021).

HRW (2020). "'I Want to Continue to Study": Barriers to Secondary Education for Syrian Refugee Children in Jordan'. https://www.hrw.org/report/2020/06/26/i-want -continue-study/barriers-secondary-education-syrian-refugee-children-jordan (accessed 15 October 2021).

INEE (2002). 'Education in Emergencies Facilitators' Guide'. https://inee.org/system /files/resources/doc_1_89_IRC_EiE_Facilitator_Guide.pdf (accessed 15 October 2021).

INEE (2010). 'Minimum Standards for Education: Preparedness, Response, Recovery'. https://inee.org/system/files/resources/INEE_Minimum_Standards_Handbook _2010%28HSP%29_EN.pdf (accessed 15 October 2021).

INEE (2020). 'Education in Emergencies Timeline'. https://timeline.ineesite.org/#event -unrwa-establised-1950-05-01 (accessed 15 October 2021).

Kagan, M. (2011). "'We Live in a Country of UNHCR": The UN Surrogate State and Refugee Policy in the Middle East', UNHCR: Research Paper No. 201. https://www .refworld.org/docid/4d8876db2.html (accessed 15 October 2021).

Kagawa, F. (2005). 'Emergency Education: A Critical Review of the Field', *Comparative Education*, 41(4), 487–503. https://doi.org/10.1080/03050060500317620.

Karasapan, O., & Shah, S. (2018). *Syrian Refugees and the Schooling Challenge*. The Brookings Institution. https://www.brookings.edu/blog/future-development/2018/10 /23/syrian-refugees-and-the-schooling-challenge/ (accessed 15 October 2021).

Lie, J. (2020). 'The Humanitarian-Development Nexus: Humanitarian Principles, Practice, and Pragmatics', *Journal of International Humanitarian Action*, 5(1), 1–13. https://doi.org/10.1186/s41018-020-00086-0.

Love, B. (2019). *We Want to do More Than Survive: Abolitionist Teaching and the Pursuit of Educational Freedom*. Boston: Beacon Press.

Malkki, L. (1996). 'Speechless Emissaries: Refugees, Humanitarianism, and Dehistoricization', *Cultural Anthropology*, 11(3), 377–404. https://doi.org/10.1525/ can.1996.11.3.02a00050.

Moghli, M.A., & Shuayb, M. (2020). *Education under COVID-19 Lockdown: Reflections for Teachers, Students and Parents*. Beirut: Center for Lebanese Studies, Lebanese American University.

Morrice, L. (2013). 'Refugees in Higher Education: Boundaries of Belonging and Recognition, Stigma and Exclusion', *International Journal of Lifelong Education*, 32(5): 652–68.

Nicolai, S., & Hine, S. (2015). *Investment for Education in Emergencies: A Review of Evidence*. London: Overseas Development Institute (ODI).

Nussbaum, M. (1995). 'Objectification', *Philosophy & Public Affairs*, 24(4), 249–91. https://doi.org/10.1111/j.1088-4963.1995.tb00032.x.

Papadaki, L. (2010). 'What Is Objectification?', *Journal of Moral Philosophy*, 7(1), 16–36. https://doi.org/10.1163/174046809X12544019606067.

Pherali, T., & Abu Moghli, M. (2019). 'Higher Education in the Context of Mass Displacement: Towards Sustainable Solutions for Refugees', *Journal of Refugee Studies*, 1–21. https://doi.org/10.1093/jrs/fez093.

Psacharopoulos, G. (1989). 'Time Trends of the Returns to Education: Cross-national Evidence', *Economics of Education Review*, 8(3), 225–31. https://doi.org/10.1016/0272-7757(82)90002-4.

Psacharopoulos, G. (1994). 'Returns to Investment in Education: A Global Update', *World Development*, 22(9), 1325–43. https://doi.org/10.1016/0305-750X(94)90007-8.

Psacharopoulos, G., & Patrios, H. (2004). 'Returns to Investment in Education: A Further Update', *Education Economics*, 12(2), 111–34. https://doi.org/10.1080/0964529042000239140.

Reid-Henry, S. (2014). 'Humanitarianism as Liberal Diagnostic: Humanitarian Reason and the Political Rationalities of the Liberal Will-To-Care', *Transactions of the Institute of British Geographers*, 39(3), 418–31. https://doi.org/10.1111/tran.12029.

Said, E. (1978). *Orientalism*. New York: Pantheon Books.

Sayigh, R. (1988). 'Palestinians in Lebanon: Status Ambiguity, Insecurity and Flux', *Race & Class*, 30(1), 13–32. https://doi.org/10.1177/030639688803000102.

Shuayb, M. (2014). 'The Art of Inclusive Exclusions: Educating the Palestinian Refugee Students in Lebanon', *Refugee Survey Quarterly*, 33(2), 20–37. https://doi.org/10.1093/rsq/hdu002.

Shuayb, M. (2020). 'How a Generation of Syrian Children in Lebanon Were Robbed of Their Education', *OpenDemocracy*. https://www.opendemocracy.net/en/north-africa-west-asia/how-generation-syrian-children-lebanon-were-robbed-their-education/ (accessed 15 October 2021).

Shuayb, M. (2021). 'Lebanon: "Ahmed Will Not Be Part of the One Percent"', *Daraj*. https://daraj.com/en/68496/?fbclid=IwAR3cn0KQ4e9N8MMS4jcRMOKwGt0xRNiv7VViB6BR87G3CkAME7-Xv5hSP30 (accessed 15 October 2021).

Shuayb, M., & Brun, C. (2020). 'For Young Syrian Refugees, Education and Employment Cannot Remain Apolitical', *OpenDemocracy*. https://www.opendemocracy.net/en/north-africa-west-asia/young-syrian-refugees-education-and-employment-cannot-remain-apolitical/ (accessed 15 October 2021).

Strand, A. (2020). 'Humanitarian-Development Nexus', *Humanitarianism: Keywords*, 104–6, London: Brill.

Sukarieh, M., & Tannock, S. (2019). 'Subcontracting Academia: Alienation, Exploitation and Disillusionment in the UK Overseas Syrian Refugee Research Industry', *Antipode*, 51(2), 664–80. https://doi.org/10.1111/anti.12502.

Szczepanik, M. (2016). 'The "Good" and "Bad" Refugees? Imagined Refugeehood(s) in the Media Coverage of the Migration Crisis', *Journal of Identity & Migration Studies*, 10(2), 23–33.

Tsourapas, G. (2019). 'Syrian Migration and the Rise of Refugee Rentierism', *Crisis*. https://crisismag.net/2019/10/01/syria-the-european-migrant-crisis-and-the-rise-of-refugee-rentierism/ (accessed 15 October 2021).

UNGA (1951). *Convention Relating to the Status of Refugees*. https://www.ohchr.org/en/professionalinterest/pages/statusofrefugees.aspx (accessed 15 October 2021).

UNHCR (2014). 'Resolve Conflicts or Face Surge in Life-Long Refugees Worldwide, Warns UNHCR Special Envoy'. https://www.unhcr.org/uk/news/press/2014/6/53a42f6d9/resolve-conflicts-face-surge-life-long-refugees-worldwide-warns-unhcr-special.html (accessed 15 October 2021).

UNHCR (2017). 'Left Behind: Refugee Education in Crisis'. https://www.unhcr.org/59b696f44.pdf (accessed 15 October 2021).

UNHCR (2019) *Stepping Up: Refugee Education in Crisis*. https://www.unhcr.org/steppingup/wp-content/uploads/sites/76/2019/09/Education-Report-2019-Final-web-9.pdf (accessed 15 October 2021).

UNHCR UK (2021). 'Refugees'. https://www.unhcr.org/uk/refugees.html#:~:text=Refugees%20are%20people%20fleeing%20conflict,can%20be%20difficult%20to%20imagine (accessed 15 October 2021).

UNHCR UK. (n.d.). 'Tertiary Education'. http://www.unhcr.org/uk/tertiary-education.html (accessed 15 October 2021).

UNRWA (2017). 'Protection Brief: Palestine Refugees Living in Lebanon'. https://www.unrwa.org/sites/default/files/lebanon_protection_brief_october_2017.pdf (accessed 15 October 2021).

Wagner, E. (2017). 'Refugee Education: Is Technology the Solution?', *INEE*. https://inee.org/resources/refugee-education-technology-solution (accessed 15 October 2021).

Zembylas, M., & Keet, A. (2019). *Critical Human Rights Education: Advancing Social-Justice-Oriented Educational Praxes*, Vol. 13. New York: Springer Nature.

5

Sewing Migrant Journeys in a Bulletproof Vest

The Museum as a Site of Memory and Mutual Learning in Medellín, Colombia

Veronica Cadavid-González and Jennifer Allsopp

Introduction

The lady is sitting under a canopy at a flip-top table outside the museum building, sewing in a bulletproof vest. It is not clear whether she is Venezuelan or Colombian – she says she is 'both now', although originally, she came from a small piece of Colombian farmland that was occupied by the guerrillas – seemingly the FARC – during the internal armed conflict. Having fled to Venezuela, the economic and civil-political crisis there has now brought her back to Colombia and, with homelessness rife among refugees and returnees, she is looking to reclaim her family's land. That is why she is wearing the vest, she explains. Land is power, and although legally she has rights to reclaim it, there are those who would still rather shoot her than relinquish it. On her piece of paper, she has drawn a map of the world and, having poked holes in various cities with a needle, she is now using yarn to connect them. They represent her family's many migrant journeys of domestic and international displacement, both voluntary and forced. Everyone around the table has a migration story to tell and we have come together, individuals from the local, national and international community at the Casa de la Memoria (Memory Museum) in Medellín, Colombia, to listen and learn as part of a two-day Migration Conversation event which took place in 2019 in collaboration with the London International Development Centre's Migration Leadership Team (LIDC-MLT).[1] In this chapter, we focus on the process and results of a public-facing Migration Laboratory which brought international researchers together with community members to explore, through artistic participatory methods, comparisons and synergies in localized and globalized understandings of migration and forced displacement.

Latin America has a long-standing and complex relationship with migration, comprising countries of emigration, transit, seasonal and periodical migration and immigration. A recurrent topic during the Migration Conversation concerned the ongoing displacement of over one million Colombian citizens living in neighbouring countries such as Ecuador, the United States and Canada as refugees or economic migrants (Iranzo-Dosdad, Edson-Louidor 2018: 5), and as many as nine million more living in the country as internally displaced persons (IDPs) (Gobierno de Colombia n.d.).[2]

At the time of the event in May 2019, over one million Venezuelan refugees had arrived in Colombia and the wider region in response to regime instability, conflict and destitution (Migracion Colombia 2021). For several countries, including Colombia, these significant movements of people from Venezuela (including the return of many Colombians and other regional migrants) have brought new challenges and opportunities. The Migration Laboratory sought to create an environment for mutual learning and knowledge exchange around this topic through the fostering of critical reflection among community participants based on museum materials and the juxtaposition of local and global perspectives. It sought to cross new frontiers in understandings of displacement across time and place, exploring how local, national and regional factors have shaped the treatment of mobility, development and education in this context. As well as being a pedagogic exercise for participants, the findings fed into research about global migration knowledge gaps.[3]

This chapter explores the strengths and limitations of critical museum pedagogy, specifically what new insights it offered about how we might learn about and practice empathy towards different types of migrants. We consider the politics of terminology in relation to migration in the Colombian context, exploring how participants in the Migration Laboratory identified important synergies and differences between the experiences of internally displaced persons within Colombia historically and those of newly arriving Venezuelan refugees.

Storytelling, we observe, was a powerful tool in this context for linking experiences and finding connections between different lives. We find that, where sufficient attention is given to the political nuances of each situation and participants are given adequate opportunities to be heard, museums can be important spaces to educate and foster empathy for others by drawing on individual and collective memories of mobility. Museums become, as Clover and Sanford (2016) have argued, drawing on McRobbie (2009), 'pedagogic contact zones' – 'spaces for collective power, critique and debate . . . sites of cocreated knowledge, resistance, praxis and social, pedagogical and self-reflexivity' (129). The event demonstrated the value of the arts in bringing marginalized voices to the fore and enabling the co-creation of knowledge by local and global actors in migration, and the power of memory museums in particular in creating political and public 'holding spaces' for non-hierarchical mutual education and identity building among societies.

Methodology and Ethics: Challenging the Idea of 'Experts'

The Medellín workshop was one of ten Global Migration Conversations, organized in 2018 and 2019 by the London International Development Centre Migration Leadership Team in partnership with regional and local stakeholders. The team was formed to develop a shared strategy for supporting migration- and displacement-related research by the UK's Economic and Social Research Council (ESRC) and Arts and Humanities Research Council (AHRC). The Latin American conversation was held in partnership with the Casa de la Memoria Museum based in Medellín, which works to promote knowledge exchange around armed conflict and recognize the narratives and lives of the victims of the armed conflict, including IDPs, in Colombia; and Fundación Mi Sangre, a Colombian charity, that focuses on peacebuilding through the empowerment of children and youth.[4] All discussions were conducted in Spanish and English using simultaneous interpretation.

The first day of the workshop featured four interactive panels which brought together policymakers, funders, researchers, non-governmental organizations (NGOs) and migrant community organizations, academics, government officials, civil society actors and lawyers from Colombia, Mexico, Venezuela, Chile, Brazil, Ecuador, the United Kingdom, the United States and Australia. It provided a forum to take stock of and learn from research on migration and asylum emerging in local, Latin American and global contexts. The second day involved interactive artistic activities and conversations with members of the general public in Medellín and a tour of the Casa de la Memoria Museum. A total of forty-five people participated in the event from diverse socio-economic and urban and rural backgrounds.[5]

The aim of the event was to develop a better understanding of participants' perceptions about different types of migration through participatory dialogue with activist, academic and practitioner experts on migration. The artistic practices were used to generate discussions and reflections. The laboratory also had a pedagogical purpose of introducing participants to concepts and ideas in relation to migration which they had not previously come across while equally evoking political emotions, particularly empathy, sympathy and compassion (Nussbaum 2013). The core questions of the conversation were: (i) What is the local perception of the migration phenomenon? (ii) In what ways can art be a tool for the promotion of a better-informed perception of migration?

Three workstations were set up, each with a different migratory theme and activity, and participants moved between the different activities, spending thirty minutes at each station. They then regrouped for an open discussion about the experience. Looking to mirror the experience of mobility, the participants subsequently were asked to travel around the museum. The event took place under Chatham House rules. As such, all references in this chapter are generalized. Consent was granted by participants to include anonymized information about their insights. Ethical approval for the research was granted by SOAS, and ethical protocols of the host museum were followed.

Critical Museum Pedagogies

There is a long history of academic work that traces the evolution of the museum as a site of education. While early theories of the educational role of museums tended to see them as static repositories of knowledge, more recently, the potential of museums to open up dialogue between the collection and the audience has been explored. For example, the idea of the 'contact zone' (Clifford 1997) was developed to encourage participation and dialogue, while 'public engagement' has come to be understood as 'a process for generating, improving or repairing relationships between institutions of culture and society at large' (Ashley 2014: 261). This shift from didactic to interactive, dialogic exchanges between observer and the observed has come with a blossoming of new tools for audience members to interact with exhibits – through posting notes, navigating multiple-choice computer screens and even creating their own exhibits, for example, through video messaging which is then featured in the exhibit. This shift in participation dynamics has been facilitated by a simultaneous shift in the nature and format of museum collections. Whereas in the past museums prompted ideas of cabinets full of objects, today museums commonly include audio and visual materials such as oral testimonies and videos.

One approach commonly employed by museums seeking to engage with the topic of migration involves immersive experiences which aim to place the visitor in the shoes of the subjects. These might include, for instance, asking participants to reflect on what one object they would take with them if they were forced to flee – or a 'walk through' a typical cell in an immigration detention centre. However, such attempts to foster empathy on the part of the visitor have been critiqued by some as voyeuristic and may also risk undermining the agency of migrants and refugees and instead reifying them as helpless victims at the mercy of state power (Harrell-Bond 1986). One alternative to fostering empathy through 'immersion' is the recruitment of survivors as virtual or real-life tour guides who help the visitor interpret the exhibit in relation to their experience.[6] In the case of the Casa de la Memoria Museum (one of a number of memory-focused museums in the region), all projects and exhibitions are based on consultation and implemented in collaboration with victims' organizations. Members of the public are invited to remember and come to terms with human rights abuses in recent history, many of which are linked to internal and international displacement. In Latin America, memory museums tend to arise from sites of tensions and debates among diverse groups in relation to contested histories and past and ongoing conflicts. They serve to empower individuals to confront shared traumas from a range of perspectives and to deliberate upon, rather than impose, ideas of truth within a society (Allier 2008: 106–7). As such, they operate as a vindication of the communities' stories, past traumas and wounds. In hosting our laboratory at the Casa de la Memoria, we were able to draw on a wealth of experience and practice in community participation and listening, including in relation to experiences of migration.

In the last two decades, migration, including forced migration, has become one of the defining topics of international (Castles 2009; De Haas 2012; Samaddar 2020) and local development (Taylor et al. 1996). Alongside challenges in providing education for people on the move – as discussed in other chapters in this edited volume – the mobility of peoples raises a further question of how to educate societies *about* histories and processes of migration. Scoping work for this chapter revealed that there are over 100 migration-themed museums globally, including museums dedicated to the topic of immigration (e.g. Paris' Cité Nationale de l'Histoire de l'Immigration[7]) and emigration (e.g. Rome's Museo Nazionale dell'Emigrazione Italiana[8]). In Latin America, the Chilean Museum of Memory and Human Rights (Museo de la Memoria y Derechos Humanos) created a temporary exhibition about the exile of Chilean people during the Pinochet era,[9] which included an exploration of the broader topic of migration and racism.[10] There are also museums specifically dedicated to forced displacements across borders (e.g. the Amritsar Partition Museum[11]) and within them (e.g. proposals for a museum of IDPs in northeast Nigeria to document the experiences of those displaced from their communities and their villages as a result of the Boko Haram insurgency). Other museums with wider thematic remits, from history to art, have committed significant resources in recent years to exhibitions on the topics of migration and forced displacement. A special issue of the *Journal of Museum Education*, co-edited by Lannes and Monsein Rhodes in 2019, focused on this growing thematic interest in migration among global museums including in Italy (Pegno 2019), Thailand (Sriprachya-Anunt 2019), the United States (Williams 2019) and Turkey (Levin 2019). Museums, they highlighted, 'have an opportunity to become purposeful centers of engagement and inclusion for immigrant and refugee communities' (5).

At the same time, the idea of the mobile museum as a place to talk about migration has emerged. The UK's Migration Museum, for example, has no fixed abode and is rather a touring assemblance of exhibitions. Meanwhile, annual pop-up events such as the Hargeisa Literature Festival continue to host temporary exhibitions on the theme of mobility, as was part of their 2019 line-up of exhibits on the theme of coexistence.[12]

When dealing with a complicated topic like migration, museums must consider how to balance stories in line with the thrust of their exhibit. There is always a risk that by focusing on one narrative, they end up sidelining or ignoring other dimensions of migratory experiences. In a recent exhibit, *Refugees Forced to Flee* at the Imperial War Museum in London, for example, the narratives of IDPs, asylum seekers and refugees were central, but those of economic and climate migration were not. While narrowing the focus can be effective in achieving certain educational aims and keeping the topic digestible, for example, for school groups, it also risks underselling the intersection of different types of migration. It is also common for historical exhibits to draw pedagogical parallels between *past and present* migrations (what we might call vertical acts of empathy). At the Anne Frank house in Amsterdam, for example, visitors are asked to confront current-day examples of persecution and think how they relate to Anne's experience. Similarly, exhibits commonly seek to draw parallels across different types of experience that occur *simultaneously* (what we might call horizontal acts of empathy). For example, Museo Casa de la Memoria in collaboration with the Anne Frank house curated the exhibition 'Niñez entre el conflicto y la esperanza' (Childhood: Between Conflict and Hope) to inspire, between children, a comparative look at different histories of children living in conflict situations around the world (Museo Casa de la Memoria n.d.).

The Migration Laboratory in Medellín sought to foster acts of both vertical and horizontal empathy and promote empathy and learning across *different types* of migrant experiences. Mobility dynamics in the region are extremely complex, with environmental, violence and economic factors intersecting to prompt population movements within and across borders. As well as creating a wealth of content to educate others, the conversation showed the value of creating a space for dialogue and involving the community in setting the parameters of the topic itself (Ashley 2014).

The Casa de la Memoria Museum: Place, Purpose and Pedagogy

There were a number of reasons why the Medellín Casa de la Memoria Museum was best suited to host this conversation. 'Museums', as Lannes and Monsein Rhodes (2019) explain,

> have a certain type of power within their communities. . . . They are seen as sites of public trust . . . they do have the social and cultural capital to bring people through their doors to engage in learning through their exhibits and programs . . . [they] can serve as anchor spaces for their communities, as places of belonging, or a third-place. (5–6)

A third-place here is defined as a space that is inclusive, local and brings together groups of people who may not socialize outside of them. The Medellín Casa de la Memoria Museum, as an institution that was born from a victims' initiative, has become a kind of community hub where people, including migrants in the community, already come to access services and workshops, from exercise and dance classes to sewing groups. The museum is situated in an historic part of the city where communities meet along a river. It has long been a place for remembrance and learning about the experience of the country's many people displaced through the armed conflict. Among other sections, the museum is host to a memory room which includes audio and visual samples from families whose relatives 'disappeared' during the armed conflict. At the time of our collaboration, the museum was already hosting community discussions and art fellowships on the recent Venezuelan refugee crisis and was keen to work together to think about how to open up dialogue and foster empathy across the two groups of displaced populations. The collection here was seen as a 'medium not a message' – a launch pad for a series of conversations (Lannes and Monsein Rhodes 2019: 8).

At the time of our collaboration, millions of Venezuelan refugees were fleeing the violence and economic collapse of their country. Unlike many countries in the region, Colombia offered a relatively sympathetic response, constructing camps on the border, making available over one million work visas and providing temporary protection to Venezuelan refugees. But stigma and discrimination were on the rise and public fears were surfacing about Venezuelan migrants taking Colombian jobs and bringing crime to the cities. In this context, the museum's then director, Cathalina Sánchez Escobar, explained: 'we wanted to explore parallels between different groups of migrants internally and across borders in Colombia to see if we could help people to see things in common . . . not just what is different.' She continued, 'For many of us, the question [of refugees] is a new topic but it knocks on our doors and the windows of our cars. You see it in the street. It touches the heart of our cities.'

Medellín occupies a unique place in relation to migration, mobility and displacement which shaped the conversation in important ways. Central to the museum's treatment of migration were questions of memory and history and ideas of reparation and non-repetition. Mobility was framed as part of a continuous process of evolution and post-conflict reconstruction in a way that destabilizes linear and cross-border conceptions of migration which tend to dominate migration studies literature. Indeed, the very concepts of 'immigration' and 'emigration' were challenged during the laboratory, with some arguing that the term 'immigration' failed to do justice to the multi-linear and intersecting nature of migratory flows and how these play out over space and time. 'Mobility', 'displacement' and 'movement' were all used more typically than the term 'migration' over the course of the workshop. As one participant said, 'Whatever migrant group we work with, our commonality is human rights.'

The attention to memory has fostered strong collaboration in the region between the arts, culture and knowledge exchange on the topic of mobility and displacement. Participants gave countless examples of how arts and culture have been vessels for promoting learning and citizen action around migration and mobility, including through formats such as embroidery; street art – including examples of street galleries (e.g. a series of murals documenting atrocities against indigenous communities in Colombia); satire; social media and storytelling. As one participant articulated it,

The difference between testimony and storytelling, what is it? Storytelling requires an artistic transformation between the testimony and story to put a voice to what happened to a 'me' – it is a way of linking to those who have not lived it; in Spanish, you 'gift' (regular) a testimony, but a story is told as part of collective construction process.

Findings from the Migration Laboratory

In this section, we discuss the conversations that took place across the different stations during the Migration Laboratory and synergies between them, as well as how props and artistic methods fostered the narration of stories.

Station (I): Migration Related to Environmental Issues and Development Projects

The idea of this station was to generate an understanding about migration linked to environmental phenomena and development projects. This included capturing people's memories of environmental migration, as well as identifying the gaps in understanding and challenges for society in this dynamic. The conversation began with projecting videos of Antioquia territories, from the museum's 'Nostalgic Landscapes' exhibition. Most of the images were of green mountains and countryside. The aim was to trigger an identity with the land and a sense of what it might mean to be displaced from these territories. Participants were asked to draw and describe what emotions, ideas and words came to mind as they viewed the images.

Ideas about environmental displacement were new to participants from urban settings. One participant explained that for him, the idea of environmental migrants or of being displaced people as a result of development projects in Colombia seemed 'unreal' – something he'd never really considered. Many urban participants had also never thought about the long-term impacts of environmental crises and injustices. Reflections centred on how for cases of environmental disasters, there is normally only an immediate humanitarian response without consideration for long-term measures. Participants with first- or second-hand experience of environmental displacement discussed the lack of frameworks to protect them. They disagreed about whether the answer to this was to expand the regulations for refugee protection or to come up with a distinct protection protocol for environmental refugees. Sometimes, it was said, individuals who are forcibly displaced because of development projects are compensated for the cost of their land, but identity and moral losses are not part of the equation. Participants noticed how matters about territory in Latin America primarily affect people living in rural areas and often in extreme poverty. As a result, the need to expand protections to indigenous lands for rural people was emphasized. The asymmetry in power relations in situations of development-related displacement was identified as underpinning rights violations, particularly considering the limited opposition indigenous communities can make to state decisions. The impossibility of return was also a theme that permeated these discussions.

In Colombia and Latin America more broadly, participants identified a close relationship between migration and armed conflict, development projects and environmental disasters. In the first scenario, many cases of forced displacement of rural people by armed groups and/or paramilitaries were seen to have a hidden motive of 'clearing the lands' – the same actors were commonly thought to be involved in corruption in the allocation of licences for megaprojects. In the second scenario, participants reflected on how excessive and rapid development without sustainability considerations can cause environmental disasters; one example given was the contamination of several rivers as a result of irresponsible mining and land fertilization which diminished the food supply for communities.

The convergence of these different displacement phenomena were illustrated in a map drawn by one participant, which depicts the overlapping territories of armed conflict, environmental displacement caused by industry (shown by the factory) and long-term climate change trends (depicted in the rain). While the image resonated with the experiences of some participants, it was surprising to others (Figure 5.1).

As one participant put it, 'we need to politicize the issue of environmental migration, to show how global warming is related to the economic model and advocate for a guarantee of minimal rights for environmental migrants.' There needs to be, it was argued, more factual and less sensationalized representation in the media of the impact of environmental changes and development initiatives and their related impact on migration. An international expert said she'd never seen the intricacies of mixed migration so clearly depicted.

Station (II): Economic Migration

This station aimed to explore participants' perceptions of economic migration, specifically about the conditions of migrants and the challenges and implications of migrating under this dynamic. Participants were asked to draw and weave a map representing the migration process (Figure 5.2). The questions to trigger

Figure 5.1 Drawing by a workshop participant. *Source*: Authors.

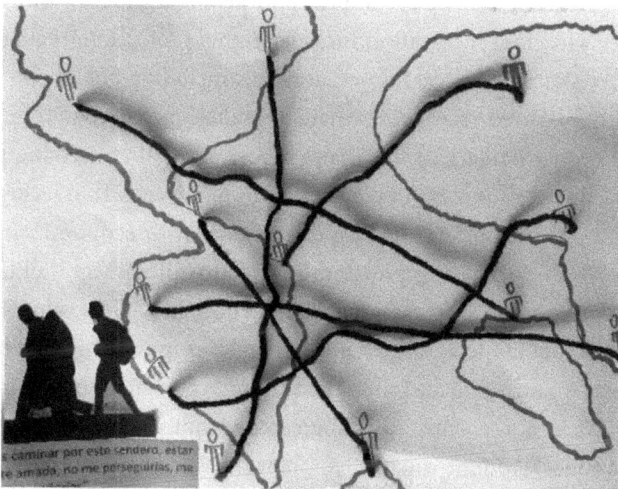

Figure 5.2 A map drawn by a workshop participant. *Source*: Authors.

the reflection were: What does a migrant feel away from their house? What kind of migration am I related to? What does it mean to migrate? What circumstances make a person migrate? When is a migrant vulnerable or not?

While participants were drawing their maps, the conversation started to flow organically and went in multiple directions, including an assessment of the current context of migration in Colombia – including newly arriving Venezuelans, and the history of emigration and immigration in the country.

Participants talked about the complete absence of a support system as the biggest factor in determining migrant vulnerability, along with the missed feeling of belonging to something and the losses from everyday life, including food, land, friends and family and social dynamics. They discerned that a lack of protection of rights for migrants stems from social and institutional factors that can lead to labour exploitation and a negative impact on physical and psychological health and well-being. These included a lack of access to health services and infrastructure to promote their well-being and provide care and treatment when required.

Integration was an important part of the discussion and was understood as an interactive process between the receiving community and migrants. Correspondingly, one common perception among participants was that integration was not just a question of time and most agreed that it was impossible to completely leave behind the feeling of being an outsider. While most of them saw migration as a great opportunity to enhance one's culture, they also considered integration to be a complex and personal process. Moreover, they considered it vital that integration includes rights protection, regularization of the migratory status and access to social rights, including public services.

Participants shared the view that migrants faced sometimes extreme discrimination, particularly if they were perceived by the receiving population to have inadequate resources or be in situations of poverty. Thus, acceptance and integration were seen to have a close relationship with economic and migrant status; those with purchasing power are wanted while others looking for jobs and part of the working class are considered to have much less value. Likewise, it was concluded that in most cases migration involves moving, at least in the short term, towards worse living and social conditions to those in their pre-migration lives even if such movement results in greater economic gains in the long term.

Participants cast doubt on the 'voluntary' aspect of economic migration. According to their assessment, a combination of economic, political and social conditions of a country force people to migrate. They stressed the importance of expanding understandings of both the 'forced' migration category and how we understand the guaranteeing of rights and protection of people. One example given was the cycle of Colombia–Venezuela migration; the 1990s Colombian context generated the expulsion of many people to Venezuela, and the current Venezuelan context is producing a massive migration to Colombia, the common theme being structural violence in both countries leading to mass forced movement at different points in time.

One key concern among participants was the role of the media regarding migration, including the media's responsibility for generating xenophobia. They spoke about the ignorance portrayed through media statements and how the media used stereotypes and particular tropes to cause alarm, for example, how they connected health and economic crises to migration when in reality such crises existed prior to the arrival of migrants to Colombia. Participants talked about the importance of education, affirming that 'we have to prepare our own to treat those who arrive well'.

Another participant stressed the need to see the positive aspects of migration and not just see it as a problem:

> It is important to see that migration contributes. It is difficult for us to see the culture, social development that a migration can bring. For example, the first thing you do when you arrive to a new place is bring new good entrepreneurship. The laboratory of cooking proved that gastronomy becomes a connecting factor.

Food emerged in every station as a connecting factor, a testament to how the experiential aspects of migration can cross types of migration. For several participants food could help bridge gaps across space and time. One participant, for example, explained her own migration story through the family menu:

> I learned how to cook outside of my native country, there are no beans or arepas in my house. My fridge has very different vegetables than those normally eaten here: plantains, yucca, my fridge and my mom's fridge are not the same. I learned how to cook with the ingredients that existed at the time when I was a migrant and they were not Colombians. What I know I learned it with my African friend.

Station (III): Forced Displacement: Refugees and IDPs

At this station, participants discussed the situation of refugees and displaced persons, considering the particularities of the Colombian context. To begin the conversation, testimonies were used from the exhibition of the Casa de la Memoria Museum, 'Colombia, paradise deprived',[6] where the issue of displacement was explored through the perspectives of survivors. To evoke political emotions such as compassion, participants were asked to write letters to those people who had to flee their territories due to the conditions of violence.

One finding for most of the laboratory participants was the acknowledgement that forced internally displaced Colombians, who in most cases are victims of armed conflict, are also migrants, which implies that Colombia has extensive experience in this area. A key reflection was: How can we use this experience of being displaced ourselves to help international refugees?

It was stressed that there were some important differences across refugee communities, in terms of both the way they were received and their support needs. One participant discussed the differential treatment accorded to Venezuelans and Haitians in Chile. While, at least on paper, Venezuelans are allowed to enter on a democratic visa, current policy is seen to discriminate against Haitians. It was felt that the political situation of Venezuelan refugees shaped their reception in many Latin American countries.

There was a widely held perception that displacement implies a violation of rights whether across or within borders. This was something especially important to Colombians, for many of whom the land represents their roots and their subsistence. Participants were keen to talk about the role of identity, reflecting on questions such as: What happens when people have been in multiple territories? How does identity change in light of geographical location? Several participants drew parallels with the first station on environmental displacement.

Participants also questioned what makes migration different from displacement. One participant commented,

> I feel that after what we have seen, in the different types of migration we have studied today there is hope to return, while with forced displacement this will creep into your soul because your hope ends, additionally of what you were. I don't want to ignore the pain that other migrants may feel but forced displacement is more aggressive and leaves a totally deep mark of it, perhaps it is not possible to recover.

Another claimed that 'the exile is also an eternal return, the idea wanting to return all the time and not being able to'.

Participants discussed the existence of invisible as well as visible borders, such as the 'invisible' borders established due to the violence of criminal groups existing in Latin American countries such as Colombia and Brazil, which divide cities and, in the case of Medellín, cause inter-urban forced displacement. In this context, they explored the difficulty of creating a city with divided territories within. One participant shared candidly that this was the first time they had

6 https://www.academia.edu/35484606/Narrazioni_da_Museo_a_Museo_
   Trasformazioni_Migranti_tra_MAXXI_e_Museo_Pigorini
7 http://www.histoire-immigration.fr/
8 http://www.museoemigrazioneitaliana.org/
9 https://web.museodelamemoria.cl/informate/exposiciones/10849/
10 https://web.museodelamemoria.cl/informate/inauguracion-otrxs-fronterxs-historia
   -sobre-migracion-racismo-y-desarraigo/
11 https://www.partitionmuseum.org/
12 http://www.hargeysaculturalcenter.org/hargeysa-international-book-fair/

References

Allier, E. (2008). 'Lugar de memoria: ¿un concepto para el análisis de las luchas memoriales? El caso de Uruguay y su pasado reciente', *Cuadernos del CLAEH*, 96–97(31), 87–109.

Ashley, S. (2014). 'Engage the World': Examining Conflicts of Engagement in Public Museums', *International Journal of Cultural Policy*, 20(3), 261–80.

Castles, S. (2009). 'Development and Migration or Migration and Development: What Comes First?', *Asian and Pacific Migration Journal*, 18(4), 441–71.

Clifford, J (1997). 'Museums as Contact Zones', in J. Clifford (Ed.), *Routes: Travel and Translation in the Late Twentieth Century*, Cambridge, MA: Harvard University Press, 188–219.

Clover, D., & Sanford, K. (2016). 'Contemporary Museums as Pedagogic Contact Zones: Potentials of Critical Cultural Adult Education', *Studies in the Education of Adults*, 48(2), 127–41.

De Haas, H. (2012). 'The Migration and Development Pendulum: A Critical View on Research and Policy', *International Migration*, 50(3), 8–25.

Gobierno de Colombia (n.d.). *Registro Unico de Victimas*. https://www
.unidadvictimas.gov.co/es/registro-unico-de-victimas-ruv/37394 (accessed 25 October 2021).

Harrell-Bond, B. E. (1986). *Imposing Aid: Emergency Assistance to Refugees*. Oxford: Oxford University Press.

Iranzo-Dosdad, A., & Edson Louidor, W. (2018). *Entre la guerra y la paz: los lugares de la diáspora colombiana*. Bogotá: Universidad de los Andes y Pontificia Universidad Javeriana.

Lannes, P., & Monsein Rhodes, L. (2019). 'Museums as Allies: Mobilizing to Address Migration', *Journal of Museum Education*, 44(1), 4–12, https://doi.org/10.1080
/10598650.2018.1563453.

Levin, I. (2019). 'Migration, Politics, and the Limits of Multiculturalism in a Turkish Museum', *Journal of Museum Education*, 44(1), 41–52.

McRobbie, A. (2009). *The Aftermath of Feminism: Gender, Culture and Social Change.* London: Sage.

Migracion Colombia. (2021). 'En un hecho sin precedentes, Colombia busca darle la mano a más de dos millones de venezolanos.' *Noticias.* https://www .migracioncolombia.gov.co/noticias/en-un-hecho-sin-precedentes-colombia-busca -darle-la-mano-a-mas-de-dos-millones-de-venezolanos (accessed 24 January 2022).

Museo Casa de la Memoria (n.d). *Sistematización proyecto expositivo Niñez entre el conflicto y la esperanza Museo Casa de la Memoria-Casa de Ana Frank 2016.* http:// colecciones.museocasadelamemoria.gov.co/repositorio/bitstream/handle/mcm /233/2.%20Sistematización%20Niñez%20entre%20el%20conflicto%20y%20la %20esperanza_Final%202016.pdf?sequence=1&isAllowed=y (accessed 24 January 2022).

Nussbaum, M (2013). *Political Emotions.* Cambridge, MA: Harvard University Press.

Pegno, M. (2019). 'Becoming a Service Provider through Partnerships and Sustained Engagement: Developing Programs with Immigrant and Refugee Audiences in Art Museums', *Journal of Museums Education,* 44(1), 13–25.

Samaddar, R. (2020). *The Postcolonial Age of Migration.* Delhi: Routledge India.

Sriprachya-Anunt, W. (2019). 'Myanmar Migrant Workers as Guests of the Nation', *Journal of Museum Education,* 44(1), 26–33.

Taylor, J. E., Arango, J., Hugo, G., Kouaouci, A., Massey, D.S., & Pellegrino, A. (1996). 'International Migration and Community Development', *Population Index,* 62(3), 397–418.

Williams, R. (2019). 'Welcoming (and Learning from) the Stranger: The Museum as a Forum for Interfaith Dialogue', *Journal of Museum Education,* 44(1), 34–40.

6

Revisiting 'Eduscape' through a Postcolonial Lens

The Influence of Globalization and Migration on Educational Offer and Demand in Senegal

Anneke Newman

Introduction

The concept of eduscape, short for educational landscape, was coined two decades ago to capture how educational processes in local settings are shaped by globalization. I build on the work of scholars in diverse disciplines who have contributed to theorizing the eduscape concept, demonstrating its applicability to multiple environments through fine-grained empirical case studies. Yet, I find there to be two Eurocentric biases in most of the literature which employs it. First, 'education' is framed in terms of the school or university inherited from the European model, neglecting non-Western or precolonial knowledges, epistemologies and learning spaces and systems. Second, when migration is considered, it is in the context of international students and academics, eclipsing alternative types of mobility for educational purposes, or other influences that migration might have on educational dynamics.

To address these biases, I provide an analysis of educational dynamics in Northern Senegal, West Africa, using a postcolonial eduscape approach which recentres the forms of knowledge and education valued by the inhabitants in this context, namely Islamic schools which predate – and operate outside of – the public school system. By grounding my analysis not in a priori decisions about the kinds of global cultural flows to focus on but in data derived from an exploratory ethnography of educational decision-making and preferences, I illuminate the forms of migration and aspects of globalization that emerged as most salient in my informants' everyday lives and their effects on educational dynamics.

By analysing education supply and family preferences in Northern Senegal through a postcolonial eduscape framework, I make two interrelated arguments. First, eduscape remains a useful concept for understanding the influence of globalization on educational phenomena, as long as 'education' and, in association, knowledges and epistemologies are defined more inclusively to overcome Eurocentric bias. Second, ethnography remains the methodology par excellence for making sense of eduscapes but should ideally be used as part of an open-ended research design to capture the kinds of global cultural flows most relevant to people on the ground in postcolonial contexts, rather than allowing the interests of researchers based in the Global North to dictate the foci of study. Of particular interest to readers of this volume on education, migration and development, a more nuanced understanding of eduscapes in specific Southern contexts could also inform policies which purposefully address power inequalities meshed in logics of coloniality and are thus better aligned with people's priorities, preoccupations and everyday realities.

Eduscape: Making Sense of Educational Landscapes in the Context of Globalization

The term 'eduscape' was first developed by Heikki Kynäslahti (2001: 25) to make sense of educational phenomena in the context of globalization. He defined it as 'a horizontal integrative landscape in the field of education which resembles the idea of "scapes" coined by Appadurai'. Appadurai's five scapes – or types of global cultural flows – include ethnoscapes, or the movement of people who are increasingly faced by 'the realities of having to move, or the fantasies of wanting to move' (1990: 297); technoscapes, or the movement of technology, 'both mechanical and informational', and commodities (1990: 297); and finanscapes, or the global movement of capital. Mediascapes refer to the distribution of communication technologies which produce and disseminate information, as well as the complex repertoires of images and narratives they promote (1990: 298). Finally, Appadurai identifies ideoscapes 'composed of elements of the Enlightenment world view, which consists of a concatenation of ideas, terms and images, including "freedom", [. . .] "rights", [. . .] and the master-term "democracy"' (1990: 299).

This is an exciting finding – it shows the value in engaging communities from all background in knowledge production and exchange and the crucial role of museums as pedagogic meeting spaces for these kinds of conversations.

Important questions were also raised as to the viability of sustaining such opportunities to learn about migration and displacement. As the example of the lady in the bulletproof vest with whom we began this chapter makes clear, there is an important safety aspect to hosting such conversations. How can a diversity of people be welcomed into a space and made to feel safe and heard? How can we make space for a plurality of voices who may disagree? For some individuals who participated who had experienced armed conflicts, the 'victim' label felt important as a vehicle for accessing future justice; for other individuals, the label felt stigmatizing, and they explained that they preferred to be referred to as survivors.

In conclusion, the museum served the role of a 'holding space' to educate and foster empathy for others by drawing on individual and collective memories of mobility. The event showed the importance of arts in offering multiple entry points for individuals to critically engage with migration topics and illustrated how museums can become 'pedagogic contact zones' (Clover and Sanford 2016), in which knowledge can be co-created by local and global migration actors and power differences within certain types of knowledge can be recognized. It is important to acknowledge the uniqueness of the geographic context of Medellín in Colombia and the opportunities it created for holding rich conversation across the contours of migration categories. The specific role of the museum as a 'House of Memories' also appears to have generated a space in which participants felt comfortable at once to share their own stories, and actively listen to and seek to relate to the stories of others.

Notes

1 For the full report of the Medellín Migration Conversation on which this chapter draws, see https://www.soas.ac.uk/lidc-mlt/outputs/file142804.pdf. A summary of this report is also available in Spanish.

2 In 2021, the official number of victims by enforced displacement is 8,176,460 (Gobierno de Colombia, n.d.).

3 https://www.soas.ac.uk/lidc-mlt/outputs/file147522.pdf

4 http://fundacionmisangre.org/

5 More information about day one can be found in the event report, online: https://www.soas.ac.uk/lidc-mlt/outputs/file142804.pdf

Discussion and Conclusion

If museums represent a selection of elements from the cultures of society which come to be recognized as 'sanctioned knowledge', whose stories get told and whose get left out is a huge question. It is important for museums to hold space for multiple narratives.

The Medellín Migration Laboratory raised several migration-related issues of specific importance to the Latin American region, among them synergies and differences between internal and international migration, environmental and development-induced migration, the economic–forced migration continuum and questions of terminology including victimhood and survival and how these play out over time. The important history of internal displacement in Colombia raised a number of questions concerning how we define individuals who have been forcibly displaced and how these concepts change over time. When, for example, is one framed as a victim or a survivor; and when do they stop being displaced and become a member of a new community? But as important as the content was the *process*. We have shown in the earlier examples how over the course of the laboratory, as participants migrated across the three stations, the stories of participants became part of the exhibition. In each station, conversations grew out of engagement with existing content in the museum and added to it. This allowed for discussions across different themes that are not possible in the more linear walk-through-style engagement with exhibits. The products of the laboratory were also displayed and kept as records in the museum's archives.

Coming together at the end of the day after they had participated in the three workstations, participants' reflections echoed that of the person who wrote the anonymous letter to the museum: that the experience had been a formative and educational one while also providing space for personal reflection and healing. One participant remarked on how the laboratory had encouraged her to think about migration more in terms of mobility through linking it to the transitions she makes in her own daily life:

> We are not divided; it is more a thought we have because there is always a thread that unites us. We all migrate, there are several factors for it. We migrate even every day, from home to work.

Perhaps one of the most striking observations of the laboratory was how similar the conclusions were from the formal migration conversation among so-called experts on day one of the event, and day two which focused on community perspectives.

6 https://www.academia.edu/35484606/Narrazioni_da_Museo_a_Museo_
   Trasformazioni_Migranti_tra_MAXXI_e_Museo_Pigorini
7 http://www.histoire-immigration.fr/
8 http://www.museoemigrazioneitaliana.org/
9 https://web.museodelamemoria.cl/informate/exposiciones/10849/
10 https://web.museodelamemoria.cl/informate/inauguracion-otrxs-fronterxs-historia
   -sobre-migracion-racismo-y-desarraigo/
11 https://www.partitionmuseum.org/
12 http://www.hargeysaculturalcenter.org/hargeysa-international-book-fair/

References

Allier, E. (2008). 'Lugar de memoria: ¿un concepto para el análisis de las luchas
   memoriales? El caso de Uruguay y su pasado reciente', *Cuadernos del CLAEH*,
   96–97(31), 87–109.

Ashley, S. (2014). 'Engage the World': Examining Conflicts of Engagement in Public
   Museums', *International Journal of Cultural Policy*, 20(3), 261–80.

Castles, S. (2009). 'Development and Migration or Migration and Development: What
   Comes First?', *Asian and Pacific Migration Journal*, 18(4), 441–71.

Clifford, J (1997). 'Museums as Contact Zones', in J. Clifford (Ed.), *Routes: Travel and
   Translation in the Late Twentieth Century*, Cambridge, MA: Harvard University
   Press, 188–219.

Clover, D., & Sanford, K. (2016). 'Contemporary Museums as Pedagogic Contact Zones:
   Potentials of Critical Cultural Adult Education', *Studies in the Education of Adults*,
   48(2), 127–41.

De Haas, H. (2012). 'The Migration and Development Pendulum: A Critical View on
   Research and Policy', *International Migration*, 50(3), 8–25.

Gobierno de Colombia (n.d.). *Registro Unico de Victimas*. https://www
   .unidadvictimas.gov.co/es/registro-unico-de-victimas-ruv/37394 (accessed 25
   October 2021).

Harrell-Bond, B. E. (1986). *Imposing Aid: Emergency Assistance to Refugees*. Oxford:
   Oxford University Press.

Iranzo-Dosdad, A., & Edson Louidor, W. (2018). *Entre la guerra y la paz: los lugares de
   la diáspora colombiana*. Bogotá: Universidad de los Andes y Pontificia Universidad
   Javeriana.

Lannes, P., & Monsein Rhodes, L. (2019). 'Museums as Allies: Mobilizing to Address
   Migration', *Journal of Museum Education*, 44(1), 4–12, https://doi.org/10.1080
   /10598650.2018.1563453.

Levin, I. (2019). 'Migration, Politics, and the Limits of Multiculturalism in a Turkish
   Museum', *Journal of Museum Education*, 44(1), 41–52.

McRobbie, A. (2009). *The Aftermath of Feminism: Gender, Culture and Social Change.* London: Sage.

Migracion Colombia. (2021). 'En un hecho sin precedentes, Colombia busca darle la mano a más de dos millones de venezolanos.' *Noticias.* https://www .migracioncolombia.gov.co/noticias/en-un-hecho-sin-precedentes-colombia-busca -darle-la-mano-a-mas-de-dos-millones-de-venezolanos (accessed 24 January 2022).

Museo Casa de la Memoria (n.d). *Sistematización proyecto expositivo Niñez entre el conflicto y la esperanza Museo Casa de la Memoria-Casa de Ana Frank 2016.* http:// colecciones.museocasadelamemoria.gov.co/repositorio/bitstream/handle/mcm /233/2.%20Sistematización%20Niñez%20entre%20el%20conflicto%20y%20la %20esperanza_Final%202016.pdf?sequence=1&isAllowed=y (accessed 24 January 2022).

Nussbaum, M (2013). *Political Emotions.* Cambridge, MA: Harvard University Press.

Pegno, M. (2019). 'Becoming a Service Provider through Partnerships and Sustained Engagement: Developing Programs with Immigrant and Refugee Audiences in Art Museums', *Journal of Museums Education,* 44(1), 13–25.

Samaddar, R. (2020). *The Postcolonial Age of Migration.* Delhi: Routledge India.

Sriprachya-Anunt, W. (2019). 'Myanmar Migrant Workers as Guests of the Nation', *Journal of Museum Education,* 44(1), 26–33.

Taylor, J. E., Arango, J., Hugo, G., Kouaouci, A., Massey, D.S., & Pellegrino, A. (1996). 'International Migration and Community Development', *Population Index,* 62(3), 397–418.

Williams, R. (2019). 'Welcoming (and Learning from) the Stranger: The Museum as a Forum for Interfaith Dialogue', *Journal of Museum Education,* 44(1), 34–40.

Revisiting 'Eduscape' through a Postcolonial Lens

The Influence of Globalization and Migration on Educational Offer and Demand in Senegal

Anneke Newman

Introduction

The concept of eduscape, short for educational landscape, was coined two decades ago to capture how educational processes in local settings are shaped by globalization. I build on the work of scholars in diverse disciplines who have contributed to theorizing the eduscape concept, demonstrating its applicability to multiple environments through fine-grained empirical case studies. Yet, I find there to be two Eurocentric biases in most of the literature which employs it. First, 'education' is framed in terms of the school or university inherited from the European model, neglecting non-Western or precolonial knowledges, epistemologies and learning spaces and systems. Second, when migration is considered, it is in the context of international students and academics, eclipsing alternative types of mobility for educational purposes, or other influences that migration might have on educational dynamics.

To address these biases, I provide an analysis of educational dynamics in Northern Senegal, West Africa, using a postcolonial eduscape approach which recentres the forms of knowledge and education valued by the inhabitants in this context, namely Islamic schools which predate – and operate outside of – the public school system. By grounding my analysis not in a priori decisions about the kinds of global cultural flows to focus on but in data derived from an exploratory ethnography of educational decision-making and preferences, I illuminate the forms of migration and aspects of globalization that emerged as most salient in my informants' everyday lives and their effects on educational dynamics.

By analysing education supply and family preferences in Northern Senegal through a postcolonial eduscape framework, I make two interrelated arguments. First, eduscape remains a useful concept for understanding the influence of globalization on educational phenomena, as long as 'education' and, in association, knowledges and epistemologies are defined more inclusively to overcome Eurocentric bias. Second, ethnography remains the methodology par excellence for making sense of eduscapes but should ideally be used as part of an open-ended research design to capture the kinds of global cultural flows most relevant to people on the ground in postcolonial contexts, rather than allowing the interests of researchers based in the Global North to dictate the foci of study. Of particular interest to readers of this volume on education, migration and development, a more nuanced understanding of eduscapes in specific Southern contexts could also inform policies which purposefully address power inequalities meshed in logics of coloniality and are thus better aligned with people's priorities, preoccupations and everyday realities.

Eduscape: Making Sense of Educational Landscapes in the Context of Globalization

The term 'eduscape' was first developed by Heikki Kynäslahti (2001: 25) to make sense of educational phenomena in the context of globalization. He defined it as 'a horizontal integrative landscape in the field of education which resembles the idea of "scapes" coined by Appadurai'. Appadurai's five scapes – or types of global cultural flows – include ethnoscapes, or the movement of people who are increasingly faced by 'the realities of having to move, or the fantasies of wanting to move' (1990: 297); technoscapes, or the movement of technology, 'both mechanical and informational', and commodities (1990: 297); and finanscapes, or the global movement of capital. Mediascapes refer to the distribution of communication technologies which produce and disseminate information, as well as the complex repertoires of images and narratives they promote (1990: 298). Finally, Appadurai identifies ideoscapes 'composed of elements of the Enlightenment world view, which consists of a concatenation of ideas, terms and images, including "freedom", [. . .] "rights", [. . .] and the master-term "democracy"' (1990: 299).

Researchers across disciplines have used and developed the eduscape concept further but often define it narrowly in terms of their scholarly interests, namely virtual learning spaces (Kynäslahti 2003), internationalization of higher education (Luke 2005; Beck 2008; Forstorp and Mellström 2013) and local reception of global policy frameworks (Ambrosius Madsen 2006). Next I summarize the main contributions of these theorists to a broad definition of eduscape.

Several scholars have stressed that key to the eduscape approach is appreciation that globalization processes entail both convergence and harmonization, and rupture and disjuncture (Carney 2009). Others underline the need to analyse power within eduscapes, evoking Appadurai's arguments about the unevenness, disjunctures and heterogeneity of scapes and flows (1990; 1996). Carney evokes how 'subjects are both empowered by global flows [. . .] and dominated [. . .] by new forms of exploitation' (2009: 64–5). Caluya et al. remind us that the study of ethnoscapes in relation to education 'raises starkly the pragmatics of who gets to come, under what circumstances' (2011: 87). In the context of glaring inequalities in people's positioning relative to power and opportunities, Ambrosius Madsen's understanding of eduscape recognizes the structural dimension – involving ideologies and policies – and an experiential, agency-based dimension including 'interpretations, adaptations and resistance' (2006: 6). In relation to social positioning, Forstorp and Mellström use the concept of 'interference' – which they consider to be a less essentializing alternative to intersectionality – to capture how 'gender, "race"/ethnicity, disability, age, and class within global eduscapes can work with or against one another, and hence either intensify or decrease oppression or privilege in various situations' (2018: 78). We will see later on how educational dynamics in Northern Senegal reflect these characteristics of globalization, and how inhabitants negotiated and resisted inequalities related to (im)mobility.

Much work focuses on the ideoscape angle of eduscapes, alternatively referred to as policyscapes (Carney 2009). In the Global South, reforms undertaken throughout the 2000s in the name of Education for All (EFA) are underpinned by neoliberal ideologies and liberalism (Ambrosius Madsen 2006; Carney 2009). In the context of such policy imperatives, the state is 'simultaneously decentred by the multiple voices that claim authority to speak about education' but also 'strengthened in its new mandate' to enact new modes of governmentality (Carney 2009: 65). Analyses using eduscape as 'policyscape' therefore expose 'potential contradictions and conflicts between the modern policies, practices and ideologies of education and local cultural values and norms [. . .] in non-Western settings' (Ambrosius Madsen 2006: 7). I explore later on how the public education system in Senegal bears the stamp of these ideologies and associated reforms.

A final contribution to the theorization of eduscape is the focus on the affective angle and social imaginaries, evoking Appadurai's observation that globalization has lent 'a peculiar new force to the imagination in social life today' (1991: 197). Caluya et al. use the term 'affective eduscapes' to draw attention to 'affective experiences as well as [. . .] emotional triggers' within educational processes (2011: 87). In their view, it is essential to recognize affective forces such as aspirations, hopes and fears (2011: 94), and how they shape, and are shaped by, educational flows. Forstorp and Mellström emphasize how eduscapes are permeated by social imaginaries, or 'important guiding principles' (2013: 338) comprising a 'network of discursive themes, images, motives and narratives available in a culture in a specific time' (Dawson 1994, cited in Forstorp and Mellström 2013: 344). Carney also speaks of 'imaginative scapes' that imbue education provision with a 'sense of urgency and potential', as well as 'hope and promise of salvation and fulfillment' (2019: 262). Indeed, in much of the Global South, the 'visions and passions of modern schooling' are quite incompatible with social realities (Ambrosius Madsen and Carney 2011: 115). Later on, I analyse how imaginaries related to migration shape the educational aspirations of youth in Northern Senegal.

A Postcolonial Critique of the Existing Eduscape Literature

While these rich contributions to eduscape theorizing provide us with a solid foundation, a flaw in this literature is its relative lack of engagement with postcolonial theory, which exhorts us to 'reconsider the colonial encounter and its continuing impact from the perspective of formerly colonized countries, regions and peoples [. . .] within the context of contemporary globalization' (Crossley and Tikly 2004: 147). The first eduscape theorist to employ an explicitly postcolonial theoretical framework was Kumari Visaka Beck (2008) who used it to understand the experiences of international students at a Canadian university. She situated supply and demand for Western educational programmes, degrees and literacies in the context of Western intellectual superiority and psychological colonization (2008) and drew on Homi Bhabha's concept of 'cultural containment' to theorize how the university 'contained' cultural diversity by accommodating it within its own frames (Beck 2008: 267–8). Similarly, Forstorp and Mellström (2018) unpacked the experiences of academics from Malaysia, noting how access to

English-language education dating from British colonization was a route to social mobility and study overseas, but placed them in in-between positions of not-quite-belonging relative to their families and home society.

Despite these examples, I argue that eduscape scholars could engage further with postcolonial approaches to analyse 'previously under-researched areas [. . .] whilst providing an epistemological challenge to existing theoretical frameworks and perspectives' (Crossley and Tikly 2004: 150). My first critique of the eduscape literature is that the form of 'education' to receive attention is invariably that inherited from the European model implanted during colonization. There are few analyses of eduscapes in the Global South; the few such studies that have been undertaken reveal the effects of global ideoscapes on schools and universities (Ambrosius Madsen 2008; Ambrosius Madsen and Carney 2011; Carney 2009; 2019; Forstorp and Mellström 2018). They deserve commendation for showing how these institutions are perceived, experienced and often resisted, in contradictory ways around the world. Yet, these studies do not engage with other forms of teaching and learning grounded within alternative epistemologies, or consider educational systems which predate colonization, or which have emerged more recently as a direct critique of, or in resistance to, educational models inherited from the colonial period.

To counter this bias, in this chapter I consider various types of 'formal' education in Senegal, but I do not follow the hegemonic definition used within international development discourse and policy, whereby formal education is linked with government-approved schools and training institutions; non-formal with community groups and other organizations; and informal with what is left, for example, interactions with family and peers (e.g. USAID and MSI 2017). In this usage, characteristics of 'formal' education 'commonly correspond with the style and characteristics associated with school-based learning that were developed in and then exported from the "industrializing West"' (Froerer 2012: 371). Instead, I use the definition of 'formal' education offered by Niyi Akinnaso, namely 'when several aspects of the learning environment and the activities that take place within it, and the content, can be said to be systematically organized in some specifiable ways' (1992: 77–8). Formal education is institutionalized, meaning that rules, regulations and conventions govern the appearance, language use and behaviour of both learners and teachers, enabling the transmission of specialized knowledge (Akinnaso 1992). This broader definition allows us to acknowledge and compare various kinds of institutionalized types of education in this postcolonial context on a level playing field, free of Eurocentric value judgements.

My second critique of the eduscape literature is the dominant way in which 'international education' is defined narrowly as students travelling across national borders to attend higher education (Luke 2005; 2006; Caluya et al. 2011; Forstorp and Mellström 2013; 2018). Despite Forstorp and Mellström's acknowledgement that studies of spatial mobility in education need to be sensitive to social class, even when they interview students from 'countries located at the peripheries of contemporary global eduscapes' (2018: 93) by focusing on individuals attending university they still privilege the experiences of a highly advantaged minority from the Global South. I argue that this focus not only ignores the majority of less privileged individuals but also eclipses other forms of migration for educational purposes as well as the alternative ways in which migration influences eduscapes, such as through remittances from the diaspora, or as an imaginary horizon which shapes youth's aspirations.

Senegal is a perfect context for investigating such dynamics. Fifty-five per cent of its population of around fifteen million live under the poverty line, and only 47 per cent are in work (USAID and MSI 2017). Migration is, therefore, often perceived as the solution to poverty. While travel within West Africa has a long history, the harsh Sahelian climate exacerbated by droughts from the 1950s pushed men from rural areas to travel further afield and for longer durations. France and West and Central African countries were the main destinations, followed by Spain, Italy and the United States. By the 1990s, members of all levels of Senegalese society migrated, including to the Middle East and Gulf countries. The phenomenon of 'boat migration' – young men in precarious craft attempting to reach southern Europe or the Canary Islands – dominated headlines during the 2000s and pushed the EU to implement various policies and programmes to stem undocumented migration (Dia 2014). While half of Senegalese migrants have no state-accredited education (Bernardini 2018), the last two decades have also witnessed emigration of highly skilled professionals; students to universities in France, the United States or Canada; and traders to Asia. While 85 per cent of Senegalese migrants are men, women are increasingly migrating through family reunification or to study abroad (Dia 2014). By 2016, 5 per cent of the population lived overseas, and 14 per cent of Senegal's GDP came from migrant remittances (Bernardini 2018), the highest proportion for any African country after Lesotho.

In what follows, I propose a postcolonial approach to the eduscape concept by recentring the knowledges, epistemologies and forms of education that my interlocutors in Senegal found valuable, as well as illuminating the kinds of migration flows which shaped educational realities there. I aim to "'re-narrativise"

(Hall 1996) the globalization story in a way that places historically marginalized parts of the world at the centre, rather than at the periphery of the education and globalization debate' as well as 'highlight forms of resistance to Western global hegemony as they have manifested themselves in education' (Tikly 2001: 151).

The following sections draw on ethnographic data collected over fifteen months in 2010–12 for my PhD on educational decision-making in the Senegal River valley basin, a zone known locally as the Futa Tooro. Fieldwork was undertaken in a commune of 5,000 inhabitants that I call by the pseudonym of Medina Diallobé, located in the administrative region of Saint Louis, department of Podor. My methods consisted of observations, semi-structured interviews and informal conversations with 130 people, including education providers, parents and youth.

The Senegalese Eduscape: Between Transnational Islam, Colonization and Education for All

The following description of the educational context in Senegal reflects calls by postcolonial scholars to compare how contemporary forms of globalization are layered upon global flows and networks from the pre-modern and early modern eras, including the spread of global religions and European colonialism (Tikly 2001: 156).

The public school system in Senegal has its roots in the system implanted during the colonial period. Based on the French principle of *laïcité* (a strict version of secularism) such schools included no religious content (White 1996). They were mainly established in towns to train an elite to manage the colony. After independence, the school system was rolled out but was marred by low cultural relevance, urban bias, gender disparities in enrolment and underinvestment at post-primary levels, which remain challenges today (Newman 2016a).

After the second EFA declaration in 2000, Senegal developed – with the World Bank and IMF – its education plan, the Programme Décennale de l'Education et de la Formation (PDEF). By 2012, gross enrolment rates of boys and girls had reached 80 per cent and 87 per cent in primary; 55 per cent and 55 per cent in *collège*; and 29 per cent and 23 per cent in *lycée* (Pôle de Dakar 2013). However, quantity, access and enrolment in primary were prioritized over quality or investment in higher levels. More schools required more teachers, and to minimize government spending the World Bank pushed for the creation of additional categories of teachers, called *volontaires* in primary and *vacataires* in secondary, who were trained for only a few months before learning in service. Half of teachers in Senegal are of this type, and their low salaries have led to repeated union strikes throughout the 2000s (Barro 2009).

In addition to public schools, Senegal has a dense network of Qur'anic schools, run by Muslim clerics, devoted to teaching recitation and memorization of the Qur'an as well as a moral education. These schools follow a model dating from the ninth century when Islam arrived in West Africa via trade routes. In sub-Saharan Africa, the spread of Islam was not accompanied by Arabization and populations therefore continued to speak their own languages. Thus, while students picked up the gist of the Qur'an's meaning over time, the learning of classical Arabic, as well as other subjects like Qur'anic interpretation and legal sciences, was taught only in specialized schools after the text was fully memorized. While this might not make sense to Western observers, classical Qur'anic schools were – and still are – based on the epistemological understanding that the value of the Qur'an is not just its literal meaning, but that the text is imbued with a sacred essence called *baraka*. Through reciting the Qur'an, students accumulate *baraka* which unlocks the potential of knowledge learned, protects the recipient from temptation and cleanses the soul. Students also learned to be good Muslims through imitation of the cleric's behaviour. Migration has always been an integral part of the Qur'anic schools' functioning, as part of a wider philosophy in the Islamic world that students be encouraged to travel to seek knowledge. Students – only boys at this time – lived for several years in the cleric's compound, worked his fields and begged for food in the village to support their studies and earn *baraka* (Ware 2014).

The French perceived Qur'anic schools to be a barrier to enrolment in their public schools and, by extension, their influence and control. They formulated policies attempting to limit the opening of Qur'anic schools and require that clerics teach in French, although these were widely ignored (White 1996). Many parents resisted the colonial school, but others – particularly lineages of customary chiefs courted by the administration – saw in it new economic and political opportunities. This led to the evolution of new forms of Qur'anic schools in urban settings, where children attended as day students and paid in cash, so they could combine a religious education with public school. However, in rural areas, live-in Qur'anic study and work for the cleric continued to be highly valued, a trend which continues today (Ware 2014).

Since the colonial period, Qur'anic schools were criticized by Western observers who did not understand the epistemology underpinning their content and pedagogy. These criticisms have been taken up by the Western school-educated urban elite and international development actors in the postcolonial period, especially since practices of child labour and begging clash with Western norms around ideal childhoods (Ware 2004). From the 1990s these critiques became internationalized, with United Nations International Children's Emergency Fund (UNICEF) and non-governmental organizations (NGOs) pushing the Senegalese government to reform the Qur'anic schools, on the grounds that they are a barrier first to child protection and later to EFA. Indeed, in Senegal, around 1.2 million children aged 6–16 have never attended state-accredited formal schooling (USAID and MSI 2017). Crucially, 70 per cent of children aged 6–11 who have never attended state school currently attend Qur'anic schools instead (ibid., 42).

Since 2002, the state has attempted various strategies to divert children attending Qur'anic schools towards government-accredited schools, which have three levels: six years of elementary (*primaire*), four years of lower secondary (*collège*) and three years of upper secondary (*lycée*). The first tactic has involved adapting the state school offer, including by integrating a few hours of optional religious instruction into the otherwise secular public schools. The Ministry of Education also opened its own religious schools in regions with the lowest enrolment rates. These include Franco-Arab schools which teach in French and Arabic and combine secular topics with religious instruction, and 'modern *daaras*' (the term for Qur'anic school in Wolof) which combine recitation of the Qur'an with secular subjects and vocational training. The second strategy has involved pushing classical Qur'anic schools to adopt an official curriculum in French and local languages and reduce Qur'anic memorization in favour of secular subjects and vocational skills. If clerics accept these terms, they gain accreditation, and their pupils are counted towards official statistics (USAID and MSI 2017).

Thus far, many Muslim clerics have opposed the reforms as they perceive the state to be a pawn of Western imperialist interests, imposing Western norms and epistemologies on their schools (Newman 2016b). Against this complex policy landscape, the following sections present trends in education supply and demand in Medina Diallobé.

Education in Medina Diallobé Commune: A Sahelian Setting Embedded in Global Flows

Education supply and demand in Medina Diallobé cannot be understood without taking into account the high rates of male outmigration from the

Senegal River valley basin. By the 2000s, 30–50 per cent of active males from the river valley basin were absent, and remittances contributed 80 per cent of household budgets (Tandian 2005). The Futa Tooro is currently among the regions in Senegal with the highest international outmigration (USAID and MSI 2017). In Medina Diallobé commune, two-thirds of its 5,000 inhabitants were women, reflecting high male absence (ANSD 2008). At the time of the research, women from the commune migrated to other parts of Senegal to marry, but few migrated internationally even for family reunification. A survey conducted by local government in 2007 documented that at least twenty affluent traders and a handful of high-level civil servants from the commune worked in Dakar; over a hundred emigrants lived in African countries; another hundred were in the United States; and thirty were in Europe (all male). By the time I did my fieldwork in 2011–12, these figures were no doubt higher.

School Supply: Between the State, Migrant Remittances and NGOs

In 2012, the formal educational offer in Medina Diallobé consisted of public state schools and Qur'anic schools but no Franco-Arab schools or modern *daaras*. There were two primary schools established in the 1950s and 2005 respectively; a *collège* opened in 2001; and a *lycée* opened in 2011. The activities of migrants were a crucial reason for the high density of state schools in Medina Diallobé. Typical of the Futa Tooro, Medina Diallobé had a Village Development Association (VDA) founded in the 1970s. The VDA members (in the commune, Dakar, and large diaspora communities) raised money, through donations or donor partnerships, to undertake local infrastructural projects. During the 1970s and 1980s, the VDA's projects were small-scale, such as buying mats for the mosque. However, in the 1990s, diaspora members became more ambitious and pushed for the creation of the *collège*, financing its construction in partnership with the state. They also raised money for the construction of the second primary school building in 2010, which since 2005 had taught under a temporary wooden awning. This phenomenon of diaspora organizations financing state school infrastructure and contributing to the expanded offer of primary and middle schools in the 2000s following EFA is a wider trend in this region. Following declines in public spending generally in the 1990s, the VDAs increasingly stepped in to fill the gap (Kane 2002). State schools have been a privileged site of investment by VDAs because diaspora members – many of whom attended Qur'anic schools – sought to fight against illiteracy in European languages which they had found to be an obstacle when looking for work overseas (Fall 2001: 206).

In addition, a small French NGO called *Operation Santé* contributed to public school infrastructure and provides a fascinating and rare example of 'international education' viewed through the eyes of development 'beneficiaries'. *Operation Santé* was set up by two academics at a French university. Introduced to Medina Diallobé through a member of the diaspora, from 2007 onwards they brought a small group of medical students to the commune for two weeks each year, who, as part of their medical training, engaged in health-related awareness-raising activities before touring Senegal's tourism hotspots. From what I could gather, while Medina Diallobé's youth loved making friends with the students, their 'development' activities were not reflective of the priorities or realities of the commune. For instance, in 2011, *Operation Santé* donated a dozen computers to the secondary schools with the aim of improving students' ICT skills. The school had nowhere to store the computers, but the mayor's deputy agreed to host them in the town hall. For several months, pupils came to use the PCs but, according to town hall staff, the students used them to consult Facebook rather than do homework. Exasperated with the administrative burden and the fact that the town hall had become a teenage hangout, they locked the room. Throughout my time in Medina Diallobé, the computers languished unused and gathering dust, much to young people's annoyance.

In addition to state schools, Medina Diallobé hosted three large Qur'anic schools founded in the early twentieth century and run by respected Sufi clerics, and seven smaller ones which were offshoots of these main ones. They hosted around 500 students in total. They were known for their quality of teaching and the reputation of the clerics, and full-time students would travel, sometimes from hundreds of kilometres away, to study there for several years. The Qur'anic schools were also funded through contributions from former students, including migrants. One cleric had several such students who had financed his house and Land Rover. Qur'anic schools also encourage strong support networks between students, and can facilitate their insertion into informal urban economies in Senegal as well as in the diaspora, thus facilitating the trajectories of internal rural-urban as well as international migrants (Newman 2019). The following section explains the educational decision-making strategies of parents and experiences of youth in the context of this diverse school offer.

School Preference and Educational Decision-Making

In 2011–12, there were 737 primary school pupils in Medina Diallobé, 56 per cent girls and 44 per cent boys. This disparity existed because although most girls attended state schools, around a fifth of boys attended Qur'anic schools full-time and never enrolled in state schools. Gender norms contributed to both girls and boys leaving school after primary or a few years into *collège:* girls to marry (Newman 2020a); boys to earn money given expectations that they be breadwinners.

Senegal is characterized by a 'culture of migration' whereby travelling is undertaken not solely for economic necessity but is embedded in the social fabric. For men, physical mobility is synonymous with the transition to adulthood and social mobility and represents the dominant 'figure of success'. The expectation to migrate means that while some voluntarily stay behind, they can be perceived as failures by others (Newman 2019). In the Futa Tooro, migrants accrue status locally through building houses, buying consumer goods and giving lavishly at lifecycle celebrations and religious festivals. In contrast, most men 'left behind' are unemployed or work for low pay in the informal economy. Girls and their parents usually prefer a migrant husband over such men, including low-paid civil servants such as teachers (Newman 2019). Migration, therefore, created a powerful imaginary and set of expectations which shaped young men's educational aspirations.

The boys and young men who attended Qur'anic schools full-time were from families of Muslim clerics, the superior group in the caste-like social hierarchy that is found in Haalpulaar society.[1] Parents of the Muslim clerical group valued Qur'anic schooling for their sons for several reasons. First, it conferred *baraka* or blessing. A Qur'anic school education was also an identity marker, a symbol of resistance against the imperialist legacy of the state, an opportunity to build networks with other prestigious families in the region and a conferrer of social status. It also taught skills useful in the informal economy, namely trade or agriculture. Many parents also assumed that their sons would migrate internationally and work in manual jobs, where there were low returns on formal education, whether public or religious. The adolescents and young men attending Qur'anic schools also aspired to migrate, whether through family reunification, by overstaying short-term visas to the United States or Europe, or through obtaining a visa within Africa. These types of migration reflected the relative wealth of this group, as well as their families' international migration histories (Newman 2019). These young men thus felt less reliant on state school diplomas, which they perceived led only to low-pay, low-status jobs in Senegal. Indeed, in Senegal generally, youth with a family member abroad are 5.5 per cent less likely to attend school than those without for similar reasons (USAID and MSI 2017: 14).

Nonetheless, Qur'anic students progressively perceived that it was necessary to have basic knowledge of French, and increasingly English, to succeed overseas. They sought private French classes if they could afford it or got informal lessons from friends in *collège* or *lycée*. Furthermore, Qur'anic school students whose families lacked the connections and capital to migrate were increasingly anxious about their prospects for finding work. Members of the diaspora who had a Qur'anic school education were also counselling their family members to send their children to state schools, given growing restrictions on low-skilled migration to the United States and Europe (Newman 2019).

In contrast to those who sent their sons to Qur'anic schools, most parents with sons in state schools were from families subordinate in the caste-like hierarchy and therefore barred by the religious elite from advanced study in local Qur'anic schools. Alternatively, they belonged to the elite Muslim clerical group but believed that state school diplomas conferred more economic advantages. Secondary school enrolment had increased significantly among Medina Diallobé inhabitants following construction of the *collège* and *lycée*, as prior attendance had required that pupils find hosts in towns or cities sometimes hundreds of kilometres away (Newman 2020b). However, adolescent boys often preferred to leave school, usually against their parents' wishes. Some were disillusioned given frequent teacher strikes, often led by *vacataires* unhappy with their work conditions. Others perceived that the massification of public schooling following EFA had reduced the value of school diplomas, and that they lacked the university degrees and clientelist contacts needed to get well-paid formal sector jobs (Newman 2019). Some youth left school to trade in the weekly market, as petty trade could evolve into successful careers in trade in Dakar or overseas. Furthermore, although the current generation of migrants without state school diplomas were encouraging their families to send their children to such schools, it was precisely these individuals who were building luxurious houses in the neighbourhood where the secondary schools were located, which inspired boys to leave school and try their luck elsewhere (Newman 2019). A few boys even left state school to transfer to Qur'anic schools, inspired by male family members who had succeeded by working in religious professions such as imams, teachers or healers in Africa and the United States (Newman 2017).

Meanwhile, there were some young men in Medina Diallobé who wanted to finish secondary school and try their luck in the formal sector in Senegal, with *vacataire* teaching posts being the most accessible option. However, they tended to be from poorer families with limited possibilities of going abroad. Their statements often reflected a hint of defensiveness, as migrating was still the dominant expectation upon young men. In fact, the 'culture of migration' in Medina Diallobé even influenced the aspirations of boys who completed secondary school, as diplomas were increasingly seen as a means of migrating to attend university and gain high-skilled employment abroad. Indeed, over the previous decade, migration from Senegal has seen a shift from low- to high-skilled individuals (Newman 2019).

Conclusion

I have drawn inspiration from eduscape theorists by showing the influence of Appadurai's five types of global cultural flows on educational processes in the commune of Medina Diallobé in northern Senegal, namely ethnoscapes (a long history of internal and international migration among Senegalese, but also foreign students coming to Senegal as part of international education projects); technoscapes (the donation of several computers for pupils' use by an NGO); finanscapes (migrant remittances which funded state and Qur'anic schools, and established migrants as 'figures of success'); mediascapes (images and narratives travelling through social media which reinforced the 'culture of migration') and ideoscapes (reform policies under EFA). I expose the power inequalities operating in this context – international restrictions on 'low-skilled' migrants, and the legacy of an education system poorly adapted to cultural realities and the needs of the population bar a small elite – and people's strategies to overcome them. I illustrate how such strategies reflected difference along the lines of gender, position in the caste-like social hierarchy, family migration histories and socioeconomic status. I also pay attention to affective dimensions of young men's imaginaries and aspirations, in particular the pride and prestige linked to being a successful breadwinner and migrant, and the shame and anxiety when these dreams remain unfulfilled.

In addition, I have combined the eduscape concept with a postcolonial approach and bottom-up ethnography to recentre the voices and perspectives of people in a global periphery to demonstrate how the continued relevance of the colonial encounter – as well as older globalization trends in the form of transnational Islam – permeated their everyday lives. I shed light on non-Western epistemologies and knowledge by highlighting preference for Islamic schools in this context. Furthermore, I pose an epistemological challenge to the eduscape concept whose use has, until now, encompassed only 'formal education' defined in a narrow, Eurocentric way which ignores alternative institutionalized education systems which predate colonization. Based on this analysis, I argue that a postcolonial eduscape approach is useful for scholars interested in researching the relationships between education, migration and development policies in the current wave of globalization.

Note

1   For more on this hierarchy, see Newman 2019: 218–19.

References

Ambrosius Madsen, U. (2006). 'Eduscape. A Challenge for Ethnographic and Comparative Education Research?', Paper Presented at Oxford Ethnography and Education Conference, Oxford, September 12–13. https://rucforsk.ruc.dk/ws/portalfiles/portal/3807928/Eduscape.pdf (accessed 18 October 2021).

Ambrosius Madsen, U. (2008). 'Toward Eduscapes: Youth and Schooling in a Global Era', in K. Hansen and Anne Line Dalsgaard (Eds), *Youth and the City in the Global South*. Bloomington: Indiana University Press, 151–62.

Ambrosius Madsen, U., & Carney, S. (2011). 'Education in an Age of Radical Uncertainty: Youth and Schooling in Urban Nepal', *Globalization, Societies and Education*, 9(1), 115–33. https://doi.org/10.1080/14767724.2010.513589.

ANSD (2008). *Direction des Statistiques Démographiques et Sociales: Répertoire des Localités, Région de St Louis (Recensement Général de la Population et de l'Habitat 2000–2002)*. Dakar. anads.ansd.sn/index.php/catalog/9/related_materials (accessed 18 October 2021).

Appadurai, A. (1990). 'Disjuncture and Difference in the Global Cultural Economy', *Theory, Culture and Society*, 7(2/3), 295–310.

Appadurai, A. (1991). 'Global Ethnoscapes: Notes and Queries for a Transnational Anthropology', in R. Fox (Ed.), *Recapturing Anthropology: Working in the Present*. Seattle, WA: School of American Research Press: Distributed by the University of Washington Press, 191–210.

Appadurai, A. (1996). *Modernity at Large: Cultural Dimensions of Globalization*, Minneapolis: University of Minnesota Press.

Barro, A. (2009). *Ecole et Pouvoir au Sénégal: La Gestion du Personnel Enseignant dans le Primaire*, Dakar: l'Harmattan-Senegal.

Beck, K. (2008). 'Being International: Learning in a Canadian University', PhD thesis, Faculty of Education, Simon Fraser University, Canada.

Bernardini, F. (2018). *In-depth Analysis: Senegal: Bastion of Democracy, Migration Priority for the EU*. Brussels: Directorate -General for External Policies, European Parliament.

Caluya, G., Probyn, E., & Vyas, S. (2011). '"Affective Eduscapes": The Case of Indian Students within Australian International Higher Education'. *Cambridge Journal of Education*, 41(1), 85–99. https://doi.org/10.1080/0305764X.2010.549455.

Carney, S. (2009). 'Negotiating Policy in an Age of Globalization: Exploring Educational "Policyscapes" in Denmark, Nepal, and China', *Comparative Education Review*, 53(1), 63–88. https://doi.org/10.1086/593152.

Carney, S. (2019). 'Writing Global Education Policy Research: Commodification, the Market and Business Involvement', in M. Parreira do Amaral, G. Steiner-Khamsi, & C. Thompson (Eds), *Researching the Global Education Industry*. London: Palgrave, Macmillan, 251–71.

Crossley, M., & Tikly, L. (2004). 'Postcolonial Perspectives and Comparative and International Research in Education: A Critical Introduction', *Comparative Education*, 40(2), 147–56. https://doi.org/10.1080/0305006042000231329.

Dia, H. (2014). 'Comment les Migrations Internationales Reconfigurent les Relations Entre Conjoints et les Identités Conjugales au Sein de Couples Sénégalais', *Cahiers Québécois de Démographie*, 43(2), 375–98. https://doi.org/10.7202/1027983aradresse copiéeune erreur s'est pro.

Fall, P. (2001). 'Migration Internationale et Développement Local dans le Nguénar Sénégalais', in M.-C. Diop (Ed.), *Le Sénégal des Migrations: Mobilités, Identités et Societés*. Paris: Karthala, 195–210.

Forstorp, P.A., & Mellström, U. (2013). 'Eduscapes: Interpreting Transnational Flows of Higher Education', *Globalization, Societies and Education*, 11(3), 335–58. https://doi.org/10.1080/14767724.2013.807039.

Forstorp, P.A., & Mellström, U. (2018). *Higher Education, Globalization and Eduscapes: Towards a Critical Anthropology of a Global Knowledge Society*. London: Palgrave Macmillan.

Froerer, P. (2012). 'Anthropology and Learning', in P. Jarvis & M. Watts (Eds), *The Routledge International Handbook on Learning*. London: Routledge, 367–75.

Hall, S. (1996). 'When Was the Post-Colonial'? Thinking at the Limit', in I. Chamber & L. Curtis (Eds), *The Post-colonial Question: Common Skies, Divided Horizons*. London: Routledge, 65–77.

ILO (2017). 'Implementation of International Labour Standards for Domestic Workers'. https://www.ilo.org/global/research/publications/what-works/WCMS_572156/lang--en/index.htm (accessed 18 October 2021).

Kane, A. (2002). 'Senegal's Village Diaspora and the People Left Ahead', *The Transnational Family: New European Frontiers and Global Networks*. Oxford and New York: Berg, 245–64.

Kynäslahti, H. (2001). 'Act Locally, Th/link Translocally: An Ethnographic View of the Kilpisjärvi', Project diss., Department of Teacher Education, University of Helsinki, Helsinki.

Kynäslahti, H. (2003). 'Considerations on Eduscape', *European Media Culture*, 8, 1–8.

Luke, C. (2005). 'Capital and Knowledge Flows: Global Higher Education Markets', *Asia Pacific Journal of Education*, 25(2), 159–74. https://doi.org/10.1080 /02188790500337940.

Luke, C. (2006). 'Eduscapes: Knowledge, Capital and Cultures', *Studies in Language and Capitalism*, 1, 97–120. doi=10.1.1.118.4193&rep=rep1&type=pdf#page=100.

Newman, A. (2016a). 'Faith, Identity, Status and Schooling: An Ethnography of Educational Decision-Making in Northern Senegal', Unpublished PhD thesis, School of Global Studies, University of Sussex, Falmer.

Newman, A. (2016b). 'Factors Influencing Clerics' Attitudes Towards Qur'anic School Reform in Northern Senegal: Ideology, Religious Authority and Socioeconomic Status', *Afrique Contemporaine*, 257, 57–75.

Newman, A. (2017). 'Passive Victims or Actively Seeking a Religious Education? Qur'anic School Students in Senegal', in A. Strhan, S. Ridgley, & S. Parker (Eds), *The Bloomsbury Reader in Religion and Childhood*. London and New York: Bloomsbury Publishing, 173–80.

Newman, A. (2019). 'The Influence of Migration on the Educational Aspirations of Young Men in Northern Senegal: Implications for Policy', *International Journal of Educational Development*, 65(3), 216–26. https://doi.org/10.1016/j.ijedudev.2018.08.005.

Newman, A. (2020a). '"Getting the Best of Both Worlds": Aspirations and Agency in Relation to Marriage and Schooling Among Haalpulaar Women in Northern Senegal', *Compare – A Journal Of Comparative and International Education*, 1–17. https://doi.org/10.1080/03057925.2020.1716306.

Newman, A. (2020b). 'Honour, Respectability and 'Noble' Work: Descent and Gender-Based Obstacles to the Education and Employment of Young Haalpulaar Women in Northern Senegal', *Children's Geographies*, 18(6), 654–66. https://doi.org/10.1080 /14733285.2020.1743820.

Niyi Akinnaso, F. (1992). 'Schooling, Language, and Knowledge in Literate and Nonliterate Societies', *Comparative Studies in Society and History*, 34(1), 68–109. https://doi.org/10.1017/S0010417500017448.

Pôle de Dakar. (2013). *Key Indicators: Senegal.* Dakar: International Institute for Educational Planning (IIEP)/Pôle de Dakar.

Tandian, A. (2005). 'Stratégies D'autonomie, Investissements Développementalistes et Besoins Collectifs. Nouvelles Figures de Migrants de la Vallée du Fleuve Sénégal', in M. Charef & P. Gonin (Eds), *Emigrés/Immigrés dans le Développement Local*. Agadir: Editions Sud-Contact, 233–55.

Tikly, L. (2001). 'Globalization and Education in the Postcolonial World: Towards a Conceptual Framework', *Comparative Education*, 37(2), 151–71. https://doi.org/10.1080/03050060124481.

USAID and MSI (2017). *Etude Nationale sur les Enfants et les Jeunes Hors du Système Éducatif au Sénégal*. Dakar: USAID Senegal. https://pdf.usaid.gov/pdf_docs/PA00TFR9.pdf (accessed 18 October 2021).

Ware, R. (2004). 'Knowledge, Faith and Power: A History of Qur'anic Schooling in 20th Century Senegal', PhD thesis, Department of History, University of Pennsylvania, US.

Ware, R. (2014). *The Walking Qur'an: Islamic Education, Embodied Knowledge, and History in West Africa*. Chapel Hill: The University of North Carolina Press.

White, B. (1996). 'Talk About School: Education and the Colonial Project in French and British Africa (1860–1960)', *Comparative Education*, 32(1), 9–26. https://doi.org/10.1080/03050069628902.

7

What Happened to the Fishing School?

Education, Mobility and Perceptions of Well-being in a Traditional Fishing Community in Western India

Nitya Rao and Ishita Patil

Introduction

Bombay duck and Pomfret are found in abundance on this coast which is why we were taught about the fishing practices and methods employed in harvesting these two species. Raapan net is not used for pomfret and Bombay duck; this is used for fish like bangda *(Indian mackerel) and* kati *(Mustached Anchovy), and the seabed is shallower in depth. We use dole nets here. We were given this knowledge in school, but now the school has been taken over by the* zilla parishad *(district government) and doesn't teach such skills. None of the teachers have such knowledge now.*

(Sitakant, 57, who completed his schooling in the Fisheries School in 1978)

The previous quote captures Sitakant's nostalgia about the coast's significance as a major breeding ground for pomfret and Bombay duck during his period at school. This chapter is based on an in-depth study of Satpati, a large fishing village in the western Indian state of Maharashtra. Home to the first fishing cooperative in the country, as well as the first 'fishing school', the village has witnessed rapid transformations, including the development of industrial estates and infrastructure projects. The fishing school sought to impart key vocational skills to facilitate innovations in the fishing enterprise alongside mainstream curriculum. It is now in decline, with little attention given to either maintenance or quality, and a student strength roughly half that in its heyday. The decline of the Fisheries School also signifies a loss of heritage, the ethics of caring and sharing, and a pride in the occupation that drove the need to learn, share and transmit its intricacies to the younger generation.

One needs to locate this phenomenon within the larger context of fisheries development in India and the study location. In keeping with the Blue Growth agenda, the overall fish production and its GDP share has been increasing in India, from 7.52 lakh[1] tons in 1950–1 to 125.90 lakh tons in 2017–18. While Maharashtra ranked first in marine fish production among Indian coastal states in 1985, it has witnessed a decline from 3.36 lakh tons in 1985 to 2.01 lakh tons in 2019 (CMFRI 2020). Now ranked fifth, Maharashtra, experiencing negative productivity (–5.83 per cent) between 2000 and 2010 (Kuriakose 2013), has been overtaken by the states of Gujarat and Kerala, which have focused on developing a range of training facilities to enhance productivity.

This decline in fisheries has created pressure on coastal rural households to diversify their sources of income. With few alternate opportunities, educational attainment has come to be perceived as critical to support diversification out of fisheries, and integration into the larger national economy. Parents increasingly aspire for their children to move out of the village, to 'skilled' jobs in the nearby metropolis of Mumbai, the state capital. As a symbol of this social and spatial mobility, many families, living in poverty, demonstrate a preference for private, English-medium schools and sacrifice their immediate consumption to pay the fees for their children (Rose 2009).

Education carries multiple meanings in people's lives, ranging from the acquisition of functional skills to earning a living (Rao and Hossain 2012), claiming social status as an 'educated person' (Jeffrey et al. 2008), building social networks and 'social capital' (Bourdieu 1987) or expanding one's capacities or 'capabilities' and in turn opportunities for shaping one's life (Dreze and Sen 1995). Formal schooling is then constructed by both the state and the community as the most important pathway for learning 'modern ways of being and doing'. Educational aspirations and choices are therefore not just material but embedded in considerations of social mobility and status enhancement. While skill-based apprenticeships or other forms of intergenerational learning may provide a safe route to employment (Marchand 2010; Rao and Hossain 2012), certification and credentials are seen to contribute to status (Jeffrey et al. 2008) and 'mobile cultural capital', which can be exchanged in a variety of labour markets (Corbett 2007: 28).

Formal education can, however, deny recognition to non-schooled or traditional knowledge such as acquired through small-scale marine fisheries in India. As an inherited, caste-based occupation, young boys and girls learn a range of skills and behaviours, including an ethic of hard work and risk-taking from observing and helping their parents (Corbett 2007; Sundar 2018). The fisher castes, while specialized and skilled in fishing, are ranked as a low caste in the social hierarchy of India. Even though fisheries and allied activities can provide economic security (Bavinck 2014) and a better quality of life compared to 'footloose' wage work in a range of informal sector activities (Breman 1996), such communities strive to challenge the construction of their social identity as 'illiterate' and 'backward' – terms attributed to many low-caste, artisanal groups in India (Kumar 2000). And in their resistance, the only option available to them is formal schooling, with a hope to secure employment that is both remunerative and respectable, outside fisheries.

This ambiguous and at times contradictory role of education (Unterhalter 1999) in securing livelihoods and creating respectable identities is particularly pertinent in the current context of globalization and widespread migration, wherein educational qualifications do not guarantee 'decent work' and, instead of intergenerational mobility, may end up reproducing pre-existing social inequalities (Rao 2011). Research with young fishermen in Tamil Nadu revealed that most young men had completed schooling and even secured engineering or other graduate degrees. Unable to secure what they perceived as 'suitable' jobs, they migrated overseas to earn money but typically found themselves in manual work and poor living and working conditions. Consequently, most returned home and entered the family occupation of fishing (Rao and Manimohan 2020). They, however, struggled with representing themselves as 'modern', so sought to improve their class position through capital investments in boats and gear, seen by the elders as contributing to unsustainable fisheries and contradicting the ethics of sharing and equity that the community prided itself for (Rao and Manimohan 2020).

An important concept that seeks to bridge the gap between spatial mobility (migration) and social mobility is that of 'motility', which represents the potential for movement or mobility, rather than necessarily its practice. Kaufmann et al. (2004: 750) define motility as the 'capacity of entities (e.g. goods, information or persons) to be mobile in social or geographic space, or as the way in which entities access and appropriate the capacity for socio-spatial mobility according to their circumstances'. Clearly, the potential for such mobility can be realized in different ways across varying sociocultural contexts, and is shaped by a range of factors, including physical aptitude or skills, accessibility to opportunities and services (including education), and aspirations, or how people interpret and act upon their skills and opportunities within specific space-time constraints. Formal educational credentials are perceived to provide basic human capabilities which can enhance the potential to move and, hence, are seen as a form of 'mobile' capital. People's educational aspirations and choices are then not deterred by the realities of sociocultural, economic and political processes, which may in reality constrain such movement, as once they are seen to have options or the potential to move, staying back can be represented as a choice rather than a necessity.

In this chapter, we examine the changing meanings of education to the fishing community in the study locality, through the lens of the fishing school. With growing challenges to fisheries and the coast, due to climate change and other transformations, these communities seek upward mobility through white-collar occupations outside fisheries. While they may or may not be successful, such mobility aspirations have impacts on education policy and systems, as well as learner experiences and well-being. We examine changes in the philosophy behind educational policies over time as they shifted from a focus on contextual relevance and social interdependence within the curriculum and pedagogy, to a more universalist curriculum meant for all sections of the population in pursuit of a 'modern' identity. This simultaneously entailed a shift away from recognizing different forms of learning, practical and theoretical, and a redefining of what constitutes 'knowledge' (Kumar 2000), in the process undermining the self-worth and self-identity of communities. Alienation from their occupational skills seems to have contributed to the simultaneous decline in the fishing school and fish production in the village from the late 1980s onwards.

Having set out the key conceptual ideas, we next describe the context of the study village and the methods used for the study. We then outline a short history of fisheries education before presenting different perceptions about the Fisheries School and its potential for enabling change alongside rationales for its neglect and decline.

Context and Methods

The Study Village

Satpati is one of the most important fishing centres on the west coast of India, in Palghar district, Maharashtra. Even in the late nineteenth century (between 1874 and 1879), the village was exporting fish worth Rs 56,670 (£5667). The first fisheries cooperative society was established here in 1937, followed by a second one in 1946 (Government of Maharashtra 1882; 1982). In 1951, the Sarvodaya

Fishermen Co-operative Society operated an ice factory and cold storage plant, later supported by a Government Service Station for repairs and maintenance (Government of Maharashtra 1982). Their boat building yard had the capacity to construct seven fishing crafts a year (Bombay State Dept. of Fisheries 1951). Around the same time, in 1950, the fisheries primary school was set up in the village, to ensure a transmission of skills, upgrading and updating them as required.

The village population of 17,032 in 2011 (Census Organisation of India 2011) appears to have almost doubled to 35,000 at present, of which 30,000 belong to the fishing community Koli. The Koli are divided into two sub-castes – Vyeti and Mangela – both similar in terms of social hierarchy and status. The remaining population comprises Muslim traders, *malis* (cultivators), *bhandari* (toddy-tappers) and *adivasi* (classified as Scheduled Tribes or indigenous) communities. Fishers who are members of the cooperatives can avail of a range of benefits, including diesel and ice at subsidized prices, fishing equipment and food rations.

Decline in Fishing, Migration and Livelihood Choices

The trawlers are not allowed to enter our oceans but as they bribe the officials, no one stops them. Our ocean was sold years ago. It is not for us anymore.

(Rina, fish vendor)

Mechanization of fisheries and the entry of trawlers and purse seiners using nets made of durable materials like nylon and synthetic thread rather than the traditional cotton, smaller mesh sizes and other modern equipment have led to overfishing and reduced the fish catch per unit (Pillai et al. 2000). Inability to access adequate fish or to enhance substantively their own investments in the fishing enterprise has adversely affected the livelihoods of small-scale fishers, whether boat owners, fish vending women or wage workers. Records of the fisher cooperative societies confirm a 62 per cent decline in the catch of pomfret between 1990 and 2019.

The loss of livelihoods is real; but it is not only due to the large trawl boats and industrial fishing. Rather, it has been aggravated by climate change as witnessed through recurring storms in the Arabian Sea, industrial pollution affecting fish stock and the lack of technological assistance and financial support to the traditional fishers. The Arabian Sea faced over seventeen major storms between 2010 and 2019. Fishermen faced huge losses of boats and equipment yet, largely uncompensated by the government, were burdened with huge debts

(Lokmat News Network 2019). Additionally, a thermal power plant, industries, amusement parks, harbours and ports have been built along this coastline in the name of growth and development. These have far-reaching effects on fishing livelihoods due to pollution, destruction of the natural habitat and displacement (Chouhan et al. 2018). Central government support for such projects has left the traditional fishers vulnerable (Warhaft 2001; Rao and Manimohan 2020), forced to diversify for survival.

While elites among the fishers can engage with trade (including exports), processing, machine repair and allied activities, such opportunities are not available to many small-scale fishers and fishing labour. Many women, earlier engaged in the drying of Bombay duck, for example, now seek work in the industrial complex at Palghar, working long hours for low wages, with hardly any leave. Given the growing precarity of the fishing enterprise, parents, especially those poor and lacking in social connections, view education as the pathway to mobility, but equally to income and livelihood security for their children.

Methods

The study used a combination of archival materials and interviews with key informants to understand the relationship between education, skills and their perceptions of mobility/immobility. The field research was undertaken between August 2019 and March 2020. The cooperative societies, which were our entry point into the village, provided a historical background of fisheries and introductions to the fishing community.

A total of sixteen interviews were conducted, six with former students, three with former teachers and the rest with community leaders, boat owners and women vendors. While some were in-person, the Covid-19 pandemic and lockdown brought the field work to a standstill, and the remaining interviews were conducted by phone between September and December 2020. Snowball sampling and key informants were used to identify respondents, especially past students of the school. Despite efforts, we were unable to speak to fisheries or education officials in the district.

Archival material, including annual reports of the Fisheries Department of the erstwhile Bombay state and syllabus of the Fisheries School, was accessed from the Asiatic Society Library and Maharashtra State Archives in Mumbai. News articles about the coast were also reviewed.

Fisheries Education in Satpati

In this section, we trace the shifts in policy thinking on fisheries education since independence, locating changes at both the national and the regional/state levels. We then focus on the Fisheries School, discussing the innovations in pedagogy and curriculum that made it unique, relevant and progressive for its time.

Fisheries Education Policies since Independence

The foundation for fisheries training was established during 'British India' with two central fisheries training centres established in 1945, followed by several State Fisheries Departments setting up their own in-service programmes to train district-level fisheries officers (Silas 1977). Post-independence, the five-year plans aimed to improve training facilities to enable fishermen to undertake longer fishing trips, use mechanized gear and commence deep sea fishing (Government of India 1951). In 1959, a Committee on Fisheries Education sought to create an integrated fisheries education system in India, to address questions of skill renewal and upgrade (Kumar 1977). The Central Institute of Fisheries Education (CIFE) and the Central Institute of Fisheries Nautical and Engineering Training (CIFNET) were established (Lok Sabha Secretariat 1968; Silas 1977). By 1967, the Central Marine Fisheries Research Institute (CMFRI), Kochi, and the Central Inland Fisheries Research Institute (CIFRI), Barrackpore, were brought under the aegis of the Indian Council of Agricultural Research (ICAR) (earlier the Imperial Council), to be developed as an integral part of agricultural research and training in India (Mruthyunjaya 2004).

Alongside these central institutions, several fisheries colleges and universities emerged across the coastal states of India, yet basic skills training at the community level was neglected. In 2008, with the establishment of the National Skills Development Corporation (NSDC), there was a new push to utilize effectively the 'demographic dividend' by addressing the non-employability of formally educated youth. The first National Policy on Skill Development, 2009, provided a framework for skills training, focusing on short-term, industry-relevant courses which would result in jobs for the trainees (Government of India 2009; Chenoy 2012). The National Policy for Skill Development and Entrepreneurship, 2015, upscaled this policy, including fisheries and aquaculture in its ambit, to promote innovation-based entrepreneurship for ensuring sustainable livelihoods (Government of India 2015). Yet unlike the Fisheries

School, these interventions are not embedded in the community and its culture and are viewed as a source of employment, rather than a way of life.

The Fisheries Schools in Maharashtra

Maharashtra was always a front runner in the development of fisheries education alongside schemes for increasing fish production, including infrastructures for storing and processing fish as well as supporting equitable returns through the development of fishermen's cooperatives (Dept. of Fisheries 1965). A unique initiative was the setting up of Fisheries Schools, providing access to basic education alongside training in fishing skills to children from fishing communities. The State Fisheries Department established eight Fisheries Primary Schools in 1950. The medium of instruction was the local language – Marathi, Gujarati or Kannada – depending on the location of the school. Certification was central to ensuring appropriation of the skills by the community and giving them value (cf. Kaufmann, Bergman and Joye et al. 2004).

The Fisheries Schools soon also became cultural centres for adult fishermen. This is because the 'technology of education, (which) consists, among other things, of the teacher, the space, the text, the teaching strategy and the rituals' (Kumar 2000: 23), were all embedded within the philosophy and ethos of the fisher community. While 'expert' fishermen were brought in as teachers, students were also provided a range of opportunities to gain exposure and experience, such as visits aboard a naval training ship to see the working of its equipment; or participating in the District Agricultural and Cattle Show, which led to the award of merit certificates (Bombay State Dept. of Fisheries 1954). Seen as an exemplar in basic fisheries education, by 1956, the student enrolment in the Satpati Fisheries Primary School had risen to 562, from 462 in its first year; with 15 teachers on its roll. Given the rising demand for fisheries education, in 1965–6, a local private school, the Adi Janata High School, was taken over by the Fisheries Department and converted into a Fisheries High School. The school at this time had 800 students and 26 teachers (Bombay State Dept. of Fisheries 1956).

The Curriculum: A Combination of Theory and Practice

The Fisheries School Certificate was awarded to students completing the seventh-grade examination for a range of fisheries-related subjects along with mathematics, science, geography, history and a second regional language

(Bombay State Dept. of Fisheries 1955a). The curriculum included both theory and practical training. Marde, the headmaster at Satpati Fisheries School in the 1960s, himself from the fishing community, would take the boys on a boat 'to show them *gholaav* (how to estimate the depth of the water) and *paakjal* (techniques) for throwing nets targeting different fish species'. The rationale was later discussed in the classroom.

Satyendra, a former student, recalls studying about different fish species and nets, navigation and wind direction, as well as learning net weaving, stitching and carpentry. Students not belonging to boat owner families would also learn these skills, and after school help boat owner families with net stitching to earn a little money for themselves.

> There is a double knot, we were taught how to tie the various knots, where to make a loop and put the string, do it in a way that our skin does not peel, and also when to use a particular loop or knot. The *kavi* net had 5 different parts, I memorized the names as a kid and still remember them – mo*hor, chirat, katra, mazvala* and *khola*. Each part is smaller than the one before, so *mohor* was the largest and *khola* so small that even your thumb would not pass through it. The smallest fish would be in the *khola*. (Satyendra, 60)

Clearly what one learnt had implications for both the ways of learning and the evaluation of this learning (Rogers 2014). While Satyendra's son is clueless about the methods and techniques used in fishing, the knowledge Satyendra gained from his school days is still fresh in his own memory.

As it was mandatory for at least one person on every boat to have a 'training certificate', in order to be eligible for subsidies for boats and gear from the National Cooperative Development Corporation, Tandel joined the Fisheries Training Centre, established in 1954. The minimum entry requirement was primary education and at least five years of fishing experience. Meant for traditional fishermen with basic knowledge of net throwing, net weaving and fishing; while some training on fishing methods, elementary principles of navigation and running and maintenance of small marine diesel engines, was included in the training, this was not covered in any depth (Silas 1977; Swaminath 1983). Speaking about the quality of the training centre, Rajesh, forty-two, a member of the Gram Panchayat, felt that it was never developed properly, hence did not benefit the community much. For those who had been to the Fisheries School, the six-month training helped consolidate their knowledge; for others it was inadequate. The link between access to credit and finance and the certification, however, meant that students had no option but to complete the course.

In 2002, the administration of the Fisheries School in Satpati was transferred to the Zilla Parishad (district council) by the Fisheries Department. While the provision of fisheries courses remains on the school curriculum, Rajesh observed: 'for years there has been no instructor to provide technical training to the children. There are no qualified teachers to teach the higher grades. Parents hence don't want to send their children to the Fisheries School.' In 2019, the school had only 310 students enrolled from the sixth to tenth grades. Of the 26 teacher positions, only 11 were filled, raising questions around the quality of provisioning.

Fishing as a Masculine Industry: Neglecting Girls' Education

Women are integral to fisheries, responsible for both preparatory and post-harvest work. Despite a high enrolment of girls in the school, there was, however, no specific practical training for them. Prema, fifty-six, who studied at the Fisheries School, recalls that boys would be taken for practical trips, while girls had none: 'I remember we had some theory on which fish is found where in the sea, how fish swim and so on. We would take notebooks from the boys and copy drawings of nets, or fish species.' The department introduced 'domestic science' as a practical subject for girls in lieu of 'carpentry' for boys, yet this course was contingent on the appointment of a 'trained lady teacher'. Deepa, fifty-six, who studied in the Fisheries School from fifth to ninth grades, said:

> What was the domestic science subject? What does it say in the syllabus? I don't know because none of it was taught. Boys had technical training, boat carpentry, net weaving, but we did not have any of it.

For girls, the learning of trade-related skills was entirely informal and intergenerational, passed on by elder women in the family. They were directly socialized into adult occupational roles as the Fisheries School curriculum did not include fish vending, drying or processing training for them. As Prema noted:

> Every boy would go on fishing trips with his father and we girls would help our mother sort fish. My mother would give me small portions of fish in the morning, to sell in the market before school. All of us learnt by observing the elders in our family.

Perhaps this exclusion of specific skills for girls in the school curriculum is because while 'women are considered active fishermen due to their major contribution to marketing activities' (Ketan Patil, Chairman of Sarvodaya Co-operative Society), they remain under-represented in the society and its decision-making mechanisms. With boats and gear being in men's domain, there was, therefore, probably no representation to the curriculum committee for including skills relevant to fisherwomen in the school. For girls, then, it was just a normal state school.

We now turn to the perceptions about fisheries education, especially the school, and its decline from the perspective of a range of stakeholders – former students, teachers and community leaders.

Perceptions about Fisheries Education

In this section we explore some of the perceptions, discourses and justifications for the state of the Fisheries School today.

Bureaucratization of Fisheries Education: Losing Contact with the Needs of Fishers

Several people from the fishing community – former teachers and students – blamed the decline of the school on the bureaucratization of fisheries education, and a lack of understanding or contact by administrators with the real needs and problems of fishers, and the new challenges they confront. Rupesh, a former chairman of the Sarvodaya Co-operative Society, commented: 'the Fisheries ministers are not experts and lack the knowledge and understanding of the fishing sector. They will not know the name of the fish or how fishing is done.'

Apart from the lack of sensitivity to or understanding of the needs of fishers, some felt the decline was due to a lack of coordination between the Fisheries and Education Departments. Satyendra noted that while the Fisheries Department expected the Education Department to streamline the training and curriculum after it took over the school in 2002, the latter had little idea about fisheries as a subject, hence let it fall into disuse. Sitakant too emphasized that in the 1960s, unlike nowadays, the provision of fishing knowledge and skills was seen as important to the growth of the industry; hence, there was a push for the inclusion of these skills in the school's curriculum. He explained:

> But as times changed, they don't feel fishing knowledge is crucial anymore. Globalization has happened, IT and software industries have grown, and options

have emerged in other fields. The government seems to have replaced fishing knowledge and skills with computers.

The lack of relevant fisheries skills training in the school, able to keep pace with contemporary changes in the complex web of fisheries relationships and technologies between the state, corporates, fisher castes, classes of labour and genders, seems also to have contributed to its decline. For other skills such as in IT or computers, parents prefer to send their children to private schools in nearby towns.

The Need for a Relevant, Professional Curriculum

In the early years, flexibility in the educational system allowed for the recruitment of local fishers to teach a range of skills in the school. This practice gave recognition to practical skills as an important part of learning and also gave visibility to the 'funds of knowledge' and 'banks of skills' that fisher children brought with them to school (Moll et al. 1992). Additionally, by creating space for intergenerational learning within the formal context of the school, the school became attractive to parents, as a symbol of their heritage, their values and 'lifeways' based on egalitarian economic relations (Corbett 2007: 25) and recognition of their traditional, artisanal knowledge, while simultaneously providing the potential for mobility.

The community nevertheless saw a case for modernizing and professionalizing the curriculum of the Fisheries School and training centre, yet this was not happening in practice. Tamore reflected:

> In the training course I attended in Cochin (in the 1960s), apart from different types of fishing, we learnt how to repair and maintain engines, but importantly, we learnt the latest techniques, for example, how to operate the Fish Finder (device). None of that is taught here. While the examinations include both practical and theoretical assessments, the syllabus has not been updated to reflect changes in modern methods and technology.

Satyendra added that while their cooperative society had a boat building yard which had successfully 'competed with private concerns and secured a contract on open tender basis for construction of fishing boats of the Saurashtra Government' (Bombay State Dept. of Fisheries 1955b), there has been no training or investment in upgrading its equipment despite the potential as a good source of employment for youth. Tamore expressed a similar sentiment:

> The youth today know English and are better educated than us. As there are no jobs, many young men return to fishing. If they have access to professional skills,

in fishing but also in allied activities, are trained and acquainted with modern tools and techniques, they will succeed and move forward.

While fisheries is a traditional occupation for the community and households in Satpati, there is an awareness of the need to update these skills with the times, especially with respect to modern technology. Community leaders recognized that in the early years, alongside facilities and equipment, there was an emphasis on skills and knowledge, as reflected in the setting up of Fisheries Schools. The objective was to develop both the fishing enterprise and the community. Clearly there is a desire for fisheries education to rebrand fisheries as a 'modern' and 'respectable' profession. Yet the state is apparently failing to hear these demands and skills programmes continue to focus on creating 'workers' rather than 'entrepreneurs' among the fishing community.

Changing Parental and Youth Aspirations in Terms of Mobility and Migration

Tamore, now seventy-three, completed his education at the Adi Janta High School in 1965, and then went to Cochin, in the southern state of Kerala, to complete his marine fisheries training course. While having a 'training certificate' was a requirement to avail benefits under governmental schemes, he attributes his success to the quality of the training he received and his ability to communicate in English. His four children studied in English-medium schools in Palghar and all but one son moved out of the fishing occupation. Sachin, now forty-six, inherited his father's boat. After studying till tenth grade in Palghar, he completed the six-month fisheries training in Satpati. While he chose to handle the family's boat and fishing business, his wife is determined to keep their two children away from fishing: 'the way our life is going, we don't want them to enter the fishing business at any cost.' Both children are now pursuing higher education outside the village. Sachin added: 'It is tough for me to sustain; I won't let my kids enter the boat. Small work is okay, I ask them to go buy nets or things, but I don't take them on the boat.'

Previously, many children dropped out of school to join the family fishing enterprise; while others like Rupesh or Ketan, both trained as engineers, or Dewan, with a postgraduate degree in commerce, chose fisheries as a business and profession. This is now rare and, given the rising costs and falling incomes, more and more parents from the fishing community actively want their children to move into other occupations.

Yet there is another side too. Tandel, fifty-five, belongs to a boat-owning family. He went to the Fisheries School in Satpati, later completed the fisheries training course and was able to acquire his boat through a loan under the NCDC scheme, which otherwise would have been difficult. While he did not send his children to the Fisheries School, his son has joined the boat business. He noted, 'Education is important, nothing will happen if they continue in fishing. But even after education, getting a job is not sure.' Perhaps if the fishing school had retained its quality, provided relevant skills and trained the fisher children to address emergent challenges on the coast, Tandel might have been open to sending his children to the fishing school. As succinctly expressed by Sitakant,

> This village is of the fishing community, illiteracy rates were high, and education was often ignored. My father was a traditional fisherman, and when he saw the fishing school giving training in fishing apart from other subjects, he pushed me to attend. But now, people see the condition of the Fisheries School, there are no teachers, fishing courses have been stopped, the community is no longer involved, so they send their children to convent schools in surrounding towns, hoping to provide them with better education. Parents now aspire that their children get jobs in Mumbai or even leave the country, as they believe that conditions won't improve if they stay in Satpati.

Arti, a fish vending woman, told us of the financial and human losses they faced when their boat drowned following an accident. They have struggled to provide good education to their three children; in English-medium schools and colleges in Palghar. She stresses the importance of quality education but also the difficulties confronted in educating children with their meagre earnings from fishing: 'The government should provide good education to our children. Education has so much value, but it is so very expensive.'

Conclusion

In the case of single industry communities, schooling is often seen as a contradictory process – providing successful students with mobile cultural capital that prepares them to leave, while those who choose to stay are invariably labelled as school dropouts (Corbett 2007). This chapter has explored a unique example of a 'fishing school' that sought to enhance the skills of children belonging to the fishing community, alongside providing them a generic education, building their motility or the potential and capacities for socio-spatial mobility, both in the community and outside. This strategy increased the choices available to fisher children; many educated young men, with higher degrees, returned to work in their family fishing businesses. At the same time, this emphasis on skills and training, and its positive valuation, contributed to the emergence of Maharashtra as the foremost Indian state in marine fish production and exports.

A point worth reiterating is the gendered nature of training in occupational skills. While even earlier, the fishing school focused on boys as 'fishermen' rather than girls as 'fish traders and marketers', this has remained unchanged. While a few women continue fish trading activities, requiring considerable skills in accounting and money management, these have been learnt not from the school but 'on-the-job'. In today's context, state-promoted self-help groups of women are a site for learning financial skills. Nevertheless, with the decline in fisheries, a majority of poor fisherwomen have now moved to unskilled work in local factories and other informal enterprises, representing a process of 'deskilling' rather than skill upgradation.

Fishing is a traditional occupation, which has seen tremendous technological advancements in recent years. Relative to agriculture and many other forms of informal employment, the returns remain significant (Bavinck 2014). The fishing community, with their traditional knowledge and seafaring skills, clearly have an advantage in seizing new opportunities in this sector, yet present-day governments, given their sectoral organization, appear to devalue traditional knowledge and skills, as reflected in homogenizing education and school curricula, often with no relevance to local needs or identities. While in its early years, the fishing school combined theoretical and practical knowledge, bringing in 'experts' from the community to 'teach' practical skills, this is no longer the case. While some fishing subjects are retained, the so-called modern knowledge and techniques are taught in a vacuum, disconnected from local skills, knowledges and practices. The devaluation and lack of recognition of their skills and capacities have also meant that the fishing community including the older generations no longer take pride in the school as reflective of their heritage. Instead, parents struggle to send their children to fee-paying English medium schools, hoping to enable their exit from fisheries into secure jobs in the city.

Clearly, investing in the education and skills of fisher communities, including technologies that support the construction of fishing as a 'modern' occupation (Rao and Manimohan 2020), alongside respectful attention to and incorporation of traditional and modern sources of knowledge in mainstream education, is vital for sustaining the growth and development of both the sector and the people. The fisheries sector in Maharashtra is a testimony to this.

Note

1   One lakh is equivalent to 100,000.

References

Bavinck, M. (2014). 'Investigating Poverty through the Lens of Riches – Immigration and Segregation in Indian Capture Fisheries', *Development Policy Review*, 32(1), 33–52. https://doi.org/10.1111/dpr.12042.

Bombay State Dept. of Fisheries (1951). *Annual Report of the Department of Fisheries (1950–1951)*. Bombay: Government Central Press.

Bombay State Dept. of Fisheries (1954). *Annual Report of the Department of Fisheries (1953–1954)*. Bombay: Government Central Press.

Bombay State Dept. of Fisheries (1955a). *Annual Report of the Department of Fisheries (1954–1955)*. Bombay: Government Central Press.

Bombay State Dept. of Fisheries (1955b). *Revised Rules for the Fisheries School Certificate Examination*. Bombay: Government Central Press.

Bombay State Dept. of Fisheries (1956). *Annual Report of the Department of Fisheries (1955–1956)*. Bombay: Government Central Press.

Bourdieu, P. (1987). *Distinction: A Social Critique of the Judgement of Taste*. Harvard: Harvard University Press.

Breman, J. (1996). *Footloose Labour: Working in India's Informal Economy*. Cambridge: Cambridge University Press.

Census Organisation of India (2011). *Population Census 2011*. https://www.census2011.co.in (accessed 18 October 2021).

Chenoy, D. (2012). *Skill Development in India: A Transformation in the Making*. New Delhi: Routledge.

Chouhan, H.A., Parthasarathy, D., & Pattanaik, S. (2018). 'Urban at the Edges: Mumbai's Coastline Urbanisms', in J. Mukherjee (eds), *Sustainable Urbanization in India. Exploring Urban Change in South Asia*. Singapore: Springer, 279–93. https://doi.org/10.1007/978-981-10-4932-3_15.

CMFRI (2020). 'Marine Fish Landings in India 2019', *CMFRI*. http://eprints.cmfri.org.in/14325/1/Marine Fish Landings in India_2020_CMFRI.pdf. (accessed 18 October 2021).

Corbett, M. (2007). *Learning to Leave: The Irony of Schooling in A Coastal Community*. Nova Scotia: Fernwood Publishing Co., Ltd.

Department of Fisheries (1965). *Advances in Fisheries of Maharashtra*. Bombay: Department of Fisheries.

Dreze, J., & Sen, A. (1995). *India: Economic Development and Social Opportunity*. New Delhi: Oxford University Press.

Government of India (1951). *First Five Year Plan*. New Delhi: Government of India, Planning Commission: Yojana Bhavan.

Government of India (2009). 'National Skill Development Policy'. New Delhi: Ministry of Labour and Employment.

Government of India (2015). 'National Policy for Skill Development and Entrepreneurship'. New Delhi: Ministry of Skilled Development and Entrepreneurship. https://msde.gov.in/en/reports-documents/policies/national -policy-skill-development-and-entrepreneurship-2015 (accessed 18 October 2021).

Government of Maharashtra (1882). *Gazetteer of the Bombay Presidency - Thana - Places of Interest*. Bombay: Government Central Press.

Government of Maharashtra (1982). 'Thane District Gazetteer'. https://cultural .maharashtra.gov.in/english/gazetteer/Thane/index.html (accessed 18 October 2021).

Jeffrey, C., Jeffery, P., & Jeffery, R. (2008). *Degrees without Freedom? Education, Masculinities and Unemployment in North India*. Stanford: Stanford University Press.

Kaufmann, V., Bergman, M.M., & Joye, D. (2004). 'Motility: Mobility as Capital', *International Journal of Urban and Regional Research*, 28(4), 745–56. https://doi.org /10.1111/j.0309-1317.2004.00549.x.

Kumar, V. (1977). 'Committee on Fisheries Education 1958 – Report', in V. Kumar (Ed.), *Committees And Commissions In India 1947–1973*. New Delhi: Concept Publishing Company, 57–60.

Kumar, N. (2000). *Lessons from Schools: The History of Education in Banaras*. New Delhi, India: Sage.

Kuriakose, S. (2013). 'Economic Sustainability of Marine Fisheries in India: A Total Factor Productivity Approach', *Journal of Aquatic Biology and Fisheries*, 2(2), 69–74.

Lokmat News Network (2019). *17 Storms in the Arabian Sea in the Last 10 Years*. Mumbai.

Lok Sabha Secretariat (1968). 'Estimates Committee 1968–1969'. 14.139.60.153/bitstr eam/123456789/966/1/ESTIMATES%20COMMITTEE%20%281968-69%29%20 %28FORTH%20LOK%20SABHA%29%20SIXTY%20SECOND%20REPORT%20_G 1146.pdf (accessed 18 October 2021).

Marchand, T.H. (2010). 'Making Knowledge: Explanations of the Indissoluble Relation between Minds, Bodies and Environment', *Journal of Royal Anthropological Institute*, 165(1), S1–S21. https://doi.org/10.1111/j.1467-9655.2010.01607.x.

Moll, L., Amanti, C., Neff, D., & Gonzalez, N. (1992). 'Funds of Knowledge for Teaching: Using a Qualitative Approach to Connect Homes and Classrooms', *Theory into Practice*, 31(2), 132–41. https://doi.org/10.1080/00405849209543534.

Mruthyunjaya, D. (2004). *Strategies and Options for Increasing and Sustaining Fisheries and Aquaculture Production to Benefit Poor Households in India.* World Fish Centre. http://eprints.cmfri.org.in/6853/1/ICAR_ICLARM.pdf (accessed 18 October 2021).

Pillai, V. N., Menon, N. G., Sehara, D. B. S., Sathiadhas, R., & Panikkar, K. K. P. (2000). 'Economic Evaluation of Different Types of Fishing Methods Along Indian Coast', *CMFRI.* eprints.cmfri.org.in/4331/.

Rao, N. (2011). 'Respect, Status and Domestic Work: Female Migrants at Home and Work', *European Journal of Development Research,* 23, 758–73. https://doi.org/10.1057/ejdr.2011.41.

Rao, N., & Hossain, M.I. (2012). '"I Want to be Respected": Migration, Mobility and the Construction of Alternate Educational Discourses in Rural Bangladesh, 2012', *Anthropology and Education Quarterly,* 43(4), 415–28. https://www.jstor.org/stable/23359078.

Rao, N., & Manimohan, R. (2020). *(Re-)Negotiating Gender and Class: New Forms of Cooperation Among Small-Scale Fishers in Tamil Nadu.* UNRISD. https://www.unrisd.org/UNRISD/website/document.nsf/(httpPublications)/8D96D7A1CEB545DB802585D1002E326E?OpenDocument (accessed 18 October 2021).

Rogers, A. (2014). *The Base of the Iceberg: Informal Learning and its Impact on Formal and Non-Formal Learning.* Berlin and Toronto: Barbara Budrich Publishers.

Rose, P. (2009). 'Editorial Introduction: Non-State Provision of Education – Evidence from Africa and Asia', *Compare,* 39, 127–34. https://doi.org/10.1080/03057920902750350.

Silas, E. G. (1977). *Indian Fisheries 1947–1977.* Cochin: The Marine Products Export Development Authority.

Sundar, A. (2018). 'Skills for Work and the Work of Skills: Community, Labour and Technological Change in India's Artisanal Fisheries', *Journal of South Asian Development,* 13(3), 1–21. https://doi.org/10.1177/0973174118804449.

Swaminath, M. (1983). 'Fisheries Development and Training in India', in U. K. Srivastava & M. D. Reddy (Eds), *Fisheries Development in India Some Aspects of Policy Management.* New Delhi: Concept Publishing Company, 327–38.

Unterhalter, E. (1999). 'The Schooling of South African Girls', in C. Heward & S. Bunwaree (Eds), *Gender, Education and Development: Beyond Access to Empowerment.* London and New York: Zed Books, 49–64.

Warhaft, S. (2001). 'No Parking at the Bunder: Fisher People and Survival in Capitalist Mumbai', *South Asia,* 24(2), 213–23. https://doi.org/10.1080/00856400108723458.

8

'They Are from Good Families Like Ours'

Educated Middle-Class Identities and (Im) Mobility among Young Dalit Women

Sugandha Nagpal

Educated Dalit Women

Over a cup of sweet milky tea, I chat with 23-year-old Kavita about her experience of living in Chaheru, a predominantly Dalit[1] village in the Doaba region of Punjab. Compared to other regions of Punjab, Doaba has the highest rates of outmigration as well as other forms of Dalit mobility, including greater strides in education, employment and social mobility. With Kavita I discuss clothing, movies and food, as well as her plans and hopes for the future. Kavita belongs to the Ad-dharmi or Chamar[2] community and has completed her MA in History from the nearby Ramgharia college. She harbours ambitions to move away from the village space through international migration and has obtained educational qualifications as a beautician and caregiver with this objective in mind. While she waits to migrate, Kavita also applies for teaching jobs in the vicinity of the village and says that in the event that migration does not work out, she wants to pursue her PhD. She belongs to a migrant middle-class family, of which many members reside abroad: Kanta, Kavita's mother, has three older daughters who are all married. Kavita's oldest sister is in the UK, and the second oldest moved to Italy to join her husband towards the end of my fieldwork. She has another older sister, Meeta, who lives in Chandigarh with her husband. Kavita's younger brother, Suresh, was training to be a chef so that upon migration to Canada he could work in his uncle's restaurant. Her older brother, Ramesh, is separated from his wife and works at a factory in Bangalore.

Towards the end of my fieldwork, Kavita recounts that a few months earlier, she received an offer to work in a bank in Chandigarh. But she was not allowed to work there because her maternal grandmother, who lives in Canada, said that she wants her to either come to Canada through the *nanny visa*,[3] work and be independent, or get married. She refused to sponsor or support Kavita's PhD studies in India. On another day, Kavita tells me that her sister who lives in Italy is pressurizing her to get married. She also points out that Ramesh will not allow her to work too far from the village. Kavita's plans and aspirations for her future are in flux and constantly evolving in response to the interventions of her relatives and gendered and class-based expectations around marriage and respectable employment.

Like Kavita, the other young women from upwardly mobile families I interacted with were either in the process of pursuing higher education or had completed their undergraduate and postgraduate education and were similarly navigating the requirements of female respectability and urban modernity. After completing their education, these young women aimed to migrate through marriage, which is seen as the most respectable way for women to migrate. They also sought 'respectable jobs', such as teaching, which are not too far from their home and do not have long working hours, allowing them to fulfil their domestic responsibilities or government jobs which were associated with stability, higher income and status. In practice, however, very few women were able to migrate as a result of marriage migration or secure government employment, their difficulties in attaining these mobility outcomes reflecting continuities in historical disadvantages. This chapter explores the ways in which young women like Kavita, a minority within their community,[4] use college education to construct middle-class identities, which are tied to the idea of mobility or the physical and cultural movement away from the village space, even though in many respects they may remain immobilized in the physical sense by structural and cultural gender norms within their communities.

Judge and Bal (2009), in their work on social change in rural and urban Dalit communities in Jalandhar and Amritsar (Punjab), note that despite generational advances in education, educational attainments have not been significant enough to propel occupational changes. In the absence of these outcomes, most young women ended up tutoring or doing stitching work from home. However, a question that emerges is, why do women continue to pursue education, even in the absence of mobility outcomes? Previous anthropological work on education and development has indicated that even in the absence of tangible outcomes, education allows young men and women to gain status in their communities (Jeffrey et al. 2008; Ciotti 2010). In drawing on this literature, the chapter explores the value of education, when it does not necessarily lead to mobility outcomes in a context with a strong culture of migration.

Much of the existing work on migration and education focuses on the ways in which migrant remittances are directed towards the education of children back home and the issue of brain drain (Yang 2004; Thieme and Wyss 2005; Rao 2010). Some work points out how education choices become defined by the desire to migrate and subsequent migration trajectories (Ali 2007; Corbett 2007). In this chapter, I draw on the construct of middle classness to explore young women's everyday discourses and interactions around mobility as the mental and cultural movement away from the village space. The chapter is based on an eleven-month ethnographic study, which involved residing in and spending extended periods of time in young women's homes. I assert that while education is an important pathway to migration in Chaheru, in the absence of migration opportunities education also serves as an important way for women to carve out modern middle-class identities while remaining in the village space. The extent to which they are able to use education as a pathway to physical mobility, however, is shaped by their family's social and economic positioning.

Education, Development and Migration

In the context of development, education has often been conceived through its link with tangible outcomes such as employment, increase in women's age at marriage and the ability to impact social change (Dreze and Sen 1995; Chopra and Jeffery 2005). Especially for Dalits, education has been seen as a crucial aspect of social mobility, allowing them to attain achieved status and overcome their ascribed status or identities (Ciotti 2006; Judge and Bal 2009). Explorations of the links between education and migration have not extensively and qualitatively engaged with the question of how young people, especially from marginalized communities, engage with education as a site of mobility, in a context where there is a strong culture of migration.

The existing work with different populations suggests that in migration cultures educational choices become defined by the desire to migrate (Ali 2007; Corbett 2007). Ali (2007), for example, finds that in Hyderabad the educational choices of young men and women to pursue computer programming or medical sciences are guided by opportunities for migration in the United States. In turn, educational facilities and options in Hyderabad also adapt to increasing migration to Gulf countries. For instance, there has been a proliferation of private schools in Hyderabad and many of them have adopted Arabic as the primary medium of instruction. In his seminal work with coastal communities in Nova Scotia, Corbett (2007) argues that there is a 'migration imperative' in rural education, drawing people away from home communities, cultures, livelihoods and familiar environments. He identifies education and migration as two strong disciplinary forces in the modernization of rural people. Among rural young men, he equates resistance to education with the unwillingness to migrate and fulfil the conditions of manhood set by the community. These works point to the close links between education and migration, wherein education serves as a precursor to migration trajectories. However, what happens when there is a long or uncertain gap between the pursuit of education and the act of migration? Rao (2010) points out the importance of attending to the 'social processes through which migration and education interact to shape people's lives, identities and status in society' (137). In the context of Chaheru, young women's educational aspirations are not confined to the act of migration but also entail aspirations for social mobility, status and processes of self-making. Thus, exploring the links between education, migration and development in Chaheru entails attending to young women's everyday meanings and associations of education and mobility

Education and Middle Classness

Previous anthropological work has pointed out that while it is often difficult to tie education with tangible mobility outcomes, nonetheless, education allows young men and women to gain status in their communities (Jeffrey et al. 2008; Ciotti 2010; Franco 2010). For instance, Ciotti (2010), based on her work with Manupur Chamars in Uttar Pradesh, India, asserts that even though a majority of the young Chamar women are unable to pursue a college degree and do not find employment outside their homes, they do not think of their education as being useless. Education allows them to acquire knowledge, a cultural capital that will stay with them throughout their lives, to attain economic self-sufficiency and to distance themselves from the 'lower class other' and engage in middle-class formation (239–42).

In her work with college-going girls and their families in Bangladesh Franco (2010) finds that, among better-off households, daughters' education is an enhancer of status and allows for marriage to be postponed until higher secondary certificate or a university degree is obtained. For the college-going girls, unlike their parents, education was not tied to marriage but its ability to open up opportunities for employment and economic independence. The young girls had aspirations to become teachers, college professors or nurses and expressed their self-esteem and self-worth through declarations of their plans to find a job after completion of their education (156). However, much like the case of Chaheru, a large majority of these girls were unable to secure employment. Despite the mismatch between aspirations and outcomes, Franco (2010) asserts that young women are able to effectively use education to develop 'awareness of their wishes and needs and increase their capacity to negotiate different ways of being part of the society' (62). These studies demonstrate that even in the absence of tangible outcomes, education can serve as a useful tool for self-making and establishing affinity to high-status cultures. The present chapter situates itself in this literature and probes the self-making of two differently positioned young women in Chaheru.

Migration and Mobility Imaginaries

Chaheru is a predominantly Ad-dharmi village located at a distance of 5 kilometres from Phagwara city. The village's location in the Doaba region of Punjab[5] and its proximity to a city imply that ideas of urbanity and especially migration circulate and acquire prominence in the village space. The village has a strong culture of international migration going back to the 1970s, when the first labour migrants left for Gulf countries. Villagers see the migration to the Gulf and Western countries as having brought *sudhar*, or development, to the village. Community members often use the discourse of migration to highlight the ways in which they have charted autonomous paths of mobility that were not reliant on government support.[6] Contemporary migration trends from Chaheru include continued migration to the Gulf and to other traditional migrant destinations like the United States, the United Kingdom, Canada and Australia along with migration to a large number of countries in southern and eastern Europe (Kapuria and Birwal 2017). Due to its lower costs, young men in Chaheru often construct migration to the Gulf as a back-up option and instead set their sights on migrating to Western countries to compete with the affluence and status of the upper castes.

Among upwardly mobile families in Chaheru there are two dominant mobility imaginaries. Given the strong migration culture in Chaheru, international migration emerges as the main pathway for moving away. Compared to employment and further education, it also signals a more permanent move away from the village. Young women from upwardly mobile families seek migration as it allows them access not only to wealth but also to urban Western lifestyles and culture. In the absence of migration, however, young women, especially from more secure middle-class families, attempt to establish proximity to the local urban space by seeking opportunities for employment and further education. These opportunities are associated with ideas of urban modernity, urban leisure, open interaction with members of the opposite sex, greater levels of awareness and cultural sophistication. Young women's imaginaries of mobility rely on specific constructions of the local urban space, the West and the village. These imaginaries of mobility are referenced and used by young women to carve middle-class identities in the village space.

The Middle Class in Chaheru

In Chaheru, the production of middle-class status emerges as the enterprise of young women, between the ages of eighteen and thirty-five from upwardly mobile families. Their orientation towards education and local employment sets them apart from the young men in the community who are more invested in accumulation of wealth through migration. In their negotiations with education, young women engage with status production work (Papanek 1979; Osella and Osella 2000; Chopra 2011) and create a respectable middle-class identity. In this context, the middle-class ethos is defined as one that facilitates movement outside the village, enhances status and is distinctive from the backward lower classes. Middle-class culture in Chaheru is inextricably linked to discourses of caste, class and gender that allow young women to physically and culturally distinguish themselves from the [*lower class*] 'vernacular' young women, who are bound by rural traditions and norms (Ciotti 2010: 218). Previous work on middle-class culture speaks to this very project of fashioning an in-between identity (Liechty 2003).

In defining the framework for middle-class identity in Chaheru, occupation and proximity to migration are important indicators of a family's ability to consume, its access to educational facilities and its type of household structure. The middle class in Chaheru is a diverse group composed of migrant families (with family members in the Gulf or Europe[7]), professionally employed families in government jobs and well-to-do business families. These families are referred to as migrant, educated and self-employed families, respectively. These groups vary not only in their choice of occupation but also in the ways that they negotiate the middle-class requirements of consumption and distinction.

All middle-class families pursue the education of young women to the extent that it is affordable. In fact, as soon as an upwardly mobile family is able to accrue some wealth, they invest in the education of their daughters. However, for migrant families, the education of women in itself is not a source of distinction. Rather, the building of large urban houses, hosting grand weddings and investments in property are the markers of status. In contrast, educated families see the education of their children as a crucial metric of distinction. They also invoke the construct of *jankari*, or awareness, and exposure to urban cultures with regard to education, fashion and food. It allows them to establish proximity to the cultured and urban middle class. Self-employed families can be seen as occupying an in-between cultural space. Similar to the migrant families, they value explicit markers of wealth like large houses and celebrations of social events like weddings. However, they also facilitate the higher education of their children at prestigious institutes, even though in most self-employed families the parents are illiterate.

Another factor that differentiates middle-class families is the security with which families can claim middle-class status. While almost all upwardly mobile families in Chaheru were engaged in the process of acquiring the ability to emulate 'appropriate' class practices, their level of cultural competence was dependent on economic resources, with less secure families lacking the means to reliably perform middle-class consumption. Through the experiences of Somika and Kavita, I explore how young women from less secure migrant and more secure educated middle-class families respectively occupy middle-class positioning.

Looking Down

Somika is twenty-four years old and belongs to an educated and secure middle-class family. She is the daughter of Balveer, a government bank clerk and a well-respected member of the community. The house that she resides in Chaheru belongs to her maternal grandmother. The family moved to Chaheru when Somika was in school to take care of her ailing grandmother. The environment in Somika's house is relatively open and egalitarian. In other households, young women often have a formal relationship with their fathers and are careful to conduct themselves in a demure way. In contrast, Somika talks freely in the presence of her father and even feels comfortable enough to interject when her father is talking with me.

Somika has completed her MA from a college in Jalandhar, a nearby city located 23 kilometres from Phagwara, and is preparing to take competitive exams for government posts. She also tutors children in the evenings. Somika often expresses frustration at the low levels of education in the village, and many of our discussions centre on the lack of female education. Like many educated young women in the village who are 'waiting' for opportunities for high-status employment to materialize, she often complains about the lack of mobility in her career trajectory and expresses that is it is difficult to sit at home for so long and not do anything. During my field work period she prepares and sits for the Life Insurance Corporation of India and government bank exams. Somika says she has taken these exams multiple times before. She also plans to prepare and sit for the railway exams.

Unlike other young women who face greater restrictions around their mobility, Somika has the support from her parents to pursue opportunities that may require her to travel further distances from the village. Towards the end of my fieldwork, Somika began classes for competitive government exams at the Ambedkar institute in Phagwara. When representatives from the institute came to talk to people in the village about the coaching that they offer, they held a meeting at Somika's house. Somika laments that while many girls showed up to find out about the classes, no one is coming to the classes because they think it is too far (the classes are being held in Phagwara town). She says,

> the girls here don't know there is special coaching for competitive exams like the bank exam . . .even the other girl that went with me [*from a poorer family in the village*] didn't know . . . even I have been raised here and have the same education yet I knew these things . . . if you have to do something you have to do it regardless of how hot it is [*in reference to Kavita's reason for not going because it is too hot*] . . . I have a banking exam for the position of a clerk . . . I've been trying for the last 5-6 years but I am confident I will get it.

In this excerpt, Somika presents herself as a girl who, despite growing up in the village, is well informed, confident and determined. She distinguishes herself from other young women in the village, who are characterized as restricted, unaware and unmotivated. Interestingly, Somika locates the other young women 'here' within the village space, while specifying that even though she has grown up in the village she does not imbibe other young women's concerns and restrictions. This desire to mark oneself as distinct from the village, both culturally and physically, underlies the narrative of young women, especially from secure middle-class families.

Middle-class families often describe the village space as one beset with backwardness, immorality, violence and drugs and seek to distance themselves from it. For instance, Somika's parents' concern about social interactions in the village translates to Somika's brothers only spending time with the sons of one other family. By way of explanation, Somika says, 'they are from a good family like ours.' The category of 'good families' is reserved for similarly placed secure middle-class families and the insinuation of pollution and immorality is linked to lower-class villagers. This illustrates the efforts of secure middle-class families to carve a middle-class identity that is dissociated from the stigma attached to lower castes. In fact, Somika herself only socializes with her neighbours and says she does not have any friends in the village, unlike young women from less secure families in the village who reported having friends that they have grown up with and meet occasionally.

Being Middle Class

In order to unravel Somika's middle-class identity and contrast it with Kavita's, it is important to place their narratives about education in the context of their family's social and economic positioning. In contrast to migrant or self-employed families, secure educated families had better links with the urban space. Many of Somika's relatives, for example, lived in Jalandhar, and she regularly visited them and explored urban leisure sites such as movie theatres and malls. Moreover, Somika's father's employment in a government bank translated to a secure pathway to middle-class consumption. In contrast, Kavita belongs to a less secure migrant middle-class family with limited and unreliable access to economic resources. Her younger brother Suresh was unemployed and waiting to migrate at the time of my field work. While Kavita and her mother claimed that her older brother Ramesh worked in Bangalore, the gossip in the village was that he was in jail for drug-related crimes. This family's insecure economic and moral positioning translated into weaker links to urban modernity.

Somika's family used their access and exposure to urban modernity as social capital and demonstrated openness to urban Western fashions and food habits.[8] In contrast, while Kavita's mother Kanta lacked the economic resources of more secure migrant families, she displays a preference for claiming proximity to Western migrant lifestyles in her grooming and upkeep of the house. Kanta's house was one of the only houses in the village among those that I visited to have toilet paper and mosquito repellent, which, she explained, was a consequence of frequent interactions with migrant relatives.

However, in contrast to other educated young women in the community who attempt to showcase their exposure to urban culture in their clothing, demeanour and movement within the village, Kavita appeared detached from projections of urban modernity. Unlike other young women from middle-class families who typically limit their movement within the village and look forward to planning trips to the city, engaging in urban leisure activities and adorning more urban clothes, Kavita was more comfortable walking around the village and her visits outside were limited to when her sisters were visiting and needed to go shopping. Similarly, in her everyday behaviour Kavita reflects rural styles of talking, gesticulating and working. The only time she slips into an urban style is when she goes shopping to the local market with her sisters or with me. On these occasions, she dresses in a pair of jeans and a top. Somika, on the other hand, would often don jeans and a sleeveless top even while at her home in the village. These behaviours serve to position Kavita differently within the community, and often other educated young women living there express surprise over Kavita's educational qualifications and do not evaluate her as having the same social positioning as them.

Moreover, Kavita's and Somika's conversations around education and mobility also revealed different concerns. While Somika used her educatedness to mark her distinction from lower-class women in the village, Kavita pointed to the difficulties she encountered in negotiating access to education and employment opportunities. Kavita's ability to pursue opportunities for employment, education and migration were closely determined by her migrant relatives. In explaining the power that they exercised Kavita said, 'You don't get it, over here people who live abroad and who have more money make the decisions in the family . . . in our house, the Italy sister makes the decisions.' As recounted at the beginning of the chapter, Kavita often discussed her inability to take up certain opportunities due to the control exercised by her migrant relatives. In addition, she also had to manage the concerns raised and presented by her non-migrant family members. For instance, Kavita expressed her inability to take the Chandigarh job, not only because of the decision of her migrant relatives but also because of her responsibility to Kanta. She says, 'I cannot do that job because I cannot leave her (referring to her mother) like that . . . she needs help with house work.' Kavita's mother has polio and Kavita divided the daily household chores with her. When I asked her what would happen if she went to Canada, Kavita tells me her older brother, Ramesh, would get remarried and *bhabhi* (her brother's wife) would come and do the work. Kavita also frequently referred to 'getting permission' from Ramesh to pursue any employment opportunity that involved travelling to another city. Thus, unlike Somika who had better access to opportunities and greater permissibility to travel longer distances for education and employment, Kavita's conversations pertained to the obstacles she had to encounter. She often expressed a sense of helplessness saying, *hum peeche reh gaye* ('we have been left behind'). This statement captures the sense of immobility and stuckness Kavita feels as she navigates and accommodates to the preferences of her family.

Thus, while both Somika and Kavita drew upon their educatedness to claim a middle-class positioning in Chaheru, they occupy this middle classness very differently. While Kavita referenced movement to spaces outside the village, her everyday discourses pertained to negotiating access to education and further employment rather than using her educational status to carve a distinctive identity. In contrast, Somika and similarly placed women were more engaged in using education as a site of distinction. Specifically, by emphasizing the importance of young women's ability to travel independently and pursue opportunities for education and employment, Somika was able to claim proximity to an urbanized or modern idea of female mobility. In her work with Manupur Chamars, Ciotti (2010) also asserts that upwardly mobile Chamar women are attempting to appropriate the 'modern' that is linked to the city space, while distancing themselves from the village (220). Given that several young women from educated and secure middle-class families in Chaheru had close links with urban spaces, appropriating ideas of urban modernity appears like a natural extension of their aspirations for mobility. However, even young women from these families were confined by ideas of 'appropriateness' and familial responsibilities. For example, towards the end of my fieldwork Somika began working at a private company in Jalandhar. But when there was a death in her family, she left her job to be able to attend to all the visitors who were coming over to her house to express their condolences. Thus, despite claims of female mobility, it is implicit that this mobility is conditional on being able to fulfil one's responsibilities at home. This harkens back to Radhakrishnan's (2008) idea of the modern woman who straddles both work and home.

Education and Mobility?

The differential interactions of Somika and Kavita with education have one point of commonality; in both cases, education at least in the short term has not translated to the desired mobility outcomes. Following my fieldwork, I learned that Kavita had secured employment at a local private school, while Somika continued to work towards passing the government employment exams. In most cases, even when young women are able to attain undergraduate and postgraduate education, it does not coincide with commensurate occupational opportunities opening up for them. This speaks to continuities in historical disadvantages. Dalit women are often unable to access elite educational institutes due to their insecure economic status. Consequently, they are unable to develop English fluency, competence in urban and Western mannerisms, and strong social networks of well-placed Dalits (Heyer 2014; Still 2015). In addition to compromised educational access, gendered norms around physical mobility make it difficult for young women to travel to different cities for educational and employment opportunities. Most young women seek opportunities for education and employment in proximity to the village and within Phagwara, as they are often disallowed by parents from moving to another city. Somika's pursuit of her degree in Jalandhar is an anomaly rather than the norm.

Thus, young women's plans and choices around education do not appear as individualized assertions of autonomy but are instead nestled in family plans and concerns around mobility and status. In fact, even the extent to which young women are able to perform educatedness is shaped by their family's economic and social positioning. This echoes previous work on young women and education in India, which pinpoints the importance of family considerations around status, class and female respectability in shaping young women's interactions with education (Chopra 2011; Froerer 2012; Osella and Osella 2000; Still 2011; Vijayakumar 2013).

In returning to the question posed in the introduction, despite the obstacles to attaining government employment or marriage migration, education continues to be valued by young women and even their parents. For parents, the importance of education is located in its instrumental value for marriage migration and accruing middle-class status. For young women, while education is an important part of working towards the goals of employment and migration, it is also seen as an important tool for developing cultural knowledge and status. As Franco (2010) points out, young women's plans and aspirations around education are significant because they reveal that 'the girls are saying that they can imagine their lives and themselves not only as mothers and wives, whose interests and needs are embedded in those of their families, but also as active participants in wider networks of social relations' (157). While Kavita, limited by the economic resources at her disposal, makes less strong claims to educational mobility, the discourse presented by Somika operates as an ideal that is referenced and selectively emulated by differently located young women in Chaheru. Thus, in expanding our focus to incorporate the non-tangible aspects of educational mobility, it is possible to see young women as invested in a more complex process of social change and identity formation. Despite its inability to guarantee mobility outcomes, education allows some young women in Chaheru to access urban spaces, develop familiarity with urban cultural mores, emulate aspects of the urban middle class and position themselves as the cultured middle class.

Notes

1 The caste system is a defining feature of social and labour relations in rural India. While there are fewer upper-caste groups, the majority of caste groups fall within the lower-caste realm, which can be further differentiated into scheduled castes (SC) or Dalits and other backward castes (OBC or BC). Scheduled tribes (ST) or Adivasis refer to India's aboriginal population that falls outside the caste system but are often couched together with scheduled castes in policy and government speak under the banner of SC and ST. These two groups are benefactors of affirmative action and government programmes due to their historically marginalized status (Chakravarti 2003).

2 In this study the Chamars in Chaheru are referred to as Ad-dharmis or Dalits based on respondents' self-identification. The hereditary occupation of Chamars consists of the snaring of skins and hides, tanning and leatherwork. Among Punjab's Dalit communities, Ad-dharmis are the most numerous and fare better on education, employment and other indicators of development. The economic mobility of Punjabi Ad-dharmis is complemented by their religious and social assertions (Jodhka 2002; Judge and Bal 2009; Ram 2009; Singh et al. 2012).

3 This was the term used by Kavita to refer to the caregiver visa.

4 The historical and contemporary work on Dalit education in Punjab has shown that education, as a site of social mobility, is available to a minority of better-placed Dalits (Judge and Bal 2009; Pimpley 1976).

5 A celebratory narrative of migration is pervasive in Punjabi popular culture, state discourse and everyday parlance in Punjabi villages and towns. This strong culture of migration dates back to Punjab's economic decline, which began in the 1980s. In the early 1980s as agricultural productivity and incomes began dwindling, agrarian protest coincided with the political unrest and persecution that followed Operation Bluestar. This coincidence of economic and political turmoil conspired to create social uncertainty and led to the exodus of young men from Punjab. Doaba is the

region of Punjab with the highest number of outmigrants (Chopra 2011; Gill 2005; Gill 2009; Singh et al. 2007).

6　Kumar (2004) points out that in Dalit communities, migration is even more valued because it is seen to be crucial in allowing lower castes to attain economic mobility and override caste stigma.

7　Those families that had migrated to North America no longer lived in the village and only came to visit.

8　Educated and secure middle-class families tend to incorporate dishes from different regions of India in their home food, and this is an important part of demonstrating their exposure to urban culture.

References

Ali, S. (2007). '"Go West Young Man": The Culture of Migration among Muslims in Hyderabad, India', *Journal of Ethnic and Migration Studies*, 33(1), 37–58. https://doi.org/10.1080/13691830601043489.

Chakravarti, U. (2003). *Gendering Caste: Through a Feminist Lens*. Calcutta: Sage.

Chopra, R. (2011). *Militant and Migrant: The Politics and Social History of Punjab*. New Delhi: Routledge.

Chopra, R., & Jeffery, P. (Eds) (2005). *Educational Regimes in Contemporary India*. New Delhi: Sage Publications.

Ciotti, M. (2006). 'In the Past We Were a Bit "Chamar"': Education as a Self- and Community Engineering Process in Northern India', *Journal of the Royal Anthropological Institute*, 12(4), 899–916. https://doi.org/10.1111/j.1467-9655.2006.00369.x.

Ciotti, M. (2010). *Retro-Modern India: Forging the Low-Caste Self*. London: Routledge.

Corbett, M. (2007). *Learning to Leave: The Irony of Schooling in a Coastal Community*. Canada: Fernwood Publishing Co., Ltd.

Dreze, J., & A. Sen. (1995). *India: Economic Development and Social Opportunity*. New Delhi: Oxford University Press.

Franco, D. N. (2010). 'Aspirations and Self-Hood: Exploring the Meaning of Higher Secondary Education for Girl College Students in Rural Bangladesh', *Compare*, 40(2), 142–65. https://doi.org/10.1080/03057920903546005.

Froerer, P. (2012). 'Learning, Livelihoods, and Social Mobility: Valuing Girls' Education in Central India', *Anthropology and Education Quarterly*, 43(4), 344–57. https://www.jstor.org/stable/23359073.

Gill, A. (2009). 'Punjab Peasantry: A Question of Life and Debt', *Journal of Punjab Studies*, 16(1), 71–88.

Gill, S.S. (2005). 'Economic Distress and Suicides in Rural Punjab', *Journal of Punjab Studies*, 12(2), 219–37.

Heyer, J. (2014). 'Dalit Women Becoming "Housewives": Lessons from the Tiruppur Region 1981/2 to 2008/9', in C. Still (Ed.), *Dalits in Neoliberal India: Mobility or Marginalization?* Abingdon: Routledge, 208–35.

Jeffrey, C., Jeffery, R., & Jeffery, P. (2008). *Degrees without Freedom : Education, Masculinities and Unemployment in North India.* New Delhi: Orient Blackswan Pvt. Ltd.

Jodhka, S. S. (2002). 'Caste and Untouchability in Rural Punjab', *Economic and Political Weekly*, 37(19), 1813–23. https://www.jstor.org/stable/4412102.

Judge, P., & Bal, G. (2009). *Mapping Dalits: Contemporary Reality and Future Prospects in Punjab.* Jaipur, India: Rawat Publications.

Kapuria, S., & Birwal, D. (2017). 'International Migration from Punjab: Trends and Challenges', *Researchpaedia*, 4(1), 27–36.

Kumar, V. (2004). 'Understanding Dalit Diaspora', *Economic and Political Weekly*, 39(1), 114–16. https://www.jstor.org/stable/4414473.

Liechty, M. (2003). *Suitably Modern: Making Middle Class Culture in a New Consumer Society.* Princeton and Oxford: Princeton University Press.

Osella, F., & Osella, C. (2000). *Social Mobility In Kerala: Modernity and Identity in Conflict.* London: Pluto Press.

Papanek, H. (1979). 'Family Status Production: The "Work" and "Non-Work" of Women', *Signs*, 4(4), 775–81. https://doi.org/10.1086/493663.

Pimpley, P.N. (1976). 'Social Characteristics of the Scheduled Caste Students in the Punjab', *Indian Journal of Social Work*, 37(1), 49–54.

Radhakrishnan, S. (2008). 'Examining the "Global" Indian Middle Class: Gender and Culture in the Silicon Valley/Bangalore Circuit', *Journal of Intercultural Studies*, 29(1), 7–20. https://doi.org/10.1080/07256860701759915.

Ram, R. (2009). 'Ravidass, Dera, Sachkhand Ballan and the Question of Dalit Identity in Punjab', *Journal of Punjab Studies*, 16(1), 1–34.

Rao, N. (2010). 'Migration, Education and Socio-Economic Mobility', *Compare*, 40(2), 137–45.

Singh, G., Simon, C., & Tatla, D.S. (2012). *New Forms of Religious Transnationalism and Development Initiatives: A Case Study of Dera Sant Sarwan Dass, Ballan, Punjab, India.* CORE. https://core.ac.uk/display/2793894. (accessed 18 October 2021).

Singh, L., Singh, I., & Ghuman, S.R. (2007). 'Changing Character of Rural Economy and Migrant Labour in Punjab', *Migrant Labor*, 57–69. https://punjab.global.ucsb.edu/sites/default/files/sitefiles/journals/volume16/no1/3-LakhwinderGill16%201%20%282%29.pdf.

Still, C. (2011). 'Spoiled Brides and the Fear of Education: Honour and Social Mobility among Dalits in South India', *Modern Asian Studies*, 45(5), 1119–46. https://www.jstor.org/stable/25835714.

Still, C. (Ed.). (2015). *Dalits in Neoliberal India: Mobility or Marginalization?* New Delhi: Routledge.

Thieme, S., & Wyss, S. (2005). 'Migration Patterns and Remittance Transfer in Nepal: A Case Study of Sainik Basti in Western Nepal'. *International Migration*, 43(5), 59–98. https://doi.org/10.1111/j.1468-2435.2005.00342.x.

Vijayakumar, G. (2013). "'I'll be Like Water": Gender, Class, and Flexible Aspirations at the Edge of India's Knowledge Economy', *Gender & Society*, 27(6), 777–98. https://doi.org/10.1177/0891243213499445.

Yang, D. (2004). *International Migration, Human Capital, and Entrepreneurship: Evidence from Philippine Migrants' Exchange Rate Shocks*. Ann Arbor: University of Michigan Press. https://eml.berkeley.edu/~webfac/emiguel/e271_s04/yang.pdf (accessed 18 October 2021).

9

Internal Migration and Children's Education in Bangalore, India

Jyotsna Jha, Archana Purohit and Sowmya J.[1]

Introduction

The linkages between internal migration and educational outcomes in India, a highly populated and developmentally diverse country, need deeper exploration, particularly as inter-state and rural–urban migration, linked to urbanization and the changing economy, increases. This chapter explores the links between internal migration and educational status of children in migrant families, based primarily on a quantitative survey of a small number of households (369) in low-income jobs in Bangalore, a South Indian city, known as the IT (Information Technology) capital of the country.

Bangalore has emerged as an important destination for migrant labour from all parts of India in recent years.[2] When the lockdown was imposed across India without much notice in March 2020, large-scale return migration of thousands of workers from the cities became one of the most talked-about issues and a visually disturbing sight highlighting their vulnerability. Our survey therefore also explored the impact of the pandemic and lockdown on migrant workers' livelihoods and their children's education.

The relationship between internal migration and educational outcomes is important to understand specifically as international and internal migration have been shown to have differing effects on human capital outcomes, with international migration exhibiting a more significant positive impact (Schapiro 2009). The channels through which migration can affect education are multiple. Remittances from migration can help families spend more on education and thus may lead to better educational outcomes. Migration can also help develop aspirations for a better life which might lead to greater educational investment.

On the other hand, migration can also have a detrimental impact on educational outcomes due to children being absent from school when they migrate seasonally or due to lack of parental guidance and attention when the children are left behind while parents migrate.

In India, migration is often circular in nature and the way the cycles of migration and annual educational cycles overlap might differ depending on the occupational sectors (Smita 2008). Similarly, due to the diversity of languages in different parts of India, the language of instruction in the destination might be different from the language of the migrant family and this creates a barrier in access to public low-cost educational facilities for migrant children (Jha and Minni 2019). Some evidence suggests that the nature of migration, whether single or family migration, or whether for piece-rate employment or daily wages, and family perceptions about returns from educational investment also shape household choices regarding children's education (Jha and Jhingran 2005; Rao 2010; Roy et al. 2015). Other features that influence education decision-making processes, such as gender, caste, community and social norms, and location, may also be important.

Taking cognizance of these factors, our survey focused on understanding three key aspects of migrant workers' lives in Bangalore: (1) livelihoods, work environment, living conditions and income; (2) children's schooling status and links to parental migratory nature of work and (3) the Covid-19 pandemic and its implications for migrant workers' lives and their children's education. What is most revealing here is that although we approached workers in particular industries known to have a high proportion of migrant workers, all our respondents turned out to be migrants. Where they differed was in the duration of migration, with many having migrated to the city more than fifteen years previously. This means that a large proportion of people living in poverty in urban settings in India are likely to be migrants. Nonetheless, that the majority of low-income workers are a 'permanently temporary workforce' (Pani 2018) remains largely unacknowledged in the policymaking ecosystem of India. We delve into this issue in our analysis of data, which helps us understand the particular vulnerabilities of migrant workers and their interlinkages with children's education.

Sectoral, Social and Age Profile of Respondents

The discussion here is based on findings of an exploratory survey conducted between March and April 2021. We adopted a purposive sampling strategy and identified five occupational categories, from which to select respondents. The five sectors or occupations to which our respondents belong are (1) construction, (2) garment factories, (3) private security services, (4) hospitality and (5) domestic help. While initially we had planned to have equal number of respondents across all the categories, the final numbers have more representation from construction, garments and hospitality sectors as we had to stop the study abruptly due to Covid-19 restrictions. Sixty-two per cent of the sample was male and 38 per cent female (Figure 9.1).[3] This could be because on excluding marriage-related migration, internal migration in India is largely employment- and male-oriented (Srivastava 2011).

The distribution of respondents across religions (88 per cent Hindu, 11 per cent Muslims and 1 per cent Christians (Figure 9.2)) is similar to the proportions for India's population (80 per cent Hindus, 14 per cent Muslims and 2 per cent Christians, according to 2011 census). The caste-wise distribution of the respondents shows an overrepresentation of scheduled tribes (ST), scheduled castes (SC) and other backward castes (OBCs), which together comprise 80 per cent of our sample (Figure 9.3); this reflects known trends whereby these groups are overrepresented among unskilled migrant workers. The presence of respondents from different age groups shows a bias towards younger people, as the majority of our sample (68 per cent) was between twenty and forty years of age (Figure 9.4).

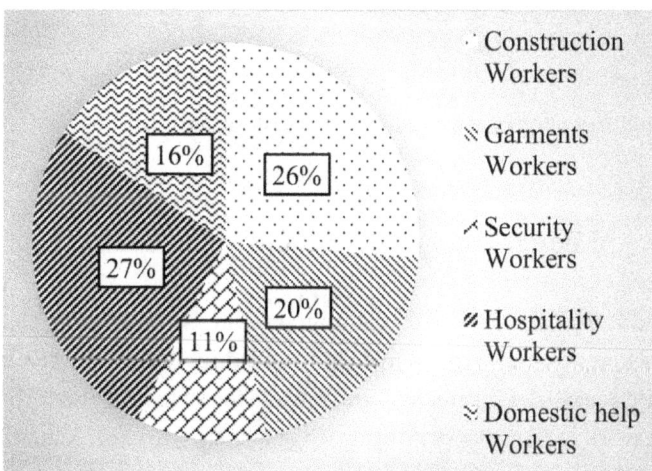

Figure 9.1 Distribution of respondents across occupational categories.

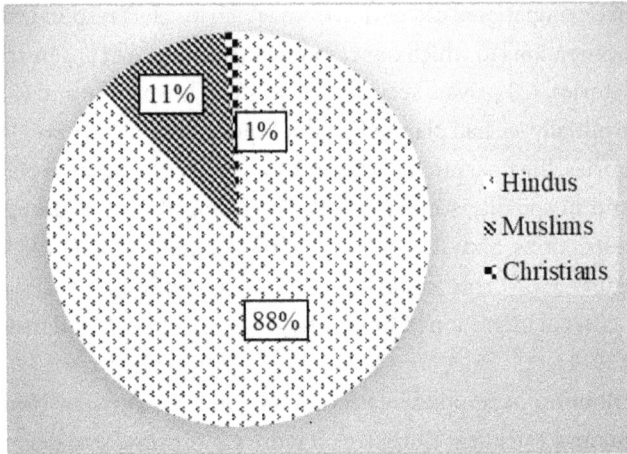

Figure 9.2 Distribution of respondents across religious groups.

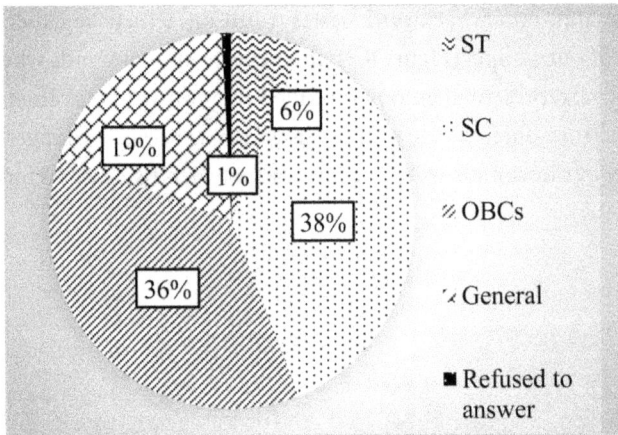

Figure 9.3 Distribution of respondents across caste groups.

Living, Work, Income and Vulnerability

One of the important aspects of the migrant's life is linked with identity and sense of belonging, and we explored this by distinguishing between migration from within Karnataka (intra-state) and outside the state (inter-state) by looking at years of work in Bangalore and knowledge of local language, Kannada. In our sample, 40 per cent were intra-state migrants while 60 per cent were inter-state migrants. The presence of inter-state migrants is relatively higher in security,

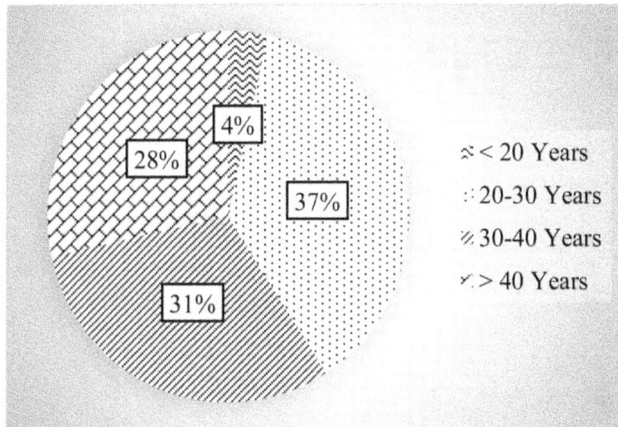

Figure 9.4 Distribution of respondents across age groups.

hospitality and domestic work sectors, while it is nearly equally distributed for construction and garment work (Table 9.1).

Although women made up 38 per cent of total respondents, their proportion was understandably higher among intra-state migrants (48 per cent) as compared to inter-state migrants (32 per cent). The practice of single male migration has been more common for those coming from distant states: Bihar, Odisha, West Bengal (Government of Kerala 2013; Pani 2020). Women coming from both within and outside the state are concentrated in domestic and garment work, while those from within the state are also present in construction. With the exception of construction, these occupations are highly gendered: hospitality and security have high concentrations of men, while garment and domestic work have a higher concentration of women workers (Table 9.1).

A higher proportion of intra-state migrants (60 per cent) have been in Bangalore for more than ten years, although this proportion is also significant for inter-state migrants (40 per cent). However, inter-state migrants seem to outnumber intra-state migrants among neo-migrants, those who have been in the city for five or less years (Table 9.2).

The choice of occupation and destinations among internal migrants is known to be driven by social networks (Litchfield et al. 2015; Munshi 2020) and supply arrangements by labour contractors (Deshingkar 2006; Mishra 2020), which proved to be true for this survey. When it comes to living status, the gaps between intra-state and inter-state migrants are wide: nearly 86 per cent of intra-state migrants live with families as against only 55 per cent of inter-state migrants. Almost all those working in garment and domestic sector live

Table 9.1 Distribution of Migrant Workers across Occupation, Place of Origin (Intra-state or Inter-state) and Gender

Place	Gender	Construction workers	Garment workers	Security workers	Hospitality workers	Domestic helps	All
Intra-state	Male	31	8	6	30	2	77
	Female	20	32	2	2	14	70
Subtotal		51	40	8	32	16	147
Inter-state	Male	43	7	32	66	2	150
	Female	3	28		1	40	72
Subtotal		46	35	32	67	42	222
Grand Total		97	75	40	99	58	369

Table 9.2 Distribution of Migrant Workers across Years of Stay in Bangalore and Place of Origin (Intra-state or Inter-state)

Place of origin/duration	< 2 years	2–5 years	5–10 years	>10 years	Total
Intra-state	8	20	30	89	147
Inter-state	37	50	46	89	222

with families, reflecting their gendered division (Table 9.3). Construction and hospitality sector workers from other states are largely single migrants living with co-workers and friends, with implications for children's education that we discuss later.

There was a difference in the living conditions of the migrants too. Forty-two per cent of our sample lived in houses shared by four or more people, while 38 per cent lived in rooms. What we refer to as rooms here are typically covered spaces shared by many people and sometimes provided by employers. Only 6 per cent said that they live in spacious accommodation, while 39 per cent of respondents described their living space as congested and 55 per cent described that as manageable.

For those living in shared accommodation, access to amenities such as toilets and bathing space is a concern: 17 per cent used open space for toilets, and 51 per cent had access to shared and public toilets. Only 31 per cent respondents had toilets attached to their living space. Similarly, 57 per cent of respondents used open space or shared bathrooms for bathing while 43 per cent had attached bathrooms. Almost 91 per cent of the construction workers, 80 per cent of domestic helps and 65 per cent of security workers used open space or shared toilets. The proportions were only slightly better in the case of garment factory workers (57 per cent) and hospitality workers (52 per cent).

A sense of belonging also comes from ability to communicate and negotiate. The knowledge of local language, Kannada, becomes important for these purposes. Language is also important with respect to children's access to schooling, especially public schooling, which is free and follows Kannada medium of instruction. In our sample, as expected, almost all of those coming from within Karnataka could speak Kannada and about a fifth could read and write Kannada. This was very different for inter-state migrants, of whom a little less than half could speak and follow Kannada, one-third reported not knowing the language at all and almost no one could read or write Kannada (Table 9.4). Migrants coming from within South India, that is, Andhra Pradesh or Tamil Nadu, have some advantages in knowing spoken Kannada, as there are

Table 9.3 Per cent Distribution of Migrant Workers across Occupation, Place of Origin (Intra-state or Inter-state) and Living Arrangements

Place	Staying with whom	Construction workers	Garments workers	Security workers	Hospitality workers	Domestic help	Total
Intra-state	alone	2.0	2.5	0.0	6.2	0.0	2.7
	with my family	86.3	95.0	100.0	62.5	100.0	85.7
	with my friends	5.9	2.5	0.0	9.4	0.0	4.8
	with co-workers	5.9	0.0	0.0	21.9	0.0	6.8
Inter-state	alone	2.2	0.0	3.1	6.0	0.0	2.7
	with my family	28.3	97.1	75.0	16.4	97.6	55.4
	with my friends	19.6	2.9	9.4	25.4	2.4	14.0
	with other co-workers	50.0	0.0	12.5	52.2	0.0	27.9

Table 9.4 Per cent Distribution of Migrant Workers across Occupation, Place of Origin (Intra-state or Inter-state) and Knowledge of Local Language

Place	Fluency in Kannada	Construction workers	Garments workers	Security workers	Hospitality workers	Domestic workers	All
Intra-state	I don't know	2.0	0.0	0.0	0.0	0.0	0.7
	can understand	0.0	0.0	12.5	0.0	0.0	0.7
	can speak a little	2.0	0.0	0.0	0.0	0.0	0.7
	can speak fluently	84.3	67.5	87.5	84.4	100.0	81.6
	can read and/or write	11.8	32.5	0.0	15.6	0.0	16.3
Inter-state	don't know	63.0	5.7	21.9	50.7	7.1	33.8
	can understand	8.7	8.6	6.2	16.4	2.4	9.5
	can speak a little	2.2	11.4	9.4	10.4	9.5	8.6
	can speak fluently	23.9	74.3	62.5	22.4	80.9	47.7
	can read and/or write	2.2	0.0	0.0	0.0	0.0	0.4

similarities with languages spoken in these states, whereas the same is not true for those coming from the linguistic worlds of Hindi or Bengali: Bihar, Uttar Pradesh or West Bengal.

In general, migrant workers' access to public services except public transport seems to be poor. Less than half have access to the Public Distribution System (PDS) through which basic rations are provided to a targeted population, which is surprising for a state where more than 70 per cent population has access to PDS (CBPS 2019). Similarly, the state has publicly supported health insurance schemes for those living in poverty but only 5 per cent of our respondents reported having access to this means of health financing (Table 9.5). Access to services that are open access without the need for any documentation (transport, health clinics) seems to be better as compared to those that need documentation (health insurance, PDS). Inter-state migrants have less access to most of these, but the difference is not as stark as the exclusion of all migrant workers from certain services. This also means that knowledge of local language and belonging to the same state play only a limited role: migrants, as a group, remain vulnerable, because of the lack of access to public services and social security schemes.

Hopes for better income and employment are what drive migration, although recent discussions also refer to migration as being aspiration-driven, with migrants moving towards cities in search of better livelihoods and improvements in their lives more generally (Bhagat 2017). While 46 per cent of the respondents mentioned that they migrated because of lack of any employment in their native places, 44 per cent said that they did so in search of better payment (Table 9.6). It is clear that most of these migrants moved for economic reasons and aspirations for city life or better jobs played a much smaller role.

Table 9.5 Distribution of Migrant Workers across Place of Origin (Intra-state or Inter-state) and Access to Public Services

Percentage for those who have access to	Intra-state	Inter-state	All
Public Distribution System (PDS; uncooked food at subsidized rates)	53.1	43.2	47.2
Public transport	99.4	89.2	93.2
Public parks	7.5	7.2	7.3
Health insurance	6.8	4.5	5.4
Government hospital/health centres/ clinics	67.3	67.6	67.5
private hospital/doctors/clinics	63.9	47.7	54.2

Table 9.6 Reason for Migration

Reason for migration	Proportion (%)
Lack of any employment	45.6
Better payment	43.8
To supplement family income	6.6
Lack of suitable jobs	0.9
Lure of city life	0.4
Others	2.6

Although most participants moved in order to improve their economic situation, whether they were able to achieve the anticipated better income is questionable. The average monthly income across all categories in our sample was Rs 11,096, or about 152 USD, which translates roughly to 6 USD a day. Some occupational workers like domestic helps and garment factory workers are paid still less: the average monthly income of domestic workers is as low as 72 USD, less than 3 USD a day (Table 9.7). The average per capita income in India for 2019–20 was Rs 126,968 annually (USD 1739), or Rs 10,580 (USD 145) a month. According to the 2017–18 Longitudinal Ageing Study,[4] however, the bottom 20 per cent of the households earn only Rs 25,825 per capita per year (353 USD). When we compare these two figures, it immediately becomes evident that while in absolute terms the income of these migrant workers might seem precarious, relatively they are in a much better place than many of their non-migrant peers. This finding is supported later on by the data on expenditure, disposable income and remittances and also explains why many continue to choose to migrate.

Table 9.7 Average Monthly Income of Migrant Workers Based on Their Occupation and Gender

Type of occupations	Male	Female	All
Construction workers	14,126* (194)**	10,470 (144)	13,259 (182)
Garments workers	11,233 (154)	9,525 (131)	9,867 (135)
Security workers	12,624 (173)	12,000 (165)	12,593 (173)
Hospitality workers	12,711 (174)	13,667 (187)	12,740 (175)
Domestic help workers	8,250 (113)	5,005 (69)	5,228 (72)
Average Income	13,034 (179)	8,066 (111)	11,096 (152)

*In Indian Rupees

**USD

Education Status of Children

A little more than half of our respondents (52 per cent) had school-age children, numbering 364 in total (59 from 3 to 5 years, 217 from 6 to 13 years and 88 from 14 to 18 years).[5] Of these, only 78 per cent were reported to be in school or any educational institution, while the remaining 22 per cent were out of school. The proportion in-school was lowest for the early childhood years (30 per cent) and the highest for the elementary school age group (93 per cent). Only 76 per cent of secondary school-age children were in school (Figures 9.5 and 9.6). A clear gender bias can be seen as the proportion of girls in school was lower than the proportion of boys for all three age groups. When we compare these figures for the national average gross enrolment rate (GER), we find that these are comparable yet lower than national averages for both elementary and secondary levels.[6]

This is an interesting pattern if we consider education policies and entitlements. Elementary education, which covers eight years of schooling for the age group of 6–13 years, is a fundamental right in India. The Right to Education as a justiciable fundamental was introduced in 2009, and, despite the fact that implementation has been far from satisfactory, it has led to expansion of, and increased participation in, public schooling, which is evident even in this data. This suggests that legislative measures, even with limited implementation, contribute to making entitlements a reality.

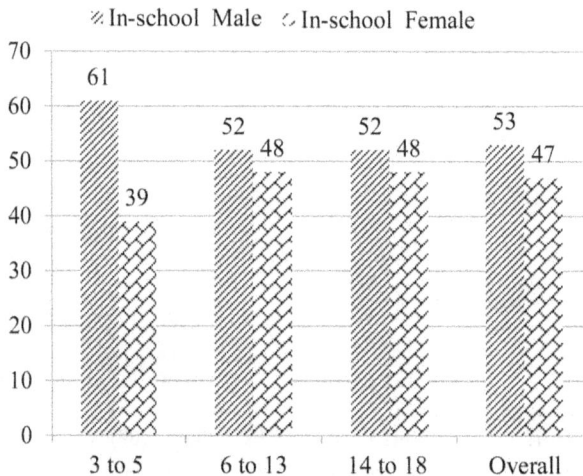

Figure 9.5 Proportion of male and female children among those in-school (different age groups).

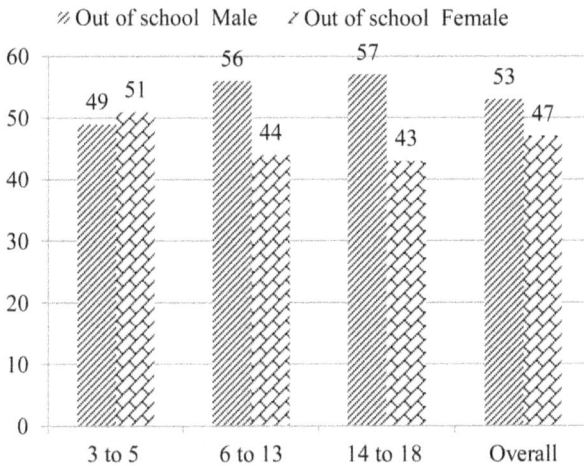

Figure 9.6 Proportion of male and female children among those out of school (different age groups).

Belonging to a social group, that is, caste or community, has been an important marker for determining schooling status or related aspirations in India. However, this association does not seem to be as strong for this group of migrant workers, except for the OBCs. While all other communities, including Muslims, SCs and STs, have about 20–25 per cent children not in school, this proportion at 14 per cent is the lowest for the OBC groups (Figure 9.7). Another outlier is the General (i.e. upper-caste Hindus) caste group, which has the highest proportion of out-of-school children at nearly 26 per cent, which goes against the usual macro

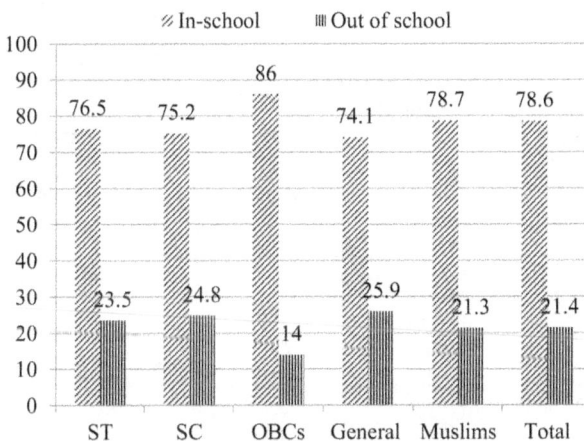

Figure 9.7 Proportion of in-school and out-of-school children in different social groups.

picture where they generally have the highest representation in educational institutions. However, the upper-caste Hindu's representation itself is low in this group, and those who are represented seem to be among the poorest, earning less than 10,000 rupees (136.71 USD) per month. OBCs and SCs have almost equal representation and also similar economic status in terms of income distribution (Table 9.8). The OBCs are politically and socially more powerful, and this may be reflected in their aspirations for their children. However, the same assertion is not reflected for girls, as both SCs and OBCs report gender disparity against girls (Table 9.9). Muslims, other than General or upper-caste Hindus, are the only group for whom the proportion of girls is notably higher among the in-school children compared to boys. This perhaps reflects the fact that many Muslim boys start working early, especially in vocations where there is a demand for traditional skill-based jobs (Jha and Jhingran 2005).

Income alone, however, does not play a decisive role in decision-making about the child's schooling. For instance, construction and hospitality workers, with the highest average monthly income, have the highest share (35 per cent and 24 per cent respectively) of out-of-school children in their families (Table 9.10). On the other hand, garment and domestic workers, despite lower

Table 9.8 Social Group-Wise Distribution of Migrant Workers across Income Classes (Indian Rupees per Month)

Caste/community	< 10,000	11,000–19,000	> 20,000
ST	11 (50.0)	10 (45.4)	1 (4.5)
SC	66 (47.5)	69 (49.6)	4 (2.9)
OBCs	57 (46.3)	58 (47.1)	8 (6.5)
General	21 (55.3)	13 (34.2)	4 (10.5)
Muslims	17 (40.5)	24 (57.1)	1 (2.4)
Total	174 (47.1)	176 (47.7)	19 (5.1)

Table 9.9 Social Group and Gender Per cent Distribution of In- and Out-of-School Children of Migrant Workers

Social groups	In school		Out of school	
	Male	Female	Male	Female
ST	50	50	50	50
SC	58.3	41.7	44.7	55.3
OBCs	51.2	48.8	64.3	35.7
General	35	65	28.6	71.4
Muslims	47.2	52.8	81.8	18.2
Total	52.8	47.2	52.6	47.4

Table 9.10 Occupation-wise Per cent Distribution of In- and Out-of-School Children of Migrant Workers

Type of occupation	In school	Out of school
Construction workers	64.7	35.3
Garments workers	86.4	13.6
Security workers	97.1	2.9
Hospitality workers	76.3	23.7
Domestic help workers	84.9	15.1

average monthly income, have almost 85 per cent children going to educational institutions. One distinguishing feature of these two sectors is that women far outnumber men, and therefore, one may surmise that women's work outside home has a positive relationship with children's education. This hypothesis appears to be further supported when we look at parents' aspirations for their children, discussed later.

We found that construction and hospitality sectors had a relatively higher presence of inter-state migrants, and workers in these two sectors are more likely to stay with co-workers and friends rather than their families. Single male migration was evidently higher in these two sectors. In contrast, garment factory workers and domestic helps mostly stayed with their families and had higher number of intra-state migrants. This suggests that potential reasons for the greater presence of out-of-school children in the first two sectors (despite higher income) could also be associated with lack of access to public education due to language differences or lack of parental presence and support when the children remain in their communities of origin.

The desire to have a salaried profession for their children was high among all those migrant workers who expressed their aspirations, but this was higher for the garment and domestic sector workers. The aspirations for boys were definitely higher in terms of more secure and higher-income jobs, except for women-concentrated garment and domestic sector workers where they wanted both their boys and girls to have secure and high-income jobs. Migration has, however, does not appear to have had an impact on their aspirations for children, as an overwhelming 94 per cent answered, 'yes' when asked, 'whether their aspirations for their children would have been the same if they had not come to Bangalore?' For the small proportion who attributed the change in their aspirations to their migration, this was linked with the 'possibility of making it happen through education'; in other words, the potential of education to enable upward mobility became apparent after coming to the city. Coming to the city also expanded their knowledge of professions and information regarding the 'choices that one could exercise'.

Does this mean the place of residence does not matter? Is there no difference between schooling status of children residing with their families in Bangalore and those living back home? Our data show that it is not true; the place of residence does matter, especially for girls. Eighty-one per cent of children who lived with their families in Bangalore were in-school as against 73 per cent of children living in their respective villages. Nearly 28 per cent girls living in the state of origin were out of school as compared to 18 per cent of girls living in Bangalore (Table 9.11).

These differences are not found when comparing intra- and inter-state migrants, where the proportions of children in and out of school were very similar (Table 9.12).

We saw earlier that while the knowledge of local language varied significantly between intra-state and inter-state migrant workers, access to public services was only slightly better for intra-state migrants. This, however, does not fully hold true for access to schooling as a larger proportion of those who can speak at least a little of the local language are in school (Table 9.13). This becomes clearer

Table 9.11 Per cent Children by Place of Residence, Gender and Schooling Status

Child's place of stay	In school			Out of school			Grand total
	Male	Female	Total	Male	Female	Total	
Living with family in Bangalore	80.1	82.0	81.0	19.9	18.0	19.0	67.9
Living with family in the state of origin	75.0	72.1	73.5	25.0	27.9	26.5	32.1
Grand total	78.6	78.5	78.6	21.4	21.5	21.4	100.0

Table 9.12 Origin of Migration, Gender and Schooling Status in Per cent

Place	In school			Out of school			Grand total
	Male	Female	Total	Male	Female	Total	
Intra-state	77.8	79.1	78.4	22.2	20.9	21.6	40.7
Inter-state	79.3	78.1	78.7	20.7	21.9	21.3	59.3
Grand total	78.6	78.5	78.6	21.4	21.5	21.4	100.0

Note: The total percentages show the percentage as of the total numbers within the respective category, and the male–female percentages show distribution within the respective totals.

Table 9.13 Parental Language (Kannada) and Status of Schooling in Per cent

Fluency in Kannada	In school	Out of school
I don't know	64.9	35.1
I can understand	65.0	35.0
I can speak a little	90.5	9.5
I can speak fluently	81.9	18.1
I can read and/or write	94.7	5.3
Total	78.6	21.4

when one analyses the distribution of school-going children between public and private schools. More than two-thirds of the school-going children attend public schools (68 per cent) while the remaining one-third go to private schools (32 per cent), but the proportion in private schools is higher for those who don't know Kannada (Table 9.14). The choice for private school is also high for those who can read and write, but the proportion of such respondents was less than 1 per cent of the sample. Although the RTE Act 2009 and the New Education Policy, 2020, promote the use of mother tongue as the medium of instruction, this is often interpreted as the use of the official local language. That this is not necessarily the mother tongue for a good section of children from marginalized communities is rarely paid any attention.

Language alone does not determine the choice of public or private schooling among migrants; affordability also matters as private schools are fee-charging schools. The proportion of in-school children goes up with average monthly income (Figure 9.8) and so does the proportion of those going to private school (Figure 9.9). The lure of private school is not limited to or pushed by the lack of knowledge of the local language alone. The attraction and demand for English-medium schooling is high in India, even among the poorest, backed by a justified rationale that it opens up opportunities for upward mobility. However, more

Table 9.14 Parental Language (Kannada) and Choice of Schooling for In-School Children in Percentage

Fluency in Kannada	Publicly funded school	Private school
I don't know	66.0	34.0
I can understand	53.8	46.2
I can speak a little	73.7	26.3
I can speak fluently	70.4	29.6
I can read and/or write	50.0	50.0
Total	67.8	32.2

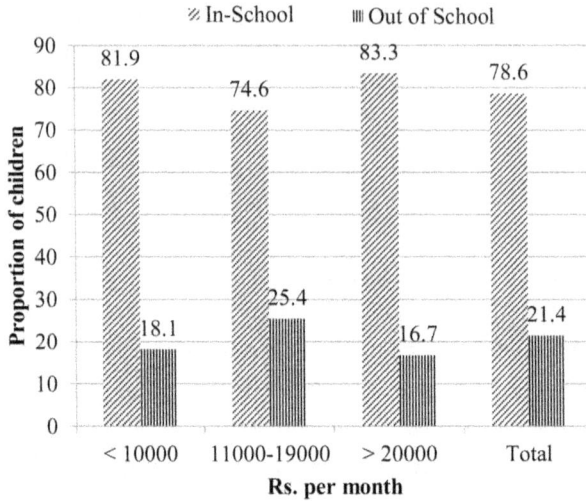

Figure 9.8 Monthly income and schooling status of their children.

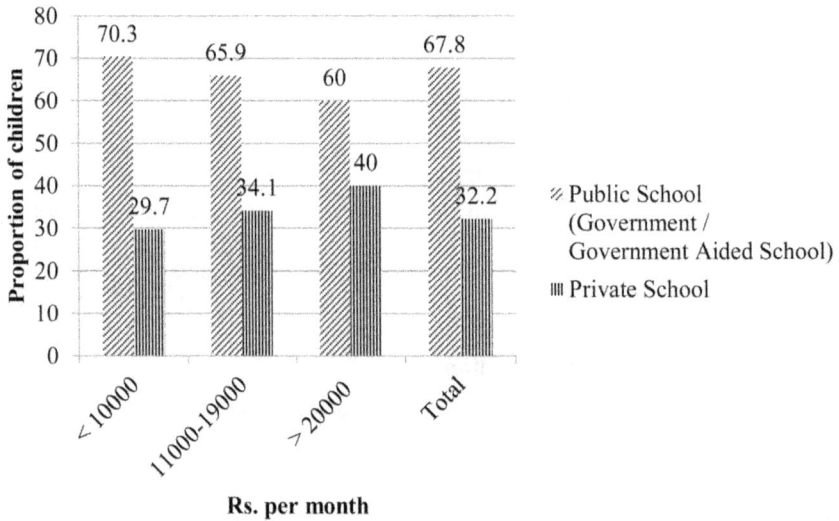

Figure 9.9 Monthly income and distribution of in-school children between public and private schools.

often than not, it is also common to offer poor quality education by charging affordable fees and admitting children from this aspiring, yet vulnerable, group (Chowdhury 2019).

It is important to recognize that so-called free public education is also not fully free. However, it still remains much more affordable compared to private school. The average per child expenditure for those attending private schools in our sample was more than ten times higher than that for those attending public schools (Table 9.15). This difference exists both for those who live in Bangalore and those who stay back home, but the average per child expenditure is significantly higher for both public and private schools in Bangalore as compared to the places of origin. Fees constitute nearly 70 per cent of total expenditure in the case of private schools in Bangalore compared to 45 per cent back home. But those in private schools back home spend more on transportation perhaps due to their rural locations and distance from school, and on additional tuition, perhaps because of the absence of educated family members to support at home.

Impact of Covid-19 on Livelihood, Income and Education

While Covid-19 and lockdowns imposed have had a devastating impact on the lives of workers in the informal sector across India, the impact on migrant lives has been even greater because of the absence of social support systems and the suddenness of lockdown that left them stranded at their workplaces (Kumar and Choudhury 2021). Among our survey participants, 65 per cent mentioned that they lost the jobs they held during the lockdown. When asked about the problems they faced during the lockdown, 41 per cent mentioned loss of employment and 12 per cent mentioned lack of sufficient food (Table 9.16).

After the lockdown was relaxed, nearly 29 per cent of the respondents chose to go back to their place of origin. The primary reasons for this were absence of any work (61 per cent), a wish to be with family during a time of difficulty (23 per cent), the inability to pay for food and other basic expenses (16 per cent) and the inability to pay rent (11 per cent). However, as we surveyed these migrants in Bangalore, it is evident that they had chosen to come back once the situation improved. Primary reasons for their choosing to return to Bangalore were lack of any employment at their native places (58 per cent) and the availability of better payment in Bangalore (49 per cent). This shows the precariousness of migrant workers' existence at destination centres where any economic shock has the potential to upset the stability and security they have gained through years of struggle. However, faced with the pressure on scarce resources in their native places, they often have no option but to pursue such employment.

Around 18 per cent of our respondents mentioned that their children had been attending online classes during the pandemic, which is higher than what other studies have reported regarding children's ability to access online education in rural India (CBPS 2020). Only 8 per cent mentioned that they were not able

Table 9.15 Spending on Education in Rupees per Child

Type of spending	Living in Bangalore			Living back home			All		
	Public school	Private school	Total	Public school	Private school	Total	Public school	Private school	Total
Fees	84	1,987	796	21	754	249	63	1,662	631
Uniform, books, notebooks	148	666	342	109	408	202	135	598	300
Transport	16	48	28	0	158	49	11	77	34
Extra tuition	16	115	53	59	158	90	30	126	64
Others	1	42	16	4	217	70	2	88	32
Total spending on education	265	2,857	1,235	192	1,695	660	241	2,551	1,062
Number of children	112	67	179	53	24	77	165	91	256

Table 9.16 Problems Faced during Lockdown between March and June 2020

Problems faced	Proportion (%)
Lack of sufficient food	12
Lack of sufficient space	1
Lack of money	27
Threat of eviction	2
Loss of employment	41
Others	4

to attend classes because of various problems such as lack of a device or internet network. Ten per cent mentioned that their child was engaged in housework and only 8 per cent had been studying on their own during the period. However, an overwhelming 76 per cent also mentioned that their child spent time simply roaming around or doing nothing when their schools/colleges were closed. This poses a real risk, as these children are highly vulnerable to trafficking or abuse (Global Fund for Children 2019).

The fact that migrant workers returned from their homes in search of employment and better income despite facing tremendous difficulties in sustaining their lives and livelihoods during the pandemic and the lockdown in 2020 reflects their precarious lives where they are forced to take similar risks again, as occurred during the rise of the second wave of the pandemic while we were still conducting our survey. This is despite the fact that these risks rarely translate into any kind of stable and secure livelihood or decent income. Still, the income they generate does allow them to send money back home for their families and extended families. On an average, respondents were remitting about one-fourth of their monthly income to their families back home. Hospitality workers and construction workers, who are mostly living with co-workers and friends, remit even higher proportions (41 and 31 per cent respectively) of their income (Table 9.17). More often than not, this remittance is at the cost of spending a low amount on their own living in the city, as discussed earlier. Since the primary objective for migrant workers is economic, and since opportunities to earn decently are limited for unskilled workers, many of them live in suboptimal conditions in order to reduce living costs at the destination city and save enough to be able to send money back home, partly to educate children there.

The average amount spent on children's education is around 7 per cent of their total income. This ranged between 4 and 9 per cent of income for workers in different sectors (Table 9.17). The average annual expense on education for respondents in our sample was Rs 12,747 which was slightly higher than

Table 9.17 Average Monthly Income in Rupees and Expenditure of Migrant Workers

Type of occupations	Income of respondent	% Total basic living expenditure*	% Disposable income	% Remittance	% Education of children
Construction workers	13,259	6,072 (46)	7,186 (54)	4,141 (31)	845 (6)
Garments workers	9,867	5,393 (55)	4,473 (45)	373 (4)	807 (8)
Security workers	12,593	8,389 (67)	4,204 (33)	1,010 (8)	572 (4)
Hospitality workers	12,740	3,993 (31)	8,746 (69)	5,254 (41)	822 (6)
Domestic help workers	5,228	4,702 (90)	526 (10)	207 (4)	470 (9)
Average	11,096	5,412 (49)	5,683 (51)	2,716 (24)	742 (7)

* Includes personal share of rent, food, travel, utilities and personal expenses.

Note: Figures in parentheses show the respective amounts as percentage of total income.

the spending reported in the 2017–18 NSS survey on Household Social Consumption.[7] This shows that even in difficult circumstances, with insecurities and facing high levels of vulnerability, migrants are spending a significant percentage of their income on children's education.

Conclusions

While it is undeniable that internal migrants lead a precarious existence in places of destination, data from our study clearly indicate that their circumstances might be somewhat better than what they have access to 'back home' in terms of the income they earn and the disposable cash they have. This was evident when migrants chose to come back to the city despite having faced innumerable problems during the pandemic. Although they always had high aspirations for their children, their responses suggest that migration has brought greater potential for them to realize these dreams.

We also see that the pathways through which migration impacts education might not be homogeneous for all migrants. Higher incomes do not necessarily translate into economic security or more investment in education for children, as was seen in case of construction and hospitality workers in our sample. The cost of living, living conditions and lack of access to public education due to constraints of language may all act as hindrances for long-distance inter-state migrants in enabling their children to have a better education.

It is also evident that the security gained through migration is vulnerable to economic shocks. There are systemic barriers that keep those living in poverty excluded from accessing social security, further enhanced by cultural and language differences, making migrant lives insecure and vulnerable. The employment loss of 65 per cent seen during the first wave of lockdown, for instance, would certainly impact our respondents' ability to continue to invest in their children's education.

Public policy and governance in such a situation need to take these unique vulnerabilities into account. Public housing, access to free medical care and education are basic entitlements that must be addressed. India and its cities are at a juncture when both the cities and the migrant workers need each other. Taking cognizance of the unique needs of migrant workers and addressing such needs to make public services, including education, more inclusive are imperative. The choice for schooling is a long-term commitment, and migration to cities has helped parents to understand the potential of education as a means to upward mobility, while giving them the means, even though limited, to realize that potential. But given the vulnerability and uncertainties in their lives and the fragility of their livelihoods, strengthening their access to social securities and public services through appropriate institutional processes is essential to ensure that their commitment to education does not fall through midway.

Notes

1   All the authors are researchers associated with the Centre for Budget and Policy Studies, Bangalore (www.cbps.in), India, and the study was funded by an internal grant. The authors wish to thank and acknowledge the significant contributions of colleagues: Sridhar R. Prasad, Vivek P. Nair and Atul Kumar.
2   This survey was to start in March 2020 when the first wave of Covid-19 started in India, leading to strict countrywide two-month lockdown. Thereafter, the fear of the likely second wave kept it on hold, and finally when we started the survey in March 2021, the second wave really engulfed us so badly that we had to stop the survey midway after covering 369, instead of the planned 500, respondents.
3   All figures and tables are sourced from the survey conducted by us unless otherwise mentioned.
4   https://www.hindustantimes.com/india-news/number-theory-how-much-does-an -average-indian-earn-101610760612856.html.
5   We took 14–18 years as age group instead of 14–17 years for the secondary and senior secondary years, as it is common for students to be a little older due to dissimilar school calendars as well as late start of schooling/grades being repeated.
6   The GER for India for 2018 (latest available) was 96.9, 80.0 and 56.2 for elementary, secondary and senior secondary stages (https://www.education.gov.in/sites/upload _files/mhrd/files/statistics-new/ESAG-2018.pdf).
7   https://accountabilityindia.in/blog/boys-still-preferred-in-families-education -spending-decisions/?utm_source=rss&utm_medium=rss&utm_campaign=boys -still-preferred-in-families-education-spending-decisions.

References

Bhagat, R. B. (2017). 'Migration and Urban Transition in India: Implications for Development', in *Population Division, Department of Economic and Social Affairs.* UN. https://www.un.org/en/development/desa/population/events/pdf/expert/27/ papers/V/paper-Bhagat-final. pdf (accessed 18 October 2021).

CBPS (2019). 'Whose Fate and Whose Wealth? An Analysis of the Bhagyalakshmi Scheme in Karnataka'. http://cbps.in/wp-content/uploads/An-analysis-of-the -Bhagyalakshmi-scheme-in-Karnataka-Report-6Jan2021-1.pdf (accessed 18 October 2021).

CBPS (2020). 'Life in the Time of Covid-19'. http://cbps.in/wp-content/uploads/Report -Final-1.pdf (accessed 18 October 2021).

Chowdhury, S. R. (2019). '"Huge Mismatch" Between What Indian Parents Seek from Private Schools and What They Get, Finds Study', *Scroll.in*, 4 January. https://scroll .in/article/905489/huge-mismatch-between-what-indian-parents-seek-from-private -schools-and-what-they-get-finds-study (accessed 18 October 2021).

Deshingkar, P. (2006). 'Internal Migration, Poverty and Development in Asia: Including the Excluded', *Institute of Development Studies*, 37(3), 88–100.

Global Fund for Children (2019). 'Scan of Issue Areas, Trends and Organisations Working in the Area of Child Trafficking in India'. https://globalfundforchildren .org/wp-content/uploads/2019/11/Toast-Advisory-India-Anti-Trafficking-Mapping -Report.pdf (accessed 18 October 2021).

Government of Kerala (2013). 'Domestic Migrant Labour in Kerala Report', Labour and Rehabilitation Department Gulati Institute of Finance and Taxation.

Jha, J., & Jhingran, D. (2005). *Elementary Education for the Poorest and Other Deprived Groups: The Real Challenge of Universalization*. New Delhi: Manohar Publish.

Jha, J., & Minni, P. (2019). 'Bridging Old Gaps, Building New Barriers: A Study on Online Admissions under the Right to Education Act', *Bangalore Urban Private Unaided Schools Education & the Urban in India,* Max Weber Stiftung.

Kumar, S., & Choudhury, S. (2021). 'Migrant Workers and Human Rights: A Critical Study on India's Covid-19 Lockdown Policy', *Social Sciences & Humanities Open*, 3(1), 1–8. https://doi.org/10.1016/j.ssaho.2021.100130.

Litchfield, J., Mahmood, R., Siddiqui, T., Egger, E. M., & Ansari, S. (2015). 'Migration and Social Networks: Evidence from Bangladesh', *Migrating out of Poverty*, 15 September. https://assets.publishing.service.gov.uk/media/57a0899740f0b64 974000174/WP31_Litchfield.pdf (accessed 18 October 2021).

Mishra, D. K. (2020). 'Seasonal Migration and Unfree Labour in Globalising India: Insights from Field Surveys in Odisha', *The Indian Journal of Labour Economics*, 63, 1087–106. https://doi.org/10.1007/s41027-020-00277-8

Munshi, K. (2020). 'Social Networks and Migration', *Annual Review of Economics*, 12(1), 503–24. https://doi.org/10.1146/annurev-economics-082019-031419.

Pani, N. (2018). 'The Permanence of Temporary Workers', *The Hindu Business Line*, January 20. https://www.thehindubusinessline.com/todays-paper/tp-opinion/the -permanence-of-temporary-workers/article8757406.ece (accessed 18 October 2021).

Pani, N. (2020). 'Thirty Years of Liberalisation: An Idea of Growth Powered by Migrant Workers', *The Wire*. https://thewire.in/labour/thirty-years-of-liberalisation-the -volatility-of-migrant-worker-based-growth.

Rao, N. (2010). *Migration, Education and Socio-Economic Mobility*. Canada: Routledge.

Roy, A. K., Singh, P., & Roy, U.N. (2015). 'Impact of Rural-urban Labour Migration on Education of Children: A Case Study of Left behind and Accompanied Migrant Children in India', *Space and Culture, India*, 2(4), 17–34. https://doi.org/10.20896/saci.v2i4.74.

Schapiro, K. A. (2009). 'Migration and Educational Outcomes of Children', *Human Development Reports*, 13 October. hdr.undp.org/en/content/migration-and-educational-outcomes-children (accessed 18 October 2021).

Smita, S. (2008). *Distress Seasonal Migration and its Impact on Children's Education*. Consortium for Research on Educational Access, Transitions and Equity. https://assets.publishing.service.gov.uk/media/57a08ba5e5274a27b2000c8b/PTA28.pdf (accessed 18 October 2021).

Srivastava, R. (2011). 'Internal Migration in India: An Overview of its Features, Trends and Policy Challenges', paper presented at National Workshop on Internal Migration and Human Development, Workshop Compendium Vol. 2. New Delhi: UNESCO and UNICEF, 1–47.

10

Internal Migration and the Educational and Social Impacts on Children Left Behind in Rural China

Xiaopeng Pang and Ziyuan Lu

Introduction

Internal rural–urban migration is considered one of the main ways to reduce poverty and a primary feature of economic development in low- and middle-income countries. Migration out of agriculture is also generally associated with improved living standards for migrant families. Outmigration can lead to increased investment in assets related to agricultural production and other investments in source communities (de Brauw and Giles 2008).

However, the effects of migration on source households and family members can be complex. For instance, one or both parents migrating out for work while leaving their children home with one parent or other relatives is very common in developing countries (Reyes 2008; Tarroja and Fernando 2013). When children remain behind, some research suggests they risk facing negative effects on their education, health and, ultimately, overall human capital accumulation (Meyerhoefer and Chen 2011; Zhao et al. 2014).

In China, migrating from rural to urban areas has been seen as an essential way to increase income and improve welfare since the 1980s (Du et al. 2005). The number of internal migrants has increased dramatically in the past decades, from about 6.6 million in 1982 to 244 million in 2017, 17 per cent of the total population.[1] It is common for migrant parents to leave their children behind in their home communities because of financial constraints, the absence of social services and the transient nature of work in urban areas (Duan and Zhou 2005).

Large-scale rural to urban migration has resulted in the phenomenon known in China as left-behind children (LBCs). These are children under the age of eighteen, who live in their original domicile, but do not live together with their parents, as either one parent or both parents have migrated for more than six months. In 2005 there were an estimated 73.31 million of them, 80 per cent of whom were living in rural areas (National Bureau of Statistics of China et al. 2017).

The overall goal of this chapter is to examine the lives and circumstances of 'left-behind' children through a systematic review of existing research in order to develop a better understanding of what is known about migration and its impact on their education and well-being in the context of China. The chapter is structured in three parts. First, we describe the background, origin and magnitude of LBCs in rural China. Second, we systematically document quantitative empirical studies which have examined the impact of migration on education and well-being of LBCs. In the last section, we consider the implications of our findings and indicate future research directions.

Background on Internal Migration and Left-behind Children in Rural China

China is a compelling place to study internal migration and its consequences for LBCs in rural areas for several reasons. First, China has unprecedented labour migration, with dramatic increases in the number of migrants in the past decades (Zhang 2000). Second, the left-behind population in China is to a large extent an outcome of institutional processes (Xiang 2007), in particular the long-standing bifurcated social institution which is usually called *hukou* (the residential registration system). The system categorizes all citizens into a rural–urban dichotomy, which has led to various structural and social barriers in migrants' access to public services in urban areas. Third, there is a strongly centralized education system which provides limited opportunities for rural migrant children.

Internal Migration and Family Decision-making

Internal migration in China was strictly controlled during the planned economy era by the *hukou* system, which categorizes people by both place (rural or urban) and type (agricultural or non-agricultural) of residency. Almost no rural resident could move to urban areas during 1958 to 1978 because the rigid *hukou* system was designed to strictly control population flows into cities. The initial *hukou* reform took place in 1988, establishing a mechanism for rural migrants to obtain legal temporary residence (LTR) in urban areas (Mallee 1995). After rural migrants could obtain LTR, they became better able to establish networks to facilitate the job search in distant labour markets (e.g. Munshi 2003).

The number of rural migrants moving to work in urban areas has soared since the *hukou* system underwent further relaxation in the 1990s (Mallee 1995). Estimates using the 1 per cent sample from the 1990 and 2000 rounds of the Population Census and the 1995 1 per cent population survey suggest that the inter-county migrant population grew from just over 20 million in 1990 to 45 million in 1995 and 78 million by 2000 (Liang and Ma 2004). Surveys conducted by the National Bureau of Statistics (NBS) and the Ministry of Agriculture, which include more detailed information on short-term migration, suggest that there were well over 100 million migrants by the early 2000s (Cai et al. 2008). During the first decade in the twenty-first century, this number doubled, increasing from 79 million in 2001 to 153 million in 2010, accounting for 12 per cent of the Chinese population.

While in the past decade the rate of increase of rural–urban migration has fallen (Figure 10.1), the total number of migrants is still huge.

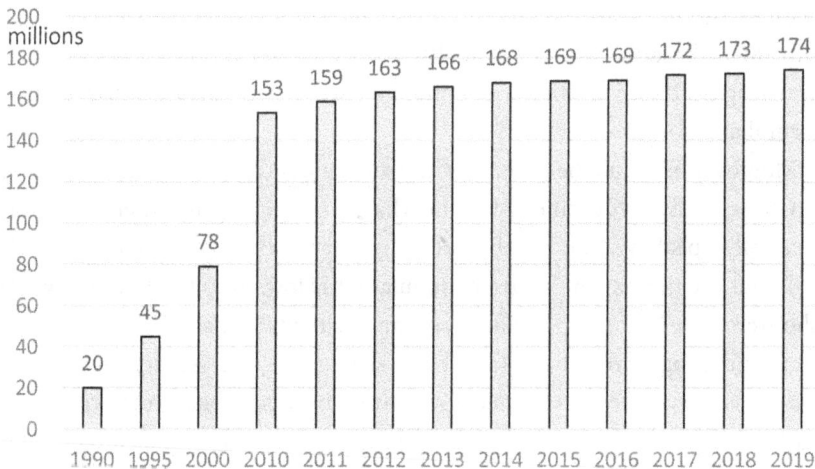

Figure 10.1 The number of rural–urban migrants. *Sources*: Data for 1990 and 2000 comes from the National Population Census; data for 1995 comes from the 1 per cent National Population Sample Survey. Other data comes from the Monitoring Reports of Rural Migrant Workers. The NBS of China.

In China, when rural residents make the decision to move to the city, they need to consider many things in relation to family members. One of the most basic decisions they need to make is whether their children should live and go to schools in their hometowns or move with them and attend schools in the city.

Under the long-standing *hukou* system in China, without urban household registration status, they face difficulties finding employment, procuring proper housing or registering their children for city schools (Cheng and Selden 1994). Even though rural migrants have been able to obtain LTR since 1990s, this status does not guarantee them access to urban health and education services or social safety nets because these benefits are still linked to *hukou* status (World Bank 2009).

In this context, when migrant parents have made the decision to bring their child to the city, the next decision (which is often out of their control) is to put children into urban public schools or to enrol them into private, for-profit so called migrant schools that have emerged for the very reason of educating migrant children. Although facilities in these schools are not always poor, tuition costs can be high. Moreover, teacher turnover is often high and there is little, if any, regulation or oversight by urban education officials. In general, there is reason to believe that the quality of education in migrant schools may be low (Wang et al. 2017). Furthermore, migrant workers often have low incomes, live in crowded living conditions and cannot afford to bring children with them. Because of these difficulties and the high costs of schooling and arranging child care in cities, many migrant parents leave their children behind in rural areas.

Moreover, it should be noted that the movement of rural labourers to cities in China is distinctly different from what is happening in other countries. Generally speaking, the number of temporary urban workers in China is high, but the permanent 'migrant' population is low. Very few of the migrant labourers can become permanent urban residents. This is largely because rural and urban areas have long been segregated with separate economic and social structures. As for most migrant workers, urban areas are merely workplaces, not homes (Jingzhong and Lu 2011). Most of China's migration is by individuals instead of entire families. These temporary migrant flows to and from the urban and rural areas seasonally are often compared to migratory birds. Meanwhile, as migrants have no choice but to leave some of their family members behind, a unique 'left-behind' population of women, children and the elderly has formed in rural areas.

Education Policies and Internal Migration in China

Due to the institutional segregation between rural and urban areas through the *hukou* system, whether one lives in an urban or a rural area is crucial in determining educational opportunities in China (Knight and Li 1996). Rural areas are characterized by relatively high educational costs, limited and lower-quality educational opportunities, and a strong gender bias favouring boys' education (Hannum and Park 2007). Although the compulsory education law stipulates that six years of primary school and three years of middle-school public education must be tuition free, education in China has never been completely free, and educational expenses (e.g. uniforms, books and supplies) shouldered by parents have continued to rise (Tsang 2000). This situation becomes more pronounced at the middle-school level, where fees are often more than twice as high as at the primary level. Educational expenses are even higher at the high school level, where compulsory schooling ends (Lu 2012). Although since 2000 the central Chinese government has ordered local governments to enforce the provision of nine years of compulsory education in rural areas free of charge, this goal has yet to be fully achieved (Lu 2012).

One measure adopted by rural local governments in order to achieve the goal of compulsory education was to restructure public primary and middle schools at county level, with the effect of closing many village primary and junior middle schools. According to statistical data from the Ministry of Education of China, the number of rural primary schools was reduced by half from 1997 to 2009. Schools located in township and county seats, which have better facilities and more qualified teachers, were built or enlarged to accept students from villages. Moreover, both central and local governments developed policies to provide additional educational support for rural children from migrant families. For example, since 2004, the central government implemented a project to build boarding schools in rural west and central provinces to ensure that school-age children who live in remote villages with no local school could attend school.

The Law of Compulsory Education (issued in 1986) requires that all children should have free access to schools until the ninth grade. Before 1996 migrant children were prohibited from enrolling in state city schools but subsequently admitted on an experimental basis. According to government requirements, urban public schools should accept migrant children when their parents' have jobs near the school. However, the education budget for compulsory education in China is allocated through local governments and is not transferable. This means that local governments have no incentives to share their resources with those without urban *hukou* registration, and urban schools with a limited education budget are reluctant to accept rural migrant children unless their parents compensate for the additional costs. As a result, although rural migrant children are no longer officially denied access to urban public schools, parents are requested to pay 'education endorsement fees' for children attending school in places other than their place of household registration, and these fees can be prohibitive for poor migrant families. Therefore, although policies have varied over time regarding how welcome migrant children are to enrol in urban public schools, the fact is that a large proportion of migrant children are still not able to attend public schools in many of China's large cities (Chen and Feng 2013; Lai et al. 2014) and can only go to either private schools in cities by paying a high tuition fee, which most migrant workers cannot afford, or to 'migrant schools', which are usually run by local entrepreneurs with a subsidized fee (Wu and Zhang 2017).

Another education policy which affects migrants is that students are required to take the college entrance examination (CEE) in their *hukou* registration area. This means that, even if migrant parents are able to bring their children to the city and enrol them in an urban school, when these students finish senior high school, they must go back to the place of their *hukou* registration to take the CEE. Moreover, the textbook and examination requirements are very different between destination cities and rural source communities. As a consequence, all migrant children must return to their *hukou* registration area for middle school unless they don't plan to take the CEE.

Rural Left-behind Children and Their Living Arrangements

Children remaining behind in rural areas when their parents migrate for work has been a phenomenon since the mid-1980s, and their numbers have increased alongside the expansion of rural urban migration since the 1990s. However, it was not until 2004, when a series of tragic events, including abuse, suicide and accidents, were reported in the press, that these children came to the attention of the public and the policy community.

Although at least three institutes collect data on LBCs and their reported number varies, all estimates suggest that the number is in the multimillions. According to data from the NBS of China, 58.6 million children, accounting for 70 per cent of rural children, were affected by parental migration in 2005.

Table 10.1 Rural Children Affected by Migration (Millions)

Year	Rural LBCs	Migrant children	% of Rural LBCs/children affected by migration
2000	27.0	19.8	57.7
2005	58.6	25.3	69.8
2010	48.3	35.8	57.4
2015	40.5	34.3	54.1

Source: The 1 per cent National Population Sample Survey (also called 'mini-census') conducted by the NBS of China in 2005 and 2015, as well as from previous Population Censuses in 2000 and 2010 (National Bureau of Statistics of China et al. 2017).

Table 10.2 Structure of Rural Left-behind Children's Families (%)

Year	2000	2015
Living with father	10.5	20.4
Living with mother	33.3	30.6
Living with grandparents	20.6	26.3
Living alone	4.4	3.3
Living with other children	–	7.0
Living with other adults	–	12.5

Source: Data for 2000 is re-calculated by authors based on the estimation of Duan and Zhou 2005; data for 2015 comes from the National Bureau of Statistics of China et al. 2017.

In 2015, the number came down to 40.5 million, representing 54.1 per cent of the children of rural migrant parents (Table 10.1).

As for living arrangements, in 2015, 51 per cent of the LBCs lived with one of their parents, 26.3 per cent lived with grandparents and 12.5 per cent lived with other adults. Another 10.3 per cent were left alone or lived with other children. Compared with the situation in 2000, the percentage of LBCs living with father and grandparents increased, while the percentage of LBCs living with mother and other children and adults decreased (Table 10.2). Living with mother is the main living arrangement among migrant families, while grandparents are the main caregivers of LBCs where both parents migrate.

Different child-rearing arrangements may have different effects on children's development. For instance, the average age of grandparents who are main caregivers of LBCs when both parents migrated was sixty years, with more than half having completed only primary-level education. The majority, in addition to taking care of their grandchildren, worked and were responsible for ensuring their household's livelihood. For the LBCs who lived alone or with other children, safety, health, living and learning conditions are of particular concern. Meanwhile, although the Chinese government has given subsidies to establish boarding schools for educating rural LBCs since 2011, very little empirical research has explored the impacts of this measure.

Impact of Migration on the Education and Health of Left-behind Children

According to statistics of the Ministry of Education, one-third of LBC are enrolled in compulsory education (Li et al. 2017) and the education of LBCs has attracted considerable attention from many researchers since 2004. In recent years, researchers have also paid increasing attention to the health of LBCs as well as other measures of well-being, including life satisfaction and time use. However, the results are mixed as the impact of migration on children's education depends on many different factors, such as age and sex of the child, duration of parents leaving homes and parental migration patterns. In this section, we systematically review quantitative empirical studies which use multi-regression analysis methods to examine the impact of migration on education and well-being of LBCs in rural China.

A number of steps were taken to identify literature for this review: First, a search was conducted of literature written in English from the Web of Science, by using the search terms 'left-behind children' and 'China'. This produced 185 articles published between 2006 and 2020. Second, all literature which uses rigid regression analysis method to estimate the impact of different parental migration pattern on rural LBCs' educational outcomes, physical health, mental health and well-being was selected. This produced thirty-one articles. Third, the same key words were used to search articles from database of Springer, Wiley Online Library, Elsevier Science Direct, JSTOR and EBSCO, and selected using the same criteria. This produced an additional five articles. In total, we reviewed the thirty-six articles to examine the impact of different types of parental migration on rural LBCs' educational outcomes, health and lives. We classify parental migration into four types: one (either) parent migrated, mother migrated, father migrated and both parents migrated. We further document the impact on children's education by their grade and sex.

We recognize that there are some limitations to this approach in that the analysis only included quantitative studies and those that were reported in English. As a result, the review is limited with respect to offering the sorts of explanations of the quantitative findings which typically emerge from qualitative studies, and may also be limited by the exclusion of other perspectives and insights afforded through studies reported in other relevant languages.

Educational Outcomes

A relatively large share of studies concerned with the relationship between rural LBCs and educational outcomes indicate that parental migration had a negative effect on these children's academic performance measured by scores in both maths and Chinese (Table 10.3). Moreover, the longer the duration of parental absence, the lower the test scores (Zhou et al. 2014). LBCs were reported to have lower academic performance when both parents are absent (Wu and Zhang 2017). However, when only the father migrates out of agriculture, a positive impact can be seen on children's test scores (Chen et al. 2009). Interestingly, Yu Bai et al. (2018) found that no matter whether it is the mother or father or both parents that migrate, the impact on English test scores is positive.

The impact on LBCs' academic performance also varies according to sex and grade. For children in primary school, girls were reported to have lower academic performance than boys (Feng Hu 2013; Wu and Zhang 2017). When junior high school students are included, boys experienced greater negative influence (Meng et al. 2015; Wang and Mao 2018). However, remittances can partially offset this negative influence especially for girls (Feng Hu 2013) by increasing investment in better quality education and enabling girls to attend school by reducing family budget constraints.

Besides the impact on LBCs' academic performance, researchers also found that parental migration has a negative impact on the likelihood of children continuing to senior high school (de Bryant and Giles 2008) and on their timely enrolment in school. Compared with boys, girls are more likely to experience grade-level lag relative to expected progress (Meyerhoefer and Chen 2011), even though boys are more likely to drop out of school (Wang 2014).

Although internal migration can increase rural families' incomes, this does not necessarily enhance the share of spending on education and may mean an increase in expenditure on consumer goods. This is particularly the case among the wealthiest rural households. The reasons for this are that migrant parents may observe low returns to education in the labour market, and so may consider spending more on children's education to be of little

Table 10.3 The Impact on LBCs' Academic Performance

Outcomes	Types of migration				Age and sex of LBCs				References
	At least one	Mother	Father	Both	Primary school	Middle school	Boys	Girls	
Math	X				No				Chen et al. 2009; Zhou et al. 2015; Chang et al. 2019
	X				(−)				Feng Hu 2013; Zhao et al. 2014; Meng et al. 2015; Wu et al. 2017; Wang et al. 2018; Chang et al. 2019
	X					No			Chen et al. 2009; Zhou et al. 2015
	X					(−)			Meng et al. 2015; Wang et al. 2018; Chang et al. 2019
	X						(−)		Feng Hu 2013); Meng et al. 2015; Wang et al. 2018
	X							(−)	Feng Hu 2013; Wu et al. 2017
		X			(−)				Zhao et al. 2014; Xie 2019
		X				(−)			Lili Li et al. 2017; Xie 2019
			X		(−)				Lili Li et al. 2017; Xie 2019
			X			(−)			Lili Li et al. 2017; Xie 2019
			X		(+)				Chen et al. 2009
				X	(−)				Zhou et al. 2014; Wu et al. 2017; Xie 2019
				X		(−)			Zhou et al. 2014; Wu et al. 2017; Lili Li et al. 2017; Xie 2019
				X			(−)		Zhou et al. 2014

						References
Chinese	X		(-)			Feng Hu 2013; Wu et al. 2017; Meng et al. 2015; Wang et al. 2018
	X		No			Zhou et al. 2015; Chen et al. 2009; Wang L. et al. 2019; Chang et al. 2019
	X			(-)		Meng et al. 2015; Wang et al. 2018
	X			No		Chen et al. 2009; Zhou et al. 2015
	X				(-)	Feng Hu 2013; Meng et al. 2015; Wang et al. 2018
	X			No	No	Chen et al. 2009
				No	No	Chen et al. 2009
English	X		(+)			Zhou et al. 2014; Wu et al. 2017
		X	(-)			Zhou et al. 2015; Chang et al. 2019
	X	X	No			
	X	X	(+)			Yu Bai et al. 2017

Note: 'X' indicates the pattern of parental migration; (+) stands for positive effect, (–) stands for negative effect, 'No' means no significant impact.

value (Démurger and Wang 2016). From the perspective of human capital accumulation, internal migration might therefore have a detrimental influence on rural development.

Health Outcomes

Many different variables are used to measure health behaviour, physical health and psychological health outcomes of LBC (column 1 of Table 10.4). The results of the literature review (Table 10.4) show that migration has a significant negative effect on the health of LBCs across all types of parental migration, with the exception of one study which found that pre-school LBCs with migrant fathers have a lower risk of anaemia (Shi et al. 2020).

Some researchers found that boy LBCs were at higher risk of skipping breakfast, higher levels of physical inactivity, internet addiction, having ever smoked tobacco and suicide ideation than boys whose parents had not migrated; and that girl LBCs were more likely to drink excessive amounts of sweetened beverage, to watch more TV, to have ever smoked or currently smoke tobacco than girls whose parents had not migrated (Gao et al. 2010; Wen et al. 2012).

With regard to physical health, the results are not consistent. Li et al. (2015) found that LBCs are 20 per cent more likely to get sick or develop chronic conditions than those living with their parents, and that girls are more vulnerable than boys, and younger children more vulnerable than older children. Xie (2019) reported that only two-parent migration is associated with a slower linear growth rate. However, Mu and de Brauw (2015) found that parental migration has no significant effect on the height of children, and improved their weight. Shi et al. (2020) found that parental migration may even be beneficial to the early childhood (age 6–35 months) nutrition of LBCs. Such inconsistencies might be explained by the difference of outcome variables and the sample sizes used in the different studies.

Studies also suggest that LBCs experience poorer psychological health than children from non-migrant families. Some studies found that parental outmigration had a significant negative impact on the mental health of LBCs, and even when migrant parents return home, children's mental health saw no significant improvement compared to children whose parents never return (Shi et al. 2016). Moreover, LBCs had more depression symptoms (Wang et al. 2019; Wu and Zhang 2017) and higher anxiety levels (Wang et al. 2019).

Table 10.4 The Impact on LBCs' Health Outcomes

| | Types of migration | | | | | Age and sex of LBCs | | | | |
Outcomes	At least one	Mother	Father	Both	Pre-school	Primary school	Middle school	Boys	Girls	References
Skipping breakfast/physical inactivity/internet addiction/overweight	X						(+)			Gao et al. 2010
Smoking	X					(+)	(+)		(+)	Wen and Lin 2012
	X						(+)			Gao et al. 2010; Wen et al. 2012
Drinking/alcoholic	X					(+)	(+)		(+)	Wen et al. 2012
Suicide ideation	X						(+)			Gao et al. 2010
		X	X	X			(+)			Wang et al. 2019
WAZ (weight-for-age z scores)	X				(+)					Mu et al. 2015
Illicit drug	X					(+)	(+)			Wen et al. 2012
Illness	X	X	X	X		(+)	(+)		(+)	Li et al. 2015
HAZ (height-for-age z scores)	X	X	X	X	No					Mu et al. 2015

(continued)

Table 10.4 (Continued) The Impact on LBCs' Health Outcomes

Outcomes	Types of migration				Age and sex of LBCs					References
	At least one	Mother	Father	Both	Pre-school	Primary school	Middle school	Boys	Girls	
BMIZ (BMI-for-age z scores)	X	X	X	X	No					Mu et al. 2015
	X					(-)	(-)		(-)	Wen et al. 2012
Rate of health status	X						(-)			Lu et al. 2020
		X	X			No	No			Xie 2019
				X		(-)	(-)			Xie 2019
Self-esteem	X						(-)			Mao et al. 2012; Sun et al. 2015
Self-assessment				X			(-)			Wu et al. 2017
Depression	X						(+)			Mao et al. 2012; Sun et al. 2015
		X				(+)				Zhou et al. 2018
		X	X	X			(+)			Wang et al. 2019

Variable								Study
MHT (mental health test)	X						(−)	Shi et al. 2016
	X							Chang et al. 2019
Anxiety disorder		X	X			(+)		Wang et al. 2019
Intrinsic motivation		X	X	X		No		Wang, L et al. 2019
Instrumental motivation		X	X	X		No		Wang, L et al. 2019
Anaemia		X	X	X	(−)			Wang, L et al. 2019
							(−)	Shi et al. 2020
BPI (Behaviour Problems Index)	X	X				No		Lu et al. 2019
				X		No		Lu et al. 2019
						(+)		Lu et al. 2019

Note: 'X' indicates the pattern of parental migration; (+) stands for positive effect, (−) stands for negative effect, 'No' means no significant impact.

Table 10.5 The Impact on LBCs' Other Welfare

| Outcomes | Types of migration | | | | Age and sex of LBCs | | | | References |
	At least one	Mother	Father	Both	Primary school	Middle school	Boys	Girls	
Bullying perpetration	X				(+)	(+)			Cui et al. 2019
Emotional well-being	X				(−)	(−)			Ren et al. 2016
Satisfaction with life and study	X				(−)	(−)			Wen et al. 2012
Time of domestic work/ farm work	X				(+)	(+)		(+)	Chang et al. 2011

Note: 'X' indicates the pattern of parental migration; (+) stands for positive effect, (−) stands for negative effect, 'No' means no significant impact.

Childhood Lives (Life Satisfaction, Childhood, Time Use and Labour Supply)

It is not only LBCs' education and health outcomes but also their daily lives that are affected by their parents' migration. Life satisfaction, time use and workload have also been examined by some researchers (Table 10.5), although there are fewer studies than those concerned with education and health. The studies do show that the migration of household members increased the time spent on farm work and domestic work by LBCs, with the increase in work time being greater for girls than boys (Chang et al. 2011). LBCs were also disadvantaged in perceived satisfaction with life and study (Wen and Lin 2012).

Researchers also found that parental migration has a negative impact on the emotional well-being of LBCs (Ren et al. 2016) and made them more likely to engage in bullying perpetration than non-migrant children (Cui et al. 2019).

Conclusion and Implications

In this chapter, we have introduced studies which outline the reported impacts of internal migration on education, health and the childhood lives of rural LBCs in the context of China. We have systematically documented empirical studies which use rigid regression analysis to examine the impact of different types of migration on LBCs' education, health and well-being. Although the results are different for different types of parental migration on left-behind boys and girls at different ages, our analysis shows that, overall, parental migration is reported to have a negative effect on rural LBCs' academic performance, physical and mental health, and their childhood lives.

These results suggest the need for policy to be strengthened in order to secure children's basic education and health rights. Ultimately measures should be promoted to offer the children of internal migrants who live in China's cities better access to urban schools so parents do not have to leave their children behind. Along with economic growth, the reform of the *hukou* system and the enrichment of education resources for migrant children in urban areas would reduce the number of rural LBCs. The limitation to our work is that only materials in English and quantitative research findings are included. This means that it is difficult to account for discrepancies in findings across different quantitative studies and there is limited scope to provide explanations for these findings. So while there are clear strengths to studies employing quantitative regression analyses, mixed-methods approaches to research will be valuable in filling some of the explanatory gaps in our understanding of the impacts of migration on children living in rural China.

Note

1 Data for 1982 comes from the 1 per cent National Population Sample Survey; data for 2017 comes from the report of the National Bureau of Statistics. https://china .unfpa.org/zh-Hans/report/20190816.

References

Bai, Y., Zhang, L., Liu, C., Shi, Y., Mo, D., & Rozelle, S. (2018). 'Effect of Parental Migration on the Academic Performance of Left Behind Children in North Western China', *The Journal of Development Studies*, 54(7), 1154–70.

Cai, F., Park, A., & Zhao, Y. (2008). 'The Chinese Labor Market in the Reform Era', in Loren Brandt & Thomas Rawski (Eds), *China's Great Economic Transformation*. Cambridge: Cambridge University Press, 167–214.

Chang, H., Dong, X.Y., & MacPhail, F. (2011). 'Labor Migration and Time use Patterns of the Left-behind Children and Elderly in Rural China', *World Development*, 39(12), 2199–210.

Chang, F., Shi, Y., Shen, A., Kohrman, A., Li, K., Wan, Q., Kenny, K., & Rozelle, S. (2019). 'Understanding the Situation of China's Left-Behind Children: A Mixed-Methods Analysis', *The Developing Economies*, 57(1), 3–35.

Chen, X., Huang, Q., Rozelle, S., Shi, Y., & Zhang, L. (2009) 'Migration, Money and Mother: The Effect of Migration on Children's Educational Performance in Rural China', *Comparative Economic Studies*, 51, 322–43.

Chen, Y., & Feng, S. (2013). 'Access to Public Schools and the Education of Migrant Children in China', *China Economic Review*, 26(C), 75-88.

Cheng, T., & Selden, M. (1994). 'The Origins and Social Consequences of China's Hukou System', *The China Quarterly*, 139, 644–68.

Cui, K., & To, S.M. (2019). 'Migrant Status, Social Support, and Bullying Perpetration of Children in Mainland China', *Children and Youth Services Review*, 107, 104534.

de Brauw, A., & Giles, J. (2008). *Migrant Opportunity and the Educational Attainment of Youth in Rural China*. Policy Research Working Paper Series; No. 4526. Washington, DC: The World Bank. Https://doi.org/10.1596/1813-9450-4526.

Démurger, S., & Wang, X. (2016). 'Remittances and Expenditure Patterns of the Left Behinds in Rural China', *China Economic Review*, 37, 177–90.

Du, Y., Park, A., & Wang, S. (2005). 'Migration and Rural Poverty in China', *Journal of Comparative Economics*, 33(4), 688–709.

Duan, C., & Zhou, F. (2005). 'A Study on Children Left Behind', *Population Research*, 29(1), 29–36 (in Chinese).

Hu, F. (2013). 'Does Migration Benefit the Schooling of Children Left Behind? Evidence From Rural Northwest China', *Demographic Research*, 29, 33–70.

Gao, Y., Li, L.P., Kim, J.H., Congdon, N., Lau, J., & Griffiths, S. (2010). 'The Impact of Parental Migration on Health Status and Health Behaviours Among Left Behind Adolescent School Children in China', *BMC Public Health*, 10(1), 1–10.

Hannum, E., & Park, A. (Eds). (2007). *Education and Reform in China*. Oxford: Routledge.

Jingzhong, Y., & Lu, P. (2011). 'Differentiated Childhoods: Impacts of Rural Labor Migration on Left-behind Children in China', *The Journal of Peasant Studies*, 38(2), 355–77.

Knight, J., & Shi, L. (1996). 'Educational Attainment and the Rural-urban Divide in China', *Oxford Bulletin of Economics and Statistics*, 58(1), 83–117.

Lai, F., Liu, C., Luo, R., Zhang, L., Ma, X., Bai, Y., Sharbono, B., & Rozelle, S. (2014). 'The Education of China's Migrant Children: The Missing Link in China's Education System', *International Journal of Educational Development*, 37, 68–77.

Li, L., Wang, L., & Nie, J. (2017). 'Effect of Parental Migration on the Academic Performance of Left-behind Middle School Students in Rural China', *China & World Economy*, 25(2), 45–59.

Li, Q., Liu, G., & Zang, W. (2015). 'The Health of Left-behind Children in Rural China', *China Economic Review*, 36, 367–76.

Liang, Z., & Ma, Z. (2004). 'China's Floating Population: new Evidence From the 2000 Census', *Population and Development Review*, 30(3), 467–88.

Lu, Y. (2012). 'Education of Children Left Behind in Rural China', *Journal of Marriage and Family*, 74(2), 328–41.

Lu, W., Zhang, A., & Mossialos, E. (2020). 'Parental Migration and Self-reported Health Status of Adolescents in China: A Cross-sectional Study', *EClinicalMedicine*, 22, 100371.

Lu, Y., Yeung, J. W. J., Liu, J., & Treiman, D. J. (2019). 'Migration and Children's Psychosocial Development in China: When and why Migration Matters', *Social Science Research*, 77, 130–47.

Mallee, H. (1995). 'China's Household Registration System under Reform', *Development and Change*, 26(1), 1–29.

Mao, Z. H., & Zhao, X. D. (2012). 'The Effects of Social Connections on Self-rated Physical and Mental Health Among Internal Migrant and Local Adolescents in Shanghai, China', *BMC Public Health*, 12(1), 1–9.

Meng, X., & Yamauchi, C. (2015). *Children of Migrants: The Cumulative Impact of Parental Migration on Their Children's Education and Health Outcomes* (No. 15-07). National Graduate Institute for Policy Studies.

Meyerhoefer, C.D., & Chen, C.J. (2011). 'The Effect of Parental Labor Migration on Children's Educational Progress in Rural China', *Review of Economics of the Household*, 9(3), 379–96.

Mu, R., & De Brauw, A. (2015). 'Migration and Young Child Nutrition: Evidence From Rural China', *Journal of Population Economics*, 28(3), 631–57.

Munshi, K. (2003). 'Networks in the Modern Economy: Mexican Migrants in the US Labor Market', *The Quarterly Journal of Economics*, 118(2), 549–99.

National Bureau of Statistics of China, UNICEF China, UNFPA China (2017). *Population Status of Children in China in 2015: Facts and Figures*. 1–20.

Ren, Q., & Treiman, D. J. (2016). 'The Consequences of Parental Labor Migration in China for Children's Emotional Wellbeing', *Social Science Research*, 58, 46–67.

Reyes, M. (2008). *Migration and Filipino Children Left Behind: A Literature Review*. Manila: Miriam College-Women and Gender Institute for the United Nations Children's Fund (UNICEF).

Shi, Y., Bai, Y., Shen, Y., Kenny, K., & Rozelle, S. (2016). 'Effects of Parental Migration on Mental Health of Left-behind Children: Evidence From Northwestern China', *China & World Economy*, 24(3), 105–22.

Shi, H., Zhang, J., Du, Y., Zhao, C., Huang, X., & Wang, X. (2020). 'The Association Between Parental Migration and Early Childhood Nutrition of Left-behind Children in Rural China', *BMC Public Health*, 20(1), 1–11.

Sun, X., Tian, Y., Zhang, Y., Xie, X., Heath, M.A., & Zhou, Z. (2015). 'Psychological Development and Educational Problems of Left-behind Children in Rural China', *School Psychology International*, 36(3), 227–52.

Tarroja, M. C. H., & Fernando, K. C. (2013). 'Providing Psychological Services for Children of Overseas Filipino Workers (OFWs): A Challenge for School Psychologists in the Philippines', *School Psychology International*, 34(2), 202–12.

Tsang, M. C. (2000). 'Education and National Development in China Since 1949: Oscillating Policies and Enduring Dilemmas', in L. Chung-Ming & S. Jianfa (Eds), *China Review*. Hong Kong: Chinese University Press, 579–618.

Wang, X., Luo, R., Zhang, L., & Rozelle, S. (2017). 'The Education gap of China's Migrant Children and Rural Counterparts', *The Journal of Development Studies*, 53(11), 1865–81.

Wang, J., Zou, J., Luo, J., Liu, H., Yang, Q., Ouyang, Y., Hu, M., & Lin, Q. (2019a). 'Mental Health Symptoms Among Rural Adolescents With Different Parental Migration Experiences: A Cross-sectional Study in China', *Psychiatry Research*, 279, 222–30.

Wang, L., Zheng, Y., Li, G., Li, Y., Fang, Z., Abbey, C., & Rozelle, S. (2019a). 'Academic Achievement and Mental Health of Left-behind Children in Rural China: A Causal Study on Parental Migration', *China Agricultural Economic Review*, 11(4), 1–160.

Wang, S., Dong, X., & Mao, Y. (2017). 'The Impact of Boarding on Campus on the Social-emotional Competence of Left-behind Children in Rural Western China', *Asia Pacific Education Review*, 18(3), 413–23.

Wang, S., & Mao, Y. (2018). 'The Effect of Boarding on Campus on Left-behind Children's Sense of School Belonging and Academic Achievement: Chinese Evidence From Propensity Score Matching Analysis', *Asia Pacific Journal of Education*, 38(3), 378–93.

Wang, S. X. (2014). 'The Effect of Parental Migration on the Educational Attainment of Their Left-behind Children in Rural China', *The BE Journal of Economic Analysis & Policy*, 14(3), 1037–80.

Wen, M., & Lin, D. (2012). 'Child Development in Rural China: Children Left Behind by Their Migrant Parents and Children of Nonmigrant Families', *Child Development*, 83(1), 120–36.

World Bank (2009). *From Poor Areas to Poor People: China's Evolving Poverty Reduction Agenda*. Washington, DC: World Bank.

Wu, J., & Zhang, J. (2017). 'The Effect of Parental Absence on Child Development in Rural China', *Asian Economic Policy Review*, 12(1), 117–34.

Xie, W. (2019). *Left-Behind Villages, Left-Behind Children: Migration and Child Health and Development in Rural China*. Doctoral Dissertation, The George Washington University.

Xiang, B. (2007). 'How far Are the Left-Behind Left Behind? A Preliminary Study in Rural China', *Population, Space and Place*, 13: 179–91. https://doi.org/10.1002/psp .437.

Zhang, W.W. (2000). *Transforming China: Economic Reform and its Political Implications*. Basingstoke: Palgrave Macmillan UK.

Zhao, Q., Yu, X., Wang, X., & Glauben, T. (2014). 'The Impact of Parental Migration on Children's School Performance in Rural China', *China Economic Review*, 31, 43–54.

Zhou, C., Sylvia, S., Zhang, L., Luo, R., Yi, H., Liu, C., . . . Rozelle, S. (2015). 'China's Left-behind Children: Impact of Parental Migration on Health, Nutrition, and Educational Outcomes', *Health Affairs*, 34(11), 1964–71.

Zhou, M., Sun, X., Huang, L., Zhang, G., Kenny, K., Xue, H., Auden, E., & Rozelle, S. (2018). 'Parental Migration and Left-behind Children's Depressive Symptoms: Estimation Based on a Nationally-representative Panel Dataset', *International Journal of Environmental Research and Public Health*, 15(6), 1069.

Zhou, M., Murphy, R., & Tao, R. (2014). 'Effects of parents' Migration on the Education of Children Left Behind in Rural China', *Population and Development Review*, 40(2), 273–92.

11

Migrant Women's Journeys for Education and Career Opportunities in Chile

Sondra Cuban

Introduction

This chapter focuses on migration, education and gender at the nexus of development in the Latin American and Caribbean (LAC) region, specifically Chile. The research draws on data from a Fulbright Commission study conducted in 2017 of fifty-five migrant women from LAC countries residing in Chile which explored their reasons for migrating as well as their experiences of adapting to a new place of settlement. I use a mobilities framework and narrative interviews to illustrate how education and career opportunities were important drivers for women's migrations, adaptations and social mobility.

The majority of participants were from the LAC region representing its historically strong feminized migration flow (Cerrutti and Parrado 2015; Lube-Guizardi and Torralbo 2019). The feminization of migration in this region reflects increases in women's autonomous migration internationally, as well as in many Global South migration corridors (Donato and Gabbacia 2016; Mansouri and Tittensor 2017). The predominant focus in the South–South literature, however, has been on East Asian and West Asian migration corridors, with LAC countries given little attention. The overarching research question guiding this exploration is: What role do education and career opportunities play in LAC women migrants' stories of moving to Chile, adapting to life there and altering their social mobility?

Chile is one of the fastest-growing migrant destinations in the region as well as in the world (United Nations 2017; Doña Reveco 2018). Migrants doubled their presence between 2002 and 2014, and by 2019, they composed over a million in a population of nearly nineteen million (INE 2020). Yet rarely is Chile discussed in the literature as a new migrant destination. This is because historically Chile has been recognized as a migrant 'sending country', rather than a 'recipient country'. During the Pinochet era (1973–90) thousands of Chileans fled the brutal dictatorship. Moreover, its geographic isolation at the 'end of the world' meant that it never previously became country of immigrants like its neighbour, Argentina (Salazar 2013: 233).

Chile's popularity as a new place of settlement is due to its relative political stability with historically strong institutions and constitutional governance, its reputation as a safe place in South America and its 'economic jaguar' status (Sznajder 1996; Vasquez et al. 2016). In 2010 Chile became an Organization for Economic Co-operation and Development (OECD) member and was fully integrated into the international global market, with the World Bank ranking it as an 'upper middle income' country. In the Southern Cone it is an ABC economic power (along with Argentina and Brazil), especially through the Mercado Común del Sur (MERCOSUR), which is a regional pact for the free movement of goods, people and services, including international students (Horna 2013). All of these factors, plus, proximity, informal networks, income differentials and political conflict, initiated the new migration to Chile, with over 70 per cent of its migrants representing the LAC region; long-time migrant communities from Peru, Ecuador, Bolivia and Argentina and, more recently, Colombians, Haitians and Venezuelans (INE 2020). Furthermore, as popular destinations for LAC migrants like the United States, Spain and Italy have further restricted migration, the opening up of Chile created new opportunities within the LAC region for migrating populations. The LAC region contains ten million intraregional migrants, a majority of which are women (United Nations 2017; Alvarez and Hernandez 2019).

Little research exists, however, about the barriers migrant women face in moving countries within the LAC region and the ways in which their social mobility may be constrained. Chile is one of the most unequal of OECD members, has some of the most regressive gender inequities in the region and, moreover, has one of the oldest migration policies in the world which stems from the Pinochet era of the 1970s and is called Decree 1094. It focuses exclusively on national security and the entry of migrants into the country rather than on their integration (Diaz Tolosa 2016). Generally, research on migration into Chile has been piecemeal and has largely excluded issues such as gender, class, race and social mobility.

Literature on Education and Employment
in Chile and within the LAC Region

Education in Chile and the LAC Region

Chile, like other Southern Cone countries, contains some of the highest female literacy rates in the world, with equal gender parity to males (UNESCO 2019a; 2019b; Bárcena et al. 2020). Likewise, the education system, ranging from primary to tertiary levels, is well established and expansive across Chile, and access has been fluid for women whose enrolments are typically high. This gender parity was due at first to Ibero-European enlightenment ideas and then Chile shifting to an industrialized country with urbanization and international networks (Avalos 2003). However, education still remains expensive and gender-segmented.

Chile has guaranteed an education through its government services and funds since the 1830s. However, it wasn't until over a century later, when education became compulsory, that secondary education reached gender parity. In the 1980s, Chilean education was changed forever with tiered systems of schooling that contributed to gender inequities, especially in technical and vocational education and STEM programmes that have had little female participation. With the transfer of schooling from centralized government to municipalities, responsibility shifted from the state to individuals and households in a market-driven education system that embraced vouchers and private education (Collins and Lear 1995; Inzunza et al. 2019). It wasn't until 2006 that a large student protest arose, Revolución Pingüina, the *penguin revolution* (due to the black-and-white uniforms) and again in 2011, which culminated in the largest of all protests in 2019 to equalize education and redress social inequalities (Inzunza et al. 2019). While under President Bachelet, the government instituted educational reforms to grant children equal access to schools (the Inclusion Law) (OECD 2017), the neoliberal model has continued to reinforce inequities.

Since 2008, Chilean law stipulates that migrant children have access to public education (UNESCO 2019a). However, they have difficulties integrating due to poverty as well as racial discrimination (Cabieses et al. 2017). Children born in Chile with at least one migrant parent are accorded citizenship through 'jus soli' (of being born in Chile). Yet they are often considered racialized outcasts, and children's parents who are irregular are vulnerable to deportation (Balart and Espejo 2012; Diaz Tolosa 2016; Pavez-Soto and Chan 2018). Also, since resource allocation is governed through local bureaucracies schooling can be difficult for families to access.

Chile's higher education follows similar neoliberal changes (Gregorutti et al. 2016; Muñoz 2016; Simbürger and Donoso 2018). The 1981 education reform under Pinochet's Chicago Boys (a group of Chilean economists who studied free-market policies at the University of Chicago) pushed universities to self-finance, thereby hiking tuition fees. Private universities were expanded, and student loans and scholarships were either reduced or eliminated. Chile's reputation for privatized higher education is well known, but what is less well understood are the cost to families with 50 per cent of all household income devoted to tuition (Espinoza and Gonzalez 2013; UNESCO 2019a). Internationalization has grown rapidly within the last decade through multilateral agreements such as Chile's National Commission for Scientific and Technological Research (CONICYT) and the Chilean International Cooperation Agency (AGCI), thus expanding university enrolments and programmes as well as visibility and revenue (Holm-Nielsen et al. 2005; Contreras 2015). Yet little research has focused on international students studying in the Global South, especially LAC exchange students studying in the LAC.

More women than men are enrolled at Chile's universities which is a trend reflected across the LAC region. Yet, there are large gender gaps in STEM subjects (Bárcena et al. 2020). This is due to conservative social attitudes about women going into socially reproductive fields (Avalos 2003). Dropout is also a problem because of the university fees, pregnancy and discrimination within university cultures where few women lead (Maldonado-Maldonado and Acosta 2018). In 2019 women students protested sexual harassment with the demand for non-sexist education.

Women and Employment in Chile

The labour market has not kept up with women's high rates of education across the LAC region, and women in the region have some of the highest rates of unemployment and underemployment in the world (Novta and Wong 2017). Chile has one of the lowest rates of female participation in the labour force of all (OECD) members and falls below most other LAC countries, despite women's high levels of education (Contreras and Plaza 2010). The factors limiting women's labour market integration include restrictive laws, poor leadership and *machista* attitudes (Contreras and Plaza 2010; World Economic Forum 2014). The lack of childcare is also a problem (Rucci and Urzúa 2015; Martinez and Perticara 2017). Findings show that after-school childcare programmes, longer school hours and free pre-schools increase women's employment hours and opportunities (Berthelon et al. 2020). While women's paid labour activities have increased, much of this is due to the growth of non-standard work (OECD 2017; ECLAC/ILO 2019). Migrant women, especially those who are undocumented, tend to work in the informal economy (Upegui-Hernández 2011).

A Mobilities Lens and Narrative Approach

The women who participated in the study were moving short distances across borders in an unevenly developed region with their 'mobile capital' (Sheller 2014, 796). In so doing they experienced 'interdependent mobilities' that combined their migratory mobility, with their physical mobility and their social mobility (Urry 2007, 47). *Migratory mobility* refers to 'migration across key nodes within a given diaspora' (Urry 2007: 8–9). Physical mobility is the ability to move and which connects to crossing borders (Cresswell 2006). These mobilities are dependent on policies and the risks involved in migrating. They also link to social mobility wherein women migrants' human capital and social trajectories move upwards or downwards when they migrate (Torche 2005). Or they may not move at all, due to occupational segmentation within the informal economy.

The participants were selected through convenience sampling techniques, as well as through various venues, including non-profit organizations, personal networks and institutional sources in order to capture a range of socio-demographic factors across Chile's migrant population. The characteristics of the sample were therefore diverse with regard to age, race, social class and marital and parental status. They also represented Chile's newest nationalities: Venezuelans (9), Colombians (13) and Haitians (13). There were also Mexicans (6), Ecuadorians (5), as well as two participants each from Cuba, Argentina and Peru, and one each from Uruguay and Brazil. Most of the participants first arrived to Santiago, and then moved south towards Temuco and its metropolitan area in the Araucanía region, where the research was conducted. The sample also represented women's high rates of education in the LAC region; twenty-one participants possessed university degrees with several more stopping short of graduation. Four exchange students were earning bachelor's degrees in Chile, and several high-skilled participants were in postgraduate programmes. Ten participants had high school diplomas, with several more receiving two-year technical degrees or certificates. Seven participants didn't complete high school, and four additional participants had a primary or middle-school education.

Narrative interviews were chosen to capture the participants' action sequences of attempting to advance their education and careers but also their 'passive mobilities', including waiting for paperwork to arrive in the mail, anticipating hearing back from an employer or scheduling a time to validate their qualifications (Bissell 2010, 58). The narratives also captured the 'emotional geographies of the participants as they evaluated their lives and described critical events' (Sheller 2004, 223). I compiled stories about their consequential decisions and events following their migrations and created profiles which were compared and contrasted to develop themes (Riessmann 1993; Braun and Clarke 2006).

Findings: Education and Career Opportunities Were Important Drivers for Migration

The following four themes emerged about women migrants' mobilities: (1) seeing windows of career opportunities; (2) anchoring education for autonomy; (3) opening doors for greater human capital; (4) building foundations for generational outcomes.

Seeing Windows of Career Opportunities

The high-skilled participants possessed degrees across disciplines in natural and physical sciences (i.e. engineering), social sciences (i.e. communications/psychology) and professions (i.e. teaching). Before migrating, nearly all of these participants worked in fields in which they received degrees in their countries, with some combining more than one field, for example, a participant with a sociology degree and a teaching certificate whose position in a toy company focused on children's learning. Yet the conditions of their work did not often match their career ambitions, and they were often underpaid, partially employed and overworked, all of which were push factors for migrating.

Long hours, little support and pressure to do more from top management were a common complaint among those who were middle managers. They had reached thresholds in their positions that they could no longer tolerate. One Colombian, Alejandra, was a director and said, 'I was burned out. I was exhausted. I had a really long schedule and worked a lot to support my daughters.' An Argentinian participant stated: 'I am creative, and I am moving around and doing things and people are bothered by it. He [her boss] lowered my position and reduced my salary and it was all political. . . . then I quit and it's a huge change, no salary, no support.' Lovelie, a Haitian participant with a nursing degree, couldn't locate work and her mother residing in the United States had to support her. She said of Chile: 'I thought about it, and it came fast. It was just because I didn't have a job.' She had 'heard people talking about Chile how there were easier jobs, it was safe and easy to come'. Lack of advancement was also a factor. A Cuban academic, Yanet, said: 'You can't develop yourself further because you can't do your experiments. It's also the reading material; not that much and the internet is limited and if you're doing a research project, any place else it would be 2 months and in Cuba, 2 years.' Chile was viewed as a place where they could improve their professional lives. Some successfully adapted their professions, for example, a lawyer who became a law faculty member. But most participants were unable to become professionals again; a Venezuelan petroleum engineer became a baker and a street vendor, a Haitian banker became a bathroom cleaner and a Colombian saleswoman became a hairdresser.

Anchoring Education for Autonomy

Having dropped out of school or university in their countries, a number of the participants sought an opportunity to finish and advance their education in Chile. Of the four participants who dropped out of their university studies, all of them married Chileans and then moved to Chile. Rosa[1] completed two years of law school in Colombia. But when her Chilean partner was offered a job in Chile, she 'blindly quit' her studies. When she arrived in Chile her husband prevented her from studying. Her mother, however, urged her to, 'keep studying because he is not going to change'. Rosa was desperate to continue so she enrolled at a university despite his protests. She recounted: 'When I wanted to study, he would also push me down so much so whenever I tried to validate my studies, the papers, the diplomas I brought with me disappeared.'

For the eleven participants who did not finish primary or secondary school, their dropout was directly related to family poverty. One Argentinian woman, Martina, was in her forties. She left school at age thirteen like many children of poor families to be a domestic through a system known as *criadazgo* (Blofield and Jokela 2018). She recollected: 'We needed money so that's why we started working at such young age, my sister and I, to support the family . . . there's no demand to study.' While she believed that it was 'never too late to finish my education', her janitorial job made this ambition difficult to achieve due to her schedule. An indigenous Ecuadorian, Paulina did not finish secondary school, due to having to support her family, similar to other adolescent girls in Ecuador (Mullery 2018). She worked in a rose processing plant and at seventeen was raped and gave birth to a daughter; gender violence is not atypical in Ecuador (UNICEF 2019). She migrated because her parents 'did not accept me because I became pregnant'. She became a domestic worker for a Chilean family and then a street vendor, but often ran from the police because her livelihood was criminalized. In the future, she said, 'My dream would be able to go back to school, finish school and become a professional; my most desired profession is to be a police officer.'

Opening Doors for Greater Human Capital

The majority of Mexican women in the study were students, reflecting an increase in their participation in higher education so as to adapt to the global economy (Henne-Ochoa 2016; OECD 2019). Mexican universities have been adapting too, with new international programmes to service these students' ambitions for cultural exchange opportunities abroad. Graciela was studying communications in a Chilean university to boost her credentials, cosmopolitanism and global job opportunities, in her words, 'to know a culture, it really makes you realize about living somewhere different from where you grew up'. She migrated through an agreement between Mexico and Chile that gave her a scholarship. She considered country rankings, 'so my top places were in Spain and the second one was Cuba.' She chose Chile because the cost of living was similar to Mexico. In weighing her return to Mexico from Chile she declared, 'if they were to offer a job I would gladly stay. I'm not attached to be in Mexico. You need to go anywhere to get a good job offer.' Yet, like other Mexican students, she did not like the disparaging comments made about Mexicans. Another student reported that Chileans shouted, 'tacos, and beer, let's go party' sort of thing . . . they yell, 'tacos and cabrón'.

  Raquel, a divorced Venezuelan in her late thirties, had migrated in the middle of a severe crisis with her young son to get her master's degree in communication sciences in Chile. She reasoned, 'at the beginning I thought I would go to Ecuador, and I got the letter, and said, ok ok, Chile.' While she enjoyed her master's programme, her son struggled to adjust because his Chilean schoolmates said, 'oh Venezuela is so bad!' She also heard discriminatory comments like 'foreigners are coming to steal jobs.' Nonetheless, her goal was 'to improve my path and social connections. . . . I am open to all possibilities'.

Building Foundations for Generational Outcomes

Children's education was also a driver for migration. An Argentinian participant, Alicia, said: 'we saw that there was a better future as far as the education goes, and that's why I decided, it was mostly for my kids.' Likewise, a Uruguayan participant described Montevideo: 'where there is crime and bad education and we thought if we stayed there, it would be hard.' The participants also migrated to support their children's schooling back home. An Ecuadorian mother, Angela, said she was 'pushed' to migrate and 'grew desperate because of my daughter's school fees'. She didn't bring her to Chile because 'she wouldn't be able to get into school, so it's the healthcare and the education, like we're cut off from that.' She added: 'my reason for being here is so I can progress along with my daughter because we will not be able to in Ecuador, and I want to give her better opportunities than what I had.'

Child migrants had problems culturally transitioning to the Chilean educational system, which is not uncommon as 'the risk of education disruption increase[s] with migration' (UNESCO 2019a). As parents, the women in the study also had problems adjusting, with one Colombian, Luciana, claiming: 'students don't respect teachers, students stand on chairs. If the teacher tells them to do something, they say something back . . . we don't like that.' They also had problems working due to the lack of childcare, with employers refusing to hire them if they were mothers. A Peruvian, Cristina, thought she had a job 'until they ask you, "do you have children?" . . . and they say, "they're too young" and the interview ends there'. Patricia, from Uruguay, had in-laws who refused to watch her children while she worked. She thought: 'I don't know what they [her in-laws] think I'm doing. . . . That bothers me. I come from a place where it doesn't matter [that women work].'

Participants with children at universities in their countries were also paying for their tuition fees. One participant, Daniela, had a daughter and son studying at different Colombian universities. She said she expected to 'work my ass off until I get my kids educated and finish university. The only thing you can give your kids is education. I don't want to make money and buy a house. I just want to give them their education'. Other participants sent their children back to their countries to go to university because it was free or more affordable than Chile.

Discussion

Decisions to Migrate: A Combination of Engendered, Economic and Educational Factors

The findings illustrated that education and career opportunities were factors in the participants' migrations and social mobility. A process of 'less positive selection' occurred whereby with the lower costs of migrating to Chile from lower-income countries to an upper-middle-income country in the same region, they believed they could progress their lives and those of their children (Feliciano 2008: 141). These decisions were also engendered; for example, the mothers desired better lives for their children, including educational opportunities and those who dropped out of school aspired to continue their education in Chile. Participants with a high school education or less banked on their social mobility improving with available jobs in Chile, while high-skilled participants gambled on greater professional opportunities. Yet both groups were often pulled into work within the informal economy.

What Happened: Discrimination and Disillusionment

The success story reputation of Chile rubbed against the reality for many participants who expected to integrate into Chile's system, but struggled to adapt; one participant, Xaviera, admitted she had a 'fairy tale' impression after she heard 'talk about Chile as well placed worldwide and a country with more opportunities'. She said she 'never thought about barriers'. These participants' high hopes that Chile's 'miracle' reputation would advance them were shattered by the discrimination they faced after they arrived (Richards 2013: 1). They had not considered that as LAC migrants, regardless of their skills and education levels, they would be cast as outsiders fit only to work in Chile's gender-segmented labour market in sectors like domestic services which have a long colonial, patriarchal history there (Courtis and Pacecca 2014; Marchetti 2018). They also experienced cultural discrimination in terms of their languages and dialects and Afro-decedent participants experienced racial prejudices. This was because a majority of Chileans saw themselves as white Europeans superior to other LAC nationalities (Walsh 2019). Further, discrimination towards migrant mothers led to workplace exclusion. And high-skilled participants were often unable to find professional work, further reducing their earnings and capital accumulation which blocked their social and occupational mobility (Cuban 2013; Hennebry and Petrozziello 2019).

Fragmented Approaches to Women Migrants' Mobilities at Regional and International Levels

The experiences of the women in the study reflect the fact that policies generally do not address migrant women's education, career and opportunity interests in the LAC region. The literature shows that at an international level, it is a similar story. The disconnect between migrant women's problems and the policies stems from three problems.

The first is that *intersectional issues are not usually addressed in social policies*. Migrant women are typically not viewed as whole people, across the lifecycle; my study showed that the young, single migrant participants had fundamentally different needs than the older ones with children. While the former dealt with cultural discrimination, the latter experienced workplace discrimination. Also, migrant women of different nationalities and races are often treated as a homogenous group. The participants with racialized identities in this study experienced double and triple disadvantages in all sectors of society, which affected their integration in Chile. A systemic and robust analysis of policies that are gender-sensitive and intersected by class, age and race is warranted, along with migrant women's labour rights protections (Basok and Piper 2012).

The second problem is that *international policies do not often transfer to regional, state or local levels, and implementation problems exist*. There were clear disconnects between international social policies, Chilean institutional regulations and migrant women's needs and interests. In the LAC region, disconnects exist between rhetoric and practice in global governance for women migrants' social and economic rights (Basok and Piper 2012). One problem is that most of the attention in international policies is given to irregular migration, particularly human trafficking. UN Women Americas and the Caribbean reported that despite some legislative progress on gender issues, implementation is fragmented (UN Women 2020). The Sustainable Development Goals (SDGs), or Los Objetivos de Desarrollo Sostenible in Latin America, also do not fully link international organizations to state governments as actors (Ojeda Medina 2019).

The third problem is that *social policies contain neoliberal, market-based and donor-driven approaches*. This means that entrenched infrastructural issues are not addressed, for example, through social welfare programmes from which migrant women could benefit. Most of the international migration policies operate in a neoliberal framework focusing primarily on the monetary gains of migrants to national economies ignoring their rights, protections and opportunity structures (Hennebry et al. 2019). The SDGs do not go far enough in challenging liberal financialization laws and corporations that create privatized services that prevent gender equality like Chile's universities (Bidegain Ponte and Rodríguez 2016). The SDGs do include migration, in Goal 10, Reducing Inequalities; Goal 8, Economic Sustainability and Decent Work; and Goal 5, Gender Equality and Women's empowerment. Yet the policy emphasis remains on controlling and managing the movement of people and the prevention of trafficking (Piper 2017). Questions remain about how these goals connect to transnational social protections (Gammage and Stevanovic 2019). Furthermore, the goals are not ambitious enough or able to tackle systemic issues that migrant women face, especially poverty, gaps which are 'the inborn faults of a capitalist system . . . in a way they would need to be if they are to inspire action' (Koehler 2016, 3). Policies also do not incorporate the hidden issues that affect migrant women such as cultural and racial discrimination (Girard 2017).

SDG Goal 4 demonstrates a lack of attention to systemic issues and gender equality, defined mostly by enrolments and completion rates rather than costs and risks involved in attending education institutions (Global Education Monitoring Report Team 2018). While in Latin America more low-income girls complete lower and upper secondary school, they still fall short in subject selection, like STEM. Education expenditures are also uneven across the region and are important to consider as well as household remittance patterns for schooling in Latin America (UNESCO 2019ab). Furthermore, SDG lifelong and adult education goals, in focusing on market-driven technical and vocational skills, only minimally address marginalized groups like migrant women and their needs and interests (Elfert 2019).

Conclusion

Migrant women, as this study illustrates, were in pursuit of building their capacities, as well as those of their children, and they migrated to improve their education and career opportunities as part of their greater social mobility. To support this, a decolonizing and transnational feminist pedagogy is needed across all levels of education focusing on migrant women's 'intellectual and political moorings' as they move across borders in the LAC (D'Arcangelis and Huntley 2012: 43). This education could incorporate the politics of care, the informal economy, identity work, and could lead to many different kinds of opportunity structures that support them to progress their lives. Yet without strong social infrastructural systems, like welfare and equitable migration policies, as well as cultural interventions to prevent gender, racial and class discrimination, migrant women will be left on their own to pursue their interests. Furthermore, a stronger analysis of gender inequities across a wider spectrum of dimensions than the current Leave No One Behind doctrine within the SDGs should be developed (Cochrane and Rao 2018) to assist migrant women to achieve greater social mobility.

Note

1   All names are pseudonyms to protect participants' anonymity.

References

Alvarez, C.A., & Hernandez, J.I. (2019). 'Introduction', in C. Álvarez Alonso & J.I. Hernández (Eds), *Latin American Geopolitics: Migration, Cities and Globalization.* Cham: Palgrave Macmillan, 1–12.

Avalos, B. (2003). 'Gender Parity and Equality in Chile: A Case Study', *UNESDOC.* https://unesdoc.unesco.org/ark:/48223/pf0000146745_eng?origin=publication _detail (accessed 18 October 2021).

Balart, A., & Espejo, N. (2012). *The Rights of Migrant Children: Challenges for Chilean Migration Law Santiago, Chile.* Santiago: UNICEF.

Bárcena, A., Cimoli, M., García-Buchaca, R., & Castillo, M. (2020). 'Women's Autonomy in Changing Economic Scenarios', *United Nations ECLAC.* https://repositorio.cepal .org/handle/11362/45037 (accessed 18 October 2021).

Basok, T., & Piper, N. (2012). 'Management Versus Rights: Women' s Migration and Global Governance in Latin America and the Caribbean', *Feminist Economics*, 18(2), 35–61. https://doi.org/10.1080/13545701.2012.690525.

Berthelon, M., Kruger, D., Lauer, C., Tiberti, L., & Zamora, C. (2020). 'Longer School Schedules, Childcare and the Quality of Mothers' Employment: Evidence from School Reform in Chile'. Partnership for Economic Policy Working Paper No. 2020-07. https://ssrn.com/abstract=3631391 (accessed 18 October 2021).

Bidegain Ponte, N., & Rodríguez, C. E. (2016). 'Agenda 2030: A Bold Enough Framework towards Sustainable, Gender-Just Development?', *Gender & Development*, 24(1), 83–98. https://doi.org/10.1080/13552074.2016.1142227.

Bissell, D. (2010). 'Narrating Mobile Methodologies: Active and Passive Empiricisms', in B. Fincham, M. McGuinness, & L. Murray (Eds), *Mobile Methodologies*. London: Palgrave Macmillan, 53–68.

Blofield, M., & Jokela, M. (2018). 'Paid Domestic Work and the Struggles of Care Workers in Latin America', *Current Sociology Monograph*, 66(4), 531–46. https://doi .org/10.1177/0011392118765259.

Braun, V., & Clarke, V. (2006). 'Using Thematic Analysis in Psychology', *Qualitative Research in Psychology*, 3(2), 77–101. http://dx.doi.org/10.1191 /1478088706qp063oa.

Cabieses, B., Chepo, M., Oyarte, M., Markkula, N., Bustos, P., Pedero, V., & Delgao, I. (2017). 'Health Inequality Gap in Immigrant versus Local Children in Chile', *Revista Chilena de Pediatria*, 88(6), 707–16. https://doi.org/10.4067/S0370 -41062017000600707.

Cerrutti, M., & Parrado, E. (2015). 'Intraregional Migration in South America: Trends and a Research Agenda', *The Annual Review of Sociology*, 41, 399–421. https://doi.org /10.1146/annurev-soc-073014-112249.

Cochrane, L., & Rao, N. (2018). 'Is the Push for Gender Sensitive Research Advancing the SDG Agenda of Leaving No One Behind?', *Forum for Development Studies*, 46(1), 45–65.

Collins, J., & Lear, J. (1995). *Chile's Free Market Miracle: A Second Look*, Oakland: Institute for Food and Development Policy.

Contreras, D., & Plaza, G. (2010). 'Cultural Factors in Women' s Labor Force Participation in Chile', *Feminist Economics*, 16(2), 27–46. https://doi.org/10.1080 /13545701003731815.

Contreras, P. (2015). 'Conceptualización y experiencia de la Internacionalización en el Pregrado Chileno', *Calidad en la Educación*, 43, 169–200. http://dx.doi.org/10.31619 /caledu.n43.47.

Courtis, C., & Pacecca, M.I. (2014). 'Domestic Work and International Migration in Latin America: Exploring Trajectories of Regional Migrant Women in Domestic Service in Argentina', *Women's Studies International Forum*, 46, 24–32. https://doi .org/10.1016/j.wsif.2014.01.002.

Cresswell, T. (2006). *On the Move: Mobility in the Modern Western World*. New York: Routledge.

Cuban, S. (2013). *Deskilling Migrant Women in the Global Care Industry*. Basingstoke: Palgrave Macmillan.

D'Arcangelis, C. L., & Huntley, A. (2012). 'No More Silence: Towards a Pedagogy of Feminist Decolonizing Solidarity', in S. Walters & L. Manicom (Eds), *Feminist Popular Education in Transnational Debates: Building Pedagogies of Possibility*. New York: Palgrave Macmillan, 41–58. https://doi.org/10.1057/9781137014597_3.

Diaz Tolosa, R.I. (2016). 'A New Chilean Migration Act: An Approach to International Standards', *International Migration*, 54(6), 109–21. https://doi.org/10.1111/imig .12259.

Doña Reveco, C. (2018). 'Amid Record Numbers of Arrivals, Chile Turns Rightward on Immigration', *Migration Policy Institute*, January 17. https://www.migrationpolicy.org/article/amid-record-numbers-arrivals-chile-turns-rightward-immigration (accessed 18 October 2021).

Donato, K.M., & Gabaccia, D. (2016). 'The Global Feminization of Migration: Past, Present, And Future', *Migration Information Source.* https:// www.migrationpolicy.org/article/global-feminization-migration-past-present-and-future (accessed 18 October 2021).

ECLAC/ILO ILO/ECLAC (2019). 'Employment Situation in Latin America and the Caribbean: Evolution of and Prospects for Women's Labour Participation in Latin America', *CEPAL.* https://www.ilo.org/wcmsp5/groups/public/---americas/---ro-lima/---sro-santiago/documents/publication/wcms_746274.pdf (accessed 18 October 2021).

Elfert, M. (2019). 'Lifelong Learning in Sustainable Development Goal 4: What Does it Mean for UNESCO's RightsBased Approach to Adult Learning and Education?', *International Review of Education*, 65(5), 537–56. https://doi.org/10.1007/s11159-019-09788-z.

Espinoza, L., & Gonzalez, E. (2013). 'Access to Higher Education in Chile: A Public vs. Private Analysis', *Prospects*, 43, 199–214. https://doi.org/10.1007/s11125-013-9268-8.

Feliciano, C. (2008). 'Gendered Selectivity: U.S. Mexican Immigrants and Mexican Nonmigrants, 1960–2000', *Latin American Research Review*, 43(1), 139–60. https://www.jstor.org/stable/20488112.

Gammage, S., & Stevanovic, N. (2019). 'Gender, Migration and Care Deficits: What Role for the Sustainable Development Goals?', *Journal of Ethnic and Migration Studies*, 45(14), 2600–20. https://doi.org/10.1080/1369183X.2018.1456751.

Girard, L. (2017). 'Achieving Gender Equality through Migration Governance: Opportunities and Solutions in Support of the Sustainable Development Agenda', *Migration in the 2030 Agenda*, 59–70. https://www.iom.int/sites/g/files/tmzbdl486/files/about-iom/gender/Migration-in-the-2030-Agenda-SDGs-Achieving-Gender-Equality-through-Migration-Governance.pdf (accessed 18 October 2021).

Global Education Monitoring Report Team (2018). *Meeting our Commitments to Gender Equality in Education.* UNESCO. https://en.unesco.org/gem-report/2018_gender_review (accessed 18 October 2021).

Gregorutti, G. Espinoza, O., González, L. E., & Loyola, J. (2016). 'What if Privatising Higher Education Becomes an Issue? The Case of Chile and Mexico', *Compare*, 46(1), 136–58.

Henne-Ochoa, C. (2016). 'To Emigrate or not to Emigrate: A Sociocultural Understanding of Mexican Professionals' Logic of (Im)mobility', *Norte América*, 11(2), 31–62. https://doi.org/10.20999/nam.2016.b002.

Hennebry, J., & Petrozziello, A. (2019). 'Closing the Gap? Gender and the Global Compacts for Migration and Refugees', *International Migration*, 57(6), 115–38. https://doi.org/10.1111/imig.12640.

Holm-Nielsen, L.B., Thorn, K., Brunner, J. J., & Balan, J. (2005). 'Regional and International Challenges to Higher Education', in H. de Wit, J. H. de Wit, & I. C. Jaramillo (Eds), *Higher Education in Latin America: The International Dimension*. Washington, D.C.: World Bank Publications, 39–70.

Horna, H. (2013). *A People's History of Latin America*. Princeton: Markus Wiener Publishers.

INE (2020). 'Estimación De Personas Extranjeras Residentes Habituales En Chile Al 31 De Diciembre 2019', *Estimate of Regular Foreign Residents in Chile as of December 31, 2019*. https://www.ine.cl/docs/default-source/demografia-y-migracion/publicaciones -y-anuarios/migraci%C3%B3n-internacional/estimaci%C3%B3n-poblaci%C3%B3n -extranjera-en-chile-2018/estimaci%C3%B3n-poblaci%C3%B3n-extranjera-en-chile -2019-metodolog%C3%ADa.pdf?sfvrsn=5b145256_6 (accessed 18 October 2021).

Inzunza, J. Assael, J., Cornejo, R., & Redondo, J. (2019). 'Public Education and Student Movements: The Chilean Rebellion under a Neoliberal Experiment', *British Journal of Sociology of Education*, 40(4), 490–506. https://doi.org/10.1080/01425692.2019 .1590179.

Koehler, G. (2016). 'Tapping the Sustainable Development Goals for Progressive Gender Equity and Equality Policy?', *Gender & Development*, 1–16. https://doi.org/10.1080 /13552074.2016.1142217.

Lube-Guizardi, M., & González Torralbo, H. (2019). 'Women in (Dis)placement: The Field of Studies on Migrations, Social Remittances, Care and Gender in Chile', *Revista de Estudios Sociales*, 70, 100–14. https://doi.org/10.7440/res70.2019.09.

Maldonado-Maldonado, A., & Acosta, F. (2018). 'An Agenda in Motion: Women's Issues in Latin American Higher Education', *International Higher Education*, 94, 2–4. https://doi.org/10.6017/ihe.2018.0.10552.

Mansouri, F., & Tittensor, F. (2017). 'Introducing and Contextualizing Feminised Migration', in D. Tittensor & F. Mansouri (Eds), *The Politics of Women and Migration in the Global South*. London: Palgrave, 1–10.

Marchetti, S. (2018). 'Gender, Migration and Globalisation: An Overview of the Debates', in A. Triandafylidou (Ed.), *Handbook of Migration and Globalisation*. Cheltenham: Edward Elgar Publishing, 443–57.

Martinez, C., & Perticara, M. (2017). 'Childcare Effects on Maternal Employment: Evidence', *Journal of Development Economics*, 126, 127–37. https://doi.org/10.1016/j .jdeveco.2017.01.001.

Mullery, S. (2018). '10 Facts About Girls' Education in Ecuador', *The Borgen Project*, 15 December. https://borgenproject.org/10-facts-about-girls-education-in-ecuador/#:~ :text=Approximately%202%20percent%20of%20girls,of%20girls%20completed %20secondary%20school. (accessed 18 October 2021).

Muñoz, D.A. (2016). 'Assessing the Research Efficiency of Higher Education Institutions in Chile: A Data Envelopment Analysis Approach', *International Journal of Educational Management*, 30(6): 809–25. https://doi.org/10.1108/IJEM-03-2015 -0022.

Novta, N., & Wong, J.C. (2017). 'Women at Work in Latin America and the Caribbean', IMF Working Paper. https://www.imf.org/en/Publications/WP/Issues/2017/02/14/Women-at-Work-in-Latin-America-and-the-Caribbean-44662 (accessed 18 October 2021).

OECD (2017). *Employment Outlook, Chile, 2017.* https://www.oecd.org/chile/Employment-Outlook-Chile-EN.pdf (accessed 18 October 2021).

OECD (2019). *Education at a Glance: Mexico.* https://www.oecd.org/education/education-at-a-glance/EAG2019_CN_MEX.pdf (accessed 18 October 2021).

Ojeda Medina, T. (2019). 'El Rol Estratégico de los Gobiernos Locales y Regionales en la Implementación de la Agenda 2030: Experiencias Desde la Cooperación Sur-Sur y Triangular', *Oasis*, 31, 9–29. https://doi.org/10.18601/16577558.n31.03.

Pavez-Soto, I., & Chan, C. (2018). 'The Second Generation in Chile: Negotiating Identities, Rights, and Public Policy', *International Migration*, 56(2), 82–96. https://doi.org/10.1111/imig.12410.

Piper, N. (2017). 'Migration and the SDGs', *Global Social Policy*, 17(2), 231–8. https://doi.org/10.1177/1468018117703443.

Richards, P. (2013). *Race and the Chilean Miracle: Neoliberalism, Democracy, and Indigenous Rights.* Pittsburgh: University of Pittsburgh Press.

Riessman, C. K. (1993). *Narrative Analysis.* Newbury Park, CA: SAGE Publications.

Rucci, M. P., & Urzúa, S. (2015). 'The Effect of Mandated Childcare on Female Wages in Chile', IDP Working Paper No. 594. https://publications.iadb.org/publications/english/document/The-Effect-of-Mandated-Child-Care-on-Female-Wages-in-Chile.pdf (accessed 18 October 2021).

Salazar, N.B. (2013). 'Imagining Mobility at the "End of the World"', *History and Anthropology*, 24(2), 233–52. https://ssrn.com/abstract=2223694.

Sheller, M. (2004). 'Automotive Emotions: Feeling the Car', *Theory, Culture & Society*, 21(4–5), 221–42. https://doi.org/10.1177/0263276404046068.

Sheller, M. (2014). 'The New Mobilities Paradigm for a Live Sociology', *Current Sociology Review*, 62(6), 789–811. https://doi.org/10.1177/0011392114533211.

Simbürger, E., & Donoso, A. (2018). 'Key Elements in the Naturalization of Neoliberal Discourse in Higher Education in Chile', *Discourse: Studies in the Cultural Politics of Education*, 41(2), 559–73. https://doi.org/10.1080/01596306.2018.1512953.

Sznajder, M. (1996). 'Dilemmas of Economic and Political Modernization in Chile: A Jaguar That Wants to Be a Puma', *Third World Quarterly*, 17(4), 725–36. https://www.jstor.org/stable/3993282.

Torche, F. (2005). 'Unequal but Fluid: Social Mobility in Chile in Comparative Perspective', *American Sociological Review*, 70, 422–50. https://www.jstor.org/stable/4145389.

UNESCO (2019a). *Migration, Displacement & Education: Building Bridges, Not Walls.* https://en.unesco.org/gem-report/report/2019/migration (accessed 18 October 2021).

UNESCO (2019b). *Building Bridges for Gender Equality: Global Education Monitoring Report.* https://en.unesco.org/gem-report/2019genderreport (accessed 18 October 2021).

UNICEF (2019). 'Violence Against Children and Gender-Based Violence: Ecuador Case Study'. https://gdc.unicef.org/resource/violence-against-children-and-gender-based-violence-ecuador-case-study (accessed 18 October 2021).

United Nations (2017). *International Migration Report*. https://www.un.org/en/development/desa/population/migration/publications/migrationreport/docs/MigrationReport2017_Highlights.pdf (accessed 18 October 2021).

UN Women (2020). *Progress of the Worlds Women 2019–2020*. https://www.unwomen.org/en/digital-library/progress-of-the-worlds-women (accessed 18 October 2021).

Upegui-Hernández, D. (2011). 'What Is Missing in the Transnational Migration Literature? A Latin American Perspective', *Feminism & Psychology*, 22(2), 228–39. https://doi.org/10.1177/0959353511415831.

Urry, J. (2007). *Mobilities*. Cambridge: Polity Press.

Vasquez, A., Cabieses, B., & Tunstall, H. (2016). 'Where are Socioeconomically Deprived Immigrants Located in Chile? A Spatial Analysis of Census Data Using an Index of Multiple Deprivation from the Last Three Decades (1992–2012)', *PLoS ONE*, 11(1), 1–19. https://doi.org/10.1371/journal.pone.0146047.

Walsh, S. (2019). 'The Chilean Exception: Racial Homogeneity, Mestizaje and Eugenic Nationalism', *Journal of Iberian and Latin American Studies*, 25(1), 105–25. https://doi.org/10.1080/14701847.2019.1579499.

World Economic Forum (2014). *Global Gender Gap Report, 2014 – Chile*. http://reports.weforum.org/global-gender-gap-report-2014/.

12

Imagining Possible Selves

Perceptions of Education among Young Migrant Women in South Africa

Faith Mkwananzi

Introduction

Over the years, women have become increasingly significant in international migration and this is evidenced by a shift in the gendered nature of migrants and refugees. Although female migrants represent a high number of remittance senders in some countries (World Health Organisation 2017), the increase in women's migration should be considered not only in relation to their economic contribution but also with regard to the altering of social and cultural development spheres. Consequently, a gender focus on migration and development enables us to pay attention to the importance of broader social factors involved in influencing women's roles, experiences, aspirations and access to resources (Dannecker and Sieveking 2009). This chapter focuses on the perceptions of Zimbabwean refugee and asylum-seeking women on education and its contribution to their desired possible selves.

Although global trends show women migrating mainly for domestic work (North and Joshi, Chapter 2), migration can bring multiple other prospects to women, including education and entrepreneurship opportunities, as well as various possibilities that may challenge and disrupt historical perceptions of women by society. To illustrate these possibilities, the chapter draws on a qualitative study in Johannesburg, South Africa, which looked at refugee and asylum-seeking young men and women's aspirations for post-secondary education. Contrary to their male counterparts who valued formal university education, women in the study valued vocational training as a trajectory for future possibilities. Vocational training was seen as necessary for practical skills, which would advance opportunities for self-employment in a region with high unemployment rates. Drawing on Dunkel and Kerpelman's (2006) assertion that individuals create their developmental pathways towards the future, the concept of possible selves is used together with the capability approach to understand the influences on how women view themselves and their possible futures. The aim is to illustrate the migration and education nexus and its impact on shifting gender and power relations in decision-making processes in relation to individual lives and communities.

In South Africa, where irregular migration and asylum seeking are common, one individual may pass through several migrant classifications during their stay and may fall into more than one category at a time (UNDP 2010). This has made categories of migration and the distinction between different types of migrants less and less definitive (Birchall 2016). Henceforth, in the chapter, the term 'migrant women' is used in reference to refugees, asylum seekers and undocumented migrants.

The chapter is structured as follows: it starts by providing the context of migration within the Southern African context, followed by a discussion of Zimbabwe–South Africa migration trends. The chapter then turns to outlining the theoretical positions framing the study, followed by the methodology. Next, the findings section considers women's reasons for migrating and discusses the perceptions of education that feature in their narratives. Finally, before concluding, the chapter provides a discussion of the women's experiences through the lens of possible selves and capabilities.

Context

Migration has long been an intrinsic component of the developmental process in Southern Africa. Wentzel and Tlabela (2006:74) note that at the beginning of the twentieth century, extensive migration patterns had emerged across Southern Africa based on labour possibilities around the industrial sector. Mines, such as in the Copperbelt in Zambia, drew thousands of labourers from within the region (Crush, Chikanda and Tawodzera 2015). In South Africa, the colonial regime exclusively used regional migrant labour with development and wealth resulting from various types of Black labour (Trimikliniotis et al. 2009), and in the 1990s, Eastern Free State farmers relied on seasonal migrant labour, particularly from Lesotho (Ulicki and Crush 2010). These trends have continued to the present day, with the Limpopo province relying on seasonal labour from neighbouring Zimbabwe. However, until the turn of the century, there was very little attention given to the movement of women in labour migration discourses.

Overtime, with fewer restrictions on immigration such as visas combined with intensifying economic and political instability within the Southern African region, the migration of both men and women has increased. Despite the relaxation of some migration requirements, mounting economic instabilities in sending countries have resulted in an increase of irregular migration, although statistics and matters pertaining to such migration are poorly understood because of inadequate and unreliable data (Ratha and Shaw 2007). Consequently, the number of undocumented migrants in South Africa is based on unverified estimates. Migration patterns to South Africa are thus complex, involving men and women, regular and irregular movement, refugees and asylum seekers, skilled and unskilled migrants, and shaped by multiple and diverse environmental, political and social-economic factors (Khan 2007).

The women whose perspectives are presented in this chapter migrated because of different push factors from Zimbabwe and pull factors to South Africa. Although some of the women migrated because of family challenges, the most notable factor was the political and economic instability in Zimbabwe at the turn of the millennium, which resulted in high levels of unemployment and caused many people to live in poverty (Besada 2011; UNICEF 2009). Nonetheless, although for the women in the study migration was driven by a desire for better and decent livelihoods, we cannot disregard other aspirations. For almost all the participants, education, in its diverse forms, was seen as one potential pathway towards achieving their socio-economic aspirations. Unlike most of the men in the study who had migrated as minors, the women had migrated primarily as young adults, with the youngest migrating at the age of sixteen and the oldest at thirty. This may have influenced their desire to pursue vocational education as some already had family responsibilities, and some believed they were too old to return to secondary school to acquire the grades necessary to access formal post-schooling opportunities such as university. For the migrant women, vocational opportunities (e.g. hairdressing and dressmaking) were seen to provide entrepreneurial opportunities in a city like Johannesburg, the economic hub of South Africa (Peberdy, Crush and Msibi 2004).

Imagining Possible Selves through the Capability Approach

The capability approach (CA) provides a comprehensive framework to consider the diverse and complex challenges of migration, cutting across and beyond social, political, cultural and economic contexts. The use of the CA in this chapter not only acknowledges the complex nature of migration but also demonstrates that human mobility, in addition to being a capability in its own right, is an integral part of both human and women's development (Mkwananzi 2019). This is illustrated by an assessment of available opportunities for the women to expand their choices, as well as their capacity to improve other dimensions of their lives, necessary for them to become their desired possible selves.

The chapter draws on the work of both Amartya Sen (1999; 2009) and Martha Nussbaum (2011). Sen's (1999) conceptualization of the capability approach emphasizes the expansion of individual freedoms and opportunities (*capabilities*) for one to lead the life one has reason to value. It is these opportunities and freedoms that determine whether or not individuals are able fully to realize their possible selves. While the central notion of the CA is to evaluate the achievements (*functionings*) and freedoms that individuals have to do that which they have reason to value, different institutional and internal factors (*conversion factors*) make it possible or challenging for migrant women to convert resources into valued functionings in the process of fully realizing who they desire to be. Influencing conditions such as environment, social connections and other individual differences come into play. Robeyns (2017) groups these various conditions into three types of conversion factors: personal (e.g. gender, age), environmental (e.g. physical environment and geographical location) and social (e.g. policies, gender norms). One of the ways to respond to both capabilities and conversion factors is through agency: the freedom to bring about one's valued achievements (Sen 1999). In operationalizing agency, the migrant women need to 'act and bring about change' in relation to their current and futures selves. Such action is often indicative of one's aspirations (Mkwananzi and Cin 2020), and the results need to be judged in terms of the women's values and objectives (Sen 1999). This chapter draws on the concepts of agency and conversion factors to understand how migrant women in this study described having to manoeuvre in order to realize their possible selves in a foreign land.

The analysis also draws on three of the ten capabilities that Nussbaum (2011) identifies as the ten core central capabilities that should be incorporated in all constitutions and regarded as important entitlements (rights) that all humans should have. These are, first, *The capability for senses, imagination*: Being able to use the senses, to imagine, think and reason – and to do these things in a 'truly human' way, informed and cultivated by adequate education, including, but by no means limited to, vocational training; second, *Practical reason*: According to Walker (2006) practical reason allows one to make well-reasoned, informed, critical, independent, intellectually acute, socially responsible and reflective choices, which, for the migrant women, included identifying ways to address conversion factors and take up opportunities that respond to their aspirations, and construct a personal life project in an uncertain and complex world of migration; and third, *Control over ones environment:* This relates to refugee women's ability to participate politically and materially. Political participation focuses on their ability to participate effectively in choices that govern their lives and this could be related to family (patriarchal systems) as well as to broader local and national conditions. Material participation includes the ability to hold property (both land and movable goods) formally and in terms of real opportunities, including the right to seek employment on an equal basis with others.

The concept of possible selves emphasizes the importance of considering dynamics that influence valued future-oriented ideas and their relation to motivation for present and future action. While these ideas often reflect someone's expectations, aspirations and fears, they also help understand how they think about capabilities and the future (Markus and Nurius 1986). The descriptive capabilities of the self-concept in possible selves illuminate the concepts' influence on what someone does (or does not do) in relation to their future (Hamman et al. 2013). The relationship between the capability approach and the theory of possible selves is linked to the two questions which Hamman et al. (2010) suggest underlie the theory's efforts and ability to integrate the cognitive and motivational perspectives of individuals. These are: (i) what social and personal factors (conversion factors) give rise to specific kinds of possible selves; and (ii) in what manner do possible selves influence the regulation of behaviour (agency)? As Hamman et al. (2010) note, often researchers addressing the possible selves questions are interested in ways to improve and influence outcomes for people whose lives are experiencing transition, such as was the case with the migrant women in this research. Agency, freedom and the three capabilities of senses and imagination; practical reason and control over one's environment can help us understand the transition process to their possible selves. This may include the formation of new identities as women imagine themselves differently from their past, free, for example, from patriarchal domination or restrictive gendered roles.

Methods

The research presented in this chapter was conducted in central Johannesburg between 2014 and 2016, focusing on migrant youth who lived by or accessed

Table 12.1 Biographies

Name	Reason (s) given for migrating	Age during interview	Type of documentation	Age at arrival	Occupation at the time of interview
Tracy	Political instability Unemployment	30	Asylum Seekers' Permit	25	Part-time domestic worker
Sara	Unemployment in home country	22	No documents	20	Helps blind mother to beg
Rita	Unemployment in home country	21	No documents	20	Seeking work/Housewife
Lorna	Unemployment in home country	23	Asylum Seekers' Permit	16	Running fruit and vegetable stall
Ruth	Unemployment in home country	33	Asylum Seekers' Permit	30	Child-minder
Feli	Better job opportunities in South Africa	27	No documents	21	Seeking work
Leya	Better job opportunities in South Africa	25	Overstayed passport	26	Doing piece jobs
Angela	Better life in South Africa	25	No documents	17	Fruit vendor
Neo	Better job opportunities in South Africa	27	Expired Asylum Seekers' Permit	21	Seeking work/housewife
Susan	Unemployment in home country	27	No documents	23	Vegetable vendor
Nancy	Better job opportunities in South Africa	27	No documents	21	Doing piece jobs

services at the Central Methodist Church (CMC) through its refugee shelter. While it had been hoped that both men and women would volunteer to participate, the first round of data collection yielded only one migrant woman. As gender was not a deciding factor for participation, this was not a limitation but resulted in curiosity about women's 'almost invisibility' in the study. As the initial coding was done, it became clear that gender issues were indeed significant. This called for a second phase of participant recruitment and further data collection between August and September 2015. Snowball sampling was used to identify female participants, with the initial contact person being one of the male participants interviewed during phase 1. In phase 2, eleven young migrant women, and fifteen young migrant men were interviewed. In addition to the migrant men and women, two organizational representatives were interviewed: Dr Gasi[1] from the refugee shelter and Dr Mbatha from the refugee school. Since Dr Gasi worked closely with the shelter, he was familiar with migrant youths' experiences based on daily interactions, while interviewing Dr Mbatha helped explore the purposes and functions of the refugee school.

Table 12.1 provides a summary of the women who participated in the study, highlighting their migrant status and reasons for migrating at the time of interview.

Reasons for Migrating

The women's narratives revealed that their reasons for migrating were multifaceted and influenced by overlapping factors. While the underlying challenge reported was political instability, this instability impacted on economic opportunities. Most of the women noted the desire for opportunities that could afford them a decent lifestyle compared to the one they experienced in Zimbabwe. The host country was seen to have better employment opportunities, despite challenges such as documentation. The opportunity for income generation was needed to manage their day-to-day lives, for example, buying food, clothing and finding decent shelter, which had been a challenge in Zimbabwe. Ruth and Leya explained:

> The living is good here. You can afford to buy food because you can get a loaf of bread for R5. [In Zimbabwe] food is very expensive because the dollar is not buying that side (in Zimbabwe). (Ruth)

Here you can live through doing piece jobs if you are not yet permanently employed, but in Zimbabwe you cannot. (Leya)

Accessing basic needs improves individual well-being and dignity which, as highlighted by Nussbaum (2011), is inherently valuable. For most women, income is also sent back to Zimbabwe as remittances for the consumption and sustenance of other family members (Waddington and Sabates 2003; Skeldon 2008). Such income-generating opportunities allow migrant women to exercise their agency and freedom towards the achievement of their well-being. This is important as it allows the women to decide and act on what they perceive to be in line with their possible selves. In South Africa, opportunities for employment and pursuing entrepreneurial activities were the kind of opportunities that the women were looking for, and which would allow them to have enough money for basic needs such as food, shelter and clothing for themselves and their extended families. However, the women felt that these opportunities for income generation could be expanded through opportunities for skills training through vocational education or programmes.

Perceptions of Vocational Education

For many of the women, experiences in South Africa influenced the value they placed on education. They believed that the instrumental role of education would help them escape poverty and equip them with resources necessary to live decent lives. The value they placed on education, however, was also influenced by experiences of gender socialization, as some of the women believed formal education was more important for equipping men as providers. They felt that women could do 'crafty skills' such as knitting, sewing and baking, and hence desired vocational education.

Migrating to South Africa gave the women the opportunity to imagine possibilities about their present lives and their futures as the new environment widened opportunities in diverse ways. Therefore, although there was little emphasis on the intrinsic value of formal education among the women, their imagined futures included the opportunities that come with vocational skills and entrepreneurship opportunities. Beyond the instrumental value of employment, vocational education and training were seen as adding to the quality of life of individuals, including both those that obtain it and those that benefit indirectly. In the case of migrant women, although they are the immediate beneficiaries of such education, the benefits may also be enjoyed indirectly by those around them, for example, their families, as can be seen in the following comments from Ruth and Susan:

> If I get my interior decor certificate, I will be happy. I will be looking forward to getting a [new] job. I want my children to enjoy their life. I want them to feel that I am everything even if their father is not there, I don't want my children to think that their father has deserted them. (Ruth)

> I would study computers or fashion. I never studied sewing but I can sew without a sewing machine and my clothes still look as if I used a machine. It's inborn for me. So I know even if I am a single mother, I can be someone. I have been married before and realised that marriage does not solve anything. (Susan)

Vocational skills were seen as important to expanding the women's opportunities to be gainfully employed or confident to start their businesses without requiring validation from culture or customary practices. The women shared that for a long time they had been socialized to believe that men are the financial providers in the home; hence, some of them had resorted to marriage as a way to escape poverty. However, their experiences of marriage made them realize the importance of and need for self-sufficiency.

Women's Perceptions of Future Selves

Analysis of the women's experiences and aspirations reveals that multiple and interacting factors influence how migrant women identify and connect with their future selves. In addition to stringent structural influences, the current self-perceived identity of migrant women influences actions related to their futures (Hamman et al. 2013). In discussing the experiences of girls and young women in Tanzania, DeJaeghere (2016: 3) uses the concept of 'imagining alternative futures', which here is useful for understanding not only the reasons for migrating but also the possible selves imagined by the women as they migrated to South Africa. The process of the women thinking about and reflecting on their possible future selves propels them to take action (or not) towards these futures. Often, this agency requires navigating obstructions and overcoming known and unknown fears. As explored in the following discussion, navigating these barriers (conversion factors) and taking action (agency) expand the freedom(s) available to advance the capabilities for practical reason, senses, imagination and thought, as well as control over one's environment as part of the well-being desired by the women.

Agency

Women reported how the new environment enabled them to retain and develop new forms of agency that enhanced their capability to imagine, think and aspire to a new self, as suggested by Appadurai (1996). The development of these new agencies required negotiation between the women's circumstances and the social structures in which they live (Mkwananzi and Cin 2020). This formation of new agencies is essential in considering how the women regrouped themselves in a de-territorialized space to reconstruct their past. It is therefore safe to suggest that agency propelled the women to establish command over opportunities available to them in pursuit of possible selves. These opportunities included those that came with the opportunity to migrate, as they embraced their new found freedom to critically reflect on and re-imagine their lives without obstructions, threats or fear.

The entrepreneurial and other income-generating opportunities the women in the study engaged with gave them the ability to make resources available to their families, and in so doing challenge long-standing traditional roles that relegate women to non-income-generating activities such as caring for the home. For example, Ruth shared:

> Right now, I [own] a residential stand in Zimbabwe and I paid money for a water well, wall and a cottage. So, I thought I should focus on building the house and then do school later. (Ruth)

Ruth's statement was echoed by Dr Gasi, who noted the need to dismantle stereotypes associated with gendered roles, that men's responsibility was to bring bread home while the responsibility of women was that of household chores. This, according to his experience working with migrants, was not true:

> Our experience however of the Zimbabwean situation is you find that a lot of the women that come through come because they either lost a husband or because they are single parents and they hope that coming here will help, not many of the women in this building are political refugees per se; most of the men are. (Dr Gasi)

In other words, he suggests that while most men migrated as political refugees, most women migrated for economic reasons. Through such agency by women, a gradual shift from traditional gendered roles and expectations takes place, releasing them from gendered oppressive environments. This is reiterated by Birchall's (2016) assertion that although labour migration may come with the pressure to provide for family members left behind, it can also represent an advent of new freedoms and opportunities for women to escape restrictive gender norms. The setting and realization of goals, as well as the ability to pursue what they value, whether or not it is directly related to their personal well-being, is therefore a key dimension of the process of agency for the women (Burchardt 2005). This opportunity taken up by the women to pursue what they value defies traditional norms. From a possible selves' viewpoint, such goal-oriented agency is a necessary dimension of the women's identities as their action will be congruent to their possible selves.

Conversion Factors

Gendered expectations may pose as conversion factors with a negative impact on what women are able to do. For most women in the study, challenges related to expectations from families that they could not meet such as providing economically for the family. Nancy, for example, described the pressures she was under:

> I'm the first born at home, so my mother looks up to me to provide everything. She knows that I am here to work, not to study. She knows that I always send money home. At her age now, if she had gone to school, she could have been doing something on her own now. (Nancy)

Often these expectations and challenges are hidden within gender norms, stereotypes and expectations. The women desired freedom to be able to live the lives that they have reason to value (Sen 1999), but within such restrictive contexts, it is difficult to imagine a possible self without fear or intimidation by external factors. A possible selves' viewpoint provides insight into the ways in which conversion factors influenced the women's future outlook. To create an environment where critical reflection about possible selves is possible requires an analysis of both the material and non-material capabilities that alter the women's present living conditions and thus shape their ability to transition to their desired futures. Although available capabilities function in parallel with agency, past and present interactions of other social, economic, political and environmental factors influence the degree to which the women are able to realize the achievements they desire – in this case, accessing and advancing their skills through vocational programmes.

In Zimbabwe, for example, Susan and Ruth possessed cutting and design and dressmaking certificates and had hoped that these qualifications would make a difference in their lives. After migrating to South Africa for better opportunities, however, they had not been able to use their knowledge and thus these certificates had not yet been instrumental to their livelihoods. Susan attributed this to lack of practical experience, which she explained is crucial for a vocational training programme:

> I have a certificate in cutting and designing but could not afford to go ahead with the diploma because of funds. But even if I have the certificate, it is difficult because I don't have the experience; I just have the ideas. (Susan)

With practical experience, one would gain skills necessary to turn the educational capability into a functioning necessary for achieving possible selves. The inability to get the necessary exposure to such practical experience may be attributed to various conversion factors such as limited opportunities for workplace training or internships, which would not have been a possibility in an unstable economic context such as in Zimbabwe. Also, the women highlighted their lack of sewing machines as a barrier to what they could do with their knowledge. In the absence of a sewing machine, a qualification in dressmaking has limited value. As noted by Robeyns (2017), considering such personal and socio-environmental profiles of individuals is important for understanding their ability to convert resources into achieved functionings. Thus, these extracts also show the importance of considering conversion factors for allowing present resources and capabilities to be converted into pathways to possible selves (Sen 1999).

Senses, Imagination and Thought

The capability for senses, imagination and thought was exhibited through the women's ability to critically reflect, reason and think about the possible futures a vocational education may bring for them. Tracy, who had not successfully completed high school, reflected on what she thought was possible under her migrant circumstances:

> I now want to sew. If I could study, I would study fashion designing. I like fashion. My mother has a machine and she just attended a six-month programme and now knows how to sew and she only went up to standard level at school. That's why I want to do that too. (Tracy)

The women were aware of what it would take to lead the lives they have reason to value, including pathways to future possible selves and the specific training required. This is closely linked to the capability of knowledge and imagination. According to Wilson-Strydom (2015), this capability can occur where one's social relations are smooth and affiliation (respect and recognition in relationships) is present to build their confidence. For migrant women this would entail receiving support from social surroundings beyond the opportunity to acquire skills. Social surroundings are important as this is where individual capabilities are influenced and possible selves imagined (Stern and Seifert 2013; Sen 2009). For that reason, support received by the women would require challenging dominant patriarchal narratives that limit women's potential to traditional gender roles. As will be seen in later extracts, this ability to use imagination and thought connects with the intrinsic and instrumental value accorded to skills development. Instrumentally, skills acquired through vocational training would widen income-generating and entrepreneurial opportunities. These opportunities would result in women being able to care for themselves and extended families or being able to afford a decent home. Intrinsically, skills to create income give one a sense of accomplishment which becomes foundational to other capabilities such as confidence.

Practical Reason

According to Nussbaum (2011:39), the capability of practical reason organizes all the others in that 'the opportunity to plan one's life is an opportunity to choose and order the functionings corresponding to the various other capabilities'. Wilson-Strydom (2015) notes that it is reasonable to argue that the capability of practical reason could be seen as a foundational capability as it involves the ability to make well-reasoned, informed, critical, independent and reflective choices about personal lives and aspirations and pathways to realize these aspirations.

Practical reason was evidenced by the women's ability to form a conception of a good life and to engage in critical reflection about the planning of their individual lives. They understood that to be successful they would need a skill set in line with the opportunities and freedoms available to them. Ruth, for example, described her reasons for wanting to enrol on an interior decorating course:

> I want to do interior decorating. I am planning to buy machines for embroidery and over-locking. I can go back to Zimbabwe and open a shop. If you do well, you can get jobs and tenders in either offices or churches. It's not a course that after you complete you have nothing to do, you always get something to do. (Ruth)

According to Watts (2009), a choice to pursue a trade vocational qualification instead of a university degree should be understood as a valued alternative career resulting from a well-thought-out process and choice. Practical reason allowed the women to have good judgement in choosing the kind of training they desired. They understood the possibilities that came with their choice, exhibiting the ability to make well-reasoned, informed, critical, independent and reflective choices about vocational education, subsequent skills and opportunities.

Control over One's Environment

Most of the women noted the desire to live a good life, the ability to care for themselves and their families, and to give back to the poor in their community, highlighting the desire to control their environment. The freedom to migrate and the desire to pursue a vocational skill expanded the capability of the women to have control over their environments. A vocational skill would further equip them with other capabilities necessary to expand and strengthen their control over the socio-economic environments they inhabited. Financially, they would be able to make decisions about their own daily needs and those of their families without fear. Socially, they may have influence in their communities and within their immediate spheres, such as family and friends. Such control was seen as important to equip the women with the ability to address those conversion factors that were limiting their potential to achieve their possible selves. For example, on what she hoped to be able to do after qualifying as an interior designer, Ruth explained her hopes to get work that would improve the life she is living:

> I want to be able to tell others that I once worked in South Africa as a child minder and housekeeper. I want to tell them as a history, at that time my life will be better. That time I should have my own big things. I want to drive my own car. I want to build an 8 roomed house; I want to have my own car. I want my first-born son to go to University. (Ruth)

However, for some, controlling their respective environments was limited by external factors. For example, upon arriving in South Africa, both Ruth and Rita had resorted to marriage in order to live what they viewed as better lives, but these choices brought about limitations to their freedom of choice and consequently their ability to control their environments. So, although Rita's husband suggested that she enrolled on a nail technician programme, Rita's autonomy to make independent decisions related to her possible self was limited by an external influencing factor. She noted:

> My husband wants me to do a nail beauty program. He said it's the one that does not take long to complete, and it has the potential to bring me money. I am also

afraid that I might get arrested on my way to college because I don't have papers. (Rita)

Such limitations may open women up to multiple risks and threats such as abuse, persistent and repressive gender roles, as well as violence and limitations imposed by immigration authorities. Thus, as the chapter advocates for the expansion of freedoms for women to make independent choices about who they desire to be, now and in the future, it is important to acknowledge the external social, political and gendered influences that affect these choices.

Conclusion

The experiences of the women in the study suggest that it is not only mainstream higher education that should be regarded as important in the development of an individual's life. They point to the value of vocational courses, including in areas such as dressmaking, beautician, hairdressing and decorating, which can play a significant role in the realization of migrant women's possible selves. There are multiple reasons that migrant women value vocational education in comparison to mainstream education. One of these is associated with the *temporariness of migration* – for many migrant women it would be difficult to develop and advance long-term aspirations (especially educational aspirations), as they view being in South Africa as temporary. The familial responsibilities that most of the women had in Zimbabwe made it difficult for them to imagine permanent settlement in South Africa. This temporariness is characterized by the desire to enrol in programmes that do not require long-term obligation. Hence, vocational programmes typically require short-term commitment, yet the subsequent opportunities associated with them may lead to increased levels of independence in different dimensions of their valued well-being. For many migrant women, this independence is associated with challenging gender stereotypes and patriarchal practices. Equipping women through appropriate education and training programmes, with skills that empower them, is then important to ensure that stereotypes and gendered expectations do not limit the potential of migrant women by virtue of relegating their capabilities to those of the home.

Note

1   All names in the chapter are pseudonyms.

References

Appadurai, A. (1996). *Modernity at Large: Cultural Dimensions of Globalization.* Minneapolis: University of Minnesota Press.

Besada, H. (2011). *Zimbabwe: Picking Up the Pieces.* New York: Palgrave MacMillan.

Birchall, J. (2016). *Gender, Age and Migration: An Extended Briefing.* https://opendocs .ids.ac.uk/opendocs/bitstream/handle/123456789/10410/Gender%20Age%20and %20Migration%20Extended%20Briefing.pdf?sequence=1 (accessed 19 October 2021).

Burchardt, T. (2005). *The Education and Employment of Disabled Young People: Frustrated Ambition.* Bristol: Policy Press.

Crush, J., Chikanda, A., & Tawodzera, G. (2015). 'The Third Wave: Mixed Migration From Zimbabwe to South Africa', *Canadian Journal of African Studies*, 49(2), 363–82.

Dannecker, P., & Sieveking, S. (2009). *Gender, Migration and Development: An Analysis of the Current Discussion on Female Migrants as Development Agents.* Working Papers – Centre on Migration, Citizenship and Development. https://www.ssoar.info /ssoar/handle/document/35340 (accessed 19 October 2021).

DeJaeghere, J. (2016). 'Girls' Educational Aspirations and Agency: Imagining Alternative Futures Through Schooling in a Low-Resourced Tanzanian Community', *Critical Studies in Education.* https://doi.org/10.1080/ 17508487.2016.1188835.

Dunkel, C., & Kerpelman, J. (2006). *Possible Selves: Theory, Research and Applications.* New York: Nova Science Publishers.

Hamman, D., Gosselina, K., Romanob, J., & Bunuan, R. (2010). 'Using Possible-selves Theory to Understand the Identity Development of new Teachers', *Teaching and Teacher Education*, 26, 1349–61.

Hamman, D., Wang, E., & Burley, H. (2013). 'What I Expect and Fear Next Year: Measuring new Teachers' Possible Selves', *Journal of Education for Teaching*, 39(2), 222–34, https://doi.org/10.1080/02607476.2013.765194.

Khan, F. (2007). *Patterns and Policies of Migration in South Africa: Changing Patterns and the Need for a Comprehensive Approach.* Cape Town: University of Cape Town Refugee Rights Project. http://www.refugeerights.uct.ac.za/downloads/ refugeerights.uct.ac.za/patterns_policies_migration_FKhan.doc (accessed 19 October 2021).

Markus, H., & Nurius, P. (1986). 'Possible Selves'. *American Psychologist*, 41(9), 954–69.

Mkwananzi, F. (2019). *Higher Education, Youth and Migration in Contexts of Disadvantage: Understanding Aspirations and Capabilities.* London: Palgrave McMillan.

Mkwananzi, F., & Cin, F.M. (2020). 'From Streets to Developing Aspirations: How Does Collective Agency for Education Change Marginalised Migrant Youths' Lives?', *Journal of Human Development and Capabilities*, 21(4), 320–38. https://doi.org/10 .1080/19452829.2020.1801609.

Nussbaum, M. (2011). *Creating Capabilities: The Human Development Approach.* Harvard: Harvard University Press.

Peberdy, S., Crush, J., & Msibi, N. (2004). *Migrants in the City of Johannesburg: A Report for the City of Johannesburg.* Southern African Migration Project. https://samponline.org/wp-content/uploads/2017/12/Migrants-in-the-City-of -Johannesburg-.pdf.

Ratha, D., & Shaw, W. (2007). *South-South Migration and Remittances.* Development Prospects Group, World Bank. https://openknowledge.worldbank.org/handle/10986 /6733 (accessed 19 October 2021).

Robeyns, I. (2017). *Wellbeing, Freedom and Social Justice: The Capability Approach re-examined.* Cambridge: Open Book Publishers.

Sen, A. (1999). *Development as Freedom.* Oxford: Oxford University Press.

Sen, A. (2009). *The Idea of Justice.* Cambridge, MA: Harvard University Press.

Skeldon, R. (2008). *Migration Policies and the Millennium Development Goals.* London: Progressive Governance.

Stern, M. J., & Seifert, S.C. (2013). 'Creative Capabilities and Community Capacity', in H. U. Otto & H. Ziegler (Eds), *Enhancing Capabilities: The Role of Social Institutions.* Berlin and Toronto: Barbara Budrich Publishers, 179–96.

Trimikliniotis, N., Gordon, S., & Zondo, B. (2009). 'Globalisation and Migrant Labour in a "Rainbow Nation": A Fortress South Africa?', in R. Munck (Ed), *Globalization and Migration: New Issues, New Politics.* London and New York: Routledge Taylor and Francis Group, 95–111.

Ulicki, T., & Crush, J. (2010). 'Poverty, Gender and Migrancy: Lesotho's Migrant Farmworkers in South Africa', in J. Crush & B. Frayne (Eds), *Surviving on the Move: Migration, Poverty, and Development in Southern Africa.* Cape Town: Logo Print, 164–82.

UNDP (2010). 'The Potential Contribution of the Zimbabwe Diaspora to Economic Recovery'. Working Paper 11. Available Online: http://archive.kubatana.net/docs/ econ/undp_contribution_diaspora_eco_recovery_100511.pdf (accessed 05 April 2022).

UNICEF (2009). *Zimbabwe Education Crisis Worsens.* http://www.unicef.org/media/ media_47915.html (accessed 19 October 2021).

Waddington, H., & Sabates-Wheeler, R. (2003). *How Does Poverty Affect Migration Choice? A Review of Literature.* Working Paper 3, December. Institute of Development Studies, Sussex.

Walker, M. (2006). *Higher Education Pedagogies: A Capabilities Approach.* Maidenhead: Open University Press and the Society for Research Into Higher Education.

Watts, M. (2009). 'Sen and the Art of Motorcycle Maintenance: Adaptive Preferences and Higher Education'. *Studies in Philosophy and Education*, 28, 425–36.

Wentzel, M., & Tlabela, K. (2006). 'Historical Background to South African Migration', in P. Kok, D. Gelderblom, J.O. Oucho, & J. van Zyl (Eds), *Migration in South and Southern Africa: Dynamics and Determinants.* Cape Town: HSRC Press, 79–96.

Wilson-Strydom, M. (2015). 'University Access and Theories of Social Justice: Contributions of the Capabilities Approach', *Higher Education*, 69(1), 143–55.

World Health Organisation. (2017). 'Women on the Move: Migration, Care Work and Health'. https://apps.who.int/iris/bitstream/handle/10665/259463/9789241513142 -eng.pdf (accessed 19 October 2021).

13

Trading Futures

The Place of Education in the Trajectories of Unaccompanied Migrant Young Men Becoming Adult in England and Italy

Jennifer Allsopp and Elaine Chase

Introduction

Each year a fluctuating number of children and young people under the age of eighteen migrate without an accompanying adult into Europe and are cared for as 'unaccompanied asylum- seeking children' within welfare and care systems. They originate from a variety of countries experiencing war, corruption, intercommunal violence or economic insecurity, including, among others, Afghanistan, Eritrea, Albania, Syria, Iran and Iraq. After arriving in Europe, whether and how young people enter the welfare system and are recognized by the authorities as children requiring support is shaped by various factors including their attempts to reunite with family members in certain countries, language skills or simply the whim of smugglers. Unlike adult asylum seekers in Europe, unaccompanied minors are not required to submit their asylum application in the country of first arrival. While throughout most of the 1990s, the number of asylum-seeking children migrating alone to Europe fluctuated between 12,000 and 14,000, there have been times, such as during the so-called refugee crisis of 2015, when this rose to as many as 90,000 (Eurostat 2016). By 2020, in part due to a range of new deterrence measures aimed to combat smuggling and irregular arrivals (Carrera et al. 2018), applications in the EU from unaccompanied minors had fallen again to 13,600 (Eurostat 2020).

An unknown number of migrant children also arrive each year without family members but remain hidden to or go 'missing' from immigration and welfare authorities (Sigona and Allsopp 2016; Humpris and Sigona 2016), often refusing to be counted for a variety of reasons including the fear of detention and deportation (Allsopp and Chase 2019; Bloch and Schuster 2005; Schuster 2005; De Genova and Peutz 2010). Despite claims to common standards across the European Union (EU) for upholding the rights of unaccompanied minors, young people's outcomes and opportunities vary according to the different welfare state and immigration control architectures they encounter (Chase and Allsopp 2020).

Children and young people recognized as unaccompanied minors by state authorities are entitled to a range of welfare services which are tailored to their age and circumstances and include opportunities for education and learning. Education for migrant children and young people is framed primarily as a basic and universal human right, in keeping with Article 28 of the UN Convention on the Rights of the Child (UNCRC). It is also identified as something which is fundamentally beneficial and in the 'best interests'[1] of all children and young people.

Research to date (Canzales and Diaz-Strong 2021) has tended to focus on exploring the processes which facilitate and/or inhibit the integration of migrant children and young people into pre-existing school structures and systems, taking account of issues of pedagogy, curriculum and ethos (Ott and O'Higgins 2019). Most work is also underpinned by normative ideas about the value of education and the need to mitigate challenges to educational access for migrant children and young people, particularly in situations of emergencies and crisis (Abu Moghli, Chapter 4). Within this frame, migrant and refugee children are defined as rights holders or foreign citizens with an inherent universal right to education.

Certain assumptions about access to and the role of learning and education have, however, been problematized. For example, it has been shown that despite the intention of schools to create spaces for the integration and well-being of migrant young people, schools may actually promote exclusion of particular groups, including unaccompanied child arrivals (Canizales and Diaz-Strong 2021; Salem, Chapter 14). Moreover, difficulties in accessing learning as well as in timing and appropriateness of learning opportunities have been documented over a number of decades (Refugee Support Network 2012; Allsopp et al. 2015; Ott and O'Higgins 2019). These challenges in accessing education aside, for unaccompanied migrant children and young people education, may be one of several intersecting migration objectives to be negotiated alongside work, private life and the pursuit of safety and security (Chase and Allsopp 2020). Migrant young people's own understandings and values in relation to education respective to their migratory trajectories and futures are poorly understood, and there has been limited or no consideration of the implications of such perspectives for policy and practice. Moreover, the education of children and youth in the European tradition tends to focus on the individual learner and apply standardized curricula to which learners must adapt. Scant, if any, attention is afforded to the learners' wider relational contexts, although, as we shall see, in Italy the approach to education of unaccompanied minors is less standardized.

Based on the narratives and experiences of unaccompanied young people seeking asylum in the UK and Italy, this chapter unsettles the highly normative ideas contained within educational policy for migrant children and young people and considers how education is situated within the wider political, social and cultural realities of their lives at particular moments in time. It focuses on the factors shaping migrant young people's decisions about their pursued futures in relation to educational progress or alternative work-based trajectories. Such decisions were significantly influenced by a range of structural and institutional opportunities and constraints (fundamentally linked to their legal status and access to social rights). Moreover, these trajectories were equally determined by their broader identities as migrant young people intimately tied to others through their transnational obligations and commitments for collective better futures and, for many, their role as 'breadwinners' who had responsibility for siblings or family members abroad. Education therefore emerged as a consideration within the trade-offs which young people had to make in relation to their migrant selves, their own future and the futures of others. The chapter illustrates how by adopting this wider sociopolitical frame in relation to the perceived value given to education requires a reconsideration of how education might be made more fit for purpose in situations of multiple and intersecting transitions.

Methodology

The chapter draws on data from the Becoming Adult[2] project, a three-year longitudinal, qualitative and peer research project in England and Italy. The research explored the well-being outcomes of children and young people arriving in England and Italy on their own, and bureaucratically defined as 'unaccompanied minors', as they made their way to institutionally defined 'adulthood' at the age of eighteen years. More than 100 unaccompanied migrant young people participated in the study in England and Italy. While all participants in England were from Afghanistan, Albania and Eritrea, those participating in Italy were from a more diverse range of countries of origin. In keeping with the demographics of children and young people migrating on their own internationally, the majority of participants (90 per cent) were male. A core characteristic of the project was that it was developed in partnership with a group of young people who had similarly arrived on their own into Europe as young migrants and who played a key role in all aspects of the research, including refining the research design, data collection, analysis and writing for publication and presentation to a range of audiences.[3] The study was approved by the research ethics committee of the University of Oxford and University College London respectively.

Understanding the Value of Education through the Capabilities Approach

The capability approach is a helpful framework for considering what migrant children and young people have reason to value with respect to education as well as, importantly, the freedoms they have to achieve what they aspire to. The approach, developed by Amartya Sen (1993) and others (Nussbaum 2011; Robeyns 2016), contests ideas of human development related to solely the enhancement of human capital and instead engages with notions such as human flourishing, freedom and emancipation (Clark 2006). Sen argues that the quality of people's lives should be the ultimate goal and that production and prosperity should be seen as means to allow people to live the lives they value (Sen 1993).

The capability approach helps distinguish between the freedoms and opportunities that migrant children and young people have to be and do what they most value, so-called capabilities, and what they are able to achieve in practice, so-called functionings. The political goal should be to expand such opportunities and freedoms (Nussbaum 2002), better understand the factors constraining young people's ability to access and make the most of freedoms and opportunities (Burchardt and Vizard 2011), and engage with the power relations that determine what constitute 'genuine choices' for young people to take action (Wolff and De-Shalit 2007; Dean 2009). Moreover, the approach enables us to move beyond ideas of negative freedoms, such as protection from harm (Landau and Duponchel 2011), towards positive freedoms or the enhancement of opportunities for migrant young people to lead the lives they most value (Zimmerman 2006; Dean 2009; Walby 2012). It thus moves us beyond questions of access and quality of education and the accepted idea that it is both desirable and in young people's best interests to pursue it in its more conventional form, to consider more specifically what young people want to achieve formatively with respect to the wider contexts of their lives and the economic and social obligations that drive their migratory decisions in the first place.

Findings

Young people participating in the research had varied educational experiences before coming to Europe which were determined in large part by their economic, social, political and cultural histories. This is true despite the fact that they tend to be considered a largely homogenous group requiring similar forms of access to welfare services and support. While some young people had never studied in formal educational settings and had limited literacy skills, as was the case, for example, for some young men from Afghanistan, others had learnt these skills at Qur'anic schools or from family members. Of the two other main countries of origin of young people included in the research, all Albanians in the study had some level of pre-existing education, as did individuals from Eritrea. Many minors from Eritrea explained that it was the pending transition out of education, with its obligatory subsequent enrolment in the national army, that prompted their flight. Aaron, for example, spoke angrily of how his father had been enslaved to the military and that in his father's absence he was forced to leave school and find work to support his family. Leaving school to work in Eritrea meant he risked being conscripted indefinitely into the army himself and so Aaron felt he had no option but to go abroad.

How unaccompanied young people in the study entered education once in Europe depended on their age upon contact with authorities, or the age they were assessed to be (Kenny and Loughry 2018), as well as resources available locally and regionally (including school places, type of school and policies governing access to education) and individual proficiency in English language and literacy. In England, some young people were immersed in the local school almost immediately, finding themselves wearing a school uniform and sitting in a classroom where they understood little or nothing. Others experienced delays of weeks or even months while a school place was found for them (Ott and O'Higgins 2019). For some, school was primarily experienced through a series of ESOL (English as a Second Language) classes where they were placed in smaller groups of foreign language students in classes specifically designed to catch them up.

In Italy, by contrast, there was more variation in young people's educational trajectories across regions and within individual cities. In some cases, unaccompanied minors frequented mainstream schools, while in others they attended separate institutions or classes after mainstream school with little or no contact with Italian students. Other reception centres in the South relied almost entirely on volunteer teachers. As in England, young people often experienced delays of weeks or months while schools were found for them. During these delays, in Italy as in England, some individuals took it into their own hands to attend English and Italian classes run by NGOs or other bodies. One young man explained that he would travel around Rome to attend three different classes in one day – without learning Italian, he said, he was 'nothing' – 'nessuno'.

Barriers to Accessing Education

Even those young people who felt more ambivalent about education often struggled with issues of access. Some were unable to secure a school place, as noted earlier, because of when they arrived in the school term. Others were desperate to move on to what they perceived as more relevant curricula related to mechanics, plumbing or engineering but found themselves having to repeatedly take ESOL or Italian language classes until they could meet the required standard to be able to access more diverse curricula. Given that the majority of unaccompanied young people arrive in countries of destination in their mid-to-late teens, many were excluded from learning opportunities due to age assessments which determined them to be older than their actual age. Others were re-assessed once in the classroom as being too old or too young which led to further disruptions in their educational placements.

Idriz from Albania had been age-disputed by the local authority in which he was placed with the result that he was denied any support, including access to education, even though the UK Home Office had accepted his age as being sixteen and despite the fact that a court ruling stated that the local authority was legally obliged to accommodate and support him. He described feeling so isolated and excluded that he attempted to take his own life by walking in front of a car. Many others who reached eighteen with no secure legal status described how their educational access was abruptly curtailed from one day to the next.

Similarly in Italy, the critical role of age assessments and the variation in local services in shaping young peoples' outcomes was exemplified in the case of Midi from Senegal. He explained that after he had arrived in Southern Italy at the age of sixteen, he was held in a reception centre where educational services were very limited. He explained how a volunteer Italian teacher recognized his potential,

> She wanted me to study. If you go elsewhere, she told me, you can study properly. You know me, I'm not here to work. I want to study . . . She even got me the ticket! She gave me books and helped me a lot. Then in Rome we had the problems.

In reality, when Midi arrived in the capital and presented himself as instructed to the police, he was age-assessed a second time and found to be eighteen which disqualified him not just from school but also from youth housing. In the two years we followed Midi, his lawyer had still not been able to track down documentation of his initial age assessment and asylum claim in Southern Italy. Educational pathways for unaccompanied minors thus intersected with a range of other bureaucratic hurdles which could shift over place and time and also be subject to the whim of 'everyday bureaucrats' working in the public and private sectors (Lipsky 1980).

Aside from directly blocking access to education for many young people, the asylum system created multiple other challenges to learning, including time-consuming meetings with solicitors, social workers and other professionals; having to work to find resources to pay for legal advice when young people were no longer eligible for legal aid (or were unaware of their eligibility) and, probably most commonly, the psychological barriers that were generated by the sheer stress and uncertainty of the asylum process. Many young people spoke of difficulties in concentrating, sleepless nights that left them unable to study; or episodes of such acute anxiety that they couldn't even face going into school or college. Kamal from Afghanistan was facing the prospect of forced return to Afghanistan and spoke of the impact this had on his ability to concentrate,

> Sometimes you know I'm sat there and I'm trying to do my Maths and I get bored you know. I think, why do I do this? How will this help me if I go back to Afghanistan? And I am just looking out of the window at people going by.

Similarly, Izat, also from Afghanistan, spoke of how he put his educational plans on hold when his asylum claim was refused by the Home Office, because he could not cope with the stress and the impact it would have on what he could achieve.

> I couldn't cope with the exams and also my court case. . . . So I wanted to get one out of the way so that I could concentrate. Because I had high hopes at college and I was doing really well . . . but I did not want my court case to affect my studies.

Because there's no point doing it and you end up with getting low grades – you can't do anything with the low grade.

A further set of barriers to learning were social and generated by the educational spaces in which young people found themselves and where many experienced bullying, harassment, discrimination and exclusion. One young Afghan, for example, explained how he was repeatedly referred to as a Taliban member by classmates, while an Albanian young woman reported being the subject of sexual harassment by boys in her class – something that she felt powerless to respond to. Bilal reported an incident at his school where the police were called after he fought back against a student who constantly bullied him yet his complaints to staff had been ignored. While the involvement of police could have had serious implications for his asylum claim, he explained how this was avoided by his social worker who stood up for him.

In other cases, young people explained how individual educators had gone out of their way to provide extra support to them, including giving evidence about their moral character and successful integration into school at their asylum appeals. Somewhat counterintuitively, young people's success at school was sometimes used by the Home Office as grounds to refuse the young people, with government representatives arguing that educational achievements could be seen as evidence of requisite social capital for reintegration and for finding employment back in their countries of origin, in particular, at the time of research, in Afghanistan. For this group, the pursuit of education could thus undermine the parallel pursuits of future safety, work and private life in England.

Accommodating Education within Migratory Projects

A major challenge for many young people in the study was how best to accommodate education within their broader migratory projects which often included meeting the expectations placed on them by others. Hence the goal of getting an education had to be balanced with the urgent need to earn money – this may be to repay debts from the journey but also to help family members survive or enable others to also migrate to places of safety. Cole (2015) has shown in relation to Eritrea, for example, that the migration of one person in a family – usually a young man in a transnational breadwinner model – can provide a survival line through remittances to generations of family members.

Many young people in our study felt a strong sense of guilt at not being able to earn money to help others. In Italy, cultural mediators were sometimes able to speak to families on behalf of the young people to explain that the minors simply were not legally allowed to work and were obliged to attend school. In England, however, the situation was complicated by the fact that most young people were unwilling to share details of their family or other commitments with their social worker or key worker for fear it would be used against them as justification to return them to their country of origin. These fears were not unfounded. Social workers in England are obliged to report evidence of relationships to the Home Office, and, unlike Italy, the UK has no legislative ban on the forced return of children. As such, many young people in the study sought to manage the pressures from their family themselves, without any support. One young person described it as like having a huge weight on their back all the time. During a residential meeting of research assistants working on the project, a group of Afghans joked about the impossibilities of meeting their families' expectations by describing themselves as chickens expected to lay golden eggs.

The disconnect between how education is conceived of by policymakers and practitioners, based on highly normative ideas about what should be learned, when learning should take place and what education is for, and the lived realities of people in contexts of migration and (im)mobility relates in part to the misnomers and problems of labelling people into particular migrant categories (Zetter 2007) and in the case of young people, particularly in relation to their 'unaccompanied' status (Lems et al. 2019). Such an approach situates young people within an individualized frame, ignoring the connections, ties and responsibilities that they have to others – and how any sense of well-being and achievement is intrinsically relational and contingent on the well-being of others (White 2016). This divorce of unaccompanied minors from their relational context in the asylum system is exemplified by the fact that the UK still denies unaccompanied asylum-seeking minors the right to family reunification in the UK.

Access to education and learning is similarly seen to signify a line between childhood and adulthood, where work is assumed to be a marker of 'adulthood' and education is seen as a stage prior to, rather than simultaneous to, livelihood and career development. This problematic bifurcation of education and work mapped onto a Eurocentric reading of childhood and adulthood ignores the fact that in most cultures 'normal' practices of childhood do not exclude simultaneously contributing to livelihoods or taking on certain roles and responsibilities associated with 'adulthood' (Morrow and Boyden 2018);

and that these roles may be particularly accentuated in contexts of migration (Heidbrink 2020). As is explored in other chapters in this volume, such narrow conceptualizations of education and learning tend to dismiss the complexities of people's lives and how they intend to live them – including the realities for child workers as well as adult learners in contexts of migration.

The research demonstrated that failing to engage with and understand the wider pressures on unaccompanied children and young people to work often lead to emotional anguish – a guilt that manifested in poor sleep, poor eating, headaches and stomach aches, depression, anxiety and suicidal feelings (Chase and Allsopp 2020). One young Afghan explained how absurd he found it to be learning about Shakespeare when his little brother in Afghanistan was starving with nothing to eat. In the absence of the legal right to work, faced with delays in receiving documentation of their right to work or without the time to work because of full-time school commitments, young people in the study would sometimes take on exploitative and poorly paid evening jobs to earn what little money they could cash-in-hand, as dishwashers, carwash attendants or, in some cases, sex workers. Others would save the meagre allowances they were given as pocket money by social workers or foster carers and send home. In extreme cases, the young people would disappear off the radar, dropping out of school and supported housing to pursue work full-time – sometimes in situations that equated to modern-day slavery or trafficking. Referring to his own series of precarious jobs, one Afghan in Italy commented, 'migrants are the new slaves of the world.'

The failure of institutional mechanisms to recognize many minors' need to work meant various bureaucratic systems were not fit for purpose. One example of this is the high numbers of minors recorded as 'missing' from reception centres in Italy, in some cases simply because they failed to meet a curfew because they were working. This reality means estimates of the true number of 'missing' migrants out of social care, said to be 10,000 at the time of research in 2016 (ECRE 2016), are unreliable (Sigona and Allsopp 2016). In Italy, sometimes social workers and educators were able to help young people to find decent employment that they could manage alongside their education. In Italy, for minors refused asylum, there is an opportunity to extend their permit for a year on a rolling basis if they can prove that they meet certain eligibility criteria and are enrolled on an education or work pathway. Having a job in the run up to turning eighteen is important to build trust with an employer to convince them to sponsor a work-based extension. Finding a healthy balance between education and work then was a crucial part of 'becoming adult' for many participants in our research.

Young People's Access to 'Valuable' Learning

Non-formal educational settings, such as those run by churches, activist groups or NGO youth groups, were found to be crucial in both contexts. Not only did these spaces provide access for individuals held back from formal schooling due to bureaucratic delays, age assessments or other factors, they also created environments which some found to be more friendly, suited to their specific needs and which could be fitted into their schedules and balanced with other pursuits, such as working or family life. A youth group in a city in England, for example, where we spent time for the research, encouraged women with babies to bring them along and trained volunteers to assist with childcare during activities. The same youth group offered cooking classes where young women in the group would sometimes take on the role of peer-educators to young men less acquainted with cooking skills, a role they seemed to take pride in and enjoy. There was also evidence that the young people attending these groups were able to have more say in setting the curriculum. In Italy, young people often said that they wanted to learn English alongside Italian. As such, volunteers were found to provide a series of English classes. Another skill that was taught at multiple sites in Italy (and in other transit countries visited in the course of other research) was map reading. This was something individuals specifically asked for so that they could better understand the geography of Europe and to be able to place where family and friends might be, as well as plan potential future travels themselves.

NGO youth workers also used their own knowledge of the specific experiences of unaccompanied minors from certain backgrounds to provide specific learning opportunities suited to their skill sets and needs. One youth worker explained that each year they ran sexual health workshops to respond to young people's identified needs for further information and support on these issues. Another led regular trips to a local farm where young people from rural backgrounds were able to learn about UK livestock – something of specific interest to many of them, given their farming backgrounds. These spaces were also important to allow young people to show off specific skills they had that fell outside of traditional education models. On one farm trip, for example, a group of Eritrean young men who had grown up on farms proudly showed off their cow milking skills, taking selfies and looking visibly chuffed by our impressed response.

These informal learning spaces also allowed local communities to shape the curriculum in ways which were relevant to young people's lives. In Rome, for example, volunteers ran weekly tours around the city for recently arrived refugees, including unaccompanied youth. They believed that by helping young people learn about the local history they were performing an act of making them feel welcome. Alternative or non-formal learning spaces also prioritized therapeutic interventions including sports and art that served a dual purpose of learning and healing.

Discussion and Conclusion

The unique positioning of unaccompanied minors in relation to the education system raises issues not only about the right to and practical access to education but also, more fundamentally, about what is education for and how can it help young people balance short- and longer-term learning needs. The Becoming Adult research project revealed a stark boundary in how the immigration system treats asylum seekers – as either children – up to the age of eighteen – or adults, with little support in navigating this transition. In the field of education, too, we talk a lot of children's education and adult education, but less consideration is given to education tailored to groups who are on the cusp of adulthood and straddle needs and desires on both sides of this divide.

The research revealed that welfare systems in England and Italy had intrinsic advantages and inadequacies that created different kinds of opportunities for young people at different points in their migration journeys. On the whole, though, Italy has come further than England in recognizing the reality of the educational quandary facing unaccompanied minors. Unlike the UK, at the time of research, Italy allowed unaccompanied minors who had been refused asylum the possibility to extend their visa at the age of eighteen for a further year if they could demonstrate certain criteria, including prospects for further study or work. This served to motivate students to either stay in school or pursue vocational opportunities more aligned with their immediate work needs.

It would appear that for education to best function as a tool for integration for unaccompanied asylum-seeking young people in Europe, there is a need to better connect their lived experiences of migration to the knowledge gaps specific to their experience. While there were undoubtedly multiple examples in the research of young people keen to pursue formal study pathways, often in the face of multiple obstacles, for others, education was seen in a broader sense as the acquiring of specific competences that would help their primary migration projects of working and securing papers in the short and medium term. This included, for example, learning English as a pathway to employment or educating themselves in the asylum system so as better to exercise their rights.

While most of their fellow students can study in the knowledge that they are working towards futures that they have a right to realize in Europe, unaccompanied asylum-seeking minor students are often studying while being subjected to an asylum process that will determine that many of them are returnable to countries of origin and will ultimately be unable to legally pursue their future plans in Europe. For those assigned a form of temporary leave to remain until they are seventeen and a half in the UK, or eighteen in Italy, this uncertainty pertaining to their futures and what will happen when they come of age is a source of acute anxiety and can be demotivating for education. First, the whole process of seeking asylum is stressful and this can have a direct impact on students' ability to study and concentrate. Second, if students fear refusal and eventual detention or deportation, they may adopt one of two strategies – either studying hard to get qualifications that they feel might serve them back in their countries (something reported to be the case among many Albanians in Italy), or they may feel extra pressure to give up on education and work to accrue resources for themselves and their families while they still have the chance.

We have shown how adopting a capabilities approach may serve to better elucidate opportunities and risks for this group in their particular position in relation to formal and informal education spaces as well as more academic and vocational studies. More research could be done in this vein to explore what unaccompanied migrant learners value from their educational experiences, especially in terms of learning about their rights and skills for practically navigating the asylum system and their new place in the world. Cosmopolitan critical literacy (Bean and Dunkerly-Bean 2020; Dunkerly-Bean et al. 2014) is a helpful framework here, drawing attention as it does to the dual orientation of learning as at once situated in a specific place, time and culture, yet also moving towards the development of transnational meanings and new connections. This theory recognizes education in all forms as a 'political project'. It involves thinking beyond merely linking well-being outcomes to knowledge, to include thinking about the wider structures and factors that facilitate or undermine human flourishing.

We must nevertheless also be wary of over-fetishizing the unaccompanied migrant learner and their specific relationship to the global. As we have argued previously (Chase and Allsopp 2014), in framing unaccompanied minors as 'citizens of the world' (Drammeh 2010), certain European policies such as the European Life Project Planning framework have promoted the cosmopolitan at the expense of the need to root unaccompanied minors in their new host countries. This logic has paved the way for educational interventions which invest in the possibility of return at the expense of local integration.

Reflecting on the failure of one such targeted vocational training attempt to prepare young people for the likelihood of return to their homeland from the Netherlands, in which young people were offered cash payments, vocational training before departure or craftsman's tools to take with them, Kromhout (2011) concludes,

> The significant number of separated young people departing for unknown destinations instead of returning to their country of origin is a cause for great concern among Dutch politicians, welfare organisations, and NGOs [. . .] It is feared that they run the risk of ending up on the streets and being exploited by traffickers. (p. 27)

Educators have to recognize the specific needs of this population within and across different contexts while also being wary not to essentialize their position. Asking unaccompanied asylum-seeking young people what they value in terms of learning and personal formation, and how this sits alongside other obligations and priorities in their migratory projects, would be a good place to start.

Notes

1 As defined by Article 3(1) of the UNCRC.
2 https://becomingadult.net/.
3 For a more detailed discussion of the methodological aspects of the study, see Chase and Allsopp (2020).

References

Allsopp, J., & Chase, E. (2019). 'Best Interests, Durable Solutions and Belonging: Policy Discourses Shaping the Futures of Unaccompanied Migrant and Refugee Minors Coming of age in Europe', *Journal of Ethnic and Migration Studies*, 45(2), 293–311.

Allsopp, J., Chase, E., & Mitchell, M. (2015). 'The Tactics of Time and Status: Young People's Experiences of Constructing Futures While Subject to Immigration Control', *Journal of Refugee Studies*, 28(2), 163–82.

Bean, T.W., & Dunkerly-Bean, J. (2020). 'Cosmopolitan Critical Literacy and Youth Civic Engagement for Human Rights'. *Pedagogies: An International Journal*, 15(4), 262–78.

Bloch, A., & Schuster, L (2005). 'At the Extremes of Exclusion: Deportation, Detention and Dispersal', *Ethnic and Racial Studies*, 28(3), 491–512.

Burchardt, T., & Vizard, P. (2011). '"Operationalizing" the Capability Approach as a Basis for Equality and Human Rights Monitoring in Twenty-first-century Britain', *Journal of Human Development and Capabilities*, 12(1), 91–119.

Canzales, S., & Diaz-Strong, D.X. (2021), '*Undocumented Childhood Arrivals in the U.S.: Widening the Frame for Research and Policy*,' Immigration Initiative at Harvard Issue Brief Series no. 11. Cambridge, MA: Harvard University Press.

Carrera, S., Mitsilegas V., Allsopp, J., & Vosyliūtė, L. (2018). *Policing Humanitarianism: EU Policies Against Human Smuggling and Their Impact on Civil Society*. London: Hart.

Chase, E., & Allsopp, J. (2014). '"Future Citizens of the World"? The Contested Futures of Independent Young Migrants in Europe', RSC Working Paper Series no. 97; Barnett Papers in Social Research Working Paper 13-05, Oxford: Refugee Studies Centre; Oxford: DSPI.

Chase, E., & Allsopp, J. (2020). *Youth Migration and the Politics of Wellbeing: Stories of Life in Transition*. London: Bristol University Press.

Clark, D. (2006). 'The Capability Approach: Its Development, Critiques and Recent Advances', Global Poverty Research Group Working Paper. https://base.socioeco.org /docs/developments_critiques_advances.pdf (accessed 18 October 2021).

Cole, G. (2015). 'Refugee or Economic Migrant? Join the Dots Theresa May', *Open Democracy*, 8 October. https://www. opendemocracy.net/en/5050/refugee-or-eco nomic-migrant-join-dots- theresa-may/ (accessed 11 May 2020).

Dean, H. (2009). 'Critiquing Capabilities: The Distractions of a Beguiling Concept', *Critical Social Policy*, 29(2), 261–78.

De Genova, N., & Peutz, N. (2010). *The Deportation Regime. Sovereignty, Space, and the Freedom of Movement*. Durham, NC: Duke University Press.

Drammeh, L. (2010). 'Life Projects for Unaccompanied Migrant Minors: A Handbook for Front-line Professionals', Council of Europe, Migration Collection. http:// www.coe.int/t/dg3/migration/ archives/Source/ID10053-Life%20projects_GB.pdf (accessed 28 March 2020).

Dunkerly-Bean, J., Bean, T., & Alnajjar, K. (2014). 'Seeking Asylum: Adolescents Explore the Crossroads of Human Rights Education and Cosmopolitan Critical Literacy', *Journal of Adolescent & Adult Literacy*, 58(3), 230–41.

European Council on Refugees and Exiles (ECRE) (2016). 'Europol 14 Estimates 10,000 Underage Refugee Children Have Gone Missing, 5 February 2016'. https://www.ecre .org/europol-estimates-10000- 16 underage-refugee-children-have-gone-missing/ (accessed 1 April 2019).

Eurostat (2016). *Asylum Statistics*. http://ec.europa.eu/eurostat/en/web/products -datasets/-/TPS00189 (accessed 19 October 2021).

Eurostat (2020). *Asylum Statistics.* https://ec.europa.eu/eurostat/statistics-explained/
index.php?title=Asylum_statistics&oldid=539013#Applications_by_unaccompanied
_minors (accessed 28 September 2021).

Heidbrink, L. (2020). *Migranthood: Youth in New Era of Deportation.* Stanford: Stanford
University Press.

Humphris, R., & Sigona, N. (2016). 'Mapping Unaccompanied Asylum Seeking
Children in England', Becoming Adult Research Brief, no. 1. London: UCL.

Kenny, M.A., & Loughry, M. (2018). 'Addressing the Limitations of age Determination
for Unaccompanied Minors: A way Forward', *Children and Youth Services Review,*
92, 15–21.

Kromhout, M. (2011). 'Return of Separated Children: The Impact of Dutch Policies',
International Migration, 49(5), 24–47.

Landau, L., & Duponchel, M. (2011). 'Laws, Policies, or Social Position? Capabilities
and the Determinants of Effective Protection in Four African Cities', *Journal of
Refugee Studies,* 24(1), 1–22.

Lems, A., Oester, K., & Strasser, S. (Eds). (2019). 'Children of the Crisis: Ethnographic
Perspectives on Unaccompanied Refugee Youth in and en Route to Europe', *Journal
of Ethnic and Migration Studies,* 46(2), 315–35.

Lipsky, M. (1980). *Street Level Bureaucrats.* New York: Russell Sage Foundation.

Morrow, V., & Boyden, J. (2018). *Responding to Children's Work: Evidence From the
Young Lives Study in Ethiopia, India, Peru and Vietnam.* Summative Report. Oxford:
Young Lives.

Nussbaum, M. (2002). 'Capabilities and Social Justice', *International Studies Review,*
4(2), 123–35.

Nussbaum, M. (2011). *Creating Capabilities.* Cambridge, MA: Harvard University Press.

Ott, E., & O'Higgins, E. (2019). 'Conceptualising Educational Provision for
Unaccompanied Asylum-seeking Children in England', *Oxford Review of Education,*
45(4), 556–72.

Refugee Support Network (2012). *'I Just Want to Study': Access to Higher Education for
Young Refugees.* London: Refugee Support Network.

Robeyns, I. (2016). 'Capabilitarianism', *Journal of Human Development and Capabilities,*
17(3), 397–414.

Schuster, L. (2005). 'A Sledgehammer to Crack a nut: Deportation, Detention and
Dispersal in Europe', *Social Policy and Administration,* 39(6), 606–21.

Sen, A.K. (1993). 'Capability and Well-being', in M. Nussbaum & A.K. Sen (Eds), *The
Quality of Life.* Oxford: Clarendon Press, 30–53.

Sigona, N., & Allsopp, J. (2016). 'Mind the Gap: Why Are Unaccompanied Children
Disappearing in Their Thousands?', *openDemocracy,* 22 February. https://www
.opendemocracy.net/en/5050/mind-gap- why-are-unaccompanied-children-disa
ppearing-in-thous/ (accessed 24 February 2018).

Walby, S. (2012). 'Sen and the Measurement of Justice and Capabilities: A Problem in
Theory and Practice', *Theory, Culture & Society,* 29(1), 99–118.

White, S. (2016). *Cultures of Wellbeing: Method, Place, Policy*, Basingstoke: Palgrave Macmillan.

Wolff, J., & de-Shalit, A. (2007). *Disadvantage*. Oxford, Oxford University Press.

Zetter, R. (2007). 'More Labels, Fewer Refugees: Remaking the Refugee Label 23 in an era of Globalization', *Journal of Refugee Studies*, 20(2), 172–92.

Zimmermann, B. (2006). 'Pragmatism and the Capability Approach: Challenges in Social Theory and Empirical Research', *European Journal of Social Theory*, 9(4), 467–84.

14

The Mediating Role of Education

Learning as Syrian Refugee Young People in Jordan

Hiba Salem

I want the future as soon as possible. I want to only think about the future.
I want to only focus on what I want to become.

During an interview, Salma, sixteen years old, describes her desire to forget the past, speed through the present and live only in a future time. Her words bring to life the urgency experienced by individuals trapped within the protracted situation of forced displacement, whose aspirations and dreams are negotiated in a state of 'waiting' within a 'never-ending present' (Conlon 2011; Brun 2015). Like Salma, young refugees experience two forms of waithood: anticipating the transition from childhood to adulthood and from displaced to resettled status (Grabska 2020). As the nature of displacement continues to be extended in countries of first asylum, refugees increasingly make sense of their future trajectories in contexts shaped by temporality and restricted mobility (Bellino 2018). For young people in these complex settings, schools are significant spaces which influence how they perceive their past, present and uncertain future. This chapter presents findings from a qualitative study conducted with Syrian refugee students attending segregated, double-shift schools in Jordan. Their reflections highlight three important roles that schools enact in the lives of displaced young people by mediating relations between refugee and host communities, forging connections with time and place, and shaping aspirations. Through these three dimensions of schooling, the chapter contributes to discussions around the positioning of education in the broader national and legal context, and the ways in which schools and the interactions between schools and surrounding structures influence refugee students' outlook towards their lives and future trajectories.

Understanding Education in Uncertainty

Today, the importance of education for refugees is at the heart of humanitarian responses. Education is seen as capable of carrying multiple rights and meanings to refugees affected by conflict, including returning to structure and normalcy, creating social opportunities, advancing knowledge and skills, and preparing refugees for future resettlement or repatriation (Buckner et al. 2018). However, the structures, models and agendas of education for refugees vary widely across contexts. In refugee-hosting nations that neighbour conflict-affected countries, such as Lebanon and Jordan, experiences of refugee education are commonly situated within overstrained systems and unstable economic conditions (Dryden-Peterson et al. 2019). Education policies in host countries are also influenced by the intersections of political debates on migration and asylum, integration model preference and the host nation's position on the futures of refugees (Dryden-Peterson et al. 2019; Karsli-Calamak and Kilinc 2021).

Recent solutions to promoting educational access for refugees have shifted to reflect the prolonged nature of displacement, including a move towards the integration of refugees into national school systems, and increased attention to the importance of inclusivity and quality of learning (Cohen 2020). The UNHCR *Education 2030: A Strategy for Refugee Education* (2019: 7) states that the commitment to include refugee children within national policies and national education systems recognizes the importance of cohesive societies, safe and enabling learning environments, and access to education that 'enables learners to use their education towards sustainable futures'. However, the practical barriers that continue to exist within many refugee-hosting nations impact the ways in which education policies are implemented and experienced.

The prolonged nature of displacement and uncertain trajectories that face refugees has prompted new research into the educational experiences of refugee communities. One particularly important focus is on how aspirations and perceptions of self are changed as refugee children and young people experience uncertainty and continuous states of waiting (Maadad and Matthews 2020). Within this process of development and becoming, adolescence marks an especially significant period of meaning-making across critical transitions. During this stage of life, adolescents typically gain increasing capacity and autonomy to make their own decisions about their lives and preferences. However, the reality for refugee young people is that decision-making can be constrained, contingent on the conditions that exist within contexts (Grabska, Regt and Franco 2018).

In situations of displacement, refugee young people are particularly vulnerable to states of waiting, forced to make meaning of transitions into adulthood, while waiting for a better and uncertain future. Grabska (2020: 23) refers to the two types of waiting that displaced young people face through notions of waithood: one referring to the 'multifaceted nature of a transition from youth to adulthood', and waithood in relation to the freedom or unfreedom to be mobile, such as voluntary repatriation or resettlement. During these transitions, refugees actively make sense of their spaces and potential trajectories which inform their decisions and preferences. These forms of waithood highlight the nature of transitions over time and involve the journeys that young refugees make from their past homes and childhood ideas about adulthood, as well as how they make sense of the uncertainties surrounding their futures. However, Bellino (2018) notes that displaced young people transitioning to adulthood are faced with trajectories which are fluid and not linear. This is particularly relevant in countries of first asylum, where education access and trajectories are positioned within broader economic, political, legal and social opportunities and constraints.

Refugees may feel confined to living in an undesired present in which they are unable to reach their desired states of being (Sommers 2012; Brun 2015) and depend on strategies that provide hope in the unfortunate circumstances they are faced with. Maintaining hope and protecting aspirations are crucial to making important transitions across time, helping refugees cope with waiting and uncertainty (Brun 2015). However, the security of these same strategies is under threat as a result of exclusionary geopolitical conditions and uncertainty. Education is one of the key mediators of time, which is able to influence how children and young people make sense of their opportunities and possible futures. However, as Dryden-Peterson (2017) notes, refugee education must be reframed to help learners engage with ideas of multiple futures, acknowledging that future trajectories may not be linear and may present multiple possibilities. If reframed appropriately, education can be an important vehicle towards the 'unknowable future' that allows refugees to continuously re-imagine their future and trajectories. Recognizing that refugee status influences 'the identity and subjectivity of those who bear the label' (Pinson et al. 2010: 19), schools are in a position to mediate how refugees make sense of their current positions within the world through positive or negative strategies.

Recognizing that significant decisions and meaning-making processes are negotiated during their youth, in this chapter I examine how Syrian refugee students draw on their school spaces to understand their current and future opportunities. In particular, I seek to understand the forms of mediatory roles that schools appeared to enact during these transitions. The chapter considers the different factors in schools which influence how decision-making processes are being made and the extent to which schools were able to positively or negatively influence how young people looked onwards to their future.

Education for Syrian Refugee Students: The Double-Shift System

This research was carried out within the context of Jordan, which has pledged to protect the rights of refugee children and included a refugee response plan within its national plans and systems (Ministry of Planning and International Cooperation 2020). The government of Jordan has created educational spaces in Jordan through multiple initiatives. Syrian refugee students in non-camp settings have been largely integrated into formal schools through the double-shift system. This system has allowed for an increase in school spaces despite overstrained institutional structures (Younes and Morrice 2019). The double-shift system in Jordan, also adopted in Lebanon, allows for an increase in school capacities by operating two different shifts: morning for national citizens and afternoon for Syrian refugees. After ten years since the Syrian conflict began, Syrian students' experiences of learning continue to be influenced by the intersections between school access and surrounding structures and attitudes in their refugee-hosting nation. While Jordan has hosted refugees from previous conflicts over many decades, including Palestinian and Iraqi refugees, the depleting aid and heightened demand on the nation's infrastructure, services, and demands for employment have been reported to influence the quality of living and community cohesion among both Jordanians and Syrians (Francis 2015; Lockhart 2018). The double-shift system, while offering access to learning, has also had bearing on the learning of both Jordanians and Syrians in the country. Through these overstretched school spaces, school hours for both communities are shortened, demand for qualified teachers is vast and unmet, and students across nationalities are segregated and therefore not encouraged to meet in safe spaces (Salem 2021).

Despite increased access to schools through this double-shift system, research to date warns of high dropout rates within secondary education and overwhelmingly limited likelihood of progression towards upper-secondary education for refugee students (Small 2020). Syrian refugee students are particularly affected by the vulnerabilities faced by their families. The majority of Syrian families in Jordan, for example, live under the national poverty line and are unable to access valid work permits due to delayed changes in policies, resistance from employers and limited work opportunities in Jordan (Small 2020). Thus, although recent policy agendas focus on ideas of integration into formal schools and the importance of strengthening inclusive and quality learning to enable refugees to prepare for their futures, the disjunctions between school structures and surrounding circumstances, and the intersections between, impact how students and their families make decisions about their learning and futures.

A Focus on the Voices of Syrian Refugee Students

The importance of understanding students' experiences underpinned the methodology of this phenomenological research. Researching the experiences of students adheres to the 1991 Convention on the Rights of the Child, respecting children's rights to explore their own feelings and communicate them on matters that affect them (UNICEF 2010). Engaging children and young people's voices can inform both academic understandings and policymaking through the perspectives of children on realities that may not be visible to the eyes of adults (Lewis and Lindsday 1999; Kellet et al. 2003; Alderson and Morrow 2011). However, research with students also requires comprehensive ethical considerations, including reflections on the positionality of the researcher and a realization of power structures between the researcher and participant (Lawrence et al. 2015; Due et al. 2016). This research drew carefully on considered interviewing methods, repeated consent processes and the positionality of the researcher (Salem 2020).

The research, undertaken in 2017, examined students' understandings of their well-being in Jordan, examining the intersections between spaces within and around schools (Salem 2020). It involved semi-structured interviews conducted with seventy-eight Syrian refugee students who were between the ages of fourteen and sixteen at the time of research and were attending one of four afternoon (or second-shift) schools in Amman, Jordan. Participants were equally divided across two boys' and two girls' schools, giving attention to the nuanced experiences of female and male students. In addition to interviews with students, a reflexive journal was used throughout fieldwork to give attention to aspects of school structure and layout, and any important observations relating to relations in classrooms between students and teachers.

As Syrian refugee students attending secondary education in Jordan are at risk of dropping out (Small 2020), this study sought to examine how students within this age group perceived their education trajectories and futures. The chapter focuses on students' perceptions of their current and future opportunities, and the role that schools play in mediating these perceptions. Data analysis was conducted through an iterative process, examining both collective and individual experiences of students. Students' interviews were analysed in multiple phases: analysis of interviews within each school, analysis of interviews according to gender and analysis of interviews per student. These three readings of data were coded, identifying the ways in which students shared similar understandings of their experiences and aspirations, while also paying attention to the individuality of students and the ways in which they negotiated their prospects and experiences differently. These data are presented under three key findings that emerged through students' perceptions, which highlight the types of mediatory roles that education can have for transitions and decision-making: mediating relations between host and refugee communities, forging connections between time and place, and shaping aspirations.

School Spaces and Learning in the Face of Uncertainty

Rushing frantically, students arrive to the classroom and collapse into their seats with playful grins. The rest circle and return, carrying desks above their small bodies, their eyes peering through the fixed frames to navigate the way and find space in this overcrowded classroom. Notebooks beginning to flip, the school day begins as the afternoon sets in. Names are read out for attendance; several absences are marked down.

As writing sketches the board, students' minds engage and disengage with the worlds that lie between these spaces and the ones that await outside. The next hours are fleeting but occupied with thoughts of the past, questions about the future and learning confined to segregated spaces that serve as reminders of students' conflicting positions in Jordan. Students' reflections of their hopes, aspirations and perceptions of self in these learning spaces tell of the importance of school structures and the ways in which they reinforce surrounding conditions. This section shares students' reflections of their aspirations and perceptions of their learning spaces, drawing attention to the role that schools play in mediating relations with the host community, forging connections with time and space, and building aspirations, and the ways in which these roles intersect with structural conditions outside of schools.

Mediating Relations between Host and Refugee Communities

During afternoon schools, students learn among other Syrian classmates, sharing similar stories of Syria's conflict and loss. Students felt that the friendships they have formed with their classmates offer opportunities for care, playfulness and social opportunities in an otherwise isolating reality. Bounded by a set of school hours that separate them from others, Syrian refugee students form relations shaped by mutual understandings of their continuous experiences of displacement. Many students, especially girls, stated that their social contact outside of schools was limited, commonly repeating, 'we do not go out anywhere' and 'we do not know anyone outside of schools.' United by these school spaces and a shared sense of journey, these friendships were often framed by students in ways which symbolized collective belonging and unity:

> I hope that in the future, I see all my friends have graduated and have degrees and that they are living a life they like. That would make life better. (Sandra, female, 16)

> Last year was difficult, but one thing that was nice was being in school and having my friends. If one of us is upset, we're all sad. If one is happy, we're all happy. (Farah, female, 16)

> There are things that motivate me to study, like my friends here at school, who always offer to help me. (Bashir, male, 15)

For female students especially, these friendships offered the only opportunity to engage with others:

> *Rima, female, 16*: 'I have good friends at this school. One of my friends is the dearest thing to me. I talk to her about everything.'

> *Researcher*: 'Do you think having friendship at school is important?'

> *Rima*: 'Yes. I don't know anyone outside of the school. We don't mix with people, not even our neighbours.'

Yet, both male and female students were also reminiscent of the freedom and ease of relationships they had in Syria, stating that they feel alone, bored, and were unable to reconcile with the limited social opportunities now available. Many expressed that they did not know any Jordanians and felt confined by their school spaces which did not allow them to form connections with others despite having spent years in Jordan. While schools mediated opportunities for friendships with other Syrian students, the segregation of school spaces also perpetuated the sense of loss, otherness and marginalization that existed outside of schools:

> We don't have friends in this country, and we lost everyone. (Sandra, female, 16)

> I wish there were more and more people for us to meet. (Kareem, male, 16)

> I want to meet more people. I want to have more friends. (Nizar, male, 15)

The separation between communities imposed by double-shift systems had several implications for the ways in which students made sense of their social place and identities in Jordan. Feelings of isolation were exacerbated by the high levels of violence, harassment and bullying that students experienced as they entered and left schools (Small 2020; Salem 2021). In particular, students felt rejected in Jordan by its structures, spaces and the communities they navigated:

> They only know me as refugee, they don't know my name. It's an ugly word. I don't know what the word means but I don't like it. I always hear it from Jordanians everywhere I go. (Aziz, male, 15)

Students experienced a conflicting sense of belonging and marginalization; allowed to connect with children from Syria but segregated from the remaining country. Due to the inability to engage with Jordanian communities either in schools or outside, with the exception of negative exchanges, students felt that 'nobody likes Syrians' in Jordan. As students made sense of their place in Jordan, the unity within classrooms was contradicted by a rejection from host communities:

> *Adam, male, 15*: 'If things were ok in Syria, I wouldn't be here. I don't like this estrangement, nobody likes it.'
>
> *Researcher*: 'Do you feel estranged?'
>
> *Adam*: 'A lot . . . this isn't my country.'
>
> *Researcher*: 'What makes you feel this way?'
>
> *Adam*: 'The people. They don't want us here.'

The segregation of schools thus determined the forms of relations and connections that students were able to form. The word 'estrangement' was repeated across conversations. Despite their desires to engage and participate more actively, students felt they lacked the freedom to connect with others in society or belong in their current spaces. In a rarer and more positive example, Qusai, fifteen years old, shed light on the importance of being able to meet others in Jordan outside of school, which he felt enabled him to make more positive connections with his spaces in the present:

> In 2015, I started to feel more settled in Jordan. I made four friends and they're Jordanian. We've become like brothers, and we play together.

Forging Connections with Place and Time

Students experienced learning as they transitioned from the stability of the past and prepared for the uncertainty of the future. However, students also expressed that as they waited for the future, they were 'stuck' in their current and undesirable present (Sommers 2012). Their learning was thus situated within the bracket of these three transitions across time, facilitating the ways they connected with each. During interviews, some of the students made sense of their learning spaces as avenues which would aid in transitioning from the hardships they experienced, to more positive states in the future:

> Right now, there's no happiness, but we don't know what the future holds. Right now, every new day is worse than the past, but this might just be a phase. It's been an ugly seven years. Enough of this now. I am going to study, and I am going to change things. (Sara, female, 16)

> I want to only think about the future. I want to only focus on what I want to become. (Salma, female, 16)

The future presented the prospect of more positive opportunities, where students hoped to experience a return of normalcy. In these examples, students drew on the value of learning to their sense of agency to create change in the future. Several students felt that education would help lead to careers and jobs that may help them re-experience a sense of joy and stability with their families:

> My house is very small and we're really struggling. That's why I study as hard as I can. When I grow up, I want to have a job so I can buy a big and beautiful house. (Judy, female, 16)

However, alongside their outlook towards becoming responsible adults, students also missed a childhood they felt they lost. Students felt that their childhood had ended too quick, stripped of opportunities for safety, play and enjoyment normally available to most young people. A recurrent notion from students interviewed is their rejection of the present; students viewed the present as bleak of the freedom that the future may bring and void of the happiness that the past once represented:

> I wish I could return to the childhood that I didn't get to live. I want to go back to the past when we would laugh, play, do anything, and for people to see that it's about childhood and innocence. (Sandra, female, 16)

> I would like to live a better life in another country and enjoy every minute of my life. I want to live every moment and not let it pass by me. (Basheer, male, 15)

> I feel like there's nothing in this country to make me happy. It's just depressing. We don't go anywhere. I just sit at home and stare at the wall. (Luna, female, 16)

> I wish there was an activity in the school. For example, I wish they'd give us a project to work on, but they don't give us things to do. (Amr, male, 15)

Across these transitions of time and place, there was a sense of entrapment that depended on a 'better' future. This suspension of living in the present impacted how students engaged with their current learning spaces. Kinan, for example, stated that his ambitions and motivation would remain idle until his desired state of a future arrived, where he might reunite with his father and resettle with his family elsewhere:

> *Kinan, male, 16:* 'I don't understand myself. I feel like I don't want to study, but I do want to study. How? I don't know what happens to me when I'm in class.'
>
> *Researcher:* 'What do you think happens?'
>
> *Kinan:* 'I lose my concentration entirely. I think about our travel plans. Every day I think, 'today might be the day we get our papers' and then I get completely distracted. If I were going to Germany to join my dad, I would be motivated to study.'

While the rejection of the present in favour of waiting for a 'better future' is a common phenomenon, schools can also present opportunities that are able to return a sense of attachment and engagement with the present. Through several conversations, students stated that they wished to engage with opportunities to re-discover their hobbies and interests, to familiarize themselves with their new physical spaces, acquire new skills and return to hobbies that they enjoyed in the past:

> I have so many hobbies that I can't pursue. I am not allowed to do that here. (Lilas, female, 16)

I loved playing the piano and now I can't practice anymore. (Raneem, female, 15)

There is no space for us to play basketball or do anything anymore. (Fadi, male, 15)

Hadia, female, 16: 'What I would like to get rid of is boredom. I think this is the biggest issue that people face. I want to replace it with something useful.'

Researcher: 'What do you mean that it's the biggest issue people face?'

Hadia: 'Boredom is the biggest thing people suffer from. Every time you ask them, what's wrong? they say 'I'm bored. I'm bored.''

For many students, the ability to enjoy active learning, play and participation more widely presented opportunities for increased attachment to their current lives and spaces in the present. Yet, despite the opportunities brought by the inclusion of refugees into schools through the double-shift system, its particular structure which emphasizes *being* refugees reinforces a sense of alienation and existing as an outsider. This, in turn, may deepen students' dissatisfaction with the present and increase their longing for the past or the future.

Shaping Aspirations

Despite the uncertainty and hardships that are experienced by refugee young people, students held strong views on the importance of education and the career paths they imagined for their future. The value placed on learning within conversations portrayed the ways in which secondary education is presented as key to future trajectories (Bellino 2018). In particular, schools played a key mediator role for aspirations, helping students move on from dreams held in Syria during their early childhood to the aspirations they formed today in the context of displacement. Many students reflected on how transitioning into young adults within post-conflict settings inspired a transformative change in their aspirations. Their reflections of their current hopes drew on the importance of reducing inequalities, protecting vulnerable communities and being recognized for positive contributions in society:

When I was a child, I used to dream of becoming a spy or actor or something like that because I was inspired by the movies I used to watch. After what I saw in Syria and the people in need of help, I realized I wanted to become a Doctor. (Basheer, male, 15)

I used to think that maybe I would be an artist. Now, I would like to become a lawyer and defend women's rights. I would like to support her to become something grand in life and I want to return the sense of childhood that was stolen from all Syrian children. I want to become famous and powerful so that I can stop wrongdoings from happening. I know that I can't do it on my own, but if an idea starts and people accept it, they might help me and maybe we'll help each other rebuild our country. (Sandra, female, 16)

After what we went through, I am going to work and make money and help people in need. (Saeed, male, 15)

These changes illustrate the transitions that young people experience in relation to their aspirations, 'before' conflict and 'after' displacement. These aspirations were strongly linked to the importance of pursuing further studies, alongside goals of returning to Syria or helping individuals elsewhere:

I have seen so many disadvantaged people going through terrible things. My aspirations are different now. I want to spread happiness in the world. I want to help those in need. My ultimate goal is to become a lawyer and I want to work on the most critical cases. And I am going to come back to Jordan to give money to every person in need. (Rania, female, 16)

I want to be a teacher so that I can help the generations after mine in Syria. (Sara)

I want to invest useful things so that I can help people. (Amr, male, 15)

If I could become an architect, I could help Syria and think about a better future. (Hamzeh, male, 15)

My dream is to continue my studies. (Sima, female, 16)

However, while students drew on the importance of continuing their education to achieve their aspirations, they also felt that the plausibility of their aspirations was trapped in impossible realities. Phrases including 'not if I stay at this school' were commonly used when students discussed the likelihood of continuing their education. In contrast, their aspirations were ignited by ideas of 'becoming something', 'succeeding' and 'learning' if they were able to move abroad to in Europe, America, Canada or Australia.

I want to stay in school but if I stay at this school I won't. If I live in another country, I'll continue my education for sure. (Abd, male, 16)

There is hope that next year might be better because we might get to go to America. If I go there, I'll be a better student. There is no hope for anyone here to be good. (Iyad, male, 15)

The conditional aspirations that students held largely related to intersections between structural and living conditions for Syrian refugees in Jordan, and students' experiences in schools which further discouraged hope. Despite understanding the limited right to work and stay within Jordan, students searched for encouragement, hope and solidarity within schools, illustrating the importance of schools in helping mediate aspirations. In particular, students felt their schooling experiences were shaped by negative factors, including short classroom hours, lack of quality teaching and discriminatory attitudes reinforced by teachers and educators (Small 2020). Particular examples shared by students illustrated intersections between Syrian's limited rights and uncertain future in Jordan, and the ways in which these factors were reinforced by their exchanges with teachers:

> I would like to study abroad because schools are much better there. They give you hope that you can finish school. They don't tell you that there's no point in school. Some say there's no point in education for us Syrians, but I want to study. (Feras, male, 15)

> I don't feel encouraged here. They keep saying things like 'there's no hope or use in these girls'. (Roula, female, 16)

> They say 'You Syrians . . . why aren't you good at school?' and I think, but I was good at school when I was in Syria. (Akram, male, 15)

Schools thus frequently instilled feelings which undermined the value of education for refugees, fundamentally shaping students' sense of what they are able to do and their aspirations for their future. Despite the aspirations that students held, many stated that they began to consider dropping out of school now that they have progressed into secondary education and had begun to reflect more seriously on the realities of their future. These discussions revealed how students actively make sense of their rights and statuses in Jordan, and the ways in which they negotiated future possibilities.

> Syrians can't do anything here. They can't rent a car, they can't work, they can't do anything. It's like being imprisoned and the rules keep getting stricter. It's not our country. (Iyad, male, 16)

> I wish I could travel because a future here in Jordan is bad. There's nothing for us here. (Ahmad, male, 15)

> There is no future here. Even if I manage to pass my exams here, what would that lead to? (Kinan, male, 16)

These findings contribute to important debates on the role of education for refugees, and the ways in which schools influence students' hope and aspirations as young people make sense of their rights and freedoms in contexts of displacement. Students' expressions of their hopes and desires to learn, pursue higher education and careers, and contribute to society show that students' aspirations and agency are active and negotiated across time and space. These findings align with other studies and show that for children the meaning-making process is conducted creatively and actively during waithood, and children re-invent and continuously re-imagine their role and interaction with society (Honwana 2012; Grabska 2020). Schools create spaces and interactions that help children conceptualize what is valuable to their lives and the extent to which they have the freedom to aspire (Hart and Brando 2018). The ways in which these aspirations are negotiated influence the decisions that individuals make, which is especially critical within periods of transition between childhood and adulthood (Hale and Kadoda 2016). Decision-making within this period is influenced by the preferences that students hold, which can be shaped by 'what your society tells you about the opportunities that are likely to be open to you' (Walker 2003: 172).

Concluding Thoughts: Living While Waiting for a Better Future

Against the uncertainty and temporal statuses that refugees face during prolonged displacement, learning spaces influence the ways in which refugee students make sense of their place and connections to society. Despite increasing integration into formal schools, achieving true inclusion is challenged by surrounding sociopolitical conditions within refugee-hosting nations. Through a focus on refugee young people in second-shift secondary education and their experiences of schools, this chapter has shed light on the importance of understanding how students made meaning of their presence in Jordan as members of displaced communities, and the ways they negotiated their aspirations, rights, relations and transitions across time. The findings illustrate the ways in which relationships, time and aspiration are experienced through intersections between schools and surrounding exclusionary structures. Schools were perceived as spaces which extended some of these opportunities while simultaneously reinforcing a sense of uncertainty, lack of belonging and dismissal of the present. These findings show that both the 'present' and 'future' are important concepts which schools need to engage with.

The reflections included in this chapter show that while refugee students experience waithood and favour the future over the current unwanted present, their meaning-making, sense of agency and aspirations were constantly being actively negotiated, changed and decided by other factors shaping their lives as refugees. These findings reaffirm the importance of understanding how hope and preferences are changed over time through intersections between spaces, relations and transitions. These transformations of hope and agency, as Brun (2015) warns, must be protected 'in waiting' to help displaced communities cope with the uncertainty and waiting they face (Brun 2015). Schools are important spaces where this negotiation is experienced through multiple forms of being, given the right to learn, to socialize, to aspire, and yet faced with limited trajectories outside of school walls. This misalignment between educational opportunities for young people and uncertainty about their futures requires further thinking in relation to how schools might enact mediatory roles, including negotiating connections and relations with the host society, forging connections with physical space and time, and building aspirations. This form of mediation is central to the purpose of education, which, as Dryden-Peterson et al. (2019) note, includes reframing education to ensure that schools help cultivate skills that are transferrable across contexts and that reflect the multiple possible futures that refugees face.

Simultaneously, the reframing of education must not only focus solely on future trajectories, which may undermine the importance of how the 'present' is experienced. Students' reflections highlighted the significance of connecting with individuals in society, with physical places and with their own development over time as they explored their identities and spaces in Jordan. The level to which they were able to enjoy play, active learning, friendships and belonging influenced how they perceived their freedoms and selves; students mostly felt unable to experience meaningful interactions, positive self-growth and attachments to places. These reductions of freedoms and capacities to enjoy or 'live', as Basheer stated, can further damage refugees' abilities to engage with notions of agency and hope. In these challenging settings, education policies and structures must recognize the importance of positive interactions and activities, paying attention to the process of decision-making and changes in hope. Students' desires to be active, productive and engaged highlight that the possibilities of future trajectories and their multiplicity are also dependent on the rights and capacities to create and enjoy attachments to present spaces and relations.

References

Alderson, P., & Morrow, V. (Eds) (2011). *The Ethics of Research with Children and Young People: A Practical Handbook*. New York: Sage Publications Ltd.

Bellino, M.J. (2018). 'Youth Aspirations in Kakuma Refugee Camp: Education as a Means for Social, Spatial, and Economic (Im)Mobility', *Globalisation, Societies and Education*, 16(4), 541–56. https://doi.org/10.1080/14767724.2018.1512049.

Brun, C. (2015). 'Active Waiting and Changing Hopes: Toward a Time Perspective on Protracted Displacement', *Social Analysis*, 59(1). https://doi.org/10.3167/sa.2015.590102.

Buckner, E., Dominique, S., & Jihae, C. (2018). 'Between Policy and Practice: The Education of Syrian Refugees in Lebanon', *Journal of Refugee Studies*, 31(4), 444–65. https://doi.org/10.1093/jrs/fex027.

Cohen, E. (2020). 'How Syrian Refugees Expand Inclusion and Navigate Exclusion in Jordan: A Framework for Understanding Curricular Engagement', *Journal of Education in Muslim Societies*, 2(1), 3–29. https://doi.org/10.2979/jems.2.1.02.

Conlon, D. (2011). 'Waiting: Feminist Perspectives on the Spacings/Timings of Migrant (Im)Mobility', *Gender, Place and Culture*, 18(3), 353–60. https://doi.org/10.1080/0966369X.2011.566320.

Dryden-Peterson, S. (2017). 'Refugee Education: Education for an Unknowable Future', *Curriculum Inquiry*, 47(1), 14–24. https://doi.org/10.1080/03626784.2016.1255935.

Dryden-Peterson, S., Elizabeth, A., Michelle, J.B., & Vidur, C. (2019). 'The Purposes of Refugee Education: Policy and Practice of Including Refugees in National Education Systems', *Sociology of Education*, 92(4), 346–66. https://doi.org/10.1177/0038040719863054.

Due, C., Riggs, D.W., & Augoustinos, M. (2016). 'Experiences of School Belonging for Young Children with Refugee Backgrounds', *The Educational and Developmental Psychologist*, 33(1), 33–53. https://doi.org/10.1017/edp.2016.9.

Francis, A. (2015). *Jordan's Refugee Crisis*, Vol. 21. Washington, DC: Carnegie Endowment for International Peace.

Grabska, K. (2020). '"Wasting Time": Migratory Trajectories of Adolescence among Eritrean Refugee Girls in Khartoum', *Critical African Studies*, 12(1), 22–36. https://doi.org/10.1080/21681392.2019.1697318.

Grabska, K., de Regt, M., & Del Franco, N. (2018). *Adolescent Girls' Migration in The Global South: Transitions into Adulthood*. Cham: Springer.

Hart, C., & Brando, N. (2018). 'A Capability Approach to Children's Well-Being, Agency and Participatory Rights in Education', *European Journal of Education*, 53(3), 293–309. https://doi.org/10.1111/ejed.12284.

Hale, S., & Kadoda, S. (2016). *Networks of Knowledge Production in Sudan: Identities, Mobilities, and Technologies*. Lanham: Lexington Books.

Honwana, A. (2012). *The Time of Youth: Work, Social Change and Politics in Africa*. Washington, DC: Kumarian Press.

Karsli-Calamak, E., & Sultan, K. (2021). 'Becoming the Teacher of a Refugee Child: Teachers' Evolving Experiences in Turkey', *International Journal of Inclusive Education*, 25(2), 259–82. https://doi.org/10.1080/13603116.2019.1707307.

Kellett, M., Fraser, S., & Ding, S. eds (2003). *Doing Research with Children and Young People*. London: Sage Publications.

Lawrence, J., Kaplan, I., & Dodds, A. (2015). 'The Rights of Refugee Children to Self-Expression and to Contribute to Knowledge in Research: Respect and Methods', *Journal of Human Rights Practice*, 7(3), 411–29. https://doi.org/10.1093/jhuman/huv010.

Lewis, A., & Lindsday, G. (Ed.) (1999). *Researching Children's Perspectives*. Buckingham: Open University Press.

Lockhart, D. (2018). *Syrian Refugee Labour Inclusion Policy in Jordan: Emerging Trends Two Years in*. WANA Institute. http://wanainstitute.org/en/publication/syrian-refugee-labour-inclusion-policy-jordan-emerging-trends-two-years (accessed 19 October 2021).

Maadad, N., & Julie M. (2020). 'Schooling Syrian Refugees in Lebanon: Building Hopeful Futures', *Educational Review*, 72(4), 459–74. https://doi.org/10.1080/00131911.2018.1508126.

Ministry of Planning and International Cooperation (2020). 'Jordan Response Plan for the Syrian Crisis 2020–2022', *Relief Web*. https://reliefweb.int/report/jordan/jordan-response-plan-syria-crisis-2020-2022 (accessed 19 October 2021).

Pinson, H., Arnot, M., & Candappa, M. (2010). *Education, Asylum and the 'Non-Citizen' Child: The Politics of Compassion and Belonging*. Hampshire: Palgrave Macmillan.

Salem, H. (2020). 'The Unheard Voices of Refugee Students: Understanding Syrian Students' Well-Being and Capabilities in Jordan's Double-Shift Schools', PhD thesis, Faculty of Education, University of Cambridge. https://doi.org/10.17863/CAM.49421.

Salem, H. (2021). '"Realities of School "Integration": Insights from Syrian Refugee Students in Jordan's Double-Shift Schools', *Journal of Refugee Studies*, feaa116. https://doi.org/10.1093/jrs/feaa116.

Small, B. (2020). '"I Want to Continue to Study": Barriers to Secondary Education for Syrian Refugee Children in Jordan', *Human Rights Watch*. https://www.nolostgeneration.org/reports/i-want-continue-study-barriers-secondary-education-syrian-refugee-children-jordan (accessed 19 October 2021).

Sommers, M. (2012). *Stuck: Rwandan Youth and the Struggle for Adulthood*. Athens: University of Georgia Press.

Walker, M. (2003). 'Framing Social Justice in Education: What Does the "Capabilities" Approach Offer?', *British Journal of Educational Studies*, 51(2): 168–87. https://doi.org/10.1111/1467-8527.t01-2-00232.

UNHCR (2019). *Education 2030: A Strategy for Refugee Education.* https://www.unhcr
.org/uk/publications/education/5d651da88d7/education-2030-strategy-refugee
-education.html (accessed 19 October 2021).

UNICEF (2010). *The United Nations Convention on the Rights of the Child.* https://www
.unicef.org.uk/what-we-do/un-convention-child-rights/ (accessed 19 October 2021).

Younes, M., & Morrice, L. (2019). *The Education of Syrian Refugees in Jordan: Issues
of Access and Quality: A Review of Policies and Initiatives (2012–2018).* Brighton:
Centre for International Education, University of Sussex.

15

Zimbabwean Migrant Teachers in South Africa

Their Search for Identity

Rian de Villiers and Zenzele Weda

Introduction

Globally, the increase in international migration has resulted in a corresponding increase in worker migration, including the migration of teachers. In sub-Saharan Africa, post-Apartheid South Africa is a popular choice of host country for migrant workers, including teachers (Crush and Tevera 2010). Migrants consider South Africa to be a country of 'greener pastures' in a sub-region blighted by government corruption, political and economic instability, and war (De Villiers and Weda 2017).

Teachers who leave their home country to teach in other countries almost always encounter challenges in the process of reconstructing their personal and professional identities in the host country (Myles et al. 2006). These include challenges arising from differences between education systems (Bartlett 2014; Manik 2014a), as well as personal conditions, including a lack of previous teaching experience (De Villiers 2004), and insufficient communication skills in the language of instruction (Hutchison 2006; Sharplin 2009). Meanwhile, structural administrative circumstances such as complicated (re)qualification processes (Collins and Reid 2012) or being assigned to difficult schools can worsen the situation for migrant teachers. Moreover, studies have reported cases of discrimination (Caravatti et al. 2014) and racism/xenophobia against migrant teachers (Manik 2014a), visa restrictions and the downgrading of qualifications (Vandeyar et al. 2014), regulatory and financial discrimination (Krüger-Potratz 2013), lower salary levels (Caravatti et al. 2014) and restricted employment contracts (Krüger-Potratz 2013).

Zimbabwean teachers constitute the largest group of migrant teachers in South Africa (Campbell 2010; Crush and Tawodzera 2013; DHET 2013; Ranga 2015). In this chapter, we report on the findings of a study that aimed to find out what challenges, in the context of the teachers' educational, social and cultural backgrounds, create impediments to the reconstruction of the Zimbabwean migrant teachers' identities in South Africa. We commence the chapter with an exposition of the theoretical framework that underpinned the study, followed by a discussion of the research design and methodology. The most significant findings are then presented, analysed and discussed, and conclusions and recommendations are made.

Theoretical Underpinnings

The framework for the study was built around social identity theory. The theory describes how people perceive themselves as members of a specific social group and how those perceptions influence their opinions (Tajfel and Turner 1986). The theory outlines three major stages in this process: social categorization, social identification and social comparison (McLeod 2019). *Social categorization* concerns people automatically placing themselves and others in categories or groups (Turner et al. 1987). Normally, people think in terms of groups, locating or categorizing themselves in a social group and believing mostly in the positive aspects of that specific group. In other words, they gain an affinity for one group over others (Mangum and Block 2018). The social group in which individuals place themselves is the 'in-group' (us) and other groups are seen as the 'out-groups' (them). The process of self-categorization coincides with *social identification* in that people adopt the identity of the group in which they have categorized themselves as belonging (McLeod 2019). Social identification is a psychological attachment that entails a formal procedure for gaining entry into the group (Green and Green 1999). Successively, people engage in *social comparisons*, observing differences between their 'in-group' and 'out-groups'. It is also natural for in-group members to create a positive self-identity (Tajfel 1981). Comparisons between groups are emotionally laden, with group threats interpreted as threats to the self (Smith 1999).

Bolívar, Domingo and Pérez-García (2014) emphasize that the social and professional identity of teachers is continuously being constructed and reconstructed as social and professional circumstances are never static. Social identity theory can help to understand the relationships between the immigrant group(s) and the dominant group in the host country (Van Oudenhoven et al. 2006). In this research, we draw on the theory to understand how migrant teachers in South Africa develop a sense of who they are, based on their group membership(s) (McLeod 2019), and how they need to compare favourably with other groups in order to maintain their self-esteem.

Research Design and Methodology

A qualitative research approach within the interpretive paradigm, drawing on a multiple case study design, was used to explore the research questions posed.

The population of this study comprised fifteen migrant Zimbabwean teachers employed in schools in Gauteng (a province in South Africa). The province of Gauteng was selected because it has the highest number of Zimbabwean teachers. Both purposive and convenience samplings were used to select the teachers in this province. The purposive selection criteria were that the teachers should be teachers trained in Zimbabwe; have at least one year's teaching experience in South African schools and, at the time of the study, be teaching at a public or private secondary (high) school. The sampling was convenient as the teachers were chosen from schools in Gauteng that were easily accessible to the researchers. Another criterion was to include a more or less equal number of men and women to achieve heterogeneity. Snowball sampling was also followed as some of the successive participants were recommended by preceding individuals (Castillo 2009; Nieuwenhuis 2009).

The participants took part in semi-structured, face-to-face phenomenological, in-depth interviews. The interview schedule consisted of open-ended and closed questions, developed to solicit the teachers' demographic information; their immigration status; as well as the personal and professional challenges they experienced in South Africa. The average duration of each interview was fifty minutes. The research complied with the ethical guidelines laid down by the researchers' universities for educational research, including confidentiality, voluntary participation, anonymity, trust, informed consent and safety in participation.

The digital recordings of the interviews were transcribed verbatim, whereafter the data were analysed qualitatively through open coding. Concepts were then grouped together into categories and themes, and inductive codes emerged from the data (Nieuwenhuis 2008).

The participants were not known to the researchers. The interview questions were validated by two experts in the field and piloted before they were used in the main study. Based on the feedback from the pilot study, the interview questions were revised. Ambiguities and redundancies were removed to improve clarity in the formulation of the questions in the interview schedule. To ensure trustworthiness, the interviews were audio-recorded in order to obtain relatively complete and accurate records (Rule and John 2011). The transcriptions were checked by all of the participants.

Findings and Discussion

In this section we discuss key findings from the study, reflecting on six main themes that emerged from the analysis. These correspond to the impediments that participants described as constraining their personal and professional identities namely: immigration status; employment status; re-certification; professional and cultural marginalization; professional and cultural isolation; and holding on to former culture or ways of knowing.

Immigration Status

A common experience among the teachers was the struggle to acquire or renew the necessary legal documentation, including work permits, passports and South African identification documents (ID), to stay and work in South Africa. Even with legal documentation, several teachers reported that they found it extremely problematic to open credit accounts in most shops without a South African ID. They felt as if they 'could not be trusted' with credit and bank loans because of their temporary residential status and their short-term employment contracts. For example, a bank refused to help Munyaradzi,[1] one of the participants in this study, and informed him that 'he will run away with the car'. Gladys's bank turned down her application for a 100 per cent home loan and, consequently, she could not afford to buy a house (De Villiers and Weda 2018). Nomsa mirrored this experience regarding banks and explained that her loan application was rejected because they identified her as a non-citizen according to her passport number. Themba further explained:

> They look when your work permit is expiring and when you put forth an investment portfolio it cannot go through. You can't plan ahead; you tend to live for the moment.

The migrant teachers' inability to access loans also meant that their chances of securing reliable transport and safe accommodation were curtailed (Weda and De Villiers 2019).

Employment Status

Lack of employment, their foreign accent, settling for menial jobs in the informal sector and non-permanent contracts in the host country were all identified by teachers in the study as obstacles to the reconstruction of their professional identities in the host country.

Periodic Employment

Employment issues are known to be a major obstacle for migrant teachers (Remennick 2002; Walsh et al. 2011; Collins and Reid 2012; Manik 2014a). Phillion (2003) contends that teachers' sense of professional identity is negated when they have been unemployed for a certain period of time. In the present study, a mutual experience among the teachers was the struggle to acquire and renew the necessary legal documentation to work and stay in South Africa. As a result, some of the migrant teachers were unemployed for a period of time. Gladys, for example, had experienced challenges in securing employment as a foreigner several times, while Maria explained that she advised other foreign teachers to 'start legally, and make sure you have all your papers' to avoid long spells of unemployment.

Settling for Menial Jobs

Some migrant teachers resort to volunteering and unpaid work in the hopes of overcoming the unemployment hurdle and to secure a teaching position (Phillion 2003; Beynon et al. 2004; Pollock 2010), while others settle for menial jobs in the informal sector (Remennick 2002). It is common for migrant teachers to take these low-skilled and poorly paying jobs in order to meet their qualification accreditation requirements and daily survival needs (Manik 2014c). Securing jobs or volunteering for unskilled or partly skilled labour results in a loss of professional identity for most migrant teachers (Taraban 2004).

Some of the migrant teachers who participated in this study had, at one time or another, settled for menial jobs in the informal sector when they were unable to find teaching positions in South African schools. Some male teachers took on semi- or unskilled labour like being security guards. Collins, for example, worked as a brick layer for about a month:

> My first job was a brick layer, something I have never done in Zimbabwe, but because I just wanted to live and survive [. . .] Then I sold a house (in real estate), that was not my profession and I had no passion for that.

Maria recounted that the worst case she knew of was that of a teacher who settled for being a maid. Mlamuleli warned others, 'Don't think you are in a position to choose. Take anything that comes until you find your feet. Probably that is how we started anyway.' Several participants confirmed that it is difficult to secure a suitable teaching position.

Short, Fixed Contracts

Migrant teachers are employed in several ways in South Africa. They may be employed in public schools officially by the State through provincial education departments or by School Governing Boards on a permanent or temporary (contract) basis. Migrant teachers may also be employed directly by private schools, where they are even more vulnerable to possible exploitation because these schools' employment conditions are not regulated by the State through the South African 1998 Employment of Educators Act (Green 2014). Sisulu et al. (2007) also contend that the majority of migrant teachers in South Africa are in extremely exploitative circumstances in private schools, either not being paid at all or receiving very low salaries, with little recourse for legal action (De Villiers and Weda 2018). Many migrant teachers work in fixed-term contracts (Remennick 2002; Maylor et al. 2006) and as supply teachers (Walsh et al. 2011; Collins and Reid 2012; Manik 2014a; Janusch 2015).

The majority of the teachers who participated in this study were employed in a temporary capacity, meaning they could not access home, study and motor car loans from the banks. Staff appointed on temporary contracts are not automatically absorbed by a medical scheme, and most of the teachers saw this as a disadvantage. With tears in her eyes, Munyaradzi described her treatment at a hospital as discriminating:

> Nobody is recognizing us. Sometimes when you go to a hospital you, as a foreigner, must pay, but the person next to you don't pay.

The lack of job security opened the migrant teachers to even more exploitation in schools. Participants explained that the Gauteng Department of Education (GDE), which hired them to work in public schools, offered them mostly three-month contracts and, in exceptional cases, one-year contracts. The constant renewal of their contracts was always cumbersome (Weda and De Villiers 2019). Mlamuleli's complaint highlights migrant teachers' frustration at having to renew their contracts or apply for new ones:

> Temporary employment here refers to renewal all the time; it is not even a year thing but it's a term thing.

Nomsa also indicated that the contracts were not always very clear, while Maria explained that it was easier to get a job in a private school than in a public school, but that most private schools were bent on exploiting migrant teachers.

Re-certification

In many countries, including South Africa, the regulation of professions is subject to the possession of specific professional qualifications. One major issue is the process of recognition of previous professional qualifications and experiences (Reid and Collins 2013; Vandeyar et al. 2014). The assessment of international qualifications forms an important requirement that must be met before migrant teachers can be employed in public schools in South Africa (Keevy, Green and Manik 2014). The experiences and professional qualifications of migrant teachers are usually disregarded as they were obtained in another country (Phillion 2003). Therefore, migrant teachers are usually exposed to another round of re-certification when they arrive in the host country. They are forced to repeat or redo all or some of their professional training (Beynon et al. 2004). Furthermore, the process of (re)certification can be both costly and lengthy (Collins and Reid 2012), particularly when the authentication and translation of certificates are needed (Fee 2010). Walsh and Brigham (2007) emphasize that these processes result in the undermining of the professional identities of migrant teachers.

The Zimbabwean migrant teachers who participated in this study were improving themselves academically in order to stand a good chance of securing better jobs and for promotion possibilities. They indicated that further studies would offer them more opportunities as foreigners in South Africa (De Villiers and Weda 2017). Maria, for example, explained that she decided to improve her qualifications because 'it is not easy to be promoted as a foreigner'. The migrant teachers interviewed felt that their previous professional experience in Zimbabwe was not recognized, and they were prone to exploitation. They also complained that their expertise and high qualifications were not rewarded. Tongai explained,

> You are employed on the basis of your first degree. No experience is taken into consideration. When they interviewed you for the job, they want experience.

According to Sithembile, the discrimination in private schools is even worse and she pleaded that 'the government should intervene to look at qualifications and experience'.

Another issue brought to light by the participants was that they were not being paid the same salary as South African teachers. The fact that the migrant teachers were unhappy with their salaries could be a complaint against the devaluation of their qualifications and previous experience. Their engagement as temporary teachers, despite their high qualifications, attests to this devaluation. The devaluation of the migrant teachers' qualifications through re-certification and the disregarding of their experience do not augur well for their professional and personal reconstruction of identity.

Professional and Cultural Isolation

Most migrant teachers experience cultural and professional isolation, and the teachers' negative feelings, brought about by these two aspects, affect the reconstruction of their professional identities (Hutchison 2006). In the present study, labelling, a lack of knowledge of indigenous languages and their foreign accent and living in isolated communities in the host country were identified as obstacles to the reconstruction of migrant teachers' professional identities.

Kwerekwere

Migrant Zimbabwean teachers are often ascribed the group labelling of *Kwerekwere*, a derogatory term and antagonistic label used by Black South Africans to refer to immigrants from the rest of Africa (Manik 2014b; Vandeyar et al. 2014; Weda and De Villiers 2019). The teachers interviewed reported that once the learners discovered that they were foreigners, they tended to be disrespectful towards them and deliberately taunted them, calling them names like *Kwerekwere*. One of the participants, Collins, described his experiences:

> There is this idea of being labelled as Kwerekwere. Even our colleagues call us that. I actually had to accept that I am a Kwerekwere.

Knowledge of Indigenous Languages

Globally, the challenges experienced by migrant teachers are often further intensified by language and communication issues (Hutchison 2006; Sharplin 2009) when migrating to a country where the language of instruction in schools is not their native language. Migrant teachers may speak English with a foreign accent or may not speak fluent English (Phillion 2003). Difficulties reported in the research literature include unfamiliarity with local educational terms (Maylor et al. 2006), having an accent and not understanding cultural meanings (Abramova 2013), not feeling as articulate (Bense 2014) and poor ability in self-expression (Janusch 2015) and comprehension (Fee 2010).

The inability of many migrant teachers to understand and communicate in indigenous languages makes it very difficult for them to interact freely with fellow teachers and the local community (Sinyolo 2012). Zimbabwean migrant teachers' lack of familiarity with the indigenous languages also limits their choice of where they could work and live (Weda and De Villiers 2019). For example, Nomsa explained, 'I normally avoid townships[2] because of the language barrier.' She preferred instead to work and live in the more affluent suburbs where English is more commonly used, even though the cost of living is higher.

All of the teachers who participated in this study were fluent in English and were teaching in English medium schools; however, most of the learners they taught were not. Therefore, they reported that they felt under pressure to emulate their South African colleagues' classroom practice of code-switching. They were not familiar with the strategy of using learners as interpreters in teaching. Gamuchirai stated clearly,

> I wish I could explain in their language, but I don't know it. So, I would ask one learner to explain in their own language, but I still can't check if she understood what she is explaining properly.

Some of the Zimbabwean teachers revealed that once learners realized that they were not proficient in the learners' indigenous languages, they took advantage of the situation to poke fun at these teachers (Weda and De Villiers 2019). Munyaradzi put it as follows, 'In my first school, they could insult me in the vernacular, knowing that I don't know what they are saying.' Chipo also found it difficult to communicate with the learners in his class. He explained, 'all the time they were correcting my pronunciation and laughing at my accent and doing their best to frustrate my teaching.'

Living in Isolated Communities

Migrant teachers' feelings of professional and cultural isolation might arise because they are always in the minority in their school community (Peeler and Jane 2003). Some studies have found that migrant teachers do not always successfully integrate into the local communities in which they live and experience challenges associated with adapting to a new culture, often alien to them (Sinyolo 2012).

The Zimbabwean teachers interviewed indicated that they preferred to live in isolated communities for safety and cultural reasons. Mlamuleli expressed that he had no social life because he felt that it was better to stay at home and be safe. His fear was clearly visible when he said that he felt traumatized and harassed every time he ventured into the city to do shopping as he was stopped by the police and asked for identification. For safety reasons, some of the migrant teachers were not willing to reveal their identity as Zimbabwean. This is in keeping with Hungwe's (2013) contention that Zimbabweans feel motivated to conceal their identities as they still face xenophobia on a daily basis (Crush and Tawodzera 2013). Sithembile also preferred to stay at home and only left to go to church where she could identify with her own culture:

> I don't go much outside my workplace, except when I go to church. The church I go to is a church from home, so I feel I am at home at church. Most people are from Zimbabwe.

Gladys reported that in Zimbabwe, it is ideal to stay in a standalone house, but in South Africa, she decided to live in a cluster where there were lots of other Zimbabweans. These examples show that safety played a vital role in the teachers' ability to integrate properly into South African society.

Professional and Cultural Marginalization

Migrant teachers also suffer from professional and cultural marginalization (Kostogriz and Peeler 2007; Fee 2010; Pollock 2010). Teachers are familiar with the learning and teaching cultures of their home country (Caravatti et al. 2014) and when they make a transition from one cultural setting to another (Elbaz-Luwisch 2004), they take their existing beliefs, attitudes and values regarding education with them (Seah and Bishop 2001; Bense 2016). This transition is a period of adjustment and negotiation for most migrant teachers as they have to reconstruct their professional identity as teachers (Kostogriz and Peeler 2007; Virta 2015).

Substitute Teachers

Migrant teachers in other contexts have reported being given fewer classes to teach than they would have preferred, or they were employed as substitute teachers (Remennick 2002). Similarly, some of the temporarily appointed Zimbabwean teachers interviewed in this study pointed out that they did not see themselves as 'real teachers' because most of them were employed as substitute teachers. For example, Mlamuleli mentioned that on certain days, an average of four to five local teachers were normally absent from school: 'It is a daily thing and then you have to cover the absence for those teachers.'

Fewer Opportunities in Decision-making Forums

Professional marginalization occurs when migrant teachers are given fewer opportunities than South African–trained teachers in professional enrichment courses or in decision-making forums compared to their native counterparts (Michael 2006). Often migrant teachers are seen as the 'other' from the outset (entrance into South Africa), and this persists across all their interactions with the South African population (Manik 2014c). Being seen as the 'other' indicates a sense of not belonging and locates migrant teachers in a marginalized position and as outsiders in their host country. Michael (2006) finds that systemic barriers prevent migrant teachers from both participating in major decision-making processes and from taking key positions in schools. Sinyolo (2012) emphasizes that unfair treatment in the workplace is common, causing many migrant teachers to lose their self-esteem and feel marginalized.

The Zimbabwean teachers interviewed reported that they had fewer opportunities and limited participation in decision-making forums. This was the case as many of their colleagues rejected their opinions without due consideration. For example, when Themba made a suggestion to one of his local colleagues, it was blatantly rejected: 'You guys from Zimbabwe, you have such intelligent ideas, why don't you implement it on the other side? (in Zimbabwe).' A few of the teachers complained that they felt excluded from some school meetings because these were, at times, conducted in a local language that they did not understand.

Holding on to Their Former Culture

Migrant teachers often hold on to their former culture or way of knowing and doing things and, according to Vandeyar et al. (2014), this is another obstacle for them in the process of reconstructing their professional identities. Most of the migrant teachers who participated in the present study still maintained ties with their home country and were planning to migrate back to Zimbabwe someday – they did not accept that they had permanently left their former country and wanted to be near their extended family. For migrant teachers who are unprepared to forsake their former culture or way of knowing, the road to the reconstruction of their professional identities may be slippery (Faez 2010). Migrant teachers experience professional acculturation (Peeler and Jane 2005) in which previous practices and expectations need to be negotiated in light of new concepts (Kostogriz and Peeler 2007). This is an intense period of negotiation and/or adjustment (Virta 2015).

Most of the Zimbabwean teachers in this study seemed unprepared to forsake their former culture or way of knowing. They found it extremely difficult to build new friendships with their South African colleagues and pleaded for social support to integrate into the communities where they worked and lived. Gladys said that she had friends at church and work, but they were not considered as 'real friends'. She found it difficult to associate with people who were 'strangers' and 'would like people who share the same passions and cultures'. Gamuchirai compared her own values with those of South African learners and was not impressed: 'Just today, a certain learner asked me a question with her hands in her pockets. In my culture it is disrespectful.'

Fee (2010) and Walsh et al. (2011) suggest induction classes, which are tailored to the specific needs of migrant teachers, may be helpful. Hutchison (2006) recommends that such classes should discuss general educational and job expectations, the local educational system, assessment practices, pedagogical issues, as well as learner characteristics. The Zimbabwean teachers confirmed that they had to make a paradigm shift when teaching in South Africa. These teachers had no choice but to accept the South African education system. They therefore expressed a dire need for proper induction into the South African education system and into the culture of the individual schools where they were engaged (De Villiers and Weda 2018). They had to forsake some of what they knew and learnt during training and in practice in their home country and, resultantly, had to discard their preferred traditional way of teaching. This paradigm shift was accompanied by a reconstruction of their professional identities. The participants contended that the education system in Zimbabwe is better than that of South Africa, mainly criticizing the South African school curriculum and its assessment practices. Langa's narrative is a prime example of this: 'In Zimbabwe, we have the Cambridge syllabus that is not so condensed, and it is easy for children to absorb.'

Conclusion

Migrant Zimbabwean teachers who have moved to South Africa are suffering an identity crisis created by the need to rapidly reconstruct their identities as residents and teachers in South Africa, and their need to maintain some stability in their identities. They are still holding onto the old and familiar: their professional training and experience, their social values and their standards of behaviour. However, this is not always compatible with the culture and professional expectations of the host society. Moreover, several interrelated issues contribute to impeding the reconstruction of their personal and professional identities. These were identified as: immigration status; employment status; re-certification; professional and cultural marginalization; and professional and cultural isolation.

Zimbabwean teachers in South Africa are seen as an undesirable group worthy of the derogatory label *Kwerekwere*, which is accompanied by disrespect from learners and colleagues in schools, and xenophobic attitudes in the communities where they live. The participating Zimbabwean teachers came from a culture where teachers are still held in high esteem. Meanwhile, their employment status in South Africa is characterized by disruptions due to short contracts that do not allow for the emergence of a professional teacher identity, and at times they are forced to take up menial jobs to survive. In the process of re-certification, migrant teachers' qualifications and experience are devalued; it is therefore not surprising that they have resorted to accumulating additional educational credentials to stay competitive. They thus feel professionally and socially marginalized, denied the privileges of being teachers in South Africa. Due to their fear of xenophobia, the migrant teachers have gone into hiding – hiding their identity as Zimbabweans and actively self-isolating.

An ideal personal and professional identity leads to increased teacher motivation, performance and growth (Bolívar et al. 2014), and this underscores the importance of this study. This study, like others conducted with migrant teachers in South Africa (Vandeyar et al. 2014; Weda and De Villiers 2019), recommends that migrant teachers be assisted to integrate into the South African community as individuals and as professionals. Mentoring and detailed induction in schools are vital. Outside of school, introducing migrants to the communities where they choose to stay could be a good start.

South Africa is presently engaged in a struggle to control and minimize xenophobia. The reconstruction of social identities is intractably linked to the ever-changing conditions in which people live, work and engage in a struggle for social and economic justice (Schiller 2015). This research points to the importance of keeping the issue of xenophobia on the agenda in South Africa in order to create social conditions for the acceptance of migrant teachers in schools and communities. Assisting migrant teachers to integrate into host country communities could contribute to eroding the xenophobic tendencies of those communities and institutions.

Notes

1 All the names used are pseudonyms to protect the identity of participants.
2 Townships are high-density suburban settlements where different indigenous languages are spoken.

References

Abramova, I. (2013). 'Grappling with Language Barriers: Implications for the Professional Development of Immigrant Teachers', *Multicultural Perspectives*, 15(3), 152–7. https://doi.org/10.1080/15210960.2013.809305.

Bartlett, L. (2014). *Migrant Teachers*. Harvard: Harvard University Press.

Bense, K. (2014). 'Languages Aren't as Important Here': German Migrant Teachers' Experiences in Australian Language Classes', *The Australian Educational Researcher*, 41(4), 485–97. https://doi.org/10.1007/s13384-014-0143-2.

Bense, K. (2016). 'International Teacher Mobility and Migration: The Exploration of a Global Phenomenon', PhD thesis, University of Western Australia, Australia.

Beynon, J., Ilieva, R., & Dichupa, M. (2004). 'Re-credentialing Experiences of Immigrant Teachers: Negotiating Institutional Structures, Professional Identities and Pedagogy', *Teachers and Teaching: Theory and Practice*, 10(4), 429–44. http://dx.doi .org/10.1080/1354060042000224160.

Bolívar, A., Domingo, J., & Pérez-García, P. (2014). 'Teachers' Professional Identity: The Case of Secondary School Teachers in Spain', *The Open Sports Science Journal*, 7(1), 106–12. http://dx.doi.org/10.2174/1875399X01407010106.

Campbell, E. K. (2010). 'Irregular Migration to Southern Africa and from the African Continent to the European Union: Tapping Latent Energy of the Youth', in A. Adepoju (Ed.), *International Migration Within, to, and from Africa in a Globalised World*. Accra: Sub-Saharan Publishers, 169–207.

Caravatti, M. L., Lederer, S. M, Lupico, A., & van Meter, N. (2014). *Getting Teacher Mobility and Migration Right*. Brussels: Education International.

Castillo, L. J. (2009). 'Snowball Sampling'. https://explorable.com/snowball-sampling (accessed 19 October 2021).

Collins, J., & Reid, C. (2012). 'Immigrant Teachers in Australia', *Cosmopolitan Civil Societies: An Interdisciplinary Journal*, 4(2), 38–61.

Crush, J., & Tawodzera, G. (2013). 'The Perilous Trek: Zimbabwean Migrant Children and Teachers in South Africa', in L. Bartlett & A. Ghaffar-Kucher (Eds), *Refugees, Immigrants, and Education in the Global South: Lives in Motion*. New York: Routledge, 54–69.

Crush, J., & Tevera, D. (2010). 'Exiting Zimbabwe', in J. Crush & D. Tevera (Eds), *Zimbabwe's Exodus Crisis, Migration, Survival*. Cape Town: African Books Collective, 1–51.

DHET (2013). 'Evaluation of Qualification Sets Submitted by Migrant Teachers in 2010', *Teaching Qualifications and Policy Directorate*, South Africa.

De Villiers, J. J. R. (2004). 'South African Teachers in United Kingdom Schools: Expectations and Experiences', *Journal of Educational Studies*, 3(1), 49–66.

De Villiers, J. J. R., & Weda, Z. L. (2017). 'South-South Migration of Zimbabwean Teachers: A Transient Greener Pasture', *South African Journal of Education*, 37(3), 1–9. https://doi.org/10.15700/saje.v37n3a1410.

De Villiers, J. J. R., & Weda, Z. L. (2018). 'Zimbabwean Teachers in South Africa: Their Needs and Advice to Prospective Migrant Teachers', *Journal of International Migration and Integration*, 19, 299–314. https://doi.org/10.1007/s12134-018-0558-0.

Elbaz-Luwisch, F. (2004). 'Immigrant Teachers: Stories of Self and Place', *International Journal of Qualitative Studies in Education*, 17(3), 387–414. https://doi.org/10.1080/0951839042000204634.

Faez, F. (2010). 'Linguistic and Cultural Adaptation of Internationally Educated Teacher Candidates', *Canadian Journal of Educational Administration and Policy*, 100, 1–20.

Fee, J. F. (2010). 'Latino Immigrant and Guest Bilingual Teachers: Overcoming Personal, Professional, and Academic Culture Shock', *Urban Education*, 46(3), 390–407. https://doi.org/10.1177/0042085910377447.

Green, A.G., & Green, D.A. (1999). 'The Economic Goals of Canada's Immigration Policy: Past and Present', *Canadian Public Policy/Analyse de Politiques*, 25(4), 425–52.

Green, W. (2014). 'Employment of Migrant Teachers in Public Schools in South Africa', in J. Keevy, W. Green, & S. Manik (Eds), *The Status of Migrant Teachers in South Africa: Implications for Policy, Research, Practice*. Pretoria: The South African Qualifications Association, 89–104.

Hungwe, C. (2013). 'Survival Strategies of Zimbabwean Migrants on Johannesburg', *Journal of Community Positive Practices*, 13(3), 52–73.

Hutchison, C. B. (2006). 'Cross-Cultural Issues Arising for Four Science Teachers During Their International Migration to Teach in US High Schools', *School Science and Mathematics*, 106(2), 74–83. https://doi.org/10.1111/j.1949-8594.2006.tb18137.x.

Janusch, S. (2015). 'Voices Unheard: Stories of Immigrant Teachers in Alberta', *Journal of International Migration and Integration*, 16(2), 299–315. https://doi.org/10.1007/s12134-014-0338-4.

Keevy, J, Green, W., & Manik, S. (2014). 'Implications for Policy, Research and Practice', in J. Keevy, W. Green, & S. Manik (Eds), *The Status of Migrant Teachers in South Africa: Implications for Policy, Research, Practice*. Pretoria: The South African Qualifications Association, 89–104.

Kostogriz, A., & Peeler, E. (2007). 'Professional Identity and Pedagogical Space: Negotiating Difference in Teacher Workplaces', *Teaching Education*, 18(2), 107–22. https://doi.org/10.1080/10476210701325135.

Krüger-Potratz, M. (2013). 'Vielfalt im Lehrerzimmer- Ein Thema Nachholder Intergrationspolitik', in K. Bräu, V. B. Georgi, & C. Rotter (Eds), *Lehrerinnen und Lehrer mit Migrationhindergrund: Zur Relevanz Eines Merkmals in Theorie, Empirie und Praxis*. Münster: Waxmann, 17–36.

Mangum, M., & Block, R. (2018). 'Social Identity Theory and Public Opinion Towards Immigration', *Social Sciences*, 7(41), 1–17. https://doi.org/10.3390/socsci7030041.

Manik, S. (2014a). 'South African Migrant Teachers' Decision-Making: Levels of Influence and "Relative Deprivation"', *Journal of South African Studies*, 40(1), 151–65. https://doi.org/10.1080/03057070.2014.889360.

Manik, S. (2014b). 'We are Working Hand to Mouth: Zimbabwean Teachers' Experiences of Vulnerability in South Africa', *Migracijske I Etnicke Teme*, 2, 171–91.

Manik, S. (2014c). 'Professional Experiences of Migrant Teachers in South Africa', in J. Keevy, W. Green, & S. Manik (Eds), *The Status of Migrant Teachers in South Africa: Implications for Policy, Research, Practice*. Pretoria: The South African Qualifications Association, 105–19.

Maylor, U., Hutchings, M. James, K., Menter, I., & Smart, S. (2006). 'Culture Clash: The Experiences of Overseas-Trained Supply Teachers in English Schools', *British Educational Research Association Annual Conference*. University of Warwick.

McLeod, S. (2019). 'Social Identity Theory', *Simply Psychology*, 24 October. www.simplypsychology.org/social-identity-theory.html (accessed 5 June 2020).

Michael, O. (2006). 'Multiculturalism in Schools: The Professional Absorption of Immigrant Teachers from the Former USSR into the Education System in Israel', *Teaching and Teacher Education*, 22(2), 164–78. https://doi.org/10.1016/j.tate.2005.09.005.

Myles, J., Cheng, L., & Wang, H. (2006). 'Teaching in Elementary School: Perceptions of Foreign-Trained Teacher Candidates on Their Teaching Practicum', *Teaching and Teacher Education*, 22(2), 233–5. https://doi.org/10.1016/j.tate.2005.09.001.

Nieuwenhuis, J. (2008). 'Qualitative Research Designs and Data Gathering Techniques', in K. Maree (Ed.), *First Steps in Research*. Pretoria: Van Schaik, 70–92.

Nieuwenhuis, J. (2009). 'Qualitative Research Designs and Data Gathering Techniques', in K. Maree (Ed.), *First Steps in Research South Africa*. Pretoria: Van Schaik, 69–97.

Peeler, E., & Jane, B. (2003). 'Mentoring: Immigrant Teachers Bridging Professional Practices', *Teaching Education*, 16(4), 325–36. https://doi.org/10.1080/10476210500345623.

Peeler, E., & Jane, B. (2005). 'Mentoring: Immigrant Teachers Bridging Professional Practices', *Teaching Education*, 16(4), 325–36. https://doi.org/10.1080/10476210500345623.

Phillion, J. (2003). 'Obstacles to Accessing the Teaching Profession for Immigrant Women', *Multicultural Education*, 11(1), 41–5.

Pollock, K. (2010). 'Marginalization and the Occasional Teacher Workforce in Ontario: The Case of Internationally Educated Teachers (IETs)', *Canadian Journal of Educational Administration and Policy*, 100, 1–21.

Ranga, D. (2015). 'The Role of Politics in the Migration of Zimbabwean Teachers to South Africa', *Development Southern Africa*, 32(2), 258–73. https://doi.org/10.1080/0376835X.2014.984376.

Reid, C., & Collins, J. (2013). '"No-One Ever Asked Me": The Invisible Experiences and Contribution of Australian Emigrant Teachers', *Race Ethnicity and Education*, 16(2), 268–90. https://doi.org/10.1080/13613324.2012.674022.

Remennick, L. (2002). 'Survival of the Fittest: Russian Immigrant Teachers Speak About Their Professional Adjustment in Israel', *International Migration*, 40(1), 99–121. https://doi.org/10.1111/1468-2435.00187.

Rule, P., & John, V. (2011). *Your Guide to Case Study Research*. Pretoria: Van Schaik.

Schiller, N. G. (2015). 'Explanatory Frameworks in Transnational Migration Studies: The Missing Multi-Scalar Global Perspective', *Ethnic and Racial Studies*, 38(13), 2275–82. https://doi.org/10.1080/01419870.2015.1058503.

Seah, W. T., & Bishop, A. J. (2001). 'Crossing Cultural Borders: The Negotiation of Value Conflicts by Migrant Teachers of Mathematics in Australia', *2001 Annual Conference of the Australian Association for Research in Education*. Fremantle, Australia. http://www.aare.edu.au/data/publications/2001/sea01394.pdf (accessed 19 October 2021).

Sharplin, E. (2009). 'Bringing Them in: The Experiences of Imported and Overseas-Qualified Teachers', *Australian Journal of Education*, 53(2), 192–206. https://doi.org/10.1177/000494410905300207.

Sinyolo, D. (2012). 'A Strategy for Managing Teacher Migration in Southern Africa', PhD thesis, University of South Africa, Pretoria, South Africa. http://hdl.handle.net/10500/10360.

Sisulu, E., Moyo, B., & Tshuma, N. (2007). 'The Zimbabwean Community in South Africa', in S. Buhlungu, J. Danie, & R. Southall (Eds), *State of the Nation South Africa 2007*. Cape Town: HSRC Press, 552–73.

Smith, E. R. (1999). 'Affective and Cognitive Implications of a Group Becoming Part of the Self: New Models of Prejudice and of the Self-Concept', in D. Abrahams & M.A. Hogg (Eds), *Social Identity and Social Cognition*. Oxford, England: Basil Blackwell, 183–96.

Tajfel, H. (1981). *Human Groups and Social Categories*, Cambridge: Cambridge University Press.

Tajfel, H., & Turner, J. (1986). 'The Social Identity Theory of Intergroup Behavior', in S. Buhlungu, J. Danie, & R. Southall (Eds), *Psychology of Intergroup Relations*. Chicago: Nelson Hall Publishers, 7–24.

Taraban, S. (2004). 'Professional Integration of Foreign-Trained Teachers in Ontario: Challenges and Opportunities', *Report for the CERIS Graduate Student Research Award*.

Turner, J.C., Hogg, M.A., Oakes, P. J., Reicher, S. D., & Wetherell, M. S. (1987). *Rediscovering the Social Group: A Self-categorization Theory*. New York: Basil Blackwell.

Vandeyar, S. Vandeyar, T., & Elufisan, K. (2014). 'Impediments to the Successful Reconstruction of African Immigrant Teachers' Professional Identities in South African Schools', *South African Journal of Education*, 34(2), 1–20. https://doi.org/10.15700/201412071136.

Van Oudenhoven, J. P., Ward, C., & Masgoret, A. (2006). 'Patterns of Relations between Immigrants and Host Societies', *International Journal of Intercultural Relations*, 30(6), 637–51. https://doi.org/10.1016/j.ijintrel.2006.09.001.

Virta, A. (2015). 'In the Middle of a Pedagogical Triangle. Native-Language Support Teachers Constructing Their Identity in a New Context'. *Teaching and Teacher Education*, 46, 84–93. https://doi.org/10.1016/j.tate.2014.11.003.

Walsh, S. C., & Brigham, S. (2007). 'Internationally Educated Female Teachers who Have Immigrated to Novia Scotia: A Research/Performance Text', *International Journal of Qualitative Methods*, 6(3), 1–28. https://doi.org/10.1177/160940690700600301.

Walsh, S.C., Brigham, S. M., & Wang, Y. (2011). 'Internationally Educated Female Teachers in the Neoliberal Context: Their Labour Market and Teacher Certification Experiences in Canada', *Teaching and Teacher Education*, 27(3), 657–65. https://doi.org/10.1016/j.tate.2010.11.004.

Weda, Z., & De Villiers, J. (2019). 'Migrant Zimbabwean Teachers in South Africa: Challenging and Rewarding Issues', *Journal of International Migration and Integration*, 20, 1013–28. https://doi.org/10.1007/s12134-018-00649-6.

Conclusion

Elaine Chase and Amy North

The diverse range of foci presented in this volume has undoubtedly opened up questions and opportunities for further exploration as much as it has given substantive answers in relation to how we might fully understand the education, migration and development nexus. Nonetheless, we hope that we have begun to connect some of the dots while demonstrating the complexity of the field. In this final chapter we revisit some of the core questions presented at the start of the volume and think about future possible directions for this body of work in terms of theory, policy, practice and research. We are, of course, considering these issues in a rapidly changing social, political, economic and environmental landscape, exemplified through those chapters that have captured some of the new demands for education in the context of the Covid-19 global pandemic. As such we anticipate that new challenges and opportunities will continue to emerge with respect to education in contexts of migration and (im)mobility, requiring constant revisiting of and innovations in the field.

Our first question, What new considerations emerge for education in the context of development when we apply a migration lens?, has proved generative of many new areas for exploration. The question relates primarily to issues of spatiality and temporality and what education is for and what it looks like in situations in which people encounter mobilities and transitions. Applying a migration or (im)mobility lens to explore the intersections of education and development reveals new considerations for education across diverse global contexts.

Throughout the book we have considered different forms of migration, including internal as well as cross-border migration; and rural–rural as well as rural–urban migrations. We have exemplified situations of migration born out of choice or necessity as well as instances of forced migration, recognizing that the boundaries between these different types of movement are frequently blurred. We have also taken into account different conceptualizations of mobility relating to the spatial or geographic movement of people; social mobility essentially through which people's social and economic lives improve or conversely deteriorate over time; as well as mobility relating to identity formation and the ways in which those who move as well as those who stay may generate social and cultural capital through their own migration, the migration of others or even through the imaginaries of migration. In her work, for example, Nagpal explores questions of mobility with respect to how some young women use college education to construct middle-class identities, which are tied to the idea of mobility or the mental and cultural movement away from the village space. In reality, young women often remain immobilized in the physical sense by deeply embedded structural and cultural gender norms which perpetuate historical disadvantages within their communities. Nonetheless, education often holds significant value with respect to social mobility, linked, for example, to possibilities of marriage migration and accruing middle-class status. Education in all its forms is thus a critical component in all of these formulations of mobility and as we have seen plays its part in complex ways.

The education-development question explored through a migration/(im) mobility lens reveals a broad range of actors who adopt multiple different positionalities within the nexus and experience widely uneven outcomes. These include those who move, those who stay, those who seek education, those who provide it, those who employ educational capital to build lives in other places or create new social identities for themselves through education while remaining rooted in their places of origin. It involves those who formulate educational and migration governance policies, whether they are acting at local, national, transnational or global levels. Whether people move or remain behind while significant others in their lives migrate, migration can fundamentally impact their lives in both positive and negative ways. For instance, migration may shape the educational outcomes and trajectories of millions of children and young people through remittances, enabling new or better learning and life opportunities for future generations. At the same time the toll on those who migrate to generate such resources may be significant as they grapple with issues of discrimination, poor pay and conditions, isolation, exploitation and the devaluing of their own skills and knowledge in unequal economies across the globe. And there may also be mixed impacts on children who remain separated from their migratory parents for significant periods of time.

The imaginaries surrounding migration in a rapidly changing and globalizing world also influence how people engage with education. In the case of international students, for example, migratory aspirations might determine their educational choices in their countries of origin as they try to secure the best chances of building the educational, social and cultural capital required to facilitate migration and maximize their options within global economies. While for some students such migration may be temporary, as discussed by Datta, many may become part of knowledge diasporas in other countries and at the same time become instrumental in forging new urban morphologies, including in relation to food, housing and rental markets, cultural and leisure opportunities.

A focus on migration and mobility in the educational landscape also helps illuminate the frequent disconnects between extant educational policies and the lived realities of learners and their communities. As discussed in her chapter on pastoralists, Dyer points out that while the media and public discourses focus on cross-border migration related to questions of security and multiple 'crises'; much larger movements of people are happening within borders and very little attention has been given to the educational experiences for these populations. She points also to the emphasis in policy on urban-centric development and the sedentary bias (Malkii 1992) which underpins the highly normative framing, structure and delivery of educational policies. Such policies continue to fundamentally ignore the fact that pastoralist communities are essentially grounded in mobile and moral economies which value situated and contextual learning. In direct contradiction to such values, policies instead impose forms of education that require learners to be in the same place every day and which assume that they ultimately want and need to be part of a global economy.

Similar disconnects between policy and lived reality emerge in those chapters exploring education in contexts of displacement. In her critique of the common assumptions and ideas underpinning what has become something of an industry in educational provision for refugees, Abu Moghli illuminates the exclusionary and segregated nature of these educational infrastructures and points to the need to debunk some of the myths surrounding refugee education and notions of humanitarianism. A systemic short-termism in terms of refugee education, she argues, ignores the fact that most displaced children will retain their status as 'refugees' for the duration of their education and beyond, during which time they remain segregated from mainstream societies and excluded from sustainable opportunities for their well-being and development. The lived experiences and impacts of such policies are illustrated in Salem's chapter through the voices of Syrian refugee children attending second-shift schools in Jordan.

Equally germane to understanding the intersections of education, migration and development is the intrinsic value of non-formal and informal learning within people's migratory experiences. This is illustrated through the experiences in the chapter by North and Joshi of migrant domestic workers and the value they give to informal language classes which not only facilitate their ability to navigate their new environments but also promote wider well-being through reducing isolation and helping, in some cases, to reduce exploitation and rights violations. Women who had previously received little or no formal education were able to formulate new identities and status as they acquired literacy and numeracy skills, developed their English-language skills and became recognized for their roles in facilitating access to education for the next generation through the resources they provided through remittances.

The contributions in the book have also gone some way towards responding to our second question: What sorts of theoretical frameworks and approaches may have relevance to understanding the intersections between education, migration and development? It might be helpful to think about relevant theories through a range of macro and micro lenses that guide how we approach the education, migration and development nexus. At the macro level we have advocated for a postcolonial/decolonial approach which broadly speaks to the importance of centring history and experience in our analysis (Samaddar 2020). Some chapters in the volume directly address questions of decolonialism, while others more implicitly integrate the broad principles of a decolonizing approach through the methods and forms of enquiry they utilize, for example, their focus on bringing to the fore the lived experience and agency of the communities they have engaged with. Dyer in her work, for example, refers to her position as a *pracademic* (researcher, practitioner and learner) when working with pastoralist communities. In her chapter on 'eduscapes', Newman highlights the importance of critiquing and extending existing theories to check their value and purpose across different global landscapes. Through what she refers to as a postcolonial application of the theory to Islamic schools in the Senegal, she concludes that *eduscape* remains a useful theoretical framework for understanding the influence of globalization on educational phenomena as long as diverse notions of 'education' alongside different knowledges and epistemologies are fully taken account of in order to shift the theory beyond its Eurocentric bias.

Similarly, Datta, in her chapter exploring the dynamics of migration for those with desirable skills and knowledge in a global economy, unsettles some of the dominant ideas that have become associated with brain drain–brain gain paradigms. Instead, she suggests that the notion of *brain chains* better captures the complex ecologies of skilled migration and the multidirectional and multidimensional processes involved. She reminds us of the temporal and spatial value of skills and how these are socially constructed and politically manipulated at different points in time to stratify migration governance systems, such as through points-based immigration arrangements. Such arrangements generate new categories of migrant identities such as the 'super-skilled' who are juxtaposed with the indolent, 'low' or 'no' skilled migrant worker for the purposes of solidifying exclusionary migration and immigration politics and perpetuating dominant discourses of the 'good' and 'bad' (im)migrant.

We also see how education intersects with theories of modernity and modern identities within an increasingly globalized economy. A 'good' education has become increasingly associated with universalized curricula and pedagogies. As illustrated in the chapter by Rao and Patil on the gradual demise of the fishing school, such emphasis on decontextualized knowledges and delinking of knowledge and skills from people's social and economic realities can lead to devaluing certain forms of knowledge and skills, promotes mobility of people away from communities and builds aspirations for urbanization. When such aspirations are not sustainable, young people return to communities with knowledge and skills that are inadequate and inappropriate for local industries. Rao and Patil link these ideas to the concept of *motility* – as they consider how education and investment in education are constituted as the imaginary pathway towards spatial and social mobility, creating expectations of the 'better life'. Yet in reality, economic, political and social constraints mean that for most, such aspirations are not realizable and that 'formal', decontextualized education may result in solidifying existing inequalities. Theoretically therefore *motility* bridges the conceptual gap between spatial mobility (migration) and social mobility as it enables us to engage with the capacity to be socially or geographically mobile according to the realities of people's circumstances.

The relevance of other theoretical paradigms, which could be considered more micro level in that they help us engage with notions of individual development and flourishing (recognizing that such opportunities may impact the lives of many others), is also illuminated across the volume. Such theories include the capabilities approach (Sen 1983, 2003; Nussbaum 2000) employed by Allsopp and Chase in their analysis of the educational trade-offs that unaccompanied migrant young people in the UK make between what they value with respect to education and work and the extent to which they are able to realize their aspirations. Similarly possible selves theory, combined with the capability approach, is employed by Mkwananzi in her work with migrant young women in South Africa. A mobilities framework is used by Cuban to explore the experiences of migrant women in Chile, and social identity theory used by Villiers and Weda to make sense of the experiences and perspectives of migrant teachers from Zimbabwe in South Africa. Such theoretical approaches can help generate a better understanding of how people's aspirations to live the lives they value intersect with their educational trajectories and personal agency in contexts of migration, contexts in which they frequently come up against multiple constraints and typically spend huge amounts of resources navigating systems which frustrate such aspirations for a better life for themselves and others.

Questions relating to the opportunities and challenges for education created by migration and (im)mobility and the implications for educational policy, curricula and pedagogy as well as learner experiences and well-being are touched on throughout the chapters. We have problematized some of the normative discourses about the value and purpose of education when we consider these questions in migratory contexts. We have seen, for example, how policy structures exacerbate educational inequalities around sedentary bias and lack of flexibility for pastoralist communities across the learning trajectories (from early years to higher education); and how ill-informed, decontextualized policies can negatively impact their social, cultural and economic lives and fail to recognize their central role in addressing bigger questions for society and the planet as a whole, such as through their situated expertise in environmental stewardship.

A number of the contributions also speak to the question: What approaches to research, policy and practice are most likely to promote justice, equity and well-being in and through education in the context of migration? Various chapters, for example, highlight the need to consider education in its broadest sense, and attend to the role that multiple learning spaces and forms of education – including non-formal and vocational education as well as formal schooling – may play in supporting the aspirations and well-being of individuals and communities in contexts of migration and (im)mobility.

More broadly, underpinned by the intentions of decolonizing and unsettling thinking across the field, a number of contributors highlight how participatory forms of enquiry and engagement can help centre the human experience in migration studies (and generate better understandings of how people understand and engage with processes of migration from social, cultural and historical perspectives). The chapter by Cadavid-González and Allsopp, for example, illustrates the potential of museums as spaces to facilitate participatory engagement in order to co-construct ideas about and make sense of migratory projects and histories in all their complexity. Other contributions also illustrate the value of more quantitative analyses which can help us understand the scale of issues and shifting patterns over time. Jha, Purohit and J.'s work, for example, helps quantify the impact of the Covid-19 pandemic on the education of migrant children in India, while Pang and Lu offer a synthesis of the quantifiable dimensions of the impacts on children's education and well-being in contexts of rural–urban migration in China.

The question 'How do gendered and other inequalities intersect with the possibilities and constraints emerging from the education, migration and development nexus?' emerges as particularly salient across the different analyses. We see the diverse nomenclature surrounding different forms of migration and how class, caste, economic status, race, nationality, educational status and gender fundamentally shape migratory experiences. Transnational elites, such as skilled workers and international students, often enjoy expansive opportunities to migrate facilitated by highly selective immigration policies in receiving countries in the Global South as well as the Global North. Yet, the picture is very different for those with limited education or skills or whose skills do not 'fit' with what constitutes desirable knowledge attributes at a particular point in time. Hence we can see how skill-based immigration policies solidify and exacerbate intersecting forms of inequality, including those associated with gender and race. Migrant women in many contexts face particular insecurities and precarity in areas they are able to find employment, including domestic work, the care economy and manufacturing and garment industries. At the same time, many men as well as women experience the very real effects of deskilling and de-professionalization through migration, symptoms of a supply and demand economy when there is a surplus of skilled labour and indicative of how skills do not retain value over place and time. At the same time, we see intra-household inequalities within migrant couples and families, where highly skilled women become relegated to the status of 'dependents' through migration and their own skills and qualifications are not recognized. Covid-19 and the resultant enforced immobility have revealed the importance of virtual migration and the growth of global learning platforms. While arguably creating new opportunities for sharing ideas and knowledge, they also illuminate digital inequalities and how many people are unable to benefit from these opportunities, revealing a whole new set of challenges and inequities in terms of educational access in the digital world.

Where Next?: Future Directions in Exploring the Education, Migration and Development Nexus

As noted earlier, we have only just started to explore an ever-changing landscape of how education and development are shaped by and shape migratory processes, and we are conscious of how the field may take multiple pathways here on in. From this body of work, a number of new areas of enquiry stand out as being particularly urgent in terms of progressing the field. First, questions of climate change and climate injustices emerge as factors intersecting with other inequalities which shape migratory decisions and aspirations. A focus on climate suggests a whole range of new questions relevant to the nexus such as, among others, the purpose and place of education in contexts of climate-related displacements; the forms of curricula and pedagogies most likely to serve the needs of affected communities; and the role of education in advocating for climate justice and redressing rights violations and inequalities which drive forced displacement.

Second, there is an enormous amount of work to be explored in relation to the role of digital technologies to support education and learning in contexts of migration and (im)mobility. The potential for innovations in pedagogies, curricula and modes of engagement for learning is extensive, while at the same time questions of digital access and equity need to remain high on policy and practice agendas. A third area of enquiry relates to the place of health, well-being and care in the education, migration and development nexus. This includes the need for a greater focus on the health and well-being of those who migrate, those who remain behind and those who provide care and education for both. A clear need, for example, has come to the fore during the pandemic for an ethics of care for international students which has been lacking in many higher education policies. Some of the chapters have similarly pointed to the complex global care chains which are fundamental to understanding the intersections between education, migration and well-being. Exploring and better understanding these in relation to pedagogy and curricula, policy and practice are clearly areas requiring further consideration.

Finally, a whole new corpus of work is likely to emerge with respect to how best to integrate understandings of the migration, education and development nexus into teaching and learning, a question which has relevance at a global scale. This has multiple dimensions, including the fact that teachers and educators may be migrating themselves; how teachers and educators engage with migrant students and learners; and, of course, the role that teachers and educators have in facilitating teaching and learning about migration and its impacts on societies across the globe.

References

Malkki, L. (1992). 'National Geographic: The Rooting of Peoples and the Territorialization of National Identity Among Scholars and Refugees', *Cultural Anthropology*, 7(1), 24–44.

Nussbaum, M. (2000). *Women and Human Development: The Capabilities Approach.* Cambridge: Cambridge University Press.

Samaddar, R. (2020). *The Postcolonial Age of Migration.* India: Routledge.

Sen, A. (1983). 'Development: Which Way Now?', *Economic Journal*, 93(372), 745–62.

Sen, A. (2003). 'Development as Capability Expansion', in S. Fukuda-Parr, et al (Eds), *Readings in Human Development.* New Delhi and New York: Oxford University Press, 3–16.

Index

www.ingramcontent.com/pod-product-compliance
Lightning Source LLC
Chambersburg PA
CBHW070901080426
R18103400001B/R181034PG41932CBX00002B/3